Shaping the Wesleyan Message

John Wesley in Theological Debate

✝

Allan Coppedge

FRANCIS ASBURY PRESS
of Evangel Publishing House

Nappanee, Indiana 46550

Requests for information should be addressed to:

Evangel Publishing House
2000 Evangel Way
P.O. Box 189
Nappanee, Indiana 46550-0189

Toll-Free Order Line: (800) 253-9315
Website: www.evangelpublishing.com

Copyedited by S. David Garber
Cover design by Brad Sherman / Grand Design

ISBN 1-928915-40-X
LCCN 2002116575

Printed in the United States of America

03 04 05 06 07 08 / 9 8 7 6 5 4 3 2 1

TO MY WIFE, BETH,

*For her gracious encouragement and
support throughout the research
and writing of this book.*

Table of Contents

Introduction

For nearly two centuries, important work on Wesley has been done from a biographical and historical perspective. The distinctly theological side of Wesley received scant attention before the publication of George Croft Cell's *The Rediscovery of John Wesley* in 1935. This fresh approach heralded a new era of theological evaluation in Wesley studies. In the half century since Cell, significant work has been done on a number of major doctrines in Wesley's thought; among others, special attention has been given to Wesley's views on grace, faith, sin, justification, sanctification, Christology, the sacraments, and Christian perfection. There has yet to appear, however, a serious study dealing with Wesley's position on predestination and related doctrines. The purpose of this book is to investigate Wesley's theology of predestination in relation to his thought and ministry, with particular attention given to the tension between predestination and perfection.

There are several factors behind the recent revival of interest in Wesley's thought, not the least of which is an increasing recognition of the significance of Wesley's theology for the Christian church. It is becoming more apparent that John Wesley is a unique figure, not only because of his prominence in the leadership of the eighteenth-century revival and his establishment of a worldwide communion of Methodists, but also because in modern church history a theological system has been attached to his name in a way that is not true of any other spiritual leader of the eighteenth century. In some circles it has been fashionable to minimize Wesley's role as a theological influence within the church by referring to him as a "folk theologian," because he did not write a textbook of systematic theology like John Calvin's *Institutes of the Christian Religion*. Yet many are beginning to recognize that there is a wholeness to Wesley's thought that is matched only by such leaders in the church as Aquinas, Luther, and Calvin. Even though he did not write a theological textbook, still there is in Wesley a rather complete thought system about the Christian faith that has organization, unity, consistency, and comprehensiveness about it. What is more, it is a holistic theology that is vital and operative around the world today.

Our attention to certain of Wesley's views will allow us then to begin to understand his entire system of theology, while at the same time we will observe how certain aspects of that theology differed from that of other Christians and led to serious doctrinal debates. Further, our investigation will make it possible for the theological descendants of Wesley, as well as any member of the Christian church, to understand how doctrinal differences have been handled by devout men of other ages. In the process we hope to gain insight into some of the principles for managing theological differences.

Numerous theological issues were discussed during the eighteenth century, including deism, the roles of reason and faith, justification, and the nature of the church. However, among the leaders of the Evangelical Revival, the two most controversial questions were predestination and perfection. Accordingly, these two doctrines have been chosen as the center of our attention in this book.

Predestination has been a much-debated doctrinal matter for centuries because it deals with some of man's most significant intelligent questions, i.e., the relationship between God's sovereignty and man's freedom.[1] Since committed Christians still often differ on this important subject, its content has a special relevance for us today.

The issues related to predestination regularly surfaced throughout the eighteenth century. Four of the occasions on which such issues arose in a controversial way have been selected as the framework of this investigation. The emphasis on predestination as the subject matter for a discussion of theological debate has the additional advantage in that it forms such an integral part of Wesley's theology. By beginning with this doctrine, we gain a way into a significant part of the thought of Wesley, and at the same time we are provided with an introduction to certain doctrinal distinctives in his theology.

While some parts of Wesley's doctrinal position lend themselves to a straight theological analysis, the doctrine of predestination is so bound up with events and personal relationships in the revival that any investigation in this area must treat the historical as well as the theological aspects of the subject. Therefore, we will provide a review of the Calvinist/Arminian controversies of the eighteenth century as they related to John Wesley, and also give a summary of Wesley's views on predestination and the place of this doctrine in his theology. Although theology and history are closely interwoven throughout the book, the investigation follows essentially a chronological sequence so that the influence of the historical factors upon the doctrinal questions can be fully appreciated.

The second of the most debated theological questions of the revival was Christian perfection. Since this subject is so intimately bound up with the concept of holiness, which is the overarching theme of all of Wesley's thought, a study of the place of Christian perfection allows us to focus on an issue that is right at the heart of all of Wesley's theology. We will notice that in the eighteenth-century debates over predestination the subject of Christian perfection became a recurring theme. As Wesley began to express reservations about unconditional predestination, others countered with questions about Christian perfection, and so the two issues became very closely intertwined as a subject for controversy.

Why did the Calvinists so strenuously reject Wesley's position? What was the relation of perfection and Wesley's whole doctrine of sanctification to his views on predestination? Did Wesley's commitment to Christian holiness have any consequences for his relationship with the Calvinists or their doctrine? Some significant work has been done on the connection between antinomianism and Wesley's theology, but not enough thought has been given to the correlation of antinomianism and sanctification. Accordingly, a central purpose of this book will be to assess the relationship of these concepts to Wesley's thought, especially his views on predestination.

The opening chapter begins with the early development of Wesley's thinking on predestination, holiness, and religious authority, and deals with the two major factors influencing his position: the Wesley family and the Church of England. While short sections on the Arminianism and Calvinism of the eighteenth century are included for the purpose of defining certain terms and introducing background material, these two positions are potential subjects for full-length investigations in their own right. Further, the complex relation of Wesley's evangelical Arminianism and the Arminianism of the Church of England in his day is also a significant subject for research, but it is beyond the scope of this book.

Part I offers an interpretation of the role played by predestination in the disruption of the original unity of the eighteenth-century revival while also evaluating selected nontheological factors. Because the free-grace debate of 1739–42 was one of the two most important clashes over predestination in Wesley's lifetime, and since it shaped future relations between many evangelical leaders, the events of this controversy are reviewed in considerable detail.

It would be inappropriate to view Wesley's theology in historical isolation from the views of other leaders of the revival. His relation to the other major figures of the early Methodist movement is of unusual importance. Thus, special attention in the early chapters will be focused upon the views and influence of George Whitefield and Charles Wesley. Fresh materials on certain other figures of this period also make it possible more accurately to assess the roles played in the controversy by John Cennick, Howel Harris, William Seward, and Joseph Humphreys.

Part II, which covers the events (1742–70) between the free-grace controversy and the Minutes controversy of the 1770s, opens with a summary of Wesley's theology of predestination. While this somewhat interrupts the historical flow of events, by the early 1750s Wesley had published most of his writings on the subject, and a convenient capsule of his views may serve as a useful background for the remainder of the book. The résumé begins with the study of how Wesley's views of the character of God affect his understanding of predestination. This is followed by a review of Wesley's doctrine of providence as a closely related issue.

Because of the complex nature of the subject, rather than talk about "predestination," it is more accurate to speak of "the related doctrines of predestination." Therefore, in this investigation Wesley's views on these various "related doctrines" will be summarized under the following categories: the nature of man; original sin; election and reprobation; prevenient grace; human freedom; resistible and irresistible grace; the extent of the atonement; and final perseverance. Because of its intimate connection with a later controversy, a discussion of Wesley's position on imputed righteousness is reserved for chapter 7. Likewise, his doctrine of justification, particularly as it relates to faith and works, and to the doctrine of Christian perfection or sanctification, are discussed in the context of other controversies. While justification and perfection are related to any discussion of predestination, these two doctrines have each been the subject of separate detailed investigations by others, and therefore, in contrast to the other "related doctrines," no comprehensive theological summary is included here.

Chapters 7 and 9 deal primarily with two of Wesley's literary debates: chapter 7 with James Hervey over imputed righteousness, and chapter 9 with Augustus Toplady, which centered around human freedom and God's sovereignty.

Since predestination was such a dividing issue during the revival, the historical side of this study inevitably focuses upon the several controversies related to the doctrine. Although the nature of the subject matter makes this quite natural, it nevertheless gives the false impression that dissension was the characteristic spirit of the revival. As a corrective to this, chapter 8 is designed to show something of the generally cordial relations and cooperative endeavors of the evangelical leaders, as exemplified in the relationship between Wesley and Whitefield.

Chapter 8 also includes a section on the problem over perfection. Where the subject of perfection appears as a part of the debates over predestination, it is treated within each of those contexts. However, another difficulty arose within Wesley's own ranks when some who claimed the experience of Christian perfection began to take the doctrine to extremes. This chapter describes how Wesley handled this in-house question and dealt with members of his own Connection (group of societies) over such theological issues.

Part III, which takes the study through the 1770s, covers the lengthy debate over the Minutes of Wesley's 1770 Conference. This Minutes Controversy was easily the most explosive of the Calvinist-Arminian disagreements. In the four chapters that comprise this section, special attention is given to John Fletcher as Wesley's articulate spokesman in the debate, and the theological kinship of these two men is examined in some detail. The place of Walter Sellon and Thomas Olivers as representatives of the Arminian camp is also explored. On the Calvinist side, the focus is primarily upon the Countess of Huntingdon, Walter Shirley, and Richard Hill, with somewhat less attention given to John Berridge and Rowland Hill. The debate on the Calvinist-Arminian questions continued in moderated form throughout the century. Yet the close of the Minutes Controversy and the first issues of Wesley's *Arminian Magazine* brought to an end the sharp exchanges over predestination during Wesley's lifetime. Thus, the historical side of the study concludes at about 1780.

In addition to the review of certain aspects of Wesley's theology, there are several other significant issues related to this investigation. First, the complex mixture of theological and nontheological factors in the controversy is an important area for interpretation, and one of the purposes of our study is to examine the place of these factors in the eighteenth-century clashes over predestination and perfection. A second, and closely related matter, is the influence of the doctrines of predestination and perfection on the personal relations among the leadership of the revival. Of special relevance for this work is the divisive nature of these doctrines for Wesley's friendship with other evangelical leaders. How great was the separation of Wesley from Whitefield or Lady Huntingdon? How much of the disunity was over predestination? How much was over perfection? Was the revival one continuous controversy between Wesley and the Calvinists? How far did their honest differences preclude cooperative endeavors? These and similar questions recur throughout the book as part of the attempt to deal with these two significant issues.

The last significant overarching issue for our study is the matter of Wesley's general concern for theological questions and how they are decided. It is common to view Wesley as the great organizer of the revival, concerned primarily with "practical divinity." Although there is some truth to this view, it is often accompanied by the assumption that Wesley felt theological questions to be relatively unimportant and a waste of his valuable time. The statement usually cited is, "The distinguishing marks of a Methodist are not his opinions of any sort. . . . We think and let think." Unfortunately, what is usually left out are Wesley's other crucial words: "But as to all opinions which do not strike at the root of Christianity, we think and let think."[2] The question then becomes: What strikes at the root of Christianity? What is the difference between an essential doctrine and an "opinion" in Wesley's mind? What are his criteria for distinguishing between these two categories? Was a proper interpretation of predestination an essential doctrine or an opinion? Was there ever any shift of that doctrine from one category to another? A further purpose, then, of this investigation is to see if the controversies over predestination and perfection provide any helpful insights into Wesley's views on the importance of theology.

Intimately bound up with this matter of the importance of theology is the whole question of how theological issues were to be decided. This is the critical point related to religious authority, an issue that still has significance in our day in connection with discussions on theological pluralism. This was not an issue of theological debate among the evangelical leaders of the revival in the same way as it is in our own time. They all basically adopted the traditional Protestant position on the matter of religious authority. However, their usefulness to us on this subject comes from another direction. The fact that they debated theological subjects with a clearly defined position on the authority of Scripture and the proper place of other authorities—such as reason, experience, and tradition—allows them to serve as models for us with regard to the criteria for theological debate. This fact also indicates some of the presuppositions that guided their doctrinal discussion. What is the criterion for deciding the truth of any issue? Is there more than one criterion? If so, do these criteria have the same value? How are they to be used? These are some of the questions that are treated in the process of describing the theological controversies of the revival. How were the debates decided? In particular, was their basis for making decisions the same as the "historically accepted" approach of contemporary theological pluralism? These are some of the questions for which we hope to find answers in this study.

1. The Early Development of Wesley's Views on Predestination, Perfection, and Religious Authority

A NY serious understanding of John Wesley's doctrinal development must take into account at least four major factors. The most obvious of these is the prevailing theological climate in the Church of England at the beginning of the eighteenth century, which had a formative effect, not only upon Wesley directly, but also indirectly upon him through his family. Since his family was such a shaping force for Wesley's views, the influences upon his parents become doubly significant. A third factor shaping Wesley's personal theology was his years as a student and a fellow at Oxford. These Oxford years will be examined in some detail. Finally, for a complete understanding of how Wesley came to certain positions in his thought, his Georgia experience must be taken into account. All four of these influences upon Wesley are closely interwoven and have a cumulative effect upon the final outcome of his convictions.

Church and Family Background

The Epworth rectory provided an unusual seedbed for the theology of John Wesley because of the unique blend of theological tradition embodied in his parents, Samuel and Susannah Wesley. This distinct doctrinal heritage had its roots in the volatile ecclesiastical situation during the lifetime of both of Wesley's grandfathers. With the rise of Oliver Cromwell to power during the Great Rebellion (1642–49) and his subsequent rule as Lord Protector during the days of the Republic (1649–60), there was a corresponding increase in the influence of the Puritan party within the Church of England. At this period there was a mixture of religion with politics, scarcely known before, that unleashed an unusual outburst of spiritual energy and activity. Many of the pastors who had remained loyal to the deposed King Charles I had to vacate their parishes. At the same time, the leading Puritans—such as Richard Baxter, John Bunyan, George Fox, William Penn, and John Milton—were ascending to the zenith of their influence.

But a mere two years after Cromwell's death, the return of the Stuart monarchy from exile in France brought dramatic changes in the theological as well as the ecclesiastical climate of the nation. In 1660 Charles II, son of Charles I, who had been beheaded in 1649, returned to the throne in London, signaling an abrupt reversal of the clergy's fortunes in the Church of England.

In 1662 Charles II, with the encouragement of the Anglican party, renewed the Act of Uniformity from Queen Elizabeth's time for structuring the organization of the Church of England. It reestablished the supremacy of the king over the church, reinforced episcopal authority, and once again made the *Book of Common Prayer* the standard order for worship. The Church of England reexamined ordinations that during Cromwell's time had often been carried out in presbyterian fashion. A large number of ministers had either to be reordained episcopally or to vacate their livelihoods. Since many Puritans could not "conform" to the Act of Uniformity because of their theological convictions, they had to live with the consequences of the changing climate within the nation. From one-quarter to one-third of the clergymen, some two thousand in all, were ejected from their pulpits and forced to become Nonconformist ministers outside the Church of England.

Among those Nonconformists or Dissenters who could not consent to the recently reestablished positions of the Church of England were Bartholomew Wesley, John Wesley's great-grandfather; John Wesley, his paternal grandfather; and Dr. Samuel Annesley, his maternal grandfather. All three men represented first the Puritan party within the Church of England and then the Puritan tradition as it continued outside that church. They were also examples of a theological position and a distinct ecclesiology. The Puritans had always pressed for a more theologically "pure" church within the Reformation tradition, and they were almost all committed Calvinists. By contrast, the Anglican party under the leadership of men like William Laud had, for the most part, become modified Arminians.[1]

Samuel Wesley's father, John Wesley, had become a vicar in Dorset after completing his degree at Oxford in Oriental languages in 1658. The renewal of the Act of Uniformity caused him to lose his position after four happy years in the pastoral ministry. He became an itinerant, dissenting preacher and served as something of a model for his future namesake grandson. In spite of severe poverty, he was able to send his son Samuel to the Free School at Dorchester. After John's early death, Samuel managed to continue his education at a dissenting academy in London, with the support and encouragement of Dr. Samuel Annesley. During this part of his training, Samuel had already been designated for the Nonconformist ministry when a radical change occurred in his views. John Wesley later described this change in his father:

> Some severe invectives being written against the Dissenters, Mr. S. Wesley being a young man of considerable talents, was pitched upon to answer it. This set him on a course of reading which soon produced an effect very different from what had been intended. Instead of writing the wished-for answer, he himself conceived [and] he saw reason to change his opinions; and actually formed a resolution to renounce the Dissenters and attach himself to the Established Church.[2]

The strong family commitment to Dissenting doctrines would have brought family opposition if his new views had been disclosed. Accordingly, Samuel set out one morning for Oxford and an education within Anglicanism without informing his family of his design.[3] Although the differences over the doctrine of church and state seem to have been primarily at issue, it is also probable that he had objected to some of the traditional Calvinistic positions. The fact that Samuel Wesley became a moderate Arminian suggests that at least a secondary reason for the separation from Nonconformism was related to some of the questionable features of Calvinism.

After completing his university training, Samuel Wesley joined with John Dunton and Richard Suatt from 1691 to 1697 in publishing a twice-weekly paper for the purpose of answering questions on all departments of literature. At first named *The Athenian Gazette,* later altered to *Athenian Mercury,* this publication gave Wesley a forum for expressing his views in the areas of divinity, church history, poetry, and natural philosophy. Many of his responses to questions on these subjects were later collected and republished in four volumes as *The Athenian Oracle.* The main structure of Samuel Wesley's theology can be extracted from this source.[4]

Samuel's Arminian sympathies are quickly revealed in his repudiation of the doctrines of election and reprobation:

> We can not be satisfied by any of those Scriptures which are brought for that purpose, that there is any such election of a determinate number as either puts a force on their natures, and irresistibly saves them or absolutely excludes all the rest of mankind from salvation. We think there is no one place in the Holy Scriptures which proves that so many men, and no more, were irresistibly determined to everlasting salvation.[5]

Samuel not only made himself clear as to his views on election; he also indicated that his criterion for doing so was the Word of God. He was further convinced that "God predestinated those to salvation whom he foresaw would make good use of His grace, resolving to damn only such as He foresaw would continue impenitent."[6] On the matter of sovereignty and man's freedom, he felt that "God made man upright, and a free agent, and that God's prescience presides over man's free agency, but doth not overrule it, by saving man whether he will or no, or by damning him undeservedly."[7] He wanted to guard against making God the Author of sin.

> God necessitates no evil action, yet foresees all. If God tempts no man to evil, much less does He necessitate. Indeed, were He to do this, the nature of man would be destroyed, the proposal of rewards and punishments would be ironical, preaching would be vain, and faith also vain.[8]

Samuel Wesley was firmly committed to the doctrine of universal redemption. He believed that Jesus Christ "atoned so far for the sins of all mankind as to make them in a saveable condition."[9]

> God really wills the salvation of all men, as far as it is consistent with the liberty of man and his own purity and justice. . . . [God] has also used all the necessary means for our salvation; He offers pardon of all sin, and right to life in Christ, to all men without exception, on condition of believing and acceptance.[10]

On the question of Arminianism and free will, Samuel wrote:

> If the Arminians do really hold, that we may be Sav'd by our own natural Power or Will, without God's Grace, thro' Christ, preventing us and working with us, we think they are as far from Truth as from the good old Doctrine of the Church. . . . But the soberest of them, nay all that we e'er met with, absolutely deny any such thing, and protest they depend upon God's Grace in all their good Actions, tho Man's Will must be taken in as a subordinate Agent, and we are to work out our own Salvation, without which we shall never obtain it. However if any of them, under this fair Covert, do really hide any poisonous Pelagian doctrines, confounding Nature and Grace, their Opinions ought to be detested, as taking off Man from his dependence on the Almighty.[11]

Since John Wesley's theology resembled that of his father, Samuel, it is reasonable to suppose that Samuel heavily influenced John. Tyerman suggests that, except for some differences in phraseology and emphasis, the doctrines of father and son are substantially the same.[12]

The second major influence on John Wesley's early thought was that of his mother, Susannah, the youngest daughter and twenty-fifth child of Dr. Samuel Annesley, dean of the Puritan preachers in London during the latter half of the seventeenth century. Nurtured at the very heart of Nonconformism, she nevertheless had an independent mind on theological questions. At the age of thirteen, she examined the controversial issues between Establishment and Dissent, and leaving her religious fellowship with the latter, embraced the doctrines and forms of the Church of England. Fortunately she did not have to brave the kind of opposition from her family that Samuel Wesley had encountered. Later, when she leaned toward unitarianism, it was a young student for the ministry named Samuel Wesley who by logical argument assisted her in reestablishing a firm belief in the Trinity. So even from her early years, Susannah was interested and thoughtful about significant theological questions.[13]

During 1725, while studying the Church of England's Thirty-Nine Articles of Religion (1571) in preparation for his ordination, John Wesley had some questions arise in his mind about Article 17, "On Predestination." He shared these with his mother, and she replied by letter with a summary of her own views:

> The Doctrine of Predestination, as maintained by rigid Calvinists, is very shocking and ought utterly to be abhorred; because it charges the most holy God with being the Author of Sin. It is certainly inconsistent with the Justice and Goodness of God, to lay any man under either a physical or moral Necessity of Committing Sin, and then punish him for doing it.
>
> I do firmly believe, that God from Eternity hath Elected some to Everlasting Life; but then I humbly conceive, that this Election is founded in his Foreknowledge according to the eighth of Romans, verse[s] 29, 30. Whom, in his eternal Prescience, God saw would make a right use of their powers, and accept of Offered Mercy—he did Predestinate—

> Adopt for His Children, his peculiar Treasure. And that they might be
> conformed to the image of his only Son, He called them to Himself by
> His Eternal Word, the Preaching of the Gospel; and internally by his
> Holy Spirit.[14]

Susannah believed that this view gave proper glory to God's free grace without impairing the liberty of men. She objected to the foreknowledge of God being seen as the cause by which many perish. Knowing that the sun would rise tomorrow was not the same as causing it to rise.

A careful comparison of this letter with Wesley's publications reveals the impact of Susannah's views. As will become clear, several of Wesley's objections to the doctrine found their roots here. He seems to have been trying to indicate his agreement with his mother when he reprinted her letter in the first volume of the *Arminian Magazine* (in 1778).

The Oxford and Georgia Years, 1720–1737

While at Oxford, Wesley pored over the Articles of Religion, and his scruples about predestination and election apparently arose over part of article 17:

> Predestination to life is the everlasting purpose of God, whereby (before the foundations of the world were laid) He hath constantly decreed by His counsels secret to us to deliver from curse and damnation those whom He hath chosen in Christ out of mankind, and to bring them by Christ to everlasting salvation, as vessels made to honour.[15]

How was article 17 to be understood? A standard interpretation in Wesley's day was by Bishop Gilbert Burnet, to which Wesley and Richard Hill both referred in a later controversy.[16] Burnet argued that article 17 did not support a supralapsarian view, wherein the decrees of God came before the Creation and the Fall. He further noted that there was no specific mention of reprobation. The key issue was whether the Article based God's eternal decree on His foreknowledge. The Arminians said yes; the Calvinistic sublapsarians said no. Burnet declared it undefined and contended that it was very probable that those who wrote the article meant that the decree was absolute. However, since they did not directly state that the decree was absolute, no one was required to hold it. In other words, the article was deliberately designed to be ambiguous so that both Arminians and Calvinists could subscribe to it.[17]

Wesley arrived at a similar position, i.e., that while holding an Arminian viewpoint, he could still wholeheartedly commit himself to the creed of the Church of England. In 1745 he wrote:

> In saying, "I teach the doctrines of the Church of England," I do, and always did, mean . . . [that] I teach the doctrines which are comprised in those Articles and Homilies to which all the clergy of the Church of England solemnly profess to assert, and that in their plain, unforced, grammatical meaning.

Yet, he recognized that a Calvinist like George Whitefield could do the same. "Each of us can truly say, 'I subscribe this Article in that which I believe from my heart is its plain, grammatical meaning.' "[18]

Wesley reached this broad interpretation of article 17 before he was ordained on September 19, 1725. Nonetheless, he wrestled with the issue up to the last moment. In August he worked through *A Defence of the Thirty-Nine Articles of the Church of England,* by John Ellis, and in September he read Isaac Watts' views on predestination.[19] His diary reveals that the subject still occupied his thoughts the week after his ordination.[20]

Wesley worked through a number of doctrinal questions while he was at Oxford. These questions included the issues that divided the Calvinists from the Arminians. In the process he established certain intellectual positions in several areas that would determine the future direction of his theology, especially in regard to doctrines related to predestination. The notion that Wesley had given the subject little consideration before the free-grace controversy began in 1739 (on his sermon "Free Grace," see chap. 2) is therefore best regarded as without foundation.

A second of these convictions firmly established in Wesley's mind at Oxford was the central importance of holiness for the Christian life. His reading of Thomas à Kempis' *The Imitation of Christ,* Jeremy Taylor's *Holy Living and Holy Dying,* and William Law's *Christian Perfection* together with *A Serious Call to a Devout and Holy Life,* convinced Wesley that "holiness of heart and life" was the essence of New Testament Christianity. Following upon this insight, the strict disciplines undertaken by the early Methodists were largely designed by Wesley for the cultivation of personal sanctity.[21] Wesley described that state of holiness for which he and others were striving in a sermon before the University in 1733. It was this message on "The Circumcision of the Heart" that he later designated as his first sermon on Christian perfection. He defined his subject as follows:

> It is that habitual disposition of soul which, in the sacred writings, is termed holiness; and which directly implies, the being cleansed from sin, "from all filthiness both of flesh and spirit"; and, by consequence, the being endued with those virtues which were also in Christ Jesus; the being so "renewed in the spirit of our mind," as to be "perfect as our father in heaven is perfect."[22]

In this sermon Wesley offered the interpretation of the doctrine of Christian perfection that came to be associated with this name. While his understanding of how this doctrine became a reality in the Christian life changed somewhat after 1738, his basic views continued much the same for the rest of his life. Wesley's interpretation of Christian perfection involved three things. One was purity of intention, dealing with the motivation of the heart. Thus Wesley began to deal with purification from self-centeredness. A second element had to do with righteous living, defined in terms of the imitation of Christ, walking as Christ walked. This was the dimension of character that was manifest in terms of outward conduct. The third aspect was the love of God and of one's neighbor. It involved loving God with all the heart, together with manifesting a perfect love for one's neighbor, i.e., loving him unconditionally, as God did. These three dimensions of purity, righteousness, and love remained at the heart of Wesley's theology of Christian perfection and were expounded in his sermons and writings for nearly sixty years.

During the early 1730s, Wesley also produced *A Collection of Forms of Prayer for Every Day in the Week,* in which he reiterated his basic theme that "Christ liveth in me: This is the fulfilling of the Law, the last stage of Christian holiness: This maketh the Man of God perfect; He that being dead to the World, is alive to God, . . . who has given him his whole Heart."[23] In another sermon written in May 1734, on "The One Thing Needful," he pointed out the crucial importance of directing all our energies "to be formed anew after the likeness of our Creator, . . . to health, to liberty, to holiness." For Wesley, this was not just one emphasis in the Christian life, or even the primary one:

> Let us well observe that our Lord doth not call this our Main concern, or Great business, the Chief thing needful; but the One thing; all others being either parts of this, or quite foreign to the End of life.[24]

As Richard Heitzenrater puts it, the Methodists were those who

> had a "single intention" in life—"to please God" by improving "in holiness, in the Love of God and thy Neighbor." And to this end they were willing more or less to follow John Wesley's "method" as a means of attaining that goal.[25]

In a similar evaluation of that era, Martin Schmidt states that Wesley "was resolutely committed to one thing, the task of promoting by all possible means his own and other people's sanctification."[26]

Although it was not until 1738 that he acquired a clear understanding of the relation of sanctification to faith, Wesley's early commitment to holy living never diminished. In 1771 he reviewed the matter for Lady Huntingdon:

> Many years since, I saw that "without holiness no man shall see the Lord." I began following after it, and inciting all with whom I had any intercourse to do the same. Ten years after, God gave me a clearer view than I had before of the way how to attain this—namely, by faith in the Son of God. And immediately I declared to all, "We are saved from sin, we are made holy, by faith." I have continued to declare this for above thirty years.[27]

In 1738 Wesley's conversations with Peter Bohler brought him to a new understanding of the nature of faith for justification. Before that time he had believed in salvation by faith, but had defined faith, as many in the Anglican communion did in his day, as rational assent to the creeds and works of piety. The result had been an attempt to make oneself holy in order to earn God's pronouncement of justification. But a new understanding of faith as a trust or reliance upon the merits of the death of Christ for salvation brought Wesley to his own Aldersgate experience of saving grace. This fresh understanding of faith for justification had a corresponding effect on his understanding of sanctification. He now began to see that both justification and sanctification were works of God's grace. The instrumental means for actualizing both experiences in the life of the individual was a definite act of faith. That is why his preaching upon entire sanctification was coupled with a call for a definite act of faith by which God's grace could bring about this state of Christian perfection in the life of a believer.

But Wesley's new grasp in 1738 of the role of faith did not produce a corresponding depreciation of discipline as an essential aid to growth in holiness. On the contrary, after 1738 the "methods" he and his Oxford friends had developed from 1725 to 1735 to promote holy living, came to occupy their rightful place in the ongoing sanctification of the believer. As the following chapters will show, this central emphasis on "scriptural holiness" in Wesley's theology was a key factor in his reaction against the effects of the Calvinistic position on predestination.

A third major theological issue that Wesley faced during the Oxford years was the question of the authoritative basis for arriving at doctrinal positions. It was the matter of deciding upon a standard for truth. Because his position on that point would then shape his thinking in other areas of theology, it is an area that deserves careful attention. The basic issue is that of authority in religious matters. The question is whether Wesley adopted the classical Protestant position regarding the final authority of Scripture, or whether he viewed other standards for truth—such as reason, experience, and tradition—as coordinate authorities of equal value with Scripture. Because the basic question is so intimately bound up with Wesley's attitude toward the Scripture, our study begins with the development of his views about the Word of God.

Wesley's understanding of the role of the Bible was first shaped in the Epworth rectory under the influence of his father. Samuel Wesley had a deep personal commitment to the Scripture as the Word of God, and his own scholarly writings reflect his passion for the Bible.[28] An indication of its importance for him can be seen in his counsel that John not enter into Holy Orders unprepared. The most significant part of this preparation was a personal familiarity with the Bible, based on a knowledge of the text in the original languages. John later paid tribute to his father in a review of his own early years:

> From a child I was taught to love and reverence the Scripture, the oracles of God; and next to these, to esteem the primitive Fathers, the writers of the three first centuries. Next after the primitive church I esteem our own, the Church of England, as the most scriptural national church in the world.[29]

If what John was taught was an accurate reflection of his father's conviction about the order of religious authority, then it is clear that for Samuel Wesley Scripture was to be given priority over tradition.

This crucial importance of the Bible was reinforced for John during the Oxford years by his reading of Jeremy Taylor's *The Rule and Exercises of Holy Living*.

Taylor repeatedly returns for his fundamental authority to the Word of God, which he confines to the Bible. All commandments and revelations, promises and threatenings, stories and sermons in the Bible belong to the Word of God, and even the best books of devotion or sermons cannot be compared with it. As Martin Schmidt observed, "It was certainly of significance for John Wesley's development that in this book he was so strongly directed to the Bible."[30]

The relation of Scripture to authority was another major issue more specifically raised for Wesley at the time of his ordination. Receiving Holy Orders in the Church of England required subscription to the Thirty-Nine Articles of Religion, and one of these articles dealt with the role of Scripture in the church. Just as article 17, on predestination, had raised enough problems for him to question whether or not he could, in good conscience, subscribe to the Thirty-Nine Articles without reservation, so also the article on Scripture may have raised for him the first time the full implications of the question of authority.

It was article 6, on the Holy Scriptures, that specifically defined the Anglican position on religious authority:

> Holy Scripture containeth all things necessary to Salvation: so that whatsoever is not read therein, nor may be proved thereby, is not to be required of any man, that it should be believed as an Article of faith, or to be thought requisite or necessary to Salvation.[31]

Article 6 then makes a distinction between the canonical books "of whose authority was never any doubt in the church" and the apocryphal books. The church reads the latter "for example of life and instruction of manners; but it doth not apply them to establish any Doctrine." By this the Church of England aligned itself with classical Protestantism's commitment to *sola scriptura*. In addition to the declaration that the Scriptures contain all things necessary for salvation, the article makes it clear that no doctrine is to "be believed as an article of faith" unless it may be read in the Bible or proved thereby. So by this declaration of faith, the Holy Scriptures were definitely established as final authority in the Church of England, and clearly distinguished from tradition.

In discussing article 6, Burnet argues that the important point to be established is "the rule of this faith." He then shows how the Church of England differs from the Roman Church:

> We . . . affirm, that the scriptures are a complete rule of faith, and that the whole Christian religion is contained in them, and no where else; and although we make great use of tradition, especially that which is most ancient and nearest the source, to help us to a clear understanding of the scriptures; yet as to matters of faith we reject all oral tradition, . . . and we refuse to receive any doctrine that is not either expressly contained in scripture, or clearly proved from it.[32]

The fact that the Scripture was recognized in the Church of England as the final authority in all matters of doctrine and practice was certainly not lost upon the conscientious young Wesley as he pored over the Articles of Religion in preparation for his ordination. Further, the very action of subscribing to the articles at that time is a very strong indicator that Wesley was beginning to make the Bible his "complete rule" in matters of religious authority.

In looking back over early Methodism, Wesley pinpointed 1729 as the year in which he "began not only to read but to study the Bible as the one, the only, standard of truth and the only model of pure religion."[33] This was the year he began to meet with the Oxford Methodists for the serious study of certain key books, including the Greek New Testament. Although Heitzenrater has given solid evidence that the Oxford circle did not begin their more concentrated study of the Bible until 1734–35,[34] still 1729 is a significant point at which Wesley realized a fresh appreciation of the Scriptures.

Even so, when Wesley wrote in 1766 that it was the year 1729 in which he began to study the Bible as "the only standard of truth," even he may be placing the date too early. That certainly was his position in 1766, but in 1729 he still had not finished working through two thorny issues related to authority: (1) the relation of Scripture to experience, which was to pertain to his struggle with the mystics in the mid-1730s; and (2) the relation of Scripture to tradition, which was to relate to his evaluation of the early church during his sojourn in Georgia.

The first of these questions, the relationship of experience to Scripture, was wrapped up with Wesley's brief involvement with the mystics. Robert Tuttle has demonstrated that between 1732 and 1735 Wesley became heavily influenced by the speculative mysticism of William Law. During this period Wesley traveled several times to London for personal interviews with Law. Early on, Wesley had been attracted to Law by his books *A Serious Call to a Devout and Holy life* and *Christian Perfection*. However, by the time Law had become Wesley's spiritual director in the mid-1730s, Law had become a convert to the German mysticism of Tauler and Böhme.

Under Law's influence Wesley began to search after salvation and assurance by means of contemplation. Here the emphasis was upon the personal experience of God according to the mystical scheme of inner penance.[35] Wesley summarized the views of the mystics while writing to his brother Samuel in November 1736. In his letter he pointed out that his chief objection was that they rejected the means of grace as God's scripturally ordained instruments for communicating His favor to men. Wesley synthesized the mystics' approach:

> All means were not necessary for all men; therefore each person must use such means and such only, as he finds necessary for him. But since we can never attain our end by being wedded to the same means; therefore we must not obstinately cleave unto anything, lest it become an hindrance, not an help. Observe, farther [*sic*] when the end is attained, the means cease.[36]

One of the chief means of grace was the Scripture. This the mystics bypassed: "The Scripture they need not read; for it is only His letter with whom they converse face to face." It was this view of the means of grace, and the Scriptures in particular, that Wesley concluded was the rock that nearly shipwrecked all his faith while he was in Georgia. On his return voyage to England, he penned his evaluation of those who placed experience above Scripture:

> All other enemies of Christianity are triflers; the Mystics are the most dangerous of its enemies. They stab it in the vitals; and its most serious professors are most likely to fall by them. May I praise Him who hath snatched me out of this fire.[37]

It is important to realize that Wesley was rejecting the mystical emphasis upon experience on the ground that it set aside the means of grace. Implicit here, however, is the underlying reason that Wesley placed such a high premium on the means of grace. They were crucial in his eyes because they were "scripturally ordained":

> According to this, according to the decision of holy writ, all who desire the grace of God are to wait for it in the means which He hath ordained; in using, not in laying them aside.[38]

The authority for evaluating the importance of the means of grace was the Bible, rather than experience or tradition. Hence, by the time he returned from Georgia, Wesley had made the Scriptures the touchstone by which he tried all opinions.

This same question arose again when Wesley had to confront a mystical quietism in the early years of the revival. The debated question was how to wait upon God: with the means of grace or without them? Wesley responded:

> It cannot possibly be conceived, that the Word of God should give no direction in so important a point; or that the Son of God . . . should have left us undetermined with regard to a question wherein our salvation is so nearly concerned. And, in fact, He hath not left us undetermined, he hath shown us the way wherein we should go. We have only to consult the oracles of God; to inquire what is written there; and, if we simply abide by their decision, there can be no possible doubt remain[ing].[39]

While he made his position clear that the means of grace were essential, it must also be observed that Wesley left no doubt as to why he took this view. It was the position of Scripture, and that for him was determinative.

A second issue with which Wesley continued to grapple after 1729 was the relation of Scripture to the tradition of the early church. During the summer of 1732 he was heavily influenced by reading the Apostolic Constitutions, the Apostolic Canons, and William Cave's *Primitive Christianity*.[40]

For a time Wesley apparently began to place the tradition of the first three or four centuries on a par with the authority of Scripture. But while he was in Georgia, a reading of Bishop William Beveridge's *Synodikon* convinced Wesley that much of the early church tradition was not of apostolic origin, and that he could not place tradition, even that which was closest to the New Testament Church, on the same level of authority with the Scripture.[41] On his return to

England, he rejoiced that he had been delivered from the error of "making antiquity a coordinate rather than a subordinate rule with Scripture."[42]

So by the beginning of 1738, Wesley had squarely faced the question of the relation of Scripture to both experience and tradition. Furthermore, he had settled for himself the issue that Scripture was to be taken as the undisputed final authority in all religious matters. At this time he wrote to Lady Cox, "To anyone who asketh me concerning myself or these whom I rejoice to call my brethren, what our principles are, I answer clearly, We have no principles but those revealed in the Word of God."[43] The following year he responded to some reservations about his conduct in promoting the revival, and he clearly justified his actions upon the authority of Scripture:

> If by catholic principles you mean any other than scriptural, they weigh nothing with me. I allow no other rule, whether of faith or practice, than the Holy Scriptures. But on scriptural principles I do not think it hard to justify whatever I do. God in Scripture commands me, according to my power, to instruct the ignorant, reform the wicked, confirm the virtuous. Man forbids me to do this in another's parish; that is, in effect, to do it at all; seeing I have now no parish of my own, nor probably ever shall. Whom then shall I hear? God or man?[44]

A convincing demonstration of how the Scripture served as final authority for Wesley at this time is found in the way he dealt with theological issues just before his evangelical conversion. In March to May 1938, as Wesley wrestled with a new definition of faith and a different understanding of justification, his intellectual and spiritual pilgrimage was heavily under the influence of the Moravian Peter Bohler. Although Bohler was both persuasive and persistent, Wesley was not to be convinced by reasoned argument alone. He began to test Bohler's views against the Bible:

> The next morning I began the Greek testament again, resolving to abide by "the law and the testimony" and being confident that God would hereby show me whether this doctrine was of God.[45]

A month later Wesley struggled to comprehend Bohler's assertion that conversion could be instantaneous, and again he turned to the Scripture:

> I could not comprehend what he spoke of an instantaneous work. I could not understand how this faith could be given in a moment. I searched the Scriptures again touching this very thing, particularly the Acts of the Apostles: but, to my utter astonishment, found scarce any so slow as that of St. Paul, who was three days in the pangs of the new birth.[46]

It was confidence in the authority of Scripture that made it possible for Wesley in future years to challenge others to convince him of a different view, but only from the Bible. In the preface to his *Sermons*, which he described as "what I find in the Bible concerning the way to heaven," Wesley indicated by what standard he was willing to be corrected: "I trust whereinsoever I have been mistaken, my mind is open to conviction. I sincerely desire to be better informed. Point out a better way than I have known. Show me it is so, by plain proof of Scripture."[47]

The evidence thus seems to substantiate the conclusion that not later than 1738 Wesley had settled the question about the relationship of Scripture to other criteria for truth. Scripture was not seen as only the first in a line of coordinate criteria, but as the final authority in all religious matters. As Snyder puts it, Wesley had "Scripture as the 'norming norm' to be placed above all other authority."[48] Because of this, Wesley must be classified as standing firmly in the classical Protestant tradition on the question of religious authority. Cohn Williams, in identifying Wesley with this position, observed, "That Wesley continually subjected tradition and experience to the 'written Word of God,' even a casual reading of his works will reveal."[49]

Not only did Wesley begin the eighteenth-century revival with this classical view of authority, but he also continued to maintain this conviction throughout his lifetime. Nearly fifty years after the Methodists "began to preach that grand scriptural doctrine, salvation by faith," Wesley could reaffirm his identification with the Reformation position:

> The faith of the Protestants, in general, embraces only those truths as necessary to salvation, which are clearly revealed in the oracles of God. Whatever is plainly declared in the Old and New Testaments is the object of their faith. They believe neither more nor less than what is manifestly contained in, and approvable by, the Holy Scriptures. The Word of God is "a lantern to their feet, and a light in all their paths." They dare not, on any pretence, go from it, to the right hand or to the left. The written word is the whole and sole rule of their faith as well as practice.[50]

It is significant for contemporary Methodism to note that this was not only Wesley's personal position, but that it characterized the Methodists as a whole. During the early years of the revival Wesley wrote in "The Character of a Methodist":

> We believe, indeed, that "all Scripture is given by the inspiration of God"; and herein we are distinguished from Jews, Turks, and Infidels. We believe the written Word of God to be the only and sufficient rule both of Christian faith and practice; and herein we are fundamentally distinguished from those of the Roman Church.[51]

Thus by the close of the Oxford and Georgia years, Wesley had come to some firm convictions on a number of major theological issues that would determine his views for the remainder of his life. The three subjects most directly related to this study, i.e., predestination, holiness, and authority, were all intrinsically related throughout the revival. Predestination and holiness were a part of the two-sided debate over the application of grace. The notice of authority was an ever-recurrent theme, as it often is in the midst of theological controversy when each party refers to its own final court of appeal on matters of right and wrong.

Excursus: Arminianism and Calvinism in England during the Eighteenth Century

While a detailed study of the state of Arminianism and Calvinism in England during the eighteenth century is beyond the scope of this investigation, a short introduction is necessary to define terms and to lay out the background within which both Wesley's theology of predestination and the Arminian-Calvinist controversies may be understood.

Arminianism

Samuel and Susannah Wesley had joined the Church of England at a time when its predominant theological ethos was Arminian. With the restoration of the monarchy had come the collapse of Puritan power in polities and a corresponding sharp decline in the influence of Calvinistic theology. Calvinism had so shifted its base to Dissenters that by 1700 Anglicanism was largely an Arminian communion.[1] A well-known story has it that when Bishop Morley was asked what the Arminians held, he replied that "they held the best bishoprics and deaneries in England."[2] Arminianism, however, was a broad term and often used as a theological umbrella that provided shelter from various political and ecclesiastical thunderstorms for all who were not Calvinists.[3]

Earlier in the century Archbishop Laud, as leader of the Arminians, had used the term to refer to his high-church theories of the episcopacy as well as to the Remonstrant understanding of predestination.[4] There was also a liberal trend in Arminianism, seen in men like Jeremy Taylor and Edward Stillingfleet, which led into a rational theology.[5] Others like the Cambridge Platonists attacked much that Calvinism represented, while Latitudinarians like Tillotson called themselves Arminians.[6]

From the Calvinist viewpoint, the Arminians had stepped off the solid ground of orthodoxy into a slough of theological rationalism. Imperceptibly, Arminianism was thought to move toward unitarianism and finally to deism, or even atheism.[7] A movement toward unitarianism did begin to take place after 1720 by theologians like John Taylor, Nathaniel Lardner, and George Benson. This movement threatened to reduce Christianity to a moral code, "far more dangerous," wrote Wesley, "than open deism itself." The fact that this happened in England, as it had earlier on the continent, made the fear of Arminianism by eighteenth-century Calvinists like George Whitefield and Jonathan Edwards all that much more understandable.[8]

Wesley's Arminianism should not be identified with any of these English accretions. His own theology on doctrines related to predestination was basically that of Jacob Arminius, and that fact later caused him openly to espouse the term Arminian.[9] The essential theology of Arminiust[10] filtered through its seventeenth-century embellishments and reached Wesley via his parents,[11] although the secondary associations that the label "Arminian" had acquired probably account for the fact that Wesley did not apply the term to himself in the early part of his ministry.[12] Wesley's leadership in the evangelical revival later resulted in his theology being distinguished as evangelical Arminianism.[13]

Calvinism

While the term Calvinism was not as all-inclusive as its eighteenth-century Arminian counterpart, it also covered a wide theological spectrum. Its variant forms will become clearer as we proceed with an examination of the several writings of its exponents. "Calvinism" may be classified into three major types: Hyper-Calvinism, High Calvinism, and Moderate Calvinism.[14] While the lines between these cannot be drawn too sharply, the distinctions do serve as a useful guide amid the complex maze of theological controversy.

High Calvinism

High Calvinism was a more developed form of Calvin's theology as represented by Theodore Beza, certain Reformed theologians after him, and the Synod of Dort. While there were variations of High Calvinism among the Puritans, all High Calvinists in England during the seventeenth and eighteenth centuries were "Five-Point Calvinists"; i.e., they believed in the *t*otal depravity of man, an *un*conditional election, a *l*imited atonement, the *ir*resistibility of grace, and the final *p*erseverance of the saints (TULIP). To these points many added acceptance of a federal theology, the infallibility of the Bible, and an assurance of salvation. While some were supralapsarians, the majority were infralapsarians (or sublapsarians).[15] Most of them refused to distinguish between the secret and revealed will of God and declared that the duty of men must be deduced from God's revealed will in Scripture.[16] Although they believed in an unconditional reprobation, they did not give it a place of prominence.

During the eighteenth-century revival, this position was represented by Augustus Toplady, Martin Madan, and Richard and Rowland Hill in the Church of England, and Andrew Fuller among the Baptists.[17] Within this viewpoint, the authors who were probably the most widely read were Elisha Coles and Dr. John Edwards of Cambridge.

Hyper-Calvinism

Hyper-Calvinism[18] was likewise "Five-Point Calvinism," but it pressed the system to more logically extreme positions. It was framed to exalt the honor of God, but in this it also drastically minimized the moral and spiritual responsibility of the sinner. It placed excessive emphasis on eternal reprobation and the eternal covenant of grace, while the central place of the cross was obscured by the accent on the divine decrees. It often made the distinction between the secret and revealed will of God and attempted to understand the duty of men from its speculations on the secret, eternal decrees of God. The emphasis placed on irresistible grace was so great that man became completely passive in conversion.[19]

The excessive preoccupation with the eternal aspects of redemption led to the discouragement of evangelism and prayer for the unconverted. The belief that the unregenerate could do nothing spiritually good resulted in a refusal to urge sinners to repent, exercise faith, or pray. Even Adam, it was held, had been incapable of faith or good works before the Fall. A "warrant" to believe, i.e., a subjective conviction of the soul, was required before one could exercise faith, and a valid assurance of salvation likewise consisted of an "inner feeling" that one had been eternally elected.

Law and gospel were frequently set in the sharpest opposition to one another. Since the unregenerate were under a covenant of law, faith could not be required of them. On the other hand, while believers were under a covenant of grace, nothing from the law applied to them.[20]

Most of the Hyper-Calvinists in the eighteenth century were Baptists and included such well-known figures as Joseph Hussey, John Skepp, Richard Davis, Lewis Wayman, John Gill, and John Brine.[21] Gill and Brine were the most widely read by their contemporaries. Manning aptly characterized these men when he asked: "In a century when the solvent acids of rationalism were so potent, was it a misfortune . . . that a hard bitter rind of tough Calvinism covered their faith?"[22]

Moderate Calvinism

Moderate Calvinism began with the total depravity of the human race and believed that all of salvation was from God, including the gift of faith. The law was designed to drive men to the gospel, where Christ had satisfied its demands and where His righteousness was imputed to the believer. The central doctrine for Moderate Calvinists was justification by faith alone, and this dominated their preaching. Good works were not a meritorious cause of salvation nor a condition. Assurance followed justification as a privilege, but not as essential to saving grace. Most individuals of this particular viewpoint held to the traditional Calvinistic view of final perseverance of the saints.[23]

Moderate Calvinists emphasized their connections with Scripture, Augustine, the ancient and medieval church, and the Anglican Thirty-Nine Articles and Homilies. However, they minimized their relationship to Calvinism. They believed that many Calvinists had gone beyond Scripture on positions like predestinated reprobation and supralapsarianism. They held to particular election, but did not allow it to become the major premise of a deterministic metaphysic, nor did they concede reprobation as its corollary.[24]

Under the influence of men like Moise Amyraut[25] and Richard Baxter,[26] they often granted a hypothetical universal atonement, whereby Christ died for all men, but not all were automatically saved. To this they added a particular election, in which God elected in Christ some to respond, and then drew them to salvation by effectual grace. None were unjustly excluded, however, since all deserved damnation; God merely passed by some. Man's condemnation was thus due to his own disobedience and not to any eternal decree.[27]

The Moderate Calvinists were embarrassed when their allies among the Hyper- and High Calvinists bordered on both practical and speculative antinomianism.[28]

For this reason they pressed good works after justification as evidence of salvation. Privilege and duty, imputed righteousness and personal obedience were closely joined together, The purpose of election was to make men holy and fit for heaven.[29] This explains why many Moderate Calvinistic Evangelicals, whenever possible, avoided preaching on the doctrines of predestination, election, and final perseverance. They concentrated instead on justification by faith alone, holiness, and assurance.[30] Many leading Evangelicals of the eighteenth century were Moderate Calvinists: George Whitefield, Henry Venn, James Hervey, William Grimshaw, John Berridge, Joseph Milner, and Thomas Scott, among others.

While the distinctions among the three types of Calvinism are useful, they should not be viewed as rigidly inflexible. At different times in his career, a man might move from one category to another. George Whitefield, for example, was a Moderate Calvinist, but during the heated debate with Wesley in 1740–41, he temporarily aligned himself more closely with the High Calvinist position. Similarly, in the 1770s August Toplady sounded at times much like a Hyper-Calvinist, although it cannot be said that he really adopted that viewpoint. Thus, these definitions will be used flexibly as functional descriptions rather than as binding categories.

PART I:

THE FREE-GRACE CONTROVERSY
1739–44

Wesley vs. Whitefield

2. The Outbreak of the Controversy on Predestination

THE controversy over predestination arose between Wesley and Whitefield in the midst of their shared leadership responsibility in the early days of the revival. Since the intimacy of the two men at the outset is important for understanding the controversy, our study begins with a description of their relationship. It then moves to the events surrounding Wesley's first sermon on predestination and the effects that followed. Because John and Charles Wesley were so close in theology as well as in ministry, due attention will be given to the way in which Charles became involved in the controversy. Finally, we will review the development of George Whitefield's own views on predestination in preparation for understanding how differences among the Wesleys and Whitefield on this point led to a division within the Evangelical Revival.

First Sign of Controversy

From his ordination in 1725 until his conversion in 1738, the Arminian-Calvinistic questions occupied relatively little place in Wesley's life.[1] These years were primarily bound up with the weightier considerations of sanctification, justification, and faith. It was not until these matters were settled for Wesley that he again encountered the doctrine of predestination.

Shortly after his conversion in 1738, Wesley traveled to Germany to visit the headquarters of the Moravians at Herrnhut. While there he spent some hours with Christian David, one of the early leaders of the Moravian community, who informed him that the first doctrinal controversy among the Herrnhuters (Moravians) was over predestination. Having become a Calvinist himself, David brought most of the new community over to his views of election and reprobation. But some refused to be moved by David's exhortations on the love of God for they were afraid that, perhaps, He had not elected them and they were reprobate. When Count Zinzendorf recognized the problem, he first sent David to a nearby pastor who held firm views on the universality of Christ's atonement. Then he gathered all of the community into his house for a three-day session on the subject, during which all finally agreed that God "willeth all men to be saved."[2]

This experience only strengthened Wesley's abhorrence of the Calvinistic view. In particular, he encountered, perhaps for the first time, the practical and pastoral problems that arose from the doctrines of election and reprobation. The despair over not knowing whether one was elect or reprobate, coupled with an inability to change that fate, created for the Moravians a situation that Wesley's pastoral heart must have felt keenly. This problem was certainly one of the reasons Wesley could never appreciate the argument of the Calvinists to the effect that the doctrine of election was "full of unspeakable comfort."

While he was in Germany the first sign of controversy appeared in London. Charles dealt with the matter by opposing "the Calvinian view with such firmness, as prevented all further attempt at this time to unsettle the minds of the people respecting the universality of God's love to men."[3]

After Wesley returned from the continent, George Whitefield, fresh from his first journey to America, joined him. Together with Charles Wesley, they formed the nucleus of spiritual leadership among the religious societies in London, resuming the intimate relationship they had enjoyed at Oxford. Whitefield noted that "many who were awakened by my preaching a year ago, are now grown strong men in Christ, by the administrations of my dear friends and fellow labourers, John and Charles Wesley."[4] In reciprocal terms, John Wesley prayed that a small portion of the spirit of Whitefield might be given to him. "Oh how is God manifested in our brother Whitefield! I have seen none like him, . . . no, not in Herrnhut!"[5]

In addition to his labors in London, Whitefield had amazing success as a field preacher in the west of England during February and March, 1739.[6] Committed to returning to Georgia, yet acutely conscious of the needs of the awakened multitudes, Whitefield requested that Wesley come and assume the responsibility for the flock in Bristol. Wesley arrived on March 31, and two days later Whitefield left the city. He stopped long enough to lay the foundation stone for a school at Kingswood before he proceeded to his hometown of Gloucester. Whitefield immediately wrote a note to Wesley, asking him to take charge of the project at Kingswood.[7] Whitefield later rejoiced at "the wonderful success of my honoured friend Mr. John Wesley's ministry in Bristol."[8]

It is only in recent years that Whitefield's proper role in the leadership of the eighteenth-century revival has been properly recognized. Whitefield had experienced an evangelical conversion before either of the two Wesleys, and he seems to have been first among the three to recognize the need for a more aggressive type of evangelism. Thus, it was Whitefield who first took to the open air to proclaim the gospel of Christ, and who first made contact with the American evangelical awakening. Further, his unusual talents for public speaking made Whitefield the most outstanding preacher of the revival.

Yet, in spite of all these things, it is far from certain that Whitefield consciously saw himself as the leader of the revival movement. Whitefield did invite Wesley to Bristol in the winter of 1739, but in what capacity? Did he view Wesley as deputy to assume the responsibility for the work only while Whitefield was away? Did Wesley come as one on an equal footing with Whitefield? Or did he come as Whitefield's mentor, to aid a younger son in the faith? The data would suggest that these men saw themselves as a group of co-workers on roughly equal terms, without any one of them assuming primacy over the others.

It is especially difficult to think of Whitefield summoning Wesley to Bristol as his "appointee" in light of the difference in their ages. In 1739 Whitefield was 24, while Wesley was 36. Further, the leadership role of their previous relationship had distinctly been with Wesley as head of the Oxford Holy Club.

In fact, both of the Wesleys seem to have had a significant amount of influence over Whitefield, not only at Oxford where Charles first introduced Whitefield to the Holy Club, but also in Georgia where John later invited him. In this connection it should also be remembered that Whitefield wrote to the Wesleys, on a number of occasions during the 1730s, requesting their guidance on important decisions.

While it does not appear that John Wesley exercised the kind of leadership during the early days of the revival that he had previously at Oxford, neither is it clear that Whitefield assumed this role. The body of evidence suggests that Whitefield refused to assume administrative oversight of the new converts and asked for assistance from the leadership core in London. On the whole it would seem that these men felt themselves bound together in a common cause, and that their close personal relationships permitted them to call upon one another for various responsibilities in order that each might exercise his gifts for the benefit of the whole spiritual enterprise.[9]

Their journals reveal that the short time that Wesley and Whitefield were together in Bristol was apparently spent in close fellowship. On Wesley's arrival the two men conversed about the work of God until far into the night. The following day Wesley visited the societies with Whitefield and for the first time heard him preach in the open air. Apparently the transition was a smooth one for both leaders and people. One who had often attended Whitefield's preaching described the event:

> When I heard him preach the last sermon at Rosegreen and telling them there was one coming after him whose shoes latchett he was not worthy to unloose, I found great Love in my heart to him after that. The first opportunity I had I went to hear Mr. John Wesley, and my conscience soon told me that it was the true gospel of Christ that he preached.[10]

Whitefield evidently commended Wesley in the highest possible terms.

Another Bristol resident said she heard him recommend "Mr. Wesley to the people, as one to be prefer'd before him."[11] Whitefield's echoes of John the Baptist indicate his desire to smooth the way as much as possible for his companion. In no way do the records hint that Wesley was to be received as a temporary leader. To the contrary, if there is any clue on the leadership question, it would appear that Whitefield deferred to Wesley.

Wesley's concern to see that the new Bristol converts grew in holiness led him to divide them into bands in order to provide that intimate Christian fellowship which he believed was essential to spiritual progress. Another aid to growth in godliness was the thorough scriptural diet he began to feed them. Before Whitefield left Bristol, Wesley had begun to work through the Sermon on the Mount with the society at Nicholas Street. During his first week he initiated a series of expositions on major New Testament books, including Acts, John, Romans, and 1 John.[12] Wesley certainly felt the need for solid biblical teaching as a stabilizing element for young Christians. He worked through large portions of the New Testament with remarkable care. His teaching of basic Christian doctrine from the book of Romans in two of the Bristol societies was especially relevant to questions on sanctification and predestination.

Wesley often reminded readers of his works that the doctrine of universal redemption was a part of his message from the earliest days of the revival. Within a week of his arrival at Bristol, while preaching from Romans at the Weavers Hall, he "declared the gospel to all, which is the 'power of God unto salvation to everyone that believeth.' "[13] The preaching of universal redemption had also been his practice in London, so that upon reaching Bristol he began as was customary for him.

Wesley's Sermon on "Free Grace": The Beginning of the Division

According to his diary, Wesley spent the morning of April 15, 1739, writing on predestination.[14] Unfortunately, the exact nature of this writing is unknown, but it indicates that he felt it necessary to record his thinking with pen and ink. Questions apparently were being raised on this subject, and he seemed genuinely perplexed as to how to respond. At first he considered a forthright declaration of his own views, but then decided for the moment that it was "best to walk gently." Shortly thereafter, this decision was set aside. Accordingly, while preaching early one morning at Newgate prison, he was led to speak "strongly and explicitly of Predestination."[15]

At the noon hour following this event, Wesley expressed uncertainty concerning whether he should continue to pursue the matter publicly. When a layman, George Purdy, pressed him to speak out boldly on the subject, Wesley "appealed to God concerning Predestination" by drawing lots. The answer he received was "Preach and print." That same evening he was "pressed in spirit to declare that 'Christ gave himself a ransom for all.' "

Two days later, on Saturday, April 28, 1739, Wesley wrote his famous sermon on "Free Grace." Still reluctant to make an issue of the doctrine, he cast a further lot for guidance on whether or not to preach that particular sermon. Receiving an affirmative answer, on Sunday morning he "declared openly for the first time against 'the horrible decree.' "[16]

Since the "Free Grace" sermon marks the beginning of the division of the Methodist movement into its Arminian and Calvinistic segments, John Wesley's reasons for preaching on predestination are important for understanding subsequent events. Wesley was never uncertain over his own doctrinal convictions, but he did question how far predestination should be a part of the public proclamation of the gospel. Since he was acutely aware that divisive debate would follow any raising of the issue, why did he preach his sermon on "Free Grace"?

There were a number of good reasons for not preaching on predestination. Wesley had received strong counsel from the Fetter Lane Society, from Whitefield, and from a "Bro. Chapman" to avoid the matter. This advice came, they said, because the people of Bristol were said to be prejudiced in its favor.[17] If this prejudice were there, it strongly suggests that Whitefield himself made it an issue in his preaching. The fact that he urged Wesley to avoid the subject indicates that

Whitefield was conscious of a difference of opinion and that he was apprehensive about doctrinal disagreements over the matter. Wesley apparently shared Whitefield's apprehension for he was clearly reticent about making predestination a subject for preaching. Then, too, Howel Harris, as well as Whitefield, may have influenced Methodist thinking in Bristol. Harris came to the city to meet Whitefield in early March and recorded that he had spoken to the society "against the Arminians."[18]

There is further evidence to suggest that Wesley was not the first to raise the issue. A letter was circulated throughout Bristol that charged him "with 'resisting and perverting the truth as it is in Jesus' by preaching against God's decree of predestination." It was handed about almost a month before Wesley saw it. Therefore, it was making its influence felt from the very beginning of his ministry in the city. A second letter added to the damage of the first. In this letter yet another Bristol resident exhorted his friends to avoid Wesley as a false teacher.[19]

Pondering these unjust accusations, Wesley at first decided to walk gently and say nothing. Yet at least two issues had been raised that could not ultimately be avoided. One issue was personal, for the letters were designed specifically to undercut Wesley's influence. The revival in Bristol being at a crucial stage, Wesley felt his primary task was to consolidate the fruits of Whitefield's ministry. As Whitefield recognized when he invited Wesley to Bristol, the need was for decisive leadership, and any undermining of Wesley's position would clearly have weakened the movement.

A second issue raised by the aforementioned letters was the place of doctrine in the revival. Both Whitefield and Wesley saw the need of solid teaching for the new converts. Indeed, Wesley had assumed responsibility for such teaching from his first day in Bristol. His constant exposition of New Testament books reveals the importance he placed on a firm theological foundation for members of the societies. It is not surprising then that such doctrinal questions should ultimately arise as the new Christians grew in theological maturity.

Wesley did not at first preach on these controversial matters, either to the societies or in the open-air services. It was in the midst of his discourse at the Newgate prison that he felt led without previous design to speak explicitly on universal redemption. Amazed and perhaps a little uneasy at his own forthrightness, he prayed that God would either withhold his blessing and so repudiate this, or confirm the procedure by a positive sign. Immediately several people began dropping to the ground as though struck from heaven. After others prayed on their behalf, they received joy, peace, and righteousness into their souls.[20] But it was not just the physical manifestations that Wesley regarded as evidence of God's favor upon his conduct; rather, it was the subsequent evident conversions that impressed him.

In spite of such confirmation, Wesley was reluctant to speak further on the subject of predestination. At least one member of the society strongly urged him to declare himself boldly on the matter. As the last in a series of steps seeking guidance, Wesley cast the aforementioned lot. Having received direction to "preach and print," he proceeded to write the sermon on predestination. Even so, his caution forced him to cast yet another lot to determine if this was indeed the message he was to preach.

After preaching the sermon on "Free Grace" two or three times over a span of four days, he let the subject drop. It may be that the message raised a storm of protest, giving him second thoughts on the matter. It seems likely however, that he felt the issue had received adequate attention and that he had no desire to press a controversial topic further. Wesley himself, reviewing the affair, indicated that predestination was not central to his preaching: "Generally I speak on faith, remission of sins, and the gift of the Holy Spirit."[21]

A study of his other sermons and texts during the remainder of 1739 supports his contention. There is no record of his having preached the sermon on "Free Grace" again. Occasionally there are passages that contain references to the universal offer of grace, but the evidence is that Wesley used these before April 1739, and that they were without explicit reference to predestination. In other sermons on faith, salvation, the Holy Spirit, etc., he may also have offered salvation to all men without making an issue of the disputed points.

One further factor behind the outbreak of the controversy was Wesley's reading of John Gill, pastor of the Particular Baptist Church in Southwark, whom Toon describes as a prominent exponent of Hyper-Calvinism.[22] An ardent controversialist who later attacked Wesley on predestination, Gill published *The Doctrine of God's Everlasting Love to His Elect and Their Eternal Union to Christ* in 1732. In answer to a discourse published by Dr. Daniel Whitby, entitled *Discourse on the Five Points*, Gill wrote his four-volume treatise *The Cause of God and Truth: Being an Examination of the Principle [Principal] Passages of Scripture Made Use of by the Arminians in Favour of Their Scheme* (1734–1738). It is probable that this last treatise came to Wesley's attention.[23]

In *The Cause of God and Truth*, Gill proposed to answer Whitby's objections to Calvinism. Volume 1 was a consideration of the passages of Scripture used by his opponent "in favour of the Universal Scheme, and against the Calvinistical Scheme." Sixty different portions of the Old and New Testament were examined with a view to refuting the Arminian arguments and giving the passages a proper interpretation.[24] In volume 2 Gill took the offensive and set out an equal number of references from the Bible to support his Calvinistic viewpoint. Attention was focused on reprobation, election, redemption, efficacious grace, the corruption of human nature, the impotence of the will of man, and lastly, perseverance.[25]

After reviewing the evidence from Scripture, Gill then turned in volume 3 to the arguments from reason used by Whitby and the Arminians. He contended that the doctrines he supported "are no more disagreeable to right reason than to divine revelation." The order of his presentation again began with reprobation. Volume 4 was a survey of the early church fathers up to Augustine, to demonstrate their basic agreement with the Calvinistic position on the key doctrines under consideration. The national crisis related to the growth of Roman Catholicism in the early eighteenth century was due, Gill felt, to the influence of Pelagianism and Arminianism. This he described as "the very life and soul of Popery."[26]

An analysis of Wesley's sermon on "Free Grace" reveals that his strongest objections were directed toward the doctrine of reprobation, and the review of Gill's work demonstrates that this was one of his key doctrinal emphases. It was primarily to this Hyper-Calvinist position, as represented by Gill, that Wesley reacted so strongly in 1739, rather than to the views of the more Moderate Calvinism that characterized many Anglican Evangelicals of the period.

Wesley read Gill in May and June. This was after the initial preaching of "Free Grace," but before its publication in the late summer. It is difficult, therefore, to know what effect Gill had on him. Is it possible that Wesley's sermon in print reflected a stronger anti-Hyper-Calvinistic position than originally had been expressed from the pulpit? Did his reading of Gill influence Wesley's decision to carry on with the controversy and publish his views? Was it a Hyper-Calvinistic element in Bristol that caused Wesley to read Gill for himself? Unfortunately, the available data do not provide sure answers to these questions. Nonetheless, there is a strong suggestion that Wesley, at least in the published form of his sermon, was reacting vigorously to Gill's brand of Hyper-Calvinism. Perhaps this was partially responsible for some of the misunderstandings that arose later between Wesley and the Moderate Calvinists. On June 25 Whitefield wrote to Wesley:

> I hear, honoured Sir, you are about to print a sermon on Predestination. It shocks me to think of it; what will be the consequences but controversy? If people ask me my opinion, what shall I do? I have a critical part to act, God enable me to behave alright! Silence on both sides will be best. It is noised abroad already that there is division between you and me. Oh, my heart within me is grieved![27]

A week later he wrote again and confessed that his spirit had been "sharpened" by some of Wesley's proceedings on doctrinal matters. He had heard that Brother Stock had been excluded from the society because he held predestination, and Whitefield did not feel this was acting with a "Catholic spirit." He strongly urged Wesley to regard the peace of the church and not publish his sermon on predestination.[28]

Due to a delay in his planned departure for Georgia, Whitefield had the opportunity to return to Bristol for a week in July. He was received with great acclaim, and he had a "useful conference" with Wesley to discuss a number of matters. One of these, no doubt, was the question of predestination. Apparently Wesley agreed to at least a postponement of the publication of his sermon. Whitefield wrote afterward that he found "Bristol had great reason to bless God for the ministry of Mr. John Wesley. The congregations I observe to be much more serious and affected than when I left them; That good, great good, is done is evident."[29]

The Role of Charles Wesley

Charles Wesley and Whitefield were close in age and temperament. Their warm friendship began in 1733 at the time that Charles introduced Whitefield to the Holy Club,[30] and it had originally been planned for Charles to journey to

Georgia with Whitefield in 1737.[31] Illustrative of their mutual esteem are the four hymns Charles wrote about Whitefield during the spring of 1739,[32] when they labored together in London. A further evidence of their relationship was Whitefield's desire that Charles take charge of the London work when he embarked for America.

Shortly after Whitefield's departure, Charles Wesley visited the family of Benjamin Seward. His reflections on the occasion indicate his own leanings with regard to predestination:

> Here I cannot but observe the narrow spirit of those that hold particular redemption. I have had no disputes with them, yet they have me in abomination. Mrs. Seward is irreconcilably angry with me; "For he offers Christ to all." When Mr. Seward, in my hearing, exhorted one of the maids to a concern for her salvation, she answered, "It was to no purpose; she could do nothing." The same answer he received from his daughter, of seven years old. See the genuine fruits of this blessed doctrine![33]

Yet, the visit was not without effect. The following month Seward wrote that Charles had convinced him of the doctrine of universal redemption.[34]

At the end of August, Charles assumed leadership of the work in Bristol. Since he was just as committed as his brother to the promotion of personal holiness among the believers, he followed John Wesley's pattern and began to expound the Scripture, working his way through Isaiah, Romans, and John. In addition to showing how important solid teaching was in his eyes, this practice also reveals that Charles was systematically treating basic biblical doctrine. Inevitably, he came to the subject of predestination. On September 20 while dealing with Romans 9, he declared: "Through mercy, we could none of us see aught of the 'horrible decree' there; but only His justice in rejecting them who had first rejected Him. Christ the Saviour of all men was in the midst of us." Two days later he wrote, "Romans 11 led me unawares to speak of final perseverance, whereby some, I would hope, were cut off from their vain confidence."[35]

A letter written to Charles on September 4, 1739, indicates that the issue of predestination was very much alive in the city at the time. The author expressed strong abhorrence of predestination because

> no fruit doth it bring forth but various strifes, contentions, and this among the Children of one Lord and King. I observe that in writing as well as talking it Robs us of nobler things. O that I could never hear it mentioned more.

Yet, he saw no inconsistency in urging Wesley in the strongest terms to offer salvation to all men:

> Cry aloud, tell the people, yea tell all the people to come to this fountain of our dear Master's Blood, Freely pour'd Blessing out of Jesus for Every

Creature. O my friend, proclaim abroad glad tidings of great Joy to all the Cursed Race of Adam.[36]

Later in the autumn, at Bradford, one of Charles Wesley's sermons was apparently misunderstood, and many were representing him as a predestinarian. After consultation, the Wesleys decided that Charles should declare himself fully on this matter. Accordingly, he recorded that he had great liberty in preaching universal redemption for an hour and a half. Afterward he asserted,[37] "I believe he will no more slander me with being a predestinarian."

Whitefield's Views on Predestination

George Whitefield embarked for America on August 14, 1739. His theological position on predestination at the time of his departure has special relevance for this study. Shortly after his conversion in 1735, Whitefield read several authors who represented the Reformed theological tradition, including Burkitt's and Matthew Henry's *Expositions*, Alleine's *Alarm to the Unconverted*, Baxter's *Call to the Unconverted*, and Janeway's *Life*. His reading of these authors removed certain prejudices in Whitefield's mind toward the Calvinistic Nonconformists, and he wrote that

> the partition wall of bigotry and sect-religion was soon broken down in my heart; for, as soon as the love of God was shed abroad in my soul, I loved all of whatsoever denomination, who loved the Lord Jesus in sincerity of heart.

Of this period, Whitefield said,

> About this time God was pleased to enlighten my soul, and bring me into a knowledge of His Free Grace and the necessity of being justified in His sight by faith only. This was more extraordinary, because my friends at Oxford had rather inclined to the mystic divinity.[38]

Dallimore views this as the germ of Whitefield's early Calvinism,[39] but this is not at all clear from Whitefield's statement.[40] What does appear, however, is that Whitefield was the first member of the Holy Club to arrive at an understanding and experience of justification by faith alone.

Whitefield's early sermons give little indication that the distinctive doctrines of Calvinism played any part in his preaching before 1739.[41] There is the possibility that he preached on predestination in Bristol in February and March of 1739. If this were so, it could explain why he felt that the people there were strongly prejudiced in its favor. Apparently his preaching during 1739 began to include some references to these doctrines. On July 31, at Stoke Newington, Whitefield gave evidence of his leanings by referring prominently to the doctrine of election, and the following week in private correspondence he rejected any connection with "sinless perfection."[42]

As Whitefield left England, doctrines related to predestination were beginning to occupy a place of greater importance in his theology. Supporting this view is Wesley, who cited a letter from Whitefield to show that originally all the

Oxford Methodists "utterly abhorred" the Calvinistic position. He insisted that on the 1739 voyage to Georgia, Whitefield was "just warping toward Calvinism."[43]

In addition to Wesley, there is other evidence that on this second voyage to America, Whitefield's convictions concerning these doctrines became much stronger. During this period he read Neal's *Lives of the Puritans* with approval and he wrote to Charles Wesley that he hoped to find lives of both Luther and Calvin in order to give him some short account of the Reformation.[44] On September 29 he wrote:

> This afternoon, I was greatly strengthened by persuing some paragraphs out of a book called *The Preacher*, written by Dr. Edwards, of Cambridge. There are such noble testimonies given before that University, of Justification by Faith only, the imputed righteousness of Christ, our having no free-will, etc., that they deserve to be written in letters of gold.[45]

Dr. John Edwards seemed to have made significant impact on the thinking of Whitefield. On April 15, 1740, Whitefield read Edwards' attack on Archbishop Tillotson to a congregation in Philadelphia. In his answer to Wesley's sermon on "Free Grace," Whitefield also referred Wesley to Edwards' work *Veritas Redux*.[46]

In *The Preacher*, Edwards had spoken directly to Whitefield's reluctance to cross swords with Wesley: "A Spirit of Meekness is not inconsistent with a warm and earnest Attacking of the Adversaries of Truth. Here is no breach of Charity as is pretended, yea, it is Charity and Compassion to treat them thus." The preacher's "concern for Truth ought to be Impartial, and laying aside undue Fervours, he must be zealous in reproving all Erroneous Doctrines."[47] Among the erroneous views to be opposed were the Remonstrants, who were classed with "the Socinians, the Skepticks, the Enthusiasts, the Deists, and the Atheists."

Further, a very close connection was alleged by Edwards between Arminian theology and Roman Catholicism.[48] In answer to those who regarded predestination and its related doctrines as subjects about which one could be indifferent, he affirmed that they were in the Scripture and therefore could not be unimportant.[49] This may well have spoken to Whitefield's previous counsel to Wesley that "silence on both sides" would be best.

There is one further matter in which Edwards may have influenced Whitefield. In volume 2 of *The Preacher*, Edwards defended his earlier attack on Archbishop Tillotson by referring to the practice of the apostles when confronted with false doctrine. Paul was quoted in his opposition to Peter at Antioch: "I withstood him to the Face because he was to be blamed." Edwards said, "I question not but this is recorded in the Sacred Writings for our Imitation."[50] The fact that this same verse (Galatians 2:11) was printed on the title page of Whitefield's *Answer* to Wesley's sermon on "Free Grace" strongly suggests that Whitefield was following both Edwards' advice and example.[51]

The letters of Whitefield during the voyage reflect the progress of his thinking on these matters. To Howel Harris he wrote:

> Since I saw you, God has been pleased to enlighten me more in the comfortable doctrine of election, etc. At my return, I hope to be more explicit than I have been. God forbid, my dear brother, that we should shun to declare the whole counsel of God.[52]

To another he wrote asking:

> What was there in you and in me, that should move God to choose us before others? Was there any fitness for[e]seen in us, except a fitness for damnation? I believe not. No, God chose us from eternity; he called us in time; and, I am persuaded, will keep us from falling finally, till time shall be no more. Consider the Gospel in this view, and it appears a consistent scheme. Henceforth I hope I shall speak boldly and plainly, as I ought to speak, and not fail to declare the whole counsel of God.[53]

In correspondence with James Hervey, Whitefield referred to

> the excellency of the doctrine of election and of the saint's final persever-ance, to those who were sealed by the spirit of promise! I am persuaded, till the man comes to believe and feel these important truths, he cannot come out of himself; but, when convinced of these and assured of the application of them to his own heart, he then walks by faith indeed.[54]

The record of Whitefield's correspondence, then, as well as his reading, gives evidence that the voyage to America was an important time in the development of his thinking concerning the distinctive doctrines of Calvinism. That he be-came initially committed to these while in England in 1739 appears probable. But it was apparently on this journey that such doctrines assumed a place of central importance.

This new emphasis was reinforced during his second visit to America by Whitefield's attachment to the Calvinistic ministers of the New World.[55] In En-gland he had hitherto been identified with the Church of England, but on his arrival in America close associations were quickly formed with Dissenting minis-ters.[56] Among the Presbyterians, members of the large Tennet family[57] were espe-cially drawn to Whitefield. His first month of itinerant preaching was spent in their company, after which he wrote to Ralph Erskine[58] of Scotland:

> I believe I agree with you in the essential truths of Christianity. I bless God, His Spirit has convinced me of our eternal election by the Father through the Son; of our free justification through faith in His Blood; of our sanctification as the consequence of that; and of our final persever-ance and glorification as the result of all. These, I am persuaded, God has joined together; these neither man no[r] devils shall ever be able to put asunder.[59]

A great deal has been made of the impact of Jonathan Edwards on Whitefield's theology.[60] The only work of Edwards that Whitefield read at this time, however, was *Thoughts Concerning the Present Revival of Religion in New England*.[61] This was primarily an account of the revival under Edwards' ministry in 1734–35, and it did not treat doctrinal issues. More important is the fact that Whitefield did not make Edwards' acquaintance until October 1740, a year after his arrival in America. By this time Whitefield was already in controversy with Wesley over predestination. Whitefield's correspondence shows that his commitment to Calvinism was already firmly established before he met Edwards.

Further, it is clear that the two men did not become intimate friends. Whitefield, in fact, was reluctant to accept Edwards' counsel on certain matters. During their three days together in the autumn of 1740, Edwards cautioned Whitefield about the reliance he placed on his impulses. Edwards recorded: "I thought Mr. Whitefield liked me not so well for my opposing these things, and though he treated me with great kindness, yet he never made so much of an intimate with me, as of other men."[62] It would seem that, at most, Edwards only confirmed in Whitefield those opinions that were already established. It is quite possible that some have confused Jonathan Edwards with Dr. John Edwards of Cambridge. Evidence shows it was the latter who had a decisive impact on Whitefield's views, rather than the New England theologian.

3. The Growing Storm over Predestination

IN 1740 Wesley found himself in theological controversy on two fronts. The twin disputes would bring about a rupture of the unanimity among the leadership of the revival. One part of the controversy concerned Wesley's differences with the Moravians over their doctrine of "stillness." This chapter opens with a discussion of the Moravian aspect of the larger picture and its relevance for understanding Wesley's subsequent disagreements with the Calvinists. This is followed by a survey of Wesley's 1740 publications on predestination.

Then specific contributors of three key figures who were involved in the predestination controversies will be examined. Fresh materials that have come to light now make it possible to see more clearly the role in the controversy played by these three: William Seward, Howel Harris, and John Cennick. Finally, the growing tension between Wesley and Whitefield during the period Whitefield was in America will be reviewed.

The Controversy with the Moravians over "Stillness"

The year 1740 was one of growing theological controversy. The first half of the year saw Wesley in doctrinal debate with the Moravians, and the latter half was a time of tension over predestination with the Calvinists. In the midst of disagreements over theology, both Wesleys continued to cultivate the spiritual life of the religious societies by exposition of Scripture. In January, John Wesley recorded, "I began the Scripture in order" at the New Room, Bristol. On June 5, as an antidote to the antinomian influence of the Moravian doctrine of "stillness," he began to expound James, and over the balance of the year he preached through 1 John, 1 and 2 Peter, the Sermon on the Mount, Matthew, and Romans.[1] During this same period at the Foundry in London, Charles Wesley did a series on Isaiah and the Gospel of John for early morning expositions.[2] Especially when involved in theological controversy, the Wesleys constantly dealt with the content of Scripture. Thus, day-to-day study of the Bible heavily fortified the understanding of doctrine among the Wesleys and the Methodist Society members. Theology for them could not be isolated from the Word of God.

In the middle of the Moravian dispute, Wesley was compelled to exclude a member for insisting on a certain theological "opinion" in the society. A Calvinist in the society described the problem to the Welch evangelist Howel Harris:

> Mr. Arcourt preaches the doctrine of Predestination very frequently and warns his hearers against what he apprehends to be errors in Wesley and the Moravian Brethren. I believe he has done some good although he seems to be too rash on the one hand as Mr. Wesley is on the other.[3]

When Charles Wesley barred him from the society, Arcourt complained that he was excluded solely because he held a "different opinion," and he pointed out that others in the society also believed in unconditional election. John Wesley replied that he did not exclude anyone because they held election or any other opinion, so long as they did not dispute about it. When Arcourt insisted on the privilege of disputing, "because you are all wrong and I am resolved to set you all right," Wesley saw that no one would profit from his membership and excluded him. The following day Wesley informed the society and sought "all of them who were weak in the faith not to 'receive one another to doubtful disputations,' but simply to follow after Holiness, and the things that make for peace."[4]

Apparently, John Arcourt spread a different account. Howel Harris wrote, asking why a member had been excluded for his convictions on predestination. Wesley sent him an account of the matter from his Journal, and added:

> You see, my brother, that the reason why Mr. Arcourt was not admitted into our society was not holding Election separate from Reprobation, but openly declaring his fixed purpose to introduce and carry on the dispute concerning Reprobation wherever he came."[5]

Wesley was beginning to apply his distinction between what was essential doctrine and what he otherwise called "opinion." The questions about predestination fell into the latter category. Though Wesley did not make a certain view on this subject a requirement for admission to any of his societies, neither would he tolerate disputation concerning what he considered to be secondary theological points. The societies were designed for the promotion of holiness in believers; Wesley did not tolerate anything suspected of subverting this purpose. This seems to have been a part of Wesley's growing awareness of the practical implications of certain doctrinal positions.

In the closing weeks of 1739 and the first half of 1740, Wesley was occupied at the London Fetter Lane society in a theological disagreement with the Moravians. Since the outbreak of the revival, the Wesleys and Whitefield had been in a spiritual partnership with the Moravians, especially in the London society. But when Wesley arrived from a time in Bristol, he wrote:

> The first person I met there was one (Mrs. Turner) whom I had left strong in the faith and zealous of good works; but she now told me Mr. Molther had fully convinced her she never had nay faith at all; and had advised her, till she received faith, to be "still," ceasing from outward works; which she had accordingly done, and did not doubt but in a short time she should find the advantage of it.[6]

That evening he heard Mr. Bray commending this same "stillness" and speaking against the danger of outward works, attendance at church, and the sacrament. Behind these testimonies stood the influence of Philip Henry Molther, a former tutor to the son of Count Zinzendorf. Molther had been commissioned as a Moravian missionary to Pennsylvania. Arriving in London en route to America, he was anxious to bring the society under stronger Moravian influence. Molther taught a kind of quietism called "stillness." He was successful in persuading many that the faith they professed was not true faith; and that they must remain "still"; that they must not use any means of grace until they were given faith.[7]

Members of the society quickly felt the impact of this doctrine. One woman described an occasion when both Wesleys were away from London. "We were left as sheep without a shepherd. Those who were left to guide us led us into strange paths." She was led into confusion over her justification. Others thought her presumptuous because she refused to deny her previous experience. "Yet I dared not say I was not justified. I would not consent to leave off the ordinances though they said we should not go to Church nor pray nor receive the Sacrament."[8] Another who escaped the impact of "stillness" wrote:

> So at that time I was delivered, but I found many of my acquaintances turned out of the way. . . . They were told they had not faith, they must not go to the sacrament. So they left off prayer and going to the sacrament till they fell into sin and were almost as bad as if they were never awakened.[9]

Wesley recognized the problem, not just as a form of antinomianism, but also as a threat to all that he had designed to promote holiness of heart and life. He found it necessary, therefore, to take steps to correct it. He had a conference with Molther and Augustus Gottlieb Spangenburg in order to understand their position. After this conference he recorded in his Journal the differences between Molther and himself on the nature of faith, the way to faith, and the manner of propagating the faith. He also wrote an assessment of the fruits of the Moravian effort in England. In addition, Wesley wrote what might be called position papers on his own views with regard to the issues in dispute with the Moravians, and inserted them in the Journal. He dealt first with the matters of faith and assurance and then with the doctrine of the true church.[10]

Because Wesley recognized that the Moravians' positions were contrary to Scripture, he immediately began to challenge them. His attempts at correcting the problem were carefully constructed on a Scriptural base. He recorded that he began the year 1740 by endeavoring "to explain to our brethren the true, Christian, Scriptural stillness, by largely unfolding those solemn words, 'Be still, and know that I am God.'" Throughout the spring Wesley continued to explain in public and private the Scriptures that he considered to have been misunderstood.[11] In Wesley's view, the root of the Moravian error was that they bypassed the "means of grace" in the same manner as the mystics. Since Wesley had already worked through the implications of that view at Oxford and in Georgia, he was not unprepared for the Moravians. Beginning with 2 Timothy 3:16, "All Scripture is given by inspiration of God," he explained the ordinances of God as "means of grace":

> Although this expression of our church, "means of grace," be not found in the Scripture; yet, if the sense of it undeniably is, to cavil at the term is a mere strife of words. But the sense of it is undeniably found in Scripture. For God hath in Scripture ordained prayer, reading or hearing

of Scripture, and the receiving the Lord's Supper as the ordinary means of conveying His grace to man.[12]

Since the Scripture was final authority, to show that the means of Grace were biblical was to settle the matter for Wesley.

During the last week in June (1740), at the height of the controversy, Wesley delivered a series of morning and evening expositions specifically designed to combat the Moravian influence. In the Fetter Lane Society, he began with an account of the work of God in their midst over the past two years, making special reference to the doctrines of salvation, faith, and the ordinances. He followed this with preaching on obedience after conversion, the confidence of believers, sin in believers, Scripture as a means of grace, and the doctrine of the Lord's Supper.[13] Finally, two of Wesley's "Standard Sermons" from this period, "The Means of Grace" and "The Spirit of Bondage and of Adoption," were specifically directed to the questions raised by the Moravians.

On July 18, a company met with Wesley at his mother's home for a thanksgiving service. Afterward they "consulted how to proceed with regard to our poor brethren of Fetter Lane. We all saw the thing was now come to a crisis, and we therefore unanimously agreed what to do." On the following Sunday he attended the society's love feast. When it was over, he read a paper reviewing the errors into which they had fallen. He concluded:

> I believe these assertions to be flatly contrary to the Word of God. I have warned you hereof again and again, and besought you to turn back to the "law and the testimony." I have borne with you long, hoping you would return. But, as I find you more and more confirmed in the error of your ways, nothing now remains, but that I should give you up to God. You that are of the same judgement, follow me.[14]

Eighteen or nineteen followed him out, including William Seward and the Countess of Huntingdon.[15] Five days later he first met his own society of nearly four hundred at the Foundry. After Wesley explained his position, almost all present agreed to avoid the society at Fetter Lane.[16]

Following the division, Wesley detailed his theological difference with the Moravians in a letter to the Church at Herrnhut. Toward the close of the letter he touched on their views of Scripture:

> You receive not the Ancients but the modern Mystics as the best interpreters of Scripture, and in conformity to these, you mix much of man's wisdom with the wisdom of God; you greatly refine the plain religion taught by the letter of Holy Writ, and philosophize on almost every part of it, to accommodate it to the Mystic theory. Hence you talk much, in a manner wholly unsupported by Scripture.[17]

With his brother Charles he was even more pointed: "As yet I dare in no wise join with the Moravians . . . because their general scheme is Mystical, not scriptural,—refined in every point above what is written, immeasurable beyond the plain doctrines of the gospel."[18]

Wesley's controversy with the Moravians is relevant to this study for several reasons. *First*, it shows that while Wesley did not hastily create division over fine points of doctrine, theology was important enough to cause disruption. There was a clear limit to the latitude Wesley was willing to allow on central doctrines like salvation and the nature of faith. The Moravians dealt a potential deathblow to these essentials in Christian theology,[19] and for such Wesley was ready to separate. Correct theology, no less than a very "practical divinity," was at the center of the dispute.

Second, Wesley began to see the practical effects of false theology on the spiritual life of believers. The Moravian teaching on the role of the church, prayer, the Scriptures, good works, and the ordinances of God undercut all those "means of grace" that Wesley believed were essential for the cultivation of Christian holiness. The central importance of sanctification in his theology caused Wesley to reject Molther's views as a form of antinomianism. Whatever undermined growth in godliness, Wesley saw that as contrary to the "Oracles of God" and, consequently, to be dismissed out of hand. His theological "tolerance" of divergent views was directly related to whether such a position encouraged or discouraged holiness of heart and life.

Third, Wesley demonstrated that his standard for judging a doctrine was the Scripture. Whatever did not accord with "the law and the testimony" was not to be received. Further, it was by the Bible that Wesley sought to establish members of the societies on a solid theological foundation. The Bible was the weapon he wielded to correct erroneous doctrines. Wesley thought it quite proper to separate himself from those that refused to recognize the ultimate authority of the Word of God in doctrine and practice.

These events also indicate that Wesley was not overly impatient regarding even doctrinal differences. The fact that almost nine months passed from the beginning of the controversy to the separation shows that Wesley desired to give individuals time to weigh their own theological views. But patience was not indifference. So, after a time division occurred because the Moravian position extended beyond the latitude of Wesley's understanding of Scripture.

Finally, having confronted the developing antinomianism among the Moravians, Wesley was probably now more aware of any such tendencies among the Predestinarians. In one sense this controversy sharpened his theological sensitivities. He was now acutely aware of the practical effects of false doctrine in the life of the believer. He was also more careful to watch for the implications of theological positions. It is also possible that he began to perceive himself surrounded by theological tendencies toward antinomianism, the Moravians being on one side, and the Calvinists on the other.

Wesley's Publications on Predestination in 1740

On the last two days in October 1740, Wesley spent his mornings writing on predestination.[20] Very likely he was preparing his *Serious Considerations of the Doctrines of Election and Reprobation* for the press. In this extended extract from the work of Isaac Watts, the apparent discrepancies in Scripture over election were reconciled by granting an absolute salvation to the elect, while at the same time allowing a conditional salvation for all men.[21] This view meant that those who were not absolutely elected to eternal salvation were not predestined to eternal misery by any decree of reprobation. Such a position satisfied Wesley's strong aversion to unconditional reprobation, and he continued to maintain a similar view until the early 1750s.

A second important emphasis of this publication was that "there is an inward Sufficiency of Power given by God to everyone, to harken to the Calls of God's Grace, and by Faith to receive that Salvation."[22] It was this inward sufficiency that allowed all men to respond to God that Wesley (but not Watts) called "prevenient grace." While this came into a more prominent focus for Wesley at a later time, the concept was clearly a part of his thought in 1740.

A second 1740 publication, one that also related to the matter of predestination, was John and Charles Wesley's *Hymns and Sacred Poems*. Charles Wesley's hymn on "Universal Redemption" was included in this selection. It had first appeared in 1739, at the end of Wesley's sermon "Free Grace." The hymnbook made use of a special method of underlining certain doctrinal emphases by printing key words in italics. In the hymns Charles gave particular attention to the universal offer of grace:

> Father, whose hand on *all* bestows
> *Sufficiency* of *saving* grace;
> Whose universal love o'erflows
> The whole of Adam's fallen race;

The Wesleys' strong abhorrence of the decree of reprobation was graphically penned:

> Doom them an endless death to die,
> From which they could not flee:
> No, Lord, thine inmost bowels cry
> Against the dire decree!

> Who'er admits; my soul disowns
> The image of *torturing* God,
> Well-pleased with human shrieks and groans,
> A fiend, a Molock gorged with blood!

The basic theological position that later found its way into Wesley's sermon on "Predestination" was first outlined for singing:

> For every man he tasted death,
> *He suffered once for all;*
> He calls as many souls as breathe,
> And all *may* hear the call,

> A power to choose, and a will to obey
> Freely His grace restores;

We all may find the living way,
And call the Savior ours.

Whom His eternal mind *foreknew*,
That they the power would use,
Ascribe to God the glory due,
And not his grace refuse;

Them, only them His will *decreed*,
Them did he *choose* alone,
Ordain in Jesus' steps to tread
And to be like His Son.

Them, the elect, consenting few,
Who yield to proffer'd love,

Justified here, he *forms anew*,
And *glorifies* above.

For *as in Adam all have died*,
So all in Christ may live,
May (for the world is justified)
His righteousness *receive*.[23]

In this hymn expression was given to the doctrines of a universal atonement and a universal call (first stanza), prevenient grace (second stanza), to foreknowledge as the basis of the decree of election (third and fourth stanzas), and also to justification and glorification (fifth stanza). Finally, the universal offer of salvation was restated (sixth stanza).

The fact that so many of the hymns in this work dealt with the doctrinal matters relating to predestination is an indication that the Wesleys were acutely aware of a growing theological controversy. It also reflected an increasing awareness of the critical need to treat these doctrinal points within the Methodist societies. Predestination was no longer to be ignored as it largely had been during the prior year. Wesley's energetic attack on the problem was twofold. First, the position of the Calvinists was repudiated in the strongest terms. Second, the Wesleys took the positive role of stating their own Arminian viewpoint as persuasively as possible. The fact that both aspects were often presented in highly emotional language made the hymnbook all that much more potent as a weapon in the doctrinal clash.[24]

Participants in the Increasing Conflict

In addition to the Wesleys and Whitefield, several other men played important roles in the early Calvinistic controversy. The names of William Seward, Howel Harris, John Cennick, and Joseph Humphreys are inseparably linked with the role of predestination in the early years of the revival. The place of the first three will be considered here. Humphreys' story is reserved for chapter four.

The Role of William Seward

William Seward of Badsey, Worcestershire, was a business and financial expert employed in the South Sea office of the Treasury.[25] A nominal upper-class Anglican, he came under the influence of the preaching of Charles Wesley and was converted in November 1738.[26] Although a layman, he was present at the Conference of Oxford Methodists in January 1739. Soon afterward, he became George Whitefield's traveling companion. After itinerating several months in England, Whitefield and Seward embarked for America in August. A letter written during the voyage indicates that Seward was already leaning toward Calvinism. Of the work of God in his heart, he wrote: "Had it not been for supernatural grace I had perished forever."[27]

His constant companionship with George Whitefield seems clearly responsible for the direction of Seward's thinking. Although there is little indication that Whitefield preached specifically on the doctrines of predestination, he had begun to raise such matters with Wesley by correspondence. These potentially divisive questions had strong emotional overtones for Whitefield, and it is natural to assume that he privately shared his views with Seward.

Seward's published *Journal* accordingly reveals a distinct preoccupation with the distinctives of Calvinism.[28] One contemporary Calvinist explained that James Hutton would not publish Seward's Journal because it "was very emplicit upon the doctrine of election."[29] Seward read Elisha Coles on God's sovereignty at this time, and he described it as "a most sound, deep Book for Election, Predestination, and peculiar Redemption, as well as God's Sovereignty." Of Coles' doctrines, he wrote: "I think they are all clearly revealed in Scripture, and I firmly believe them." Yet, he recognized that other sincere Christians held opposing views. "As I know holy pious godly Souls, Men that are full of faith and the Holy Ghost, and that hazard their Lives for the Lord Jesus, who differ in some Points from the Author, I will not condemn them."[30]

In Seward's theology, God's sovereign wisdom lay behind predestination. The mystery of election and reprobation, he argued, was to be accepted by faith. "Has not the Potter power over the clay, to make one vessel to honour, and another to dishonour? Besides, if 'tis just with God to damn the Devil, or any one sinner amongst men, 'tis equally just to damn millions of sinners."[31] Seward summarized his views:

> For my Part I look upon Election, etc. as a Mystery, like the Trinity, to be firmly believed, tho' not fathom'd, for as Election is certain by God's Word; so it is as certain by the same Word, that the Almighty has no Pleasure in the Death of a Sinner; . . . and yet our very Reason will tell us, if we consider the Attributes of God, there are a certain Number of the Elect, foreknown, foreordained, and predestinated before the Foundation of the World, chosen in Christ. . . . Therefore as both these truths are so plainly Revealed, I will believe both.[32]

The doctrine of justification by faith alone, along with the Reformed position on the decrees of God, was believed by Seward to be the true doctrine of the established church.[33] He rejected the concept of free will, and was "fully convinced that our Salvation is all of God."[34] This salvation was based upon the imputed righteousness of Christ,[35] and it led to the infallible and eternal perseverance of the elect.[36] Further, he was convinced of the necessity of the new birth, the means of grace, and the evidence of good works.[37]

Seward had no hesitation in offering the free gospel to all men, however, since he considered the responsibility for reprobation to be the result of human choice.

> I do firmly believe that God is Gracious and long suffering not willing that any should perish but that all should come to the knowledge of the truth and be saved and I do as firmly believe that no man can come to Jesus Christ unless the Father draw him—I do believe that the Spirit of God striveth with all men and that few are chosen to be heirs of the Kingdom—I do believe the wicked will curse and blaspheme God forever but will be forced to own that their Damnation was of themselves.[38]

Seward arrived in London from America on June 19, 1740, and shortly thereafter published his *Journal* as an account of his voyage and as a declaration of his theological position. Apparently the published *Journal* divided Methodist ranks, Charles Wesley wrote to Whitefield on September 1: "Well-meaning Mr. Seward has caused the world to triumph in our supposed dissention, by his unseasonable journal.[39] Your zealous, indiscreet friends, instead of concealing any little difference between us have told it in Gath."[40] One whose spiritual life had been affected wrote:

> I do not remember losing this sense of my justification any otherwise than by this. While one was reading Mr. Seward's journal I sat by and found immediately I was disaffected with the author. Then I felt instantly I had lost that sweet peace which before I had enjoyed.[41]

In spite of their differences, Seward continued his friendship with and admiration for the Wesleys. He was at the society in Cardiff on September 7 and wrote of the occasion: "Hearing they had Rejected Mr. Wesley and Mr. Harris I told them they had Rejected the Servants of the Most High God who came to shew unto them the Way of Salvation."[42]

Early in September, Seward began a preaching tour in the West of England and Wales, in company with Howel Harris. At Caerleon he was struck on the right eye and temporarily blinded. Nevertheless, he continued the strenuous itinerant preaching, even though his horse had to be led. The following week he preached to about 1,500 people for two hours "upon the Sovereign Everlasting Love of God to his Elect."

On reaching Bristol, he was reunited with Charles Wesley. Wesley, noting Seward's strong opinions on predestination, did not give him a chance to speak to the society at the New Room, but later the same day invited him to speak at

Kingswood. The result, Wesley noted, did not convince him of Seward's call to preach. Returning to Bristol, he told Charles that several, including Mrs. Grevil, a sister of George Whitefield, had urged Seward to claim the New Room, apparently on the basis of his early contribution toward its construction. "But," Wesley observed, "he abhorred their baseness."

At the early preaching service the following morning, Seward recorded that Wesley was too harsh in rebuking a friend "which came with me (and holds Election)," even though the reproof was for "uncleanness." After the meeting Wesley stated, "He [Seward] told me he was in a mist; the Baptists last night having laboured hard to make him oppose me publicly. Before we parted, all was set right again."[43] Later that day Seward again joined his Calvinist friends, whom, he said,

> the Lord made a Means of opening my Eyes to see that Satan had de-
> ceived Brother Wesley by turning himself into an Angel of Light—they
> both Rejected my journal—which bore an explicit Testimony to the
> Doctrine of Election—and Mr. C. Wesley slighted all the great things
> which my Dear Jesus hath lately done by my weak hands.[44]

After they dined together that evening, Seward recalled that he told Wesley:

> I must declare for a public Separation and that seeing he was my Spiri-
> tual Father it was with much Sorrow and heaviness of Heart I spoke it,
> but that I could have not longer fellowship with him—for being called a
> Brother, and I believing him a Minister of Satan, I was commanded
> with Such a one not to Eat—came home in much tribulation.

The next day Seward's attitude toward the Wesleys grew harsher still:

> It was set home upon me that the Mr. Wesleys were Judas' False Prophets,
> Wolves in Sheeps Clothing. They crept into Houses and for a pretense
> made long Prayer. Mr. Charles Wesley being made an Instrument under
> God of opening my eyes to see the mysteries of the Gospel which had
> greatly prejudiced me in his favour but I considered that Judas was a preacher
> of the Gospel and Cast Devils out of others—tho' he was a Devil him-
> self—that tho' Mr. Wesley was an instrument of opening my Eyes—yet
> the Lord drew me to follow Mr. Whitefield and not Mr. Wesley.[45]

Being convinced that neither of the Wesleys had any more saving faith "than Mahomet," Seward publicly denounced them to about a hundred people on Rose Green. "I was moved to bear this Testimony that if Mr. Wesleys were the Minis-ters of Christ I was the Servant of Satan, but if I was the Servant of Christ then they were the Servants of Satan."

Friends tried to reconcile Seward with Charles Wesley, but to no avail. Seward said:

> It was given me to answer there was no peace saith my God to the
> wicked—I was also moved to deal plainly with his Soul and say—thou
> Child of the Devil, thou Enemy of all Righteousness—thou art in the

Gall of Bitterness and Bond of Iniquity—whereupon he desired we might pray which I at first declined to join in but after comply'd with.[46]

What lay behind Seward's sudden change of attitude and his bitter break with the Wesleys? Doctrine was certainly an important issue. After proclaiming publicly against the Wesleys, Seward "was also led to plead for God's Eternal Decrees and against the Popish Error of perfection." Charles Wesley felt this was greatly exaggerated by the agitation of Seward's Baptist friends. "He came from them, and utterly renounced my brother and me, in bitter words of hatred, which they had put into his mouth. I pray God lay not this sin to their charge."[47]

A contributing element was Seward's health. It was less than three weeks after he had been stoned and temporarily lost his eyesight. Since that time he had not rested from the strenuous task of itinerant preaching. His journal reveals that he often slept only three or four hours a night. Further, for some months he had been on a strict diet of vegetables and water. Seward himself recorded that, on the 25th, Whitefield's brother, Captain Thomas Whitefield, along with Charles Wesley, felt he should see a doctor.[48] This evidence reveals that Seward's grievances at this time were strongly aggravated by his physical weakness. His bitterness at the separation in particular was quite uncharacteristic of his attitude in times of normal health.

Seward's preaching now became primarily a crusade "against the Doctrines of Perfection, Universal Redemption and falling from Grace as held by Mr. Wesley." Opposition to Wesley's views, coupled with his own Calvinistic position on these subjects, became almost the entire content of his preaching for the following weeks. He wrote from Trevecka on October 12: "Brother Harris says he is convinced of all the errors I am sent to oppose but does not yet find a necessity laid on him to oppose them in the manner I do."[49]

Seward's death from stoning at the end of October made him the first martyr of the Methodist movement.[50] This made the pain of his renunciation all that more acute for Charles Wesley:

> I was led in the evening to preach universal redemption from those words, "the Lord is not willing that any should perish, but that all should come to repentance." A spirit mightily confirmed the irresistible truth. I then spoke with unfeigned concern of our dear departed brother; and with just abhorrence of those unhappy bigots, whose headlong zeal had robbed us of him. We sang a funeral hymn over him and were comforted in the hope of soon meeting him again, where no sower of tares, no reprobating pharisee, shall ever part us more.[51]

The Role of Howel Harris

A second important figure for the early Methodist revival was Howel Harris of Wales. Known later as the "Welsh Apostle," Harris was converted at Trevecka on Whitsunday 1735, while he was receiving the sacrament. His concern for the salvation of others led him to begin speaking to family and neighbors at his mother's home. Although he received considerable opposition from the established church, he began to preach from house to house. While teaching school during the day, Harris spent his evenings and weekends traveling about south Wales and "exhorting" men to turn to God. He soon recognized the strategic importance of gathering converts into small groups for Christian fellowship. Thus, at least as early as the autumn of 1736, he wrote to a friend: "We are beginning to set up private societies."[52]

Harris' ministry, which began several years earlier than that of Whitefield and the Wesleys, as described by William Seward:

> Mr. Howel Harris has been a means under God of raising about 30 religious Societies who all pray extempore and from what we can see of them are filled with the Spirit: he goes from place to place and preaches or exhorts on a place like a weighing post (at horse races) which they raise for him and he often appoints his meetings at such Times and places where Revels, cockfightings and the like are appointed whereby he has been a mighty Instrument of Reformation. . . . He discourses for he does not call it preaching because he is not in Orders, tho he has offered himself twice to the Bishop and was rejected. I say he discourses often for 2, 3, or 4 hours together and some times all night. He has a settled hoarseness upon him notwithstanding which he daily goes on exerting himself so as to make 1500 or 2000 hear, or more, being willing to spend and be spent for the good of souls. Oh! how my Heart burns within me to hear him and our dear Brother Whitefield tell their Experiences and to see how they resemble each other.[53]

Although they had corresponded earlier, Harris did not meet Whitefield until March 1739. Coming together at Cardiff in south Wales, the two men enjoyed fellowship their first evening until midnight. Harris recalled a "conversation relating what God has done for us. Had my soul filled with Heaven."[54] The time was just as moving for Whitefield: "When I first saw him, my heart was knit closely to him. I wanted to catch some of his fire, and gave him the right hand of fellowship with my whole heart. We spent the evening in telling one another what God had done for our souls and took an account of the several Societies, and agreed on such measures as seemed most conducive to promote the common interest of our Lord."[55] With this meeting began the association of the revival in Wales with the movement just beginning in England.

In June, Harris traveled to Bristol and met John Wesley for the first time. He listened to Wesley preach on faith. Then Harris wrote: "I believe my going here was from God so much for the benefit of my own Soul and to take Prejudice from me, and possibly from many more, for all our Countrymen were prejudiced against him that he was an Arminian."[56] Afterward he told Wesley that because many had informed him that Wesley was an Arminian and a "Free-Willer," he had to force himself to hear Wesley preach. But, Harris added, "I had not been long there before my spirit was knit to you, as it was [to] the dear Mr. Whitefield; and before you had done, I was so overpowered with joy and love that I could scarce stand."[57] It was at Harris' invitation that Wesley made his early trips to Wales in October 1739 and April 1740. Harris later mentioned to a friend, however, that it had been a qualified invitation:

> I gave the two Brothers a call to Wales, looking on them as Powerful ministers of Jesus Christ, much owned, etc. . . . Only I told Mr. J. Wesley at parting with him that if he came to Wales he must not bring his sermon on free grace with him or Preach that Doctrine, for if he did I would oppose him.[58]

Wesley so faithfully observed Harris' condition on his first visit that one who heard several of his sermons gathered the impression that "he is far from being an Arminian."[59] Wesley's subsequent evaluation of the work of God in Wales was that "God had done great things by Howel Harris," and after Harris had assisted Charles for a time in Bristol in 1740, Charles described him as a "son of thunder and of consolation."[60]

Harris' theology developed with time. Never having the benefit of a formal theological education, he maintained fluidity in his doctrinal position all his life. Reviewing his development in 1761, he wrote:

> I see I have had every truth gradually and authority in it. First the thundering, then the spirituality of the law for 2 years, then Christ Doctrinally, . . . then inviting to Christ—the freeness of His grace to sinners; forgiveness of sins and assurance after meeting Mr. Whitefield; a year after holiness and pressing to perfection and entering to outward order.[61]

In general Harris may be described as Moderate Calvinist on predestination. His Calvinism came primarily from two sources. The first was a group of men, of whom Thomas Jones, vicar of Cwmyoy, was chief. As early as 1736, Harris visited Jones and came under the influence of his sermons and personality. This, plus the preaching of Griffith Jones, Daniel Rowlands, and Thomas Lewis, first led Harris to a Calvinistic position.[62]

The second source of Harris' doctrinal views was his wide reading, especially among the Puritan divines. Writing to James Erskine in 1745, Harris said: "I think we all agree with the good old orthodox Reformers and Puritans; I have their works in great esteem." Although not read until a later date, one of his favorite works was Elisha Coles, *A Practical Discourse on God's Sovereignty*.[63]

In March 1742, after being with Wesley at Cardiff, Harris wrote down his agreements and disagreements with Wesley's views on predestination. Although his generous spirit at times caused him to modify his theology in the presence of other deeply committed Christians of differing views, these may be taken as a good résumé of his thinking. In harmony with the Wesleys, he held that "Salvation begins in Christ," not in anything human, and is all of God. He chooses men to salvation, and by his faithfulness they are kept faithful. "All are damned in Adam," "born in Sin and deserve Hell." "None can turn himself," and "none will be damned but such as willingly, obstinately and willfully reject Christ."

Further, they agreed that "Christ died for all Mankind in some sense," and that no man was converted until he had the Spirit of Adoption, till He had dominion over sin, till Christ took possession of the will, and till righteousness, peace, and joy in the Holy Ghost were in man, and he felt the fruits of the Spirit. On the security of the believer, Wesley and Harris held in common that "none shall be saved but such as are faithful to the end," that those who "turn back to Sin" and "bear no fruit will perish," and that some "may be enlightened, taste the good word and fall away." Harris felt that no reference to falling from Grace should be mentioned to the slack or the unjustified, but only to earnest mourners.[64]

But Harris differed from Wesley on certain key points. Election was not based on foreknowledge, as with Wesley, but only in the good pleasure of God. Those whom God loved, He called and "makes them irresistibly come." Yet he insisted that this was also "consistent with the free nature of the will." Those to whom faith was given also received the gift of the Spirit. Harris was convinced that God appointed certain means of grace and that by His love kept men from falling totally. He believed in predestination to life, which should make a person more watchful and humble.

With regard to offering redemption to all men by preaching, Harris believed he could "call all freely and declare that Christ is willing to receive all as will come and reject none," but "no one has a free will till 'tis given him." Harris felt he could "use all the Texts about falling from grace fully and clearly and leave the application to God."[65]

Elsewhere Harris indicates there was a change in his theology regarding reprobation. "I had previously come to see the Doctrine of Election, but now for a while I fell into believing in Reprobation; but I was weaned from the latter by reading I Timothy 2:4; II Peter 2:9, and Ezekiel 33:11."[66] Wesley reported, about this time, that Harris had renounced and now abhorred reprobation.

Though they differed over the doctrines of predestination, when Harris was with the Wesley, a spirit of love and harmony prevailed. In June 1740, Harris was with Charles Wesley in Bristol. There he wrote that he went to Mrs. Grevil's,

> where we talked sweetly about Election. O how has disputing about it quite destroyed love here. Went to Brother Charles Wesley at the New Room where he preached exceedingly sweet on I John 1:5. Showed the Danger of any one's taking the Notion that he was Elect before he had all the marks of the new Birth upon him (which I agreed with entirely), otherwise it fed carnality and negligence—as the carnal stillness does.

The following day after reading Wesley's Journal, he noted:

> We agreed in everything. He allowed God's Everlasting love and particular Election to all those that have all the marks of the new Birth in them, but that God has a love of pity to all, else we'll make us more loving than God. In private together to past 10 agreeing about Degrees of faith. I feel I have not that Power which he [C.W.] has and which I had.[67]

However, when he was not in company with the Wesleys, Harris often felt the doctrinal issues were more central. On July 16 he heard that John Wesley had excluded a man from the society "purely because he held Election," and he wrote:

> If you exclude him from the Society, and from the Fraternity of the Methodists, you must exclude Brother Whitefield, Brother Seward, and myself. It is owing to *Special, Distinguishing,* and *Irresistible Grace,* that those . . . are saved. . . . Look now to the teachings of God's Spirit in your Heart, *and less to your Reason and Learning,* and then you will soon see, that *God chose you, and not you him*: and see on which a tottering Foundation you build, viz. *Your own Faithfulness,* and not on *God's Unchangeableness.*[68]

After hearing of Seward's break with Charles Wesley, Harris wrote to John Cennick that he was thinking of declaring against the Wesleys. "I must own the Difference did not appear so great to me as 'tis now. . . . This doctrine is hellish, Popish, heretical."[69] Yet, when Charles Wesley soon after visited Wales, he could write of his meeting with Harris: "All misunderstandings vanished at the sight of each other and our hearts were knit together as at the beginning. We sang a hymn of triumph. God had prepared his heart for this meeting."[70]

Harris' account, however, was significantly different. He recalled that Charles had told him: "Brother Harris, I now believe Election and did they know at Cardiff how strong I believe in Election—as strong as you—they would no more receive me than they do you." It is difficult to avoid the conclusion that Charles, perhaps inadvertently, had misled Harris. Harris felt betrayed:

> I found Hypocrisy in Ch. . . . 1. He told me he believed Election . . . and yet contrary to that 2. sang in the Society here the Hymns against Election saying if any held Election they must be silent. 3. He said that Christ died for all and if it were not for that he would believe Election. . . . 4. He preached that Christ died as much for Judas as for Peter. 5. He preached that a man may have the five first Beatitudes and fall if they have not the pure heart. (O I must oppose this Hypocrisy to his Face.)[71]

Possibly Charles, as well as Harris, labored too hard to smooth over troublesome issues when they were together, and this tendency to maximize agreement, while playing down the controverted points, later appeared as hypocrisy when the two men were separated. Instead of waiting to oppose Charles to his face, Harris wrote a loving letter about their differences. He concluded it with the proposal: "Let us according to the grace given be diligent and watch over each other. . . . Let us always be learning."[72]

The Role of John Cennick

Another figure involved in the early predestination dispute was John Cennick of Reading. Cennick's father was from a devout Quaker family, but he joined the Church of England shortly after marriage. Thus, Cennick was brought up in the Anglican Communion. For most of his teens, Cennick "followed after Righteousness by Works," but about 1735 the Lord began to awaken him to his sinful condition. Of this time he wrote: "I more and more thought I was predestinated to Misery everlasting. . . . I said, 'Surely I am reprobate, God hath loved every Man but me.' "[73] Calvinistic theology had obviously influenced his life even before he became a Christian.

Cennick was delivered from his fears at his conversion on September 7, 1737. The following year he read Whitefield's Journals and prayed for an opportunity for friendship with the young evangelist. On a visit to Oxford, Charles Kinchin introduced him to the Wesleys and Whitefield. When John Wesley met him again in March 1739, at Reading, he was impressed by the fact that Cennick had recently formed a religious society there. In June, Cennick spent several days with Whitefield in London. When he expressed his desire to visit the Brethren in Bristol, Whitefield mentioned that Wesley was building a school at Kingswood and asked Cennick if he were willing to be one of the masters there. Although his only previous employment had been as a surveyor, Cennick said he was "obedient" to Whitefield's suggestion. When he reached Bristol on June 12, he found that Wesley had left in haste for London the day before, leaving instructions that Cennick was to be received "as his own self."

Two days after his arrival, Cennick went to Kingswood to hear a young man read a sermon to the colliers. When the young man was late in coming, some of the several hundred present wanted Cennick to preach. Although fearful of such a step, he prayed for guidance and found freedom to comply with their desire. "I then tarried no longer," he later wrote, "but rose up and went to the Congregation, the Lord bearing witness with my Word, insomuch that many believed in that Hour." He preached several more times before Wesley returned to Bristol. When Wesley arrived, many urged him to forbid Cennick's lay preaching, but, according to Cennick, he "rather encouraged me, and often took sweet Council together with me, as Friends."[74]

Through the summer of 1740, Cennick appeared to be in doctrinal agreement with the Wesleys. When Charles Wesley was preaching at Kingswood on July 17, he could say: "Before the sermon, I declared our brother Cennick's entire agreement with me in the belief of Universal Redemption; and he confirmed my saying with a hymn of his own. Never did I find my spirit more knit to him." However, by November Cennick's position had changed. Charles Wesley recorded, "While I was testifying that Christ died for all, Mr. Cennick, in the hearing of many, gave me the lie. I calmly told him afterwards, 'If I speak not the truth in Jesus, may I decrease, and you increase.' "[75] Other doctrines also became matters of dispute. Joseph Humphreys told John Wesley: "John Cennick has declared to me that he should not have meddled with that point of final perseverance had not your brother begun to speak against it."[76]

What was the cause of Cennick's change of views on the doctrines related to predestination? It is possible that Whitefield's influence was being felt. Whitefield was certainly discussing the doctrinal questions with Wesley by correspondence at this time. More important, however, was the impact of Howel Harris. On October 27 Harris wrote to Cennick:

This Week Brother Seward has been here, and tells me of his dividing with Brother Charles; he seems clear in his Conviction that God would have him do so. I have long been waiting to see if Brother John and Charles should receive farther Light, or be silent, and not oppose Election and Perseverance; . . . I plainly see we preach two Gospels, one sets all on God, the other on Man; the one on God's Will, the other on Man's Will; the one on God's chusing, the other on Man's chusing.

My dear Brother, deal faithfully with Brothers John and Charles; . . . And you must answer to your Father for everything he has taught you, to see that in this you are faithful to declare the whole Counsel of God, and teach others as God has taught you. . . . While the Doctrine of final Perseverance is not fully and clearly set forth to the Children of the Covenant, they are robbed Of the Food that their Father had prepared for them. . . . What I am contending for, is the Glory of his *Sovereign, Free, Unchangeable Love to his Elect* . . . while they are contending against it, I cannot give them the right Hand of Fellowship.

I am sure this is the Truth of God, and I must bear my Testimony against all who oppose it. And I hope our dear Lord . . .will incline your Heart likewise, to join with your poor unworthy Brother in Christ, H.H.[77]

> The letter was such a strong plea for opposing the Wesleys on the doctrine of predestination that it seems clearly to have influenced Cennick's behavior. Thus, he withstood Charles Wesley publicly on November 4.

Harris' letter assumed that Cennick was convinced of the Calvinistic position.[78] Perhaps Harris and Whitefield were responsible for the change in Cennick's views, or possibly Cennick had only accommodated himself to Wesley's theology in order to maintain harmony, as he did later in the controversy. In December, after he saw their "false foundation," he could still write:

> But because I had no mind to part from them I assured them I knew no Calvinist in the world, nor believed reprobation, or in the least doubted of universal redemption; only I told them I should be glad to find a doctrine whereby the election and universal redemption could be made to agree.[79]

The evidence suggests that Cennick may not have acted with candor or good faith in his relations with the Wesleys. He certainly knew at this time that both Whitefield and Harris were Calvinists and that they accordingly had strong reservations about universal redemption.

After the initial disagreement in November, the controversy grew more intense. Charles said that while he was preaching in Kingswood,

> the strong ones were offended. The poison of Calvin has drunk up their spirit of love. Anne Ayling and Ann Davis could not refrain from railing. John Cennick never offered to stop them. Alas! We have set the wolf to keep the sheep! God gave me great moderation toward him, who, for many months, has been undermining our doctrine and authority.

Two days later Charles had a conference with Cennick and his friends in Kingswood, but they reached no agreement even though Charles offered to drop the controversy if Cennick was willing. Charles then wrote to John "a full account of the predestination party, their practices and designs." He especially noted their desire "to have a church within themselves, and give themselves a Sacrament of bread and water."[80]

At this news John Wesley set out for Bristol in mid-December, where he "laboured to heal jealousies and misunderstandings." He wrote:

> The next evening Mr. Cennick came back from a little journey into Wiltshire. I was greatly surprised when I went to receive him, as usual, with open arms, to observe him quite cold; so that a stranger would judge he had scarce ever seen me before. However, for the present I said nothing, but did him honour before the people.

Wesley later pressed Cennick to explain his behavior. "Mr. Cennick now told me plainly he could not agree with me, because I did not preach the truth, in particular with regard to election."[81] One member of the society, who had been confused over the differences between Wesley's and Cennick's doctrine, described Cennick as "invincibly opinionated."[82] However, Cennick felt the problem was aggravated from the opposite camp.

> The Perfectionists all this while strove daily with Mr. Wesley against me, and at last before Christmas he forbade me to preach in the school any more, and without any noise I yielded.

Later he conceded that he thought this was against Wesley's will.[83]

There is some evidence to suggest that, in addition to the questions related to Calvinism, Cennick leaned toward the doctrine of "stillness" that Wesley had battled at Fetter Lane. Wesley had to censure the society at Kingswood for "slighting his ordinances" and "not speaking or praying when met together, till they were sensibly moved thereto."[84] Cennick himself records that when Wesley came to Kingswood, he felt Cennick was too close to the "Still Brethren."[85] Somewhat later the Methodists described his societies in Wiltshire as "tinctured with Antinomianism."[86] Cennick's Quaker background may have inclined him toward some of the "stillness" emphasis, and it is possible this tendency influenced his decision to leave Whitefield in order to join the Moravians in 1746.[87]

The confrontation began early in 1741. After preaching on February 22, Wesley met with Cennick and about twenty others. When he accused them of speaking about him behind his back, they replied by charging him with preaching man's faithfulness and not the faithfulness of God. Although Wesley was accused of preaching false doctrine, Cennick agreed to continue meeting the society under Wesley's authority. But at the same time he insisted on meeting separately with his own followers. To this Wesley rejoined, "You should have told me this before, and not have supplanted me in my own house, stealing the hearts of the people, and by private accusations, separating very friends."

When Cennick denied that he had privately accused him, Wesley produced a letter from Cennick to George Whitefield, dated January 17, 1741. He invited members of the society to judge for themselves. Wesley then read the letter in which Cennick had described the situation at Kingswood: "With Universal Redemption brother Charles pleases the world; brother John follows him in everything. I believe no atheist can more preach against Predestination than they; and all that believe Election are accounted enemies to God, and called so. "Fly, dear brother. I am as alone; I am in the midst of the plague. If God give thee leave, make haste."[88]

Cennick then acknowledged the letter to be his, and stated: "I do not retract anything in it, nor blame myself for sending it." At least some members of the society judged differently, and one later wrote to Charles Wesley: "The time that your Brother read the Letter in the Bands, which Mr. Cennick writ, it was of great use to me; this underhand dealing of Mr. Cennick's could never be right."[89]

They met again on February 28 with the bands at Kingswood. After a general discussion on the disagreements, Wesley read a paper that accused the Cennick party of undermining the Wesleys in their own societies while professing their esteem to their faces. He concluded:

> Therefore, not for their opinions, but for their scoffing at the word and ministers of God, for their tale-bearing, back-biting, and evil speaking, for their dissembling lying, and slandering:

> I, John Wesley, by the consent and approbation of the band-society in Kingswood, do declare the persons above mentioned to be no longer members thereof. Neither will they be so accounted, till they openly confess their faults, and thereby do what in them lies to remove the scandal they have given.[90]

Wesley claimed that the expulsion was not for doctrinal disagreements but for strife and disorderly conduct.

Somewhat shocked at first, Cennick began to accuse the Wesleys of preaching "Popery." He would not admit to having done anything amiss. Wesley then gave Cennick and his party a few days to consider the matter.

When they met again the following week, Wesley spoke plainly of the things he thought were wrong. He felt matters could no longer be postponed because of the confusion being created in the Society. Thomas Bissicks, a member of the Cennick party, replied: "It is our holding Election is the true cause of your separating from us." Wesley responded, "You know in your own conscience it is not. There are several Predestinarians in our societies both at London and Bristol, nor did I ever yet put anyone out of either because he held that opinion."[91]

When Cennick would admit no wrong conduct, nor ask pardon, Wesley offered the society a choice. After prayer, Cennick withdrew with about half of those present. This ended his relationship with the Wesleys.[92] The permanent effects on the work of this dispute can be seen in Wesley's comments almost twenty years later:

> I visited the classes at Kingswood. Here only there is no increase; and
> yet, where was there such a prospect till that weak man, John Cennick[,]
> confounded a poor people with strange doctrines? Oh what mischief
> may be done by one that means well! We see no end of it to this day.[93]

Although in Wesley's mind the separation was not over theology, Cennick
nonetheless felt doctrine to be at the root of the controversy. Moreover, Cennick's
point of view could not but affect George Whitefield who was shortly to arrive
from America. Whitefield never discussed this matter with Wesley before separating from him and therefore did not have the benefit of Wesley's side of the
question. Just how much this issue influenced Whitefield's thinking on separation is uncertain, but that it had its impact seems unquestionable.

Wesley and Whitefield: The Growing Rift

Wesley continued to work on the subject of predestination during the controversy with Cennick. For five days in December 1740, he made an extract from
the Quaker, Robert Barclay. This was published in 1741 as *Serious Considerations
on Absolute Predestination*. On December 26 he read from Dr. John Edwards, one
who had strongly influenced Whitefield. Wesley's evaluation, however, was quite
different than Whitefield's. He reflected:

> Surely never man wrote like this man! At least, none of all whom I have
> seen. I have not seen so haughty, over-bearing, pedantic a writer. Stiff
> and trifling in the same breath; positive and opinionated to the last de-
> gree; and of course treating others with more good manners than justice.
> But above all, sour, ill-natured, morose without a parallel, which indeed
> is his distinguishing character. Be his opinion right or wrong, if Dr.
> Edward's temper were a Christian temper, I would abjure Christianity
> for ever.[94]

In early March, Wesley spent several days writing on predestination. Although
he had spoken previously on universal redemption, he did not preach directly on
the subject of predestination at Kingswood until March 17.[95] His explicit dealing
with the theological issues thus did not take place until after Cennick separated
from Wesley. Theoretically, at least, Wesley still seemed to classify the important
predestination questions as "opinion" rather than as essential Christian doctrine.
All these matters, however, were very much before him when George Whitefield
landed in England on March 11, 1741.

During 1740 George Whitefield had established himself as an outstanding
evangelist in New England and the Middle Colonies. In the process he had become an influential leader of the American ministers. Along with many of these
ministers, Whitefield identified the revival as the fruit of Calvinistic theology. In
the midst of Whitefield's success as a major force in America's Great Awakening,
he regularly corresponded with the Wesleys.[96] In a letter dated March 26, 1740,
he recognized the doctrinal differences between them, but he desired there should
be no dividing controversy:

> The doctrine of election, and the final perseverance of those that are truly in Christ, I am ten thousand times more convinced of, if possible, than when I saw you last—You think otherwise; why then should we dispute, when there is no probability of convincing? . . . By the blessing of God, provoke me to it as much as you please, I do not think ever to enter the lists of controversy with you on the points wherein we differ.[97]

By the end of May, however, his close connections with the American ministers had strengthened his convictions on election and final perseverance, and his personal opinion of Wesley was obviously changing:

> I cannot entertain prejudices against your conduct and principles any longer, without informing you. The more I examine the writings of the most experienced men, and the experiences of the most established Christians, the more I differ from your notion about not committing sin, and your denying the doctrines of election, and final perseverance of the saints. I dread coming to England, unless you are resolved to oppose these truths with less warmth, than when I was there last.[98]

Wesley responded by recognizing the doctrinal differences but looked forward to the time when God would make them of one opinion:

> The case is quite plain. There are bigots both for Predestination and against it. God is sending a message to those on either side. But neither will receive it, unless from one of his own opinion. Therefore for a time you are suffered to be of one opinion and I of another. But when His time is come God will do what man cannot—namely, make us both of one mind.[99]

In the meantime Whitefield responded, strongly urging silence on all sides.

> If possible, dear Sir, never speak against election in your sermons; no one can say that I ever mentioned it in public discourses, whatever my private sentiments may be. For Christ's sake, let us not be divided amongst ourselves: nothing will so much prevent a division as your being silent on this head.

Yet, on August 25, Whitefield indicated that he had second thoughts about a truce. "I cannot bear the thoughts of opposing you: but how can I avoid it, if you go about (as your brother Charles once said) to drive John Calvin out of Bristol." Although he had heard reports of disputes in England over election and perfection, Whitefield sensed that he may not have fully understood Wesley's position: "I wish I knew your principles fully; did you write oftener, and more frankly, it might have a better effect than silence and reserve."[100]

At this time Charles Wesley wrote a warm letter to Whitefield. In spite of the forces that wanted to separate them, Charles declared that the Wesleys were in no way "cooled in our affection towards you, by all the idle stories we hear of your opposition to us." He continued: "God increase the horror he has given me of the separation! I had rather you saw me dead at your feet than openly opposing you."

On the doctrinal points he wrote: "When God hath taught us mutual forebearance, longsuffering, and love, who knows but he may bring us into an exact agreement on all things? In the meantime I do not think the difference considerable. I shall never dispute with you touching election."[101]

By the autumn of 1740, Whitefield's theological opinions were becoming more sharply focused. He was most vocal in opposition to what he thought were Wesley's views on "sinless perfection." Wesley had begun to preach on holiness in the autumn of 1739. Then in November of that year, he had written and preached his sermon, "Christian Perfection."[102] In 1740, when he and Charles published their *Hymns and Sacred Songs*, he had described the experience of Christian perfection in unusually high terms. The preaching and publication on this subject produced a strong reaction from Whitefield:

> I am sorry to hear by many letters, that you seem to own a sinless perfection in this life attainable. I do not expect to say indwelling sin is finished and destroyed in me, till I bow down my head and give up the ghost. There must be some Amalekites left in the Israelites land, to keep his soul in action, to keep him humble, and to drive him continually to Jesus Christ for pardon and forgiveness. I know many abuse this doctrine and perhaps wilfully indulge in, or do not aspire after holiness, because no man is perfect in this life. But what of that? Must I therefore assert doctrines contrary to the gospel?[103]

He continued his objections throughout the autumn.

> O that we were of one mind; for I am persuaded you greatly err. You have set a mark you will never arrive at, till you come to glory. I think few enjoy such continued manifestations of God's presence as I do, and have done, for some years; but I dare not pretend to say I shall be absolutely perfect.[104]

Regarding his own theology, Whitefield was reluctant to be labeled as a Calvinist: "I never read anything that Calvin wrote; my doctrines I had from Christ and his apostles; I was taught from God."[105] Yet, Whitefield stated his views from a distinctively Calvinistic perspective:

> Whatever men's reasonings may suggest, if they do God justice, they must acknowledge that they did not choose God, but that God chose them. And if He chose them at all, it must be from eternity, and that too without anything foreseen in them. Unless they acknowledge this, man's salvation must be in part owing to the free-will of man.[106]

Whitefield admitted that

> the doctrines of election and final perseverance hath been abused, (and what doctrine has not), but notwithstanding, it is children's bread, and ought not in my opinion to be withheld from them, supposing it is always mentioned with proper cautions against abuse.

At this time he took his strongest stand on reprobation: "What then is there in reprobation so horrid? I see no blasphemy in holding that doctrine, if rightly explained. If God might have passed by all, he may pass by some."[107] Yet, he recognized that some of his views were strong meat for believers.

> But I would be tender on this point and leave persons to be taught of God. I am of the martyr Bradford's mind. Let a man go to the grammar school of faith and repentance, before he goes to the University of election and predestination.[108]

As Whitefield's time in America drew to a close, he wavered over how vocal he should be on these matters when he returned to England. He wrote to Wesley, "I am willing to go with you to prison, and to death; but I am not willing to oppose you." Whitefield's last letter sent from America expressed his anguish:

> O that there may be harmony, and very intimate union between us! Yet it cannot be since you hold Universal Redemption. But no more of this. Perhaps, in Spring, we may see each other face to face. . . . My dear brother, for Christ's sake avoid all disputation. Do not oblige me to preach against you; I had rather die.[109]

The Wesley-Whitefield correspondence reveals that the discussion of doctrinal questions to this point was carried on in a spirit of warm affection and mutual esteem. The frequency of their letters indicates that they considered themselves as acting in concert for the promotion of the work of God. A keen fraternal spirit pervaded their communications, and each seemed especially desirous to avoid any separation. Whitefield's attitude in the midst of the controversy was unusually generous and respectful, which makes it all the more difficult to understand his Answer to Wesley, dated December 24, 1740, from Bethesda, in Georgia. He did not wait to publish this personal attack on Wesley until they had seen one another "face to face," but sent it to the printers in Charlestown and Boston just before embarking for England on January 24, 1741.

4. The Division of the Methodist Societies

THE controversy between Wesley and Whitefield finally came to a head in 1741. The stated reasons for their theological difference are found in the prior discussion of John Wesley's sermon on "Free Grace" and in Whitefield's "Answer" to Wesley. After a description of Whitefield's separation from Wesley, the reaction of the Wesleys will be considered. John Wesley's response was primarily in his writings on predestination, whereas Charles Wesley's response was seen especially in his hymns as well as in his personal support of his brother. The chapter concludes with a description of the personal reconciliation of Howel Harris to the Wesleys and the separation of Joseph Humphreys from them.

The Separation between Wesley and Whitefield

A letter from Whitefield to Wesley, dated September 25, 1740, was printed in London without the consent of either. It condemned Wesley's doctrine of perfection and the publication of his sermon "Free Grace." The letter caused quite an uproar about six weeks before Whitefield arrived in England. Wesley recorded that on reaching a society meeting at his headquarters in London, he found that

> great numbers of copies were given to our people, both at the door and in the Foundry itself. Having procured one of them, I related (after preaching) the naked fact to the congregation, and told them, "I will do just what I believe Mr. Whitefield would were he here himself." Upon which I tore it in pieces before them all. Every one who had received it did the same. So that in two minutes there was not a whole copy left. Ah! poor Ahithophel![1]

Although the motives of Wesley were unquestionable, the action was easily misinterpreted as an attack on Whitefield.[2] Wesley may have recognized this when the congregation unexpectedly followed his example and tore up all the copies of the letter, for two days later he wrote to Whitefield, most likely to explain his action and dispel any misunderstanding.[3] On his journey to England, Whitefield wrote to Ralph Erskine:

> I am now going to England, expecting to suffer great things. I hear, there are sad divisions and errors sprung up among the Brethren. In the spirit of meekness, I have answered dear Mr. Wesley's sermon, entitled "Free Grace"; and trust God will enable me to bear a full and explicit testimony to all His eternal truths.[4]

Whitefield apparently expected some kind of confrontation with the Wesleys. Further evidence of his anticipation of controversy is revealed in a letter to Charles Wesley and his brother together:

> My Dear, Dear Brethren; Why did you throw out the bone of contention? Why did you print that sermon against Predestination? Why did

you, in particular, my dear brother Charles, affix your hymns, and join in putting out your late hymn-book? How can you say, you will not dispute with me about election, and yet print such hymns, and your brother send his sermon, against election, to Mr. Garden, and others in America?[5]

Whitefield now felt he could not preach the gospel without speaking of election. He informed the brothers that his "Answer" to Wesley's sermon had already been printed in America, and that he was bringing another copy to publish in London. He disclaimed credit, however, for any separation that might follow as a result.

Whitefield's personal circumstances on arrival in England are important for understanding his subsequent conduct. He was over a thousand pounds in debt for the Orphan-house at Savannah, and he was threatened with arrest because he could not pay his creditors. His close companion William Seward had suffered martyrdom the previous autumn. In addition, Seward, who had generously assisted the work financially in the past, died without making any provision in his will for Whitefield. His publisher, James Hutton, refused to print his materials because of doctrinal differences. His injudicious censure of the late Archbishop Tillotson had caused many former admirers to desert him. Then, too, earlier outdoor congregations of more than twenty thousand were now reduced to some two hundred.[6]

Other factors also contributed to this desertion by former friends. William Holland reported that in 1740

> Mr. Whitefield wrote a letter from America to some of his Dissenting Friends in England, wherein he declared his Belief in the Doctrine of Reprobation. They took copies of the Letter and were exceeding industrious in shewing it to Mr. Whitefield's old acquaintance, triumphing as it were that they had gained him over to their Party.

The result was seen on Whitefield's return. "As he had professed to believe the doctrine of Reprobation, many of his old Friends dropped their acquaintance with him."[7]

Other problems pressed upon him: The court of Anglican Commissary Garden in Charleston had censured him; his appeal in London had not been settled. John Cennick was striving to involve him in the controversy over the Kingswood school. Elizabeth Delamotte had rejected his proposal of marriage, and she shortly thereafter married another. Finally, Whitefield's health was not good. This combination of difficulties was enough to pressure any mature man into steps he might later wish to retract. Yet Whitefield at this time was only twenty-six years old.

The center of controversy between Wesley and Whitefield was Wesley's sermon on "Free Grace." John Wesley preached this sermon in Bristol on April 29, 1739, but at Whitefield's request its publication was delayed until the autumn. Wesley justified its publication in a preface to the reader:

> Nothing but the strongest conviction, not only that what is here advanced is "the truth as it is in Jesus," but also that I am indispensably obliged to declare this truth to all the world, could have induced me

openly to oppose the sentiments of those whom I esteem for their work's sake: At whose feet may I be found in the day of the Lord Jesus![8]

From his text, Romans 8:32, "He that spared not his own Son, but delivered him up for us all, how shall he not with him also freely give us all things?" Wesley declared the free grace of God. For him it was "Free In All" and "Free For All." It was "Free In All" because it depended in no way on man's merit or works.

"But is not the grace of God also Free For All?" asked Wesley. The Predestinarians would answer "No!" Wesley summarized their position: "It is free only for those whom God hath ordained to Life." The rest of mankind was ordained to death: for them it was not free. God had absolutely decreed that some were born to be destroyed in hell; this He did of His own good pleasure. For such there was no possibility of redemption.

Wesley then dealt with the objection of some that this was not the form of predestination that they held. They would hold to a doctrine of election, but not of reprobation. Wesley showed the inconsistency of this position, maintaining that if one held to the doctrine of election, the implication of that position made it logical to accept the consequences of reprobation as well.

> Call it therefore by whatever name you please, election, preterition, predestination, or reprobation, it comes in the end to the same thing. The sense of all is plainly this, . . . by virtue of an eternal, unchangeable, irresistible decree of God, one part of mankind are infallibly saved, and the rest infallibly damned; it being impossible that any of the former should be damned, or that any of the latter should be saved.[9]

In this same sermon, Wesley enumerated a number of practical implications that he saw arising from the predestinarian position. He stated his particular objections to them:

> 1. It made all preaching vain, and thus voided one of the ordinances of God.

> 2. It lent itself to the destruction of holiness, which was the end of all the ordinances of God, by removing certain basic motives, e.g., the hope of heaven and the fear of hell.

> 3. It tended to destroy several branches of holiness, especially meekness and love. Wesley felt it inspired a sharpness of temper among those who spoke on this subject and also a contempt toward the non-elect.

> 4. It tended to destroy the comfort of religion. For the non-elect all the promises of God were of no avail, and for the rest, did not every man at some time doubt his own election?

> 5. It tended to destroy zeal for good works by cutting off one of the strongest motives for these works, viz., the hope of saving men's souls. In any case, if men were either elect or reprobate, why bother?

6. It had a tendency to overthrow the whole Christian revelation. If some were elect by the eternal decrees of God, whether or not there was a Christian revelation, then what was the need of it? If there was no need, could it be true?

7. It made Christian revelation contradict itself by positioning a predestination grounded on some texts that flatly contradicted others, as well as the whole scope and tenor of Scripture.

8. It was a doctrine full of blasphemy, because it represented Christ as a hypocrite and a deceiver of men. Christ always spoke as if he wanted all men to be saved, and he invited all to follow Him. Could Jesus have done this when he knew they could not respond? Again, it destroyed some basic attributes of God, viz., his justice, mercy, and truth, and made him more cruel and unjust than the devil.[10]

Of these objections, the first, second, third, fifth, and possibly the sixth were obviously reactions against antinomian tendencies that Wesley felt would undermine the foundations of Christian holiness. If these were indeed practical implications of the doctrine of predestination, Wesley had good reason for his strong reaction.

In addition to his objections, Wesley made two other valuable points. One dealt with the Predestinarian's question, "Why are not all men saved if universal redemption be true?" *First*, Wesley answered that men were not saved by any decree of God, or lost because it was His pleasure that they should die. Whatever the cause, if the oracles of God were true, it could not be His will that some should be born to die. *Second*, he declared that they were lost because they refused to be saved. "Therefore are they without excuse; because God would save them, but they will not be saved." Unfortunately, Wesley did not at this point elaborate his view of prevenient grace, and thereby he left himself open to the charge of holding to a doctrine of natural free will.

Another matter of consequence was Wesley's positive statement regarding what he believed to be the real decree of God. For him, God had set before men life and death, and a man might choose one or the other. All who permitted Christ to make them alive were elect according to the foreknowledge of God. Wesley felt that this understanding of the decree of God gave encouragement to good works, to all holiness, and to the ordinances of God. At the same time, it was also a source of joy, happiness, and comfort. In addition, it was worthy of God and consistent with His nature, especially in regard to God's justice, mercy, and truth. Moreover, Wesley was convinced that this position was in agreement with the whole scope and tenor of Christian revelation.[11]

Charles Wesley's hymn "Universal Redemption" was appended to the sermon "Free Grace." This hymn set forth the same objections to the doctrine of predestination as the sermon. Interestingly, as crucial as the sermon "Free Grace" was in the controversy with the Calvinists, Wesley never printed it in the *Standard Ser-*

mons. In Wesley's own edition of his works, it was placed among his controversial writings.[12]

Although George Whitefield's response had been published in America, he submitted a copy to Charles Wesley before sending it to the press in London. Charles returned it, saying, "Put up again thy sword into its place."[13] Nevertheless, Whitefield pressed forward with his original intention to print his "Answer" to Wesley, because he felt he must bear testimony to the truths of God's Word.[14] Although strongly reluctant to write against Wesley, he sensed a responsibility for those who had benefited from his own ministry, but who were now in danger of falling into error. Just as Paul rebuked Peter at Antioch, Whitefield "withstood him to the face because he was to be blamed."[15]

Whitefield did not intend to enter a long debate on the subject of God's decrees, but for the theological issues referred Wesley to *Veritas Redux,* by Dr. John Edwards. His own attention was directed more specifically to Wesley's objections. He first attacked Wesley's statement that he felt "an indispensible obligation" to publish his divisive sermon. Whitefield challenged Wesley's use of lots in the decision to preach on "Free Grace" in Bristol, accusing him of publishing solely on the basis of a lot. To raise further question about Wesley's method of guidance, he cited another occasion when Wesley had cast a lot and later admitted that it had probably been wrong. Whitefield felt that the lot over Wesley's sermon was, in like manner, a wrong one. "And if so," he said, "let not the children of God, who are mine and your intimate friends, and also advocates for universal redemption, think that doctrine true because you preached it up in compliance with a lot given out from God."[16]

Whitefield thought Wesley's text for the sermon was more adequate for proving election and final perseverance than the contrary. Thus, he objected that Wesley had abandoned a proper exposition of the Scripture and had gone on to other things. While Whitefield blamed Wesley for beginning his discussion, not with the doctrine of election, but with the obviously less popular corollary of reprobation, in the same paragraph he admitted that the two stand or fall together. He confessed to hold the basic position that Wesley had described as predestinarian:

> I frankly acknowledge, I believe the doctrine of reprobation, in this view, that God intends to give saving grace, through Jesus Christ, only to a certain number, and the rest of mankind, after the fall of Adam, being justly left of God to continue in sin, will at last suffer that eternal death, which is its proper wages.[17]

Whitefield understood this to be the correct interpretation of article 17 of the Church of England.

He next turned his attention to Wesley's reasons for rejecting the doctrine. On Wesley's first point that predestination made all preaching vain, Whitefield replied that God had appointed certain means for salvation, as well as salvation itself. He made a telling distinction between the ultimate purpose of God and the means of achieving it. From a human point of view, since preachers did not know who were elect, they were obliged to preach to all men. Further, it was possible that the doctrine would be useful even to the non-elect by restraining them from sin.

To the accusation that the doctrine of election tended to destroy holiness by removing the motives of reward of heaven and fear of hell, Whitefield contended that those who loved the Lord would strive to be holy out of love and gratitude. But also, recognizing the value of rewards, he felt that the elect would do more good works in order to attain an even greater reward in heaven. Then Whitefield spoke to Wesley's assertion that several branches of holiness tended to be destroyed, e.g., meekness, love, etc., because many who held this doctrine seem to be of narrow temper and sharp spirit. Whitefield objected to judging the truth of principles entirely from the practice of some who held them.

Next he dealt with the question of whether or not this doctrine tended to destroy the comforts of religion. He quoted article 17, "That the godly consideration of predestination, and election in Christ, is full of sweet, pleasant, and unspeakable comfort to godly persons," as evidence that the Reformers did not think election destroyed either holiness or the comforts of religion. To this, Whitefield added his own personal testimony of the comforts to this doctrine.

Wesley had objected that according to this doctrine millions, without any preceding offense of their own, were doomed to everlasting burning. Whitefield replied that since they all shared in the guilt of Adam's sin, God was quite just in imputing Adam's sin to his posterity, and He might have justly passed over all. He declared that any denial of this position would constitute disbelief in original sin. But if this view were accepted, then election and reprobation would be right, just, and reasonable; for if God could have passed by all, then He could justly have passed by some.

To the charge that good works were destroyed by this doctrine, Whitefield did not deal with Wesley's questions. He simply stated that, on the contrary, it pressed him to abound in good works.

To Wesley's accusation that predestination tended to overthrow the whole Christian revelation, Whitefield again made the distinction between means and ends. God's end design was to save men by the death of His Son, but His means were that this salvation should be applied to the elect through knowledge and faith in Him. On the particular objection that it made Scripture self-contradictory, Whitefield failed to touch on God's general invitation to all men, nor did he deal with Wesley's assertion that the texts used in support of predestination were not in harmony with the larger scope and tenor of the Christian revelation. To the texts that indicated God had no pleasure in the death of men, Whitefield protested that if they were taken in their literal sense, then no one would be damned. God did not delight simply in their death, but delighted to magnify his justice by punishing them, as they deserved.

Finally, Whitefield had no reply to the objection that the doctrine was open to the charge of blasphemy because it made Jesus a hypocrite for offering salvation to all men when He knew they could not respond. Whitefield simply reversed the charge and said it was blasphemy to assert that Christ died for those that perish:

> You cannot make good the assertion, "that Christ died for them that perish," without holding "That all the damned souls would hereafter be brought out of hell." . . . For how can all be universally redeemed, if they are not finally saved?[18]

Whitefield accused Wesley of making salvation depend not on God's free grace, but on man's free will. He closed with an exhortation that Wesley should

> put down his "carnal reasoning" and become "a little child," so that he could "print another sermon the reverse of this, and entitle it free-grace indeed. Free, not because free to all; but free, because God may withhold or give it to whom and when he pleases."[19]

While Whitefield readily identified himself with unconditional predestination, he warmly denied many of what Wesley saw as logical implications of that doctrine. He dealt clearly with the charges regarding the vanity of preaching, the destruction of holiness and its several branches, and the overthrow of the Christian revelation. But when he addressed himself to the comfort of religion, zeal for good works, revelation contradicting itself, and the charge of blasphemy, Whitefield never fully came to grips with Wesley's objections.

Wesley could argue that Whitefield had left four of his eight arguments untouched. Yet he probably overstated his case when he described Whitefield's letter as "a mere burlesque" of an answer, and declared that Whitefield had treated his "four remaining arguments in such a gentle manner as if he feared they would burn his fingers."[20]

In addition to responding to Wesley's objections, Whitefield made two other significant points. *First*, he rejected Wesley's position on Christian perfection. He argued that Wesley held an absolute or "sinless" perfection, in which a man could not sin again after conversion.[21] Although Wesley had not discussed Christian perfection in his sermon, Whitefield and later Calvinists objected to that doctrine most strenuously.

In 1741 Wesley published his sermon on "Christian Perfection." Without question it was a part of his larger campaign to promote Christian holiness. It is probable that he also intended it to be an answer to some of the charges that had been made against him, as well as to state clearly his own teaching on the subject. In this work he refuted the accusation that he held absolute perfection by showing in what sense Christians are not perfect:

> Christian perfection, therefore, does not imply (as some men seem to have imagined) an exemption either from ignorance, or mistake, or infirmities, or temptations. Indeed, it is only another term for holiness. Neither in this respect is there any absolute perfection on earth. There is no perfection of degrees, as it is termed; none which does not admit of a continual increase.[22]

He then took the offensive to show in what way Christians are perfect: "They are now in such a sense perfect, as not to commit sin, and to be freed from evil thoughts and evil tempers." In an earlier sermon on "Salvation by Faith," Wesley had included a section on salvation from the power of sin. He understood that a Christian did not sin by habitual sin, by any willful sin, by any sinful desire, nor by his infirmities, "for his infirmities have no concurrence of his will; and without this they are not properly sins."[23]

While Wesley denied the caricature of perfection that was symbolized by the term "sinless,"[24] yet it was with considerable difficulty that he completely disassociated himself from the phrase. Later he wrote: "I do not contend for the term sinless, though I do not object against it."[25]

Whitefield was reacting to Wesley's views on perfection that were included in the preface to *Hymns and Sacred Songs*, published in 1740. Wesley never expressed the doctrine in any higher terms, and afterward he modified some of his expressions when that preface was republished as a part of *A Plain Account of Christian Perfection*.[26]

It was noted above that Whitefield made two additional significant points in his response to Wesley. Besides his rejection of Wesley's doctrine of Christian perfection, he also made public some personal communications from Wesley on Wesley's use of lots. Although Whitefield justly had grave reservations about this practice, the publication of the private letters created a wide breach between the two men. Whitefield was probably right in claiming that a little more prudence on Wesley's part could have produced a different situation. Yet, a careful study of the circumstances has revealed that the use of the lot came at the end of a series of moves in which Wesley sought guidance on this question. Thus, when Whitefield raised the issue in public, he became open to his own charge, "that it was quite imprudent to publish."

Unfortunately, this personal attack on Wesley was still carried on thirty-seven years later as a result of Whitefield's revelations. In the midst of the great controversy during the 1770s, Rowland Hill and Augustus Toplady taunted Wesley over casting lots for his creed. Thomas Olivers replied for Wesley:

> It is hard not to believe that the relaters of this story are totally void of veracity, honour and conscience. The well-known fact is . . . neither more or less than this. When Mr. Whitefield, by embracing and preaching Calvinism, turned aside from the original doctrines of Methodism, it was a doubt with Mr. Wesley, not whether he should believe Calvinism, but whether he should preach and print against it. What made this a matter of doubt was [that], if he did expressly preach and print against it, he would oppose Mr. Whitefield, whom he dearly loved. On the other hand, if he did not preach and print against it, Mr. Whitefield's great influence would draw vast multitudes into his mistake. In this strait, it is true, he cast a lot, which came up to this effect, "as thou hast long believed Calvinism to be a delusion, regardless of friends and enemies, preach and print against it." Now, will good men, will men of honour, will men who make the smallest pretence to integrity, conscience, truth,

justice, or anything else that is good, call this "Casting lots for His Creed"?[27]

Whitefield's treatment of Wesley and his use of lots was even more astonishing in the light of his own remarks on this subject in a letter of 1740:

> I am no friend to casting lots; but I believe, on extraordinary occasions, when things can be determined no other way, God, if appealed to, and waited on by prayer and fasting, will answer by lot now, as well as formerly.[28]

Whitefield apparently recognized the personal affront which his indiscretion had caused and later apologized to Wesley for making the matter public.

After the publication of Whitefield's "Answer," Wesley went to see him and to allow Whitefield to speak for himself. Whitefield told him that, because they preached two different gospels, he could not give Wesley the right hand of fellowship, and he further declared his resolve to preach publicly against both of the Wesleys. When Westley Hall reminded him of an earlier promise not to oppose his friends publicly, Whitefield stated "that promise was only an effect of human weakness."[29] He was now, he said, of another mind. Some fellowship continued between them, however, for on the next day Whitefield and Cennick attended the evening love feast at the Foundry.

The following week Wesley believed that love and justice required that he respond to Whitefield, so he sought a second interview. Wesley observed that Whitefield could have published a treatise on the subject without the personal references and thus have borne his testimony to his preferred doctrines without putting additional weapons in the hands of those who loved neither man. As it was, Wesley noted, Whitefield "had said enough of what was wholly foreign to the question to make an open (and probably irreparable) breach between him and me."[30]

When Whitefield later reflected on these events, he regretfully recalled:

> I had written an answer, which though revised and much approved of by some good and judicious divines, I think had some too strong expressions about absolute reprobation, which the apostle leaves rather to be inferred than expressed. . . . Ten thousand times would I rather have died than to part with my old friends. It would have melted any heart to have heard Mr. Charles Wesley and me weeping, after prayer, that, if possible, the breach might be prevented.[31]

According to Whitefield, "Busybodies, on both sides, blew up the coals." But, though a break ensued, yet they kept from "anathematizing" each other.

In a conversation between Thomas's wife, Elizabeth, and Whitefield, Thomas Maxfield described the anguish Whitefield felt over the separation: "Oh! said Mr. Whitefield, what would I not give, or suffer, or do to see such times again upon earth!—But oh! that division, that division, what slaughter it made."[32]

When Wesley heard this, he responded, "But who made that division? It was not I. It was not my brother. It was Mr. Whitefield himself; and that notwithstanding all admonitions, arguments, and entreaties." Wesley stated that after Whitefield had published his "Answer," he made no reply. Although Whitefield began to preach against the Wesleys by name in public places, Wesley testified: "We never returned railing for railing, but spoke honourably of him at all times and in all places." According to Wesley, then, only part of the problem was doctrinal:

> It was not merely the difference of doctrine that caused the division. It was rather the manner wherein he maintained his doctrine and treated us in every place. Otherwise difference of doctrine would not have created any difference of affection; but he might lovingly have held particular redemption and we general to our lives' end.[33]

At first Whitefield felt it important to emphasize predestination in his preaching. Wesley related that

> when he preached in the very Foundry, and my brother sat by him, he preached the absolute decrees in the most peremptory and offensive manner. What was this but drawing the sword and throwing away the scabbard? Who, then, is chargeable with the contention and division that ensued?[34]

In one sense, though, the initial responsibility for the controversy lay at Wesley's door. He first publicly raised the issue by his preaching in Bristol; and then, second, by the later publication of "Free Grace" in 1739. However, Wesley began by making a doctrinal point that was not personally directed toward Whitefield. It was essentially a treatise against predestination, offered as a sermon. At this stage the controversy was confined to a discussion of purely theological differences. Thus, while the raising of the theological matters was largely Wesley's responsibility, the personal element in the dispute was not his creation.

That Wesley keenly felt Whitefield's "Answer" as a personal attack is revealed in his comment that enough wholly foreign to the doctrinal question had been included to make an open and irreparable breach between them. This referred primarily to Whitefield disclosing Wesley's use of the lot as means of guidance. Just how deeply Wesley felt this, was disclosed in his quote from Ecclesiasticus 22:22: "For a treacherous wound, and for the betraying of secrets, every friend will depart."

The estrangement was also a painful one for Whitefield because he was emotionally attached to the Wesleys, especially to Charles. His preaching on the decrees before Charles at the Foundry is difficult to explain. Perhaps he was unconsciously thinking of earlier days at the Fetter Lane Society when he had a larger share of the leadership responsibility and so felt free to speak his mind. Apparently he recognized this as an indiscretion, for there is no evidence that this was ever repeated.

Indeed, there appears to be some reason for regarding Whitefield's conduct during this time as being something less than his more mature actions. Some evidence indicates that he acted at times with an impetuosity that he often later regretted. Examples would include his self-confessed "injudicious" remarks against Archbishop Tillotson, and some expressions in his early sermons and Journals for which he later apologized.[35] Dallimore states that, on the trip to America in 1739, Whitefield had to ask forgiveness for some of his conduct during the revival in London that had been in "a style too Apostolical." To these may be added such things as the unusual method of his proposal to Elizabeth Dalarnotte,[36] together with his somewhat indiscreet letter to slaveholders in North America.[37] Much of this may be attributed to youth and inexperience, which, when compounded with the large number of difficult circumstances under which Whitefield was personally laboring, may in part account for his behavior. He later regretted some of his theological statements, as well as his revelation of the private communications between himself and Wesley. He wrote:

> My having dropped some too strong expressions concerning *absolute reprobation*; and more especially, my mentioning Mr. Wesley's casting a lot on a private occasion, known only to God and ourselves, have put me to great pain. . . . For this I have asked both God and him pardon years ago. And though I believe both have forgiven me, yet I believe I shall never be able to forgive myself.[38]

In spite of the personal attack, Wesley asserted that Whitefield did not need to fear any reprisals from him:

> This field you have all to yourself. I cannot dwell on those things, which have an immediate tendency to make you odious and contemptible. The general tenor both of my public and private exhort[at]ions, when I touch thereon at all, is, "Spare the young man, even Absalom, for my sake."[39]

When a friend encouraged Wesley to reply publicly to Whitefield's "Answer," Wesley responded, "Never. You have heard the cry, Whitefield against Wesley; but you shall never hear, Wesley against Whitefield."[40]

Although John Wesley never published a reply to Whitefield, Susannah Wesley apparently did not have the same scruples about a public response. There appeared at this time an anonymous work entitled *Remarks on Whitefield's Letters to Mr. Wesley, On His Sermon on Free Grace in a Letter From a Gentlewoman to Her Friend*. Several years later in a private conversation with Richard Viney, Wesley indicated that his mother was the author of this pamphlet.[41]

The separation between Wesley and Whitefield was organizational as well as theological. In London, Whitefield soon began to form separate societies. Some Calvinistic Dissenters purchased a piece of ground in Moorfields. Here, to screen early morning audiences from the cold and rain, they erected a temporary shed called the Tabernacle. Whitefield was very uncomfortable about the site, however, because it was so near the Foundry and gave the appearance of "one altar set up against another."[42]

Whitefield now became very close to the Dissenters. In America almost all of his associates and friends in the ministry were Nonconformists, while at the same time in England, most of the established churches were closed to his ministry. The Dissenters had financed and erected the Tabernacle, and Whitefield had become its chief minister. While Wesley was also ecclesiastically irregular, he refrained from identifying himself too closely with Nonconformists. Whitefield, by contrast, deliberately planned to assist all ecclesiastical bodies. "I have no freedom," he wrote to Joseph Humphreys, "but in going about to all denominations."[43] In order that he might preach throughout the country, he wrote to Howel Harris and invited him to assist in the work at the Tabernacle. Harris' ministry there was later supplemented when Whitefield drew other men around him.

Whitefield began to promote the interests of the Calvinistic wing of the Methodist movement through the publication of a Christian newspaper. The idea of a publication to relate the events of the revival was first suggested by William Seward as early as February 1739.[44] Nothing appeared, however, until September 1740, when John Lewis printed the first issue of *The Christian's Amusement.* Although Whitefield and Seward encouraged Lewis, Whitefield was still in America at that time. Thus, he was probably not directly involved in the venture. When he arrived in England in March 1741, however, the title of the paper was changed to *The Weekly History: or An Account of the Most Remarkable Particulars relating to the present Progress of the Gospel. By the encouragement of the Rev. Mr. Whitefield.*[45] It became from this time the unofficial voice of Calvinistic Methodism.

Its principal contributors were Whitefield, John Cennick, Howel Harris, and Joseph Humphreys.[46] Early issues of the paper were largely given to the differences over the doctrines of predestination. The Wesleys were often mentioned by name in remarks related to the controversy.[47] In the latter part of 1741, however, the emphasis changed to a more positive presentation of materials connected with the revival. Thereafter, little mention was made of doctrinal disputes.

Two contemporary judgments on the Whitefield-Wesley separation show how outsiders viewed the division. The first was by John Hutton, an earlier confidant of both Wesley and Whitefield, who spoke from a Moravian perspective: "Whitefield broke with us because we altogether rejected his doctrine of Reprobation, absolutely and in public. With Wesley also he had no peace over just this point."

From Hutton's viewpoint, the revival now had three separate branches. The first were "a special sort who leaned to Moravianism"; the second were coming out of the church and "Pelagianism," whom the Lord gave to Wesley; and "a third out of the sects and especially inclined to Calvinism," who went with Whitefield. Yet, he was convinced that God "has a true people amongst all three sorts."[48]

The second contemporary judgment on the separation was from *The Gentleman's Magazine* for June 1741. It reveals the attitude of the secular press. After a review of the theological differences of Wesley and Whitefield, the article noted:

> The controversy is grown so great a height, that Mr. Whitefield tells his auditors, that if they follow on Wesley's doctrines, they will be damned. On the other hand, Mr. Wesley tells his congregation, that if they follow Mr. Whitefield, and do not stick close to him, it will bring all to distrac-

tion and confusion at least. . . . From these circumstances it is very evident that they are both cheats, deluders and imposters.[49]

After the separation Wesley wrote to Charles that he could not leave London, because he had to "go round and glean after G. Whitefield,"[50] and he requested more copies of *Hymns on God's Everlasting Love,* an extremely important tool for teaching the societies.

Wesley's Writings on Predestination in 1741

In April and May of 1741, Wesley preached his sermon on "Predestination" at Bristol and London.[51] His sermon "Free Grace" (delivered in Bristol on April 29, 1739) was primarily an attack on the Calvinistic interpretation of predestination; but this sermon was a positive presentation of the same data from Wesley's point of view. It was a constructive piece and advanced his interpretation of the biblical terms "predestination," "election," etc.

Since Romans 8 and 9 were generally recognized to be difficult chapters, Wesley expected interpreters to be unusually sober and careful in their expositions of these passages. He discovered, however, that here they appeared most dogmatic and spoke in a manner *"ex cathedra* infallible," especially those who preached the absolute decrees. Wesley contrasted himself with this practice and modestly proposed some "hints" on understanding the passage.

He chose for his text Romans 8:29–30:

> For whom he did foreknow, he also did predestinate to be conformed to the image of his Son, that he might be the firstborn among many brethren. Moreover, whom he did predestinate, them he also called; and whom he called, them he also justified; and whom he justified, them he also glorified.

Wesley believed that Paul was not speaking of a chain of causes and effects, but rather of the method in which God works, i.e., the order in which the several aspects of salvation follow each other. In a survey of the whole work of God, Wesley *first* dealt with God's foreknowledge. He reminded his readers that this was God's accommodation to human language, and that in reality there was neither foreknowledge nor afterknowledge with God. For Him, all is present knowledge, because He sees all things at once. Men must be careful not to think that, because God knows about future events, He is the cause of them. No! Rather He knows them because they are. In no way does God's foreknowledge cause belief or unbelief. This would be analogous to one who said he caused the sun to rise because he knew that it would come up on the morrow. Further, if causation were not separated from foreknowledge, a man would have no freedom of choice and, in Wesley's eyes, could not be held accountable for his conduct. Such a person would be incapable of vice or virtue, reward or punishment.

Wesley's *second* point was the foundation of his whole argument. He believed that the unchangeable, irresistible, irreversible decree of God was that all who believed would be saved, while all who did not believe would be damned. Thus, *third*, according to this fixed decree that those who believed would be saved, those whom God knew as believers, He called. The outward call came by the word of His grace, and the inward call came by His Spirit. This inward application of the call was what some termed "effectual calling."

Fourth, God justified those who were called, i.e., He made them just and righteous. At this point Wesley's concern for holiness pressed him to inject sanctification into the sequence. He claimed that justification was to be understood in the "peculiar sense" that God conformed men to the image of His Son, or "as we usually speak, sanctified them." This was his preparation for the *final* point: those whom He justified and sanctified, He also glorified.[52]

Perhaps the most remarkable difference between this sermon and "Free Grace" is the more moderate tone used here. The former was highly emotional in flavor, deliberately designed to put its readers on their guard, with respect to the Calvinistic position on predestination. While the sermon on "Free Grace" only used a verse as a starting point from which to attack the doctrine, this message was a more thorough exposition of the text. Its carefully worded argument proceeds step by step and is an example of Wesley's logical mind functioning at its best.

From April to July 1741, Wesley continued to read and write on predestination.[53] He also made related doctrines a subject of special study. When he read an account of the Synod of Dort, he exclaimed:

> What a pity it is that the holy Synod of Trent and that of Dort did not sit at the same time; nearly allied as they were, not only as to the *purity of doctrine* which each of them established, but also as to the *spirit* wherewith they acted, if the latter did not exceed!

At Oxford he pursued his research further at the Bodleian and Lincoln College libraries. Wesley's reading concerning Calvin's part in the death of Servetus left him aghast. He recorded that Calvin

> utterly denies his being the cause of Servetus' death. "No!" says he, "I *only advised* our magistrates, as having a right to restrain heretics by the sword, to seize upon and try that archheretic. But after he was condemned, I said not one word about his execution"![54]

In the midst of this concentrated study, Wesley read Bishop Bull's *Harmonia Apostolica*, in which Bull attempted to reconcile Paul's justification by faith with James' justification by works.[55] Just as important at this period for Wesley's thinking, however, was the bishop's contention that the Calvinistic doctrines were definitely antinomian.[56]

From July 14 to 25, Wesley immersed himself in Calvin. Just after this he wrote *A Dialogue Between a Predestinarian and His Friend*.[57] Using a hypothetical discussion as his medium, Wesley has a "Friend" ask some embarrassing questions of the "Predestinarian," viz., those that pressed the implications of unconditional election to a logical conclusion. In order to show that some Calvinists carried their position to certain extreme conclusions, Wesley made each answer of the Predestinarian a direct quotation of some Calvinistic author. He used material from Calvin, Piscator, Zanchius, and others, using care to give the exact reference of each quotation. He assured his readers that they were all accurate and in context.

In their "dialogue," the friend compelled the Predestinarian to admit that (1) God ordained all events, including Adam's fall; (2) the wills of men are governed by the irresistible will of God; (3) sin was necessary and caused by actions that God decreed; and (4) election could not stand without reprobation. When the Predestinarian sought the opinion of his companion on absolute election and reprobation, the friend replied that he could not find them in Scripture and that he believed they bore dismal fruit, as in the case of the death of Servetus over a "difference of opinion" with Calvin.[58]

There is an emotional flavor to this work that is absent from the sermon on "Predestination"; yet it is not as pronounced as that in "Free Grace." Neither Whitefield nor his own research had modified any of Wesley's fears of the Calvinistic position; nevertheless, his opposition is more moderate in tone than was the case previously. By the question-and-answer method, he led the reader along to logical conclusions that many Calvinists would have been reluctant to adopt. Wesley felt, however that they must (1) swallow all these assertions; (2) renounce them all together; or (3) "equivocate, evade the questions, and prevaricate without end."[59]

During 1741 Wesley also sent out *The Scripture Doctrine Concerning Predestination, Election and Reprobation: Extracted from a late Author.* He did not reveal who the late author was, but in Benson's edition of the *Works,* it appears as one of Wesley's own compositions.[60] The most important aspect of this work is that it described Wesley's own position on free will and prevenient grace.

The last of Wesley's prose works from this period was extracted from the Quaker apologist Robert Barclay. Further copies of Barclay's *Serious Consideration on Absolute Predestination* were distributed not only to Wesley's congregation at the Foundry, but a thousand of them were also given to Whitefield's people at the Tabernacle![61]

Charles Wesley and the Calvinists

While John Wesley worked on predestination in London, Charles felt the impact of the controversy in Bristol, as evidenced by his description of Whitefield's preaching:

> One who in fear of God, and mistrust of himself, had heard Mr. W—, assured me he had preached barefaced reprobation. The people fled before the reprobating lion. But again and again, as he observed them depart, the preacher of sad tidings called them back, with general offers of salvation. Vain and empty offers indeed! What availed his telling them that, for aught he knew, they might be all elect. He did not believe them all elect; he could not; therefore he only mocked them with an empty word of invitation.[62]

Charles described one incident as an illustration of his pastoral problems over predestination.

> A woman spoke to me of her husband. He was under strong convictions, while he attended the word; but the first time he heard the *other Gospel*, [he] came home *elect* and in proof of it, *beat his wife*. His seriousness was at an end. His work was done. God doth not behold iniquity in Jacob; therefore his iniquity and cruelty abound. He uses her worse than a Turk (his predestinarian brother) and tells her, if he killed her he could not be damned.[63]

While some commentators treat this story as a lighter side of the controversy, it was just this kind of practical antinominianism that supported the Wesleys' apprehensions about the Calvinistic position.

Charles' firsthand acquaintance with Calvinist authors was disclosed in his discussion of reprobation with a Bristol resident. When the man finally confessed that there was a great mystery in it, Charles then replied: "Or to put it in Beza's words, which I then read him, 'We believe though it is incomprehensible, that it is just to damn such as do not deserve it.' " When the man could not respond to a further question, Charles read him Calvin! He concluded:

> Never did I meet with a more pitiful advocate of a more pitiful cause. And yet I believe he could say as much for reprobation as another. I told him his predestination had got a millstone about its neck, and would infallibly be drowned, if he did not part it from reprobation.[64]

Thomas Jackson declared that Charles had a "deep and solemn conviction" that the peculiarities of what is called Calvinism are unscriptural, of dangerous tendency to the souls of men, and are only neutralized in their effects by the admixture of saving truth with which they are generally proposed. Charles preached against absolute predestination and in defense of God's universal love much oftener and with far greater warmth than his brother, and expressed himself in language much stronger than John ever employed in reference to this subject. He loved Mr. Whitefield with an ardor that nothing could quench, but he could not abide his doctrinal position.[65]

A letter from Charles Wesley to John indicates that due to Whitefield's presence in Bristol, Charles was more alarmed over the controversy than his brother:

> I am exceedingly afraid lest predestination should be propagated among us in a more subtle and dangerous manner than has hitherto been attempted. Mr. Whitefield preaches holiness very strongly, and "free grace" to all; yet, at the same time, he uses expressions which necessarily imply reprobation. He wraps it up in smoother language than before, in order to convey the poison more successfully. Our Society, on this account, go to hear him without any scruple or dread. We have sufficiently seen the fatal effects of this devilish doctrine already, so that we cannot keep at too great a distance from it. For my part, by the grace of God, I never will be reconciled to reprobation, nor join with those who hold it.[66]

Charles admonished his brother for his credulity and failure to recognize the seriousness of the problem. In strong terms he urged John to renounce Whitefield from the housetop "till he renounces reprobation." John coolly endorsed the letter: "In a panic about G.W."[67]

In 1741 the Wesley brothers jointly published *Hymns on God's Everlasting Love*. This hymnbook was a major tool in the theological debate within the societies. One contemporary witness testified that she was "quickened and strengthened considerably . . . when the Hymns on Universal Redemption are sung."[68]

Speaking of this "body of practical divinity," Rattenbury says these fiery verses, when repeatedly sung, proved more formidable than any sermon could be in proving the absurdity and tragic horror of the "Horrible Decree."

> Nothing did so much to destroy popular Calvinism in England as Charles Wesley's hymns; they made it incredible to the reason, and repulsive to the heart of decent people; but immediately effective as were these ironical verses, they had not the permanent value of the positive hymns of God's Everlasting Love.[69]

These hymns of controversy revealed Charles' views on the doctrines of God and man. The God of everlasting love was set over against the picture of God presented in Hyper-Calvinism. For Charles Wesley, the Calvinist's God was basically a God of hate:

> A doctrine which asserted that God could deliberately create countless millions of human beings with the purpose of burning them in hell fire everlastingly, in the opinion of Charles Wesley, debased God; also he thought that the reduction of men and women to the status of mere automata, the playthings of a capricious and cruel Omnipotence, degraded man.[70]

The fundamental truths advanced began with the conviction that God was righteous, while man was a fallen creature, having inherited the sin of his first parents. Any with doubts about original sin needed only to look at the relations between men, and into his own heart. Next, man was unable to save himself. Yet this was not the absolute total depravity of the Calvinistic position. Instead, the preventing grace of God allowed men to respond to God in faith.

> By nature only free to ill,
> We never had one motion known
> Of good, hadst Thou not given the will,
> and wrought it by thy grace alone.[71]

Although all of salvation was by divine initiative, man did have the capacity to resist the will of God.

The very heart of the gospel for Charles Wesley was that God is Love. "PURE UNIVERSAL LOVE THOU ART" was the great discovery of "Wrestling Jacob," and that line was always printed in capital letters in this famous hymn by Charles, to distinguish it from everything else. This love was for all men, not just an elect few.

Though Charles Wesley believed that man was in revolt against God, yet God had respect for the freedom of his will. Since He did not force Himself on men, there was no irresistible grace. For Charles Wesley, a man who did not have the capacity to resist the grace of God, was no real man but an automaton. A sinner could come to God only because of the preventing grace of God, but in spite of the wooing and pleading of God, grace was nonetheless resistible.[72]

Many of Charles Wesley's hymns so strongly stressed the breadth of God's love that it is not difficult to see how Whitefield and others believed that some of them implied God would ultimately save all men. Charles' object, however, was to show that God's love reached to every man, no matter how sinful. Yet, salvation was all of God, and only by His grace was man enabled to respond.

> Father, whose *everlasting love*
> *Thy only Son for sinners gave,*
> *Whose grace to* all *did freely* move,
> And sent Him down a *world to save;*[73]

Charles' strong reaction to the Calvinistic position in "The Horrible Decree" illustrates his capacity to create an emotional, as well as intellectual, response.

> Ah! gentle, gracious Dove;
> And art thou grieved in me,
> That sinners should restrain thy love,
> And say, "It is not free:
>
> It is not free for *all;*
> The *most* Thou *passest by,*
> And mockest with a fruitless call
> Whom Thou hast doomed to die."
>
> They think Thee *not sincere*
> In giving each his day:
>
> "Thou only draw'st the sinner near,
> To cast him quite away;
>
> To aggravate his sin,
> His sure damnation seal,
> Thou show'st him heaven, and say'st, Go in,—
> And thrusts him into hell."
>
> Sinners, abhor the fiend:
> His other gospel hear—
> "The God of truth did not intend
> The thing His words declare;
>
> *He offers* grace to *all,*
> *Which* most *cannot embrace,*

Mock'd with an ineffectual call
And insufficient grace.

"The righteous God consign'd
Them over to their doom,
And sent the Saviour of mankind
To damn them from the womb:

To damn for falling short
Of what they could not do,
For not believing the report
Of that which was not true."[74]

Charles' ministry in the city of Bristol was closely tied to the controversy. To protect the societies from the Calvinistic doctrines, he first gave all the band members at Kingswood "the treatise on predestination." His second method of attack was regular preaching on related doctrines. On April 13 and 20, he preached explicitly on universal redemption. On May 7, after preaching on the text "And I, if I be lifted up from the earth, will draw all men unto me," he declared: "Was I in search after the strongest scriptures for universal redemption, I could not choose so well as Providence chose for me."[75] At the end of the summer, while he was preaching on Isaiah 53, he "was greatly assisted to purge out the leaven of Calvinism." On another occasion, while expounding Ezekiel 18, he declared, "Our Lord owned me here also, and the hammer of his Word broke the rock of absolute predestination in pieces. One, who had been long entangled with it, now testified that she had delivered her soul out of the snare of the fowler."[76] Apparently Charles' efforts made some impact, for at the end of August he wrote that he met the Kingswood bands and rejoiced in their steadfastness, "none having turned either to the right hand or to the left, either to stillness or predestination."[77]

Yet some pastoral problems that sprang from the controversy continued. Charles illustrated the Wesleys' fear of the "overconfidence" of some who believed in final perseverance.

> One serious youth I spake with today, who did run well: But from the time that he was persuaded to believe there was no falling after justification, he did began to fall, as he now confesses, into carelessness, self-indulgence, and at last into known sins.[78]

Another who had experienced conversion wrote of her experience:

> I then gave way to reasonings and reasoned myself into the belief of Election. I then thought that God had made a remnant to be saved and a remnant to be lost, and now the preachers of that Doctrine came. I went to hear them and believed all they said concerning the Elected Love as they called it and not falling from grace, but woeful experience soon told me I was fallen.[79]

These were what the Wesleys saw as the practical implications of the Calvinistic position, and they served as a powerful motivating factor in their opposition to the doctrines of Calvinism.

Howel Harris Reconciled with the Wesleys

In the middle of June 1741, Howel Harris was present at Bristol while Charles preached, and afterward he testified publicly to the power with which Charles had spoken. Someone informed Charles that, when Harris left the room, he had stopped the railing of some, saying, "He would hear nothing against his brother Wesleys for they were true ministers of Christ, and children of God!" "But," said Wesley, "Who can touch pitch, and not be defiled? The very next day he came, and threatened to declare against me as a deceiver."[80]

The following day Charles invited Harris to address the society. "He gave an account of his conversion by irresistible grace, mixing with his experience the impossibility of falling, God's unchangeableness, etc. I could not but observe the ungenerousness of my friend," wrote Charles. Wesley interrupted Harris to ask the society if he should be permitted to continue, but they would not allow it.

> "Then," said he, "You thrust me out." "No," I said, "we do not; you are
> welcome to stay as long as you please. We acknowledge you a child of
> God." Yet again he began, "If you do not believe irresistible grace;" and
> I cut off the sentence of reprobation which I foresaw coming.

After Harris left the meeting, Charles continued the service. "I acknowledged the grace given our dear brother Harris, and excused his estrangement from me through the wickedness of his counselors." A few days later, Harris "Cried for the Wesleys" and prayed that if he had wronged them, he would be able to make things right.[81]

When Harris visited London during July 1741, his Calvinistic theology aligned him closely with Whitefield and the work at the Tabernacle, but even there he was able to moderate some who censured the Wesleys. He often felt his heart knit to the brothers, yet he heard rumors that John Wesley had said: "If you would be saved stay here, if you would be damned go to the Tabernacle."[82] When he was with Wesley, his affections grew; when he was away from him, he had recurring reservations. Finally he prayed: "O Lord shew me by some means of John Wesley what he is, if he is Thy child that I may eternally join him, if not that I may not for the world hold fellowship with him."

On August 30 Harris' doubts apparently were settled. Wesley sent for him, and they "met with vast love." Harris declared: "Sure this union is of the Lord for I had no hand in it and my carnal nature and carnal reason is all against it." A month later he was reconciled to Charles Wesley. In a long theological conversation, they agreed that salvation was all of God, i.e., that God does the choosing and keeping of those who are saved. They were of one accord in ascribing damnation to a man's own sins, not to any sovereign pleasure of God. Charles was willing to qualify his statement that "faith was the cause of justification" to mean that faith was the "Instrumental Cause," and he further denied any free will in man.[83]

In March 1742, after being with Wesley in Cardiff, Harris wrote of his "feeling deep love to him and humbled for any word I said against him and felt a union such as I never felt before." They talked about election and reprobation, and "agreed we should not meddle" in controversies anywhere.[84] Later in the year, Harris described to Charles how he believed Satan's device to keep them asunder was

> by representing us to you as preaching Election and Perseverance in such a manner as to give license to sin and to feed pride and presumption and carnal security, which indeed is far from us; and so you to us as setting the creature to build on himself.

Harris then proposed, however, that they discourage all disputes, and summarized their problem with a note of optimism:

> I see that little by little the Lord will bring us together. We have been perhaps in your eyes too far leaning towards Reprobation, though we never meant it in the least, as to set man's damnation on God's decretive willing it unconditionally. We try to secure God's Glory in man's salvation; and you try to secure His Justice by setting man's damnation in his own will. It is probably the duty of all of us to be more careful with our words.[85]

From this point Harris began to record nothing but his affection for the Wesleys, as well as his labors to unite them with other members of the Calvinistic party.

Joseph Humphreys' Separation from Wesley

Another of the early preachers of the Methodist revival was Joseph Humphreys. Humphreys grew up in Oxfordshire, where his father was a minister of a Dissenting congregation. While attending a Nonconformist academy in London, he began to preach, although he was still unconverted. In May 1739, he first heard Whitefield and shortly thereafter experienced justification by faith.[86] While he continued to study, he began to serve under Wesley at Deptford and Greenwich. Wesley later wrote that Humphreys was "the first lay preacher that assisted me in England."[87]

In the midst of the dispute at Kingswood, Wesley had requested Humphreys to take John Cennick's place there. Humphreys, however, had reservations and replied:

> So far as I see at present I cannot cordially do anything in opposition to Mr. Cennick. As for his particular opinions, so long as he is silent about them, so long as they can do no harm, . . . indeed my way is not clear at present to do anything in order to exclude him from labouring in those parts; for I should think that I prevented a useful instrument.[88]

Nevertheless, Humphreys journeyed to Bristol and the following month wrote to Wesley of his ministry there. His account included his views on perseverance, perfection, and predestination. Humphreys preferred to leave predestination "quite alone so as neither to speak for it nor against it in a controversial way." Apparently this was one doctrine about which he was uncertain: "Some Scriptures which are brought for it, I pretend not to understand. There is a mystery in them." He was determined, however, to make his own election sure and to call others to do the same.[89]

In early April the "mystery" of predestination was resolved. While reading Romans 8, Humphreys was persuaded that the "peculiar, special love, called Electing Love" was best understood from the Calvinistic perspective. He did not see his commitment to election and final perseverance, however, as a new doctrine: but only à farther discovery of God's love."[90] With forthrightness he wrote immediately to Wesley of the change in his views. Wesley conversed several times with Humphreys over the points in question, and in order to clarify his own position for Humphreys. On April 10, he expounded the eighth chapter of Romans in Humphreys' presence.[91] Apparently Humphreys was not satisfied with Wesley's interpretation, for he wrote the next day to Charles Wesley:

> I believe whoever is finally saved, was chosen in Christ before the Foundation of the World. I had a precious Taste of electing, everlasting Love about a week ago. And if God has shewn me this *once* and *again*, why should I hide this Truth any longer.[92]

To another, Humphreys confessed that to avoid the conclusion that universal redemption necessarily implied universal salvation, he had turned to a view of limited election. The following month, after Humphreys had joined Whitefield, he wrote to John Wesley:

> I would have joined with you till all eternity, if I could. Nevertheless, that I may simply follow the light which God has given me, I now think it my duty no longer to join with you, but openly to RENOUNCE your peculiar doctrines.[93]

To this new theological position, Wesley replied: "I do not understand you. What doctrines do you mean? that 'Christ died for all?' or that 'He that is born of God sinneth not'? These are not peculiar to me. The first is St. Paul's, the second is St. John's."[94]

Years later Wesley summarized Humphreys' subsequent career:

> He turned Calvinist, and joined Mr. Whitefield, and published an invective against my brother and me in the newspaper. In a while he renounced Mr. Whitefield, and was ordained a Presbyterian minister. At last he received Episcopal ordination. He then scoffed at inward religion, and when reminded of his own experience, replied, "That was one of the foolish things which I wrote in the time of my madness!"[95]

5. A Limited Reconciliation between Leaders of the Debate

SEVERAL months after the immediate heat of the separation of Whitefield from Wesley, the debate began to cool down. There was a move toward partial reconciliation. Howel Harris, in particular, played a mediating role between the Calvinists and the Wesleyans during 1741 and 1742. The result was the reestablishment of personal fellowship between the Wesleys and Whitefield, although additional efforts at a closer union of the two parties over the next several years did not bear fruit. This concluding section of Part 1 closes with an evaluation of the role of doctrine for John Wesley and a discussion of how Wesley's commitment to Christian holiness affected his involvement in the controversy.

Howel Harris Serves as Mediator

Howel Harris was the central figure in attempts to reunite the Calvinists and the Wesleys. After his own reconciliation with the brothers, he immediately began to labor for union between the contending parties. He first brought Wesley and John Cennick to a measure of agreement. After meeting together with them, Harris wrote, "We agreed to preach that God is willing to receive all as are willing to submit to all the offices of Christ, and to meddle nothing further but leave it work in all Hearts. Everyone assented."[1]

In early October 1741 at Bristol, Harris was explaining to Joseph Humphreys his reconciliation with the Wesleys when John Wesley arrived at their lodgings. They discoursed until 2:00 a.m. on free will, perseverance, perfection, and reprobation, but they "parted in love," and "agreed to pray for each other and not to receive false accusation." Harris' attempts to bring Wesley and Humphreys closer together were more limited:

> Endeavoured to reconcile Bro. Humphreys and Bro. Wesley, but 'tis God's work. I reasoned much about Union, though they may be in some Errors in way of expressing yet in the main they are safe, i.e., setting Christ the foundation and looking to Him continually.[2]

Of Harris' efforts Wesley could exclaim: "Blessed be thou of the Lord, thou man of Peace!"[3] Although Wesley and Humphreys never returned to their former intimate friendship, Charles Wesley and Humphreys apparently reestablished some fellowship. Charles agreed to read and correct Humphreys' account of his spiritual experience. At the end of the year, Humphreys wrote him a warm letter, expressing his gratitude for the influence of Wesley's ministry on his life. He proposed:

> Let us wait till God shall reveal all other things unto us, and make us infinitely of one mind. At present let us go on, simply declaring to others what the Lord hath done for our souls. . . . Let us long for a union in the

Lord. Let everyone that is without be astonished at our patience with, and mildness toward, one another.[4]

At Harris' invitation, John Wesley visited Wales in mid-October to attend a "Conference" with Daniel Rowlands, Humphreys, Thomas Price, and "many others." Harris urged them to consider union, and the Welsh Calvinist Methodists appeared anxious to reach an understanding with Wesley. The English Calvinists, however, led by Humphreys and Thomas Bissicks, a former miner,[5] were staunchly opposed to reconciliation and warmly charged Harris with error. Harris confessed that "by loving John Wesley I have lost all my friends."[6] Although the conference did not fulfill Harris' intended purpose, Wesley could still write: "We parted in much love, being all determined to let controversy alone, and to preach 'Jesus Christ, and Him crucified.' "[7]

Wesley and Whitefield Reestablish Personal Fellowship

Undaunted in his efforts to promote peace, Harris wrote the same month to Whitefield in Scotland. He recounted his conversations with the Wesleys, explained that both denied free will, and mentioned Charles Wesley's loving spirit and warm regard for Whitefield. This more accurate understanding of the Wesleys' position, plus Charles' expression of affection, obviously moved the tenderhearted Whitefield, so he immediately wrote to John Wesley at Bristol:

> I have for a long time expected that you would have sent me an answer to my last; but, I suppose, you are afraid to correspond with me, because I revealed your secret about the "lot." Though much may be said for my doing it, yet I am sorry now that any such thing dropped from my pen, and I humbly ask pardon.
>
> May God remove all obstacles that now prevent our union! Though I hold particular election, yet I offer Jesus freely to every individual soul. You may carry sanctification to what degrees you will, only I cannot agree that the inbeing of sin is to be destroyed in this life.[8]

Apparently the reestablishment of friendship was becoming more important to Whitefield than their doctrinal differences. When he arrived in Bristol three weeks later, however, he found a fresh cause for contention, which he described to Harris:

> Brother Weslies (with grief I speak it) seem to be worse than ever. Just now they have published another hymn book, ... wherein are some dreadfully horrid things. We are called Advocates of the Devil, Carnal Saints etc. Christians are to be as completely holy as the Angels, and as Spotless and Sinless as Jesus himself.[9]

Yet Whitefield's genuine sorrow over the separation cannot be doubted. In the winter of 1742 Lady Huntingdon told Wesley of her meeting Whitefield in Gloucester and of his apparent shame concerning his conduct toward Wesley.[10]

Before the end of the year, he met twice with Charles Wesley and wrote again to John, longing for some friendly contact.

On the other side, Wesley's affectionate interest in George Whitefield could not be questioned. At the height of the controversy, he wrote: "I read over Mr. Whitefield's account of God's dealing with his soul. Great part of this I know to be true. Oh 'let not mercy and truth forsake thee! Bind them about thy neck! Write them upon the table of thy heart!' "[11]

In January 1742, after Whitefield heard Charles Wesley preach, he lamented: "I would meet more than half-way; but we are all too shy."[12] Perhaps this accounts for no firm record of Whitefield and John Wesley meeting until April. Wesley described the occasion:

> I spent an agreeable hour with Mr. Whitefield. I believe he is sincere in all he says concerning his earnest desire of joining hand in hand with all that love the Lord Jesus Christ. But if (as some would persuade me) he is not, the loss is all on his own side. I am just as I was; I go my way, whether he goes with me or stays behind.[13]

Apparently Wesley's friends did not succeed in keeping the two men apart. Three weeks later, together they visited the Archbishop of Canterbury and the Bishop of London. Wesley said afterward: "I trust, if we should be called to appear before princes, we should not be ashamed."[14]

A letter from Whitefield to Wesley in October 1742 confirms that the two men had reestablished personal fellowship:

> Yesterday morning, I had your kind letter, dated October 5. In answer to the first part of it, I say, "Let old things pass away, and all things become new." I can heartily say "Amen" to the latter part of it. "Let the king live forever, and controversy die." It has died with me long ago. . . . I have been upon my knees praying for you and yours.[15]

This amiable relationship was restored in spite of their doctrinal disagreements. Their friendship continued without resolving their differences on predestination. Whitefield still declared: "Mr. Wesley I think is wrong in some things; but I believe he will shine bright in glory. I have not given way to him, or to any, whom I thought in error, not for an hour; but I think it best not to dispute, where there is no probability of convincing."[16] And while Wesley's affections were clear, so were his convictions: "I love Calvin, Luther more; the Moravians, Mr. Law, and Mr. Whitefield far more than either. But I love truth more than all."[17] As Ronald Knox so aptly observed: "Never were theologians so resolved to make a molehill out of a mountain."[18]

Efforts at Closer Union between the Calvinists and the Wesleyans

Although personal fellowship was reestablished among most of the leaders of early Methodism, this never resulted in a formal union of the Calvinistic and Wesleyan parties. Efforts toward this end included a conference in London on August 20, 1743. Whitefield, Harris, and the two Wesleys met and agreed on such procedural matters as the use of lay teachers, refusal to separate from the Church of England, and the protection of the law from mob violence. But "they were not free about receiving the Sacrament together," nor did the meeting pave the way toward organizational unity. The first "Conference" of the English Calvinistic Methodists was held shortly thereafter, and Harris' account of the proceedings reveals that the question of union with the Wesleys was not even raised.[19]

Wesley, however, continued to seek a measure of theological consensus. His "strong desire to unite with Mr. Whitefield as far as possible" led him to consider again three of the major points of controversy. Under each section Wesley indicated how far he could go to reach some agreement. On unconditional election, Wesley granted that God had unconditionally elected some individuals and nations to specific privileges and responsibilities. Further, he said, "I do not deny (though I cannot prove it is so), that He has unconditionally elected some persons (thence eminently styled 'The Elect') to eternal glory." But he still staunchly denied that those "not thus elected to glory must perish."[20]

Under the subject of irresistible grace, Wesley conceded that at the moment grace brings salvation to the soul, it is irresistible, but generally the grace of God may be and has been resisted. In addition, he did not deny "that in some souls in those eminently styled The Elect (if such there be) the grace of God is so far irresistible that they cannot but believe and be finally saved."

Another disputed area was final perseverance. Here Wesley affirmed that there was a "state attainable in this life from which a man cannot finally fall," and he did not reject the assertion "that all those eminently styled The Elect will infallibly persevere to the end."[21]

On these three points Wesley went as far as he could go, allowing (1) that there is the possibility that a few persons were unconditionally elected; (2) that at a certain moment grace was irresistible; and (3) that any who were "the elect" would infallibly persevere to the end. Wesley nowhere came closer to the Calvinistic views, but in his subsequent writings he drew back from these positions.

Wesley met his own first "Conference" at the Foundry on June 25–29, 1744. The previous month he had asked Richard Viney about an agenda for the meetings, and Viney had outlined their basic concerns. "What do we meet for? To consider before God 1) What to Teach, 2) How to Teach, 3) What to do? i.e., Doctrine, Discipline, and Practice." A series of questions were proposed, some of which reflected the points of debate with the Calvinists. Under "Doctrine" he asked: "What is sanctification? Can a believer fall *totally* and *finally*? How? Is inbred sin taken away in this Life? How can we *know* that one is thus saved? Is the second Preface true?" "Discipline" was the next head: "What can we adopt from CZ [Count Zinzendorf]? Mr. Whitefield? The Kirk? The Quakers? Any other people?" Finally, under "Practice" the union question was raised: "Can we unite any further with Mr. Whitefield? With the Moravians? Is any Conference with either advisable?"[22] Though the Conference agreed that the Moravians would adamantly oppose any closer cooperation, they were willing to consider a joint conference with Whitefield to explore the possibility of union.[23]

Nevertheless, on the doctrinal matters they all agreed that they had "unawares leaned too much towards Calvinism."[24] This probably represented Wesley's view that he had gone too far in his attempt to work out a compromise with Whitefield on which the differing parties could unite. But it was also closely connected with the danger of antinomianism, which Wesley believed was latent in the Calvinistic position. In the Christian church, antinomianism was that age-old heresy holding that believers were not obligated to obey the moral demands of the Scripture, because Christ had freed them from all law. They were thus "anti-law," or antinomian, who believed that Christian liberty meant liberty from any "bondage" to the commandments of God. It was this position that the Conference described as that "which makes void the law through faith,"[25] and during the free-grace controversy Wesley saw enough examples of it as the fruit of Calvinism to instill in him a lifelong fear of its influence.

After dealing with the questions of Calvinism and antinomianism, the Conference next turned its attention to the doctrine of sanctification. They were not content to deal only with the problems of differing theological positions, but were concerned with positive promotion of holiness of heart and life within their own connection. The basic focus of this first Conference was the definition of entire sanctification, its attainment, and the assurance of the experience in this life. The following year, at the second Conference, sanctification was again discussed vis-à-vis Calvinism and antinomianism, and this time the emphasis was on when the experience of entire sanctification occurred, how it ought to be preached, and the manner in which one should wait for it.

A third major treatment of the subject by Wesley with his preachers came in 1747, when they spelled out in some detail the differences between the Wesleyan and the Calvinistic viewpoints on sanctification, along with the scriptural basis of Wesley's position.[26] The early Conferences thus continued to see a very close connection between their differences with their Calvinist brethren over predestination and their differences over perfection. These were two sides of the same theological coin, and whichever way it was turned, the other question was not far out of the picture.

The Role of Doctrine for Wesley

While Wesley's reaction to antinomianism has been made clear, this has not been properly placed in the larger perspective of his central theological emphasis.[27] Fear of antinomianism was only the negative side of Wesley's positive concern for Christian holiness. The real concern for Wesley was the cultivation of "holiness of heart and life" in the believer, and anything that hindered this growth in godliness was to be ardently opposed. Thus, while there were related issues that were perceived to undermine the sanctity of the spiritual life, Wesley's main interest was the positive promotion of holy living. This he did, not only by field preaching, biblical exposition, the band meetings, and "the means of grace," but also in his publications and by the instruction of his preachers.

In addition to his sermon on "Christian Perfection" (1741), Wesley printed another pamphlet on the same subject, but since he did not wish to give undue offense to the antiperfectionists, he gave it the innocuous title of *The Character of a Methodist* (1742). Among other publications designed to encourage personal godliness were extracts from Thomas à Kempis' *Imitation of Christ* (1741), and William Law's *Christian Perfection* (1743) and *A Serious Call to a Holy Life* (1744), all three being books that had significantly influenced Wesley's Oxford commitment to the centrality of holiness for the Christian faith.

Apparently, these publications, along with his sermons on the subject, did not go without effect. Wesley several times records in his *Journal* that Methodists were giving testimony to an experience of Christian perfection or cleansing from all sin.[28] Lastly, as we have seen, when Wesley first began to gather his preachers into Conference, there were extended discussions of the doctrine of sanctification and its place in their ministry.[29]

It is important to note that Christian holiness for Wesley was both inward and outward. The negative side of inward holiness referred to the cleansing of the heart and the purifying of the intentions, while the positive side meant a perfect love for God and man.[30] The former was the renewal "of the soul in the image of God," and the latter was that "faith which worketh by love."[31] Writing of both aspects of inward holiness, Wesley declared: "Scripture holiness is the image of God; the mind which was in Christ; the love of God and man."[32]

But holiness was not purely an inward matter for Wesley. Outward holiness was the natural result of inward sanctification, and indeed the manifestation of the inner working of the Holy Spirit. Holiness in Wesley's mind was both "of heart and life," and the evidence of "holiness of life" was obedience to the commands of God in Scripture.[33] He stated that in a word holiness was "the mind that was in Christ, enabling us to walk as Christ also walked."[34] It was the perceived tendency in Calvinism to take the urgency out of "walking as Christ walked" in obedience to the commandments of Scripture that Wesley feared would undermine the pursuit of holiness and lead to open antinomianism.

In his *A Short History of Methodism*, Wesley looked back over the 1741 division:

> Here was the first breach, which warm men persuaded Mr. Whitefield to make merely for a difference of opinion. Those, indeed, who believed universal redemption had no desire at all to separate; but those who held particular redemption would not hear of any accommodation, being determined to have no fellowship with men that "were in so dangerous errors." So there were now two sorts of Methodists, so called; those for particular, and those for general, redemption.[35]

Wesley claimed that the theological difference between Whitefield and himself was basically a "difference of opinion," for which he "had no desire at all to separate." This was in contrast to his own earlier division with the Moravians, where Wesley had judged the theological questions to be of major importance. Because of incorrect views on those doctrines that "struck at the root of Christianity," he had been ready to initiate the separation. But in the Calvinistic controversy, Wesley repeatedly styled as "opinions" the differences over the doctrines of predestination, and for such matters that were not essential to Christian doctrine, he did not wish to divide the Methodist movement.

While the place of correct theology continued to be important for Wesley, doctrinal issues were divided into two categories. The line of demarcation was the Scripture. While Wesley was willing that he and Whitefield debate the biblical passages on predestination while continuing to labor together, he firmly believed that the Moravian position on faith, the ordinances of God, the church, the Scripture and tradition, and good works was "flatly contrary to the Word of God." Within this biblical framework, Wesley felt union was possible and desirable, even though men held differing views on minor questions. But those positions that fell outside the standard of the Scripture he saw as major doctrinal deviations, and at that point theological issues became important enough to cause disruption.

In the light of this claim that predestination was only an "opinion," how are we to understand Wesley's strong reactions to Calvinism during the free-grace controversy? Apparently, for a short time in the heat of the controversy, he had mentally shifted predestination from the category of "opinion" to the category of a threat to "essential truth." In the 1760s he confessed as much to John Newton:

> Just so my brother and I reasoned 80 years ago, as thinking it our duty to oppose Predestination with our whole strength; not as an opinion, but as a dangerous mistake, which appears to be subversive of the very foundation of Christian experience, and which has, in fact, given occasion to the most grievous offences. That it has given occasion to such offences I know; I can name time place and persons.[36]

The cause of this temporary mental reclassification of predestination was its apparent adverse effect upon the spiritual lives of believers. When Calvinism was quite clearly a hindrance to personal holiness and an encouragement to corresponding antinomianism, Wesley tended to feel it was a more essential matter. This occasional adjustment from one doctrinal category to another was probably as much an emotional reaction as a rational consideration and, very likely, was directly related to the number of instances of antinomianism that Wesley personally encountered during any given period. In 1740–41, predestination became an "essential" doctrine for him; but after this, Wesley's intellectual judgment restored it to the class of "opinion," and there it remained for the next thirty years.

While related doctrines received minor attention, the theological aspect of the free-grace controversy centered on election and reprobation, the extent of the atonement, and perfection. Although Wesley began the debate as a doctrinal discussion, Whitefield reoriented its course by injecting personal factors into the disagreement. The resulting mixture of theological and nontheological ingredients emerged from the oven of discord somewhat scorched. Differences were now baked into a permanent division, and all the icing of personal friendship could not restore the appearance of the Methodist cake. For all their mutual respect and affection, the two chief leaders of Methodism could never again bring their forces into the harmony that they had known at the beginning. For the remainder of Whitefield's lifetime, they lived together in an uneasy truce, often with a remarkable degree of effectiveness in the revival campaign, but never with their original unanimity.

PART II:

THE MINOR CONTROVERSIES
1745–1770

Wesley vs. Hervey and Toplady

6. Wesley's Theology of Predestination

A SURVEY of Wesley's writings on predestination will make it possible to provide a summary of related doctrines in Wesley's thought. Accordingly, this chapter begins with the doctrine of God's sovereignty. Particular attention is given to the roles of God, in relation to His character, which form crucial introduction to Wesley's whole perspective in this area. This section is followed first by a discussion of God's providence and then by an examination of the doctrine of predestination in Wesley's theology. This review will further include summaries of Wesley's views on election, foreknowledge, the universality of redemption, original sin, prevenient grace, free will, resistible grace, final perseverance and assurance of salvation, and the question of reprobation of the non-elect. Such a summary of Wesley's theology of predestination provides a means for evaluating the further controversies in this area during the eighteenth century. It also gives a convenient capsule of Wesley's views for those who would like to compare this area with other aspects of his theology.

Wesley's Publications Related to Predestination, 1749–1765

While the period from the early 1740s until the 1770s was not the storm center of the eighteenth-century debates over predestination, it was by no means a silent period. Several sharp literary exchanges punctuated these years, and Wesley's own writings during this time help to set these disputes in a proper perspective.

From 1749 to 1755, Wesley edited *A Christian Library*. Consisting of fifty volumes of extracts from over seventy authors, this was his most extensive literary venture.[1] Since his design was to produce "the choicest pieces of practical divinity" in order to make the gospel "intelligible to plain men," Wesley granted himself wide freedom in revisions and additions to the works he abridged.[2] One factor that influenced his editorial pen was a desire "to preserve a consistency throughout" the *Library*. Theological corrections played no inconsiderable role in this process. Our narrower concern at this point, however, is with the question of how Wesley's theology of predestination affected his work as editor.[3]

A large number of Calvinistic authors from among the Puritan divines were included in the *Library*. Although Wesley differed from men like Thomas Goodwin and John Owen on predestination, he saw no reason to dismiss their valuable contributions on many aspects of the Christian life or other congenial doctrines. When he did come to objectionable theological material, he either omitted the section or made alterations in the text to bring it into line with his own views. Tyerman described this as an attempt "to separate the rich ore of evangelical truth from the base alloy of Pelagian and Calvinian error."[4] In the "Life of Philip Henry," for example, Henry's Calvinistic confession of faith was deleted. Wesley defended his practice by saying that he had clearly forewarned his readers of his editorial policy in the preface.[5]

Wesley's abridgement of the Westminster Shorter Catechism illustrates his differences with that theological tradition. Without apology, Wesley eliminated from the catechism[6] the questions on election and predestination, effectual calling, the decrees, and perfection, while elsewhere he modified certain references to those doctrines; e.g., "God's elect" became "mankind," and "they that are effectually called" became "they that truly believe."[7] Although this procedure was Wesley's usual practice in treating the Calvinistic Puritan writers, not every line touching these doctrines was excluded. Indeed, in a later controversy Richard Hill used such passages to charge Wesley with inconsistency.[8]

Another example of Wesley's editorial treatment of Calvinistic authors was his three-volume *Explanatory Notes upon the Old Testament*, which appeared in 1765. Because he did not have time to write his own full-fledged commentary, Wesley resorted to an abridgement of the expositions by Matthew Henry and Matthew Poole. In his preface he clearly listed the theology of predestination as one of the factors affecting his selection of materials. For those who had the complete work by Henry, he stated that they "have no need of any other: particularly those who believe . . . the doctrine of absolute, irrespective unconditional Predestination." Wesley believed his own work would be more "sound" than the original, however, in the sense that it would declare, "God willeth all men to be saved, and come to the knowledge of his truth." Therefore, he gave express notice to the reader that what Henry "wrote in favour of *Particular Redemption* is totally left out."[9]

At Wesley's second Conference, the question was raised, "What can we do to stop the progress of Antinomianism?" Part of the answer was, "Write one or two more dialogues."[10] As a result Wesley published in 1745 *A Dialogue Between An Antinomian and His Friend*, followed the same year by *A Second Dialogue Between An Antinomian and His Friend*. Early in 1754 Wesley completed his *Explanatory Notes upon the New Testament*. In this work he briefly outlined his theological position by way of short exegetical notes. While predestination did not receive undue attention, Wesley did take care to set forth his own views where they differed from the Calvinists. His commentary on Romans dealt mostly with related doctrines, although there were other significant notes on predestination scattered throughout the text.[11] When he became increasingly concerned with the doctrine of final perseverance, he published *Serious Thoughts Concerning the Perseverance of the Saints* (1751).

It was also during this period that Wesley wrote *Predestination Calmly Considered*, his longest work on the subject. Three factors occasioned this treatise. The first was the response of the Rev. John Gill to Wesley's work on the perseverance of the saints. By way of reply to Wesley, Gill published *The Doctrine of the Saints' Final Perseverance Asserted and Vindicated* (1752). It was to the Hyper-Calvinistic position as represented by Gill that Wesley had reacted so forcibly in his sermon "Free Grace" (1739), and this time it was Gill's presentation of infallible perseverance that moved Wesley to take up his pen. He recognized, however, that he needed to deal at length with the several doctrines related to predestination and not to isolate any one of them as he had done in his earlier *Serious Thoughts Concerning the Perseverance of the Saints*. Accordingly, he sent forth in 1752 his second reaction to the Hyper-Calvinism of Gill in the form of a treatise that touched on all the doctrines involved.[12]

A second factor behind *Predestination Calmly Considered* was a hardening of Wesley's position on unconditional election. He wrote to his brother in August 1752 that some of the Irish preachers had accused Charles of siding with Whitefield on perseverance, and perhaps also on predestination. Wesley admitted that this was probably due to the fact "that both you and I often granted an absolute, unconditional election of some, together with a conditional election of all men." He explained the shift in his own position:

> I did incline to this scheme for many years; but of late I have doubted of it more and more: (1) because all the texts which I used to think supported it, I now think prove either more or less—either absolute reprobation and election, or neither; (2) because I find this opinion serves all the ill purposes of absolute predestination, particularly that of supporting infallible perseverance.[13]

The longer treatise served as a means to show his withdrawal from an earlier and more conciliatory position.

Related to this was a third matter in which Wesley heard some echoes of his own previous view among his preachers. At the first Irish Conference at Limerick in 1752, Wesley observed a general decay in the societies that he attributed in part to the influence of antinomian and Calvinist teaching. While all ten preachers present declared that they did not believe in absolute predestination, three of them added: "We believe there are some persons absolutely elected." Although they reaffirmed the conditional election and perseverance of all men, they felt that those who were unconditionally elected could not finally fall.[14] Because this represented Wesley's own previous position, these differences were tolerated. But it was resolved that in the future no man would be received as a preacher who did not thoroughly agree to Methodist doctrine as well as practice. Thus, *Predestination Calmly Considered* was the third instance in which Wesley attempted to clarify one of the doctrinal standards for preachers serving with him.[15]

The Doctrine of God

The 1752 publication of *Predestination Calmly Considered* represented his most complete statement, and it serves as a basis on which to summarize Wesley's views on the doctrine of predestination. While it was this longer work that spelled out most thoroughly Wesley's theology of predestination, all of his writing on the subject are here included in this survey. His understanding of predestination was influenced primarily by two factors: his concept of the nature of God, drawn from Scripture; and the biblical data relating to predestination.[16] Since the picture of God revealed in Scripture was the most influential factor in shaping Wesley's views on predestination, we will begin with one aspect of that picture.

The Effect of the Roles of God on Predestination

Wesley's concept of the sovereignty of God cannot be understood apart from his view of the whole character of God. He believed that God had revealed Himself in a twofold way as both Creator and Governor of the universe.[17] While these were two distinct relationships between God and the world and were not to be confused, neither could they be separated.

As Creator, God determined all things according to His sovereign will. This included the general circumstances of creation (i.e., the time, the place, the manner of creating things), the natural endowments of men, and the outward circumstances attending birth, such as parents and relations. Further, His sovereign will was responsible for ordering all temporal things such as health, fortune, and friends, as well as such spiritual things as the dispensing of the various gifts of His Spirit for the edification of the church.[18] In His role as Creator, everything was done according to God's sovereign pleasure.

However, when God acted as Governor, He no longer acted as mere Sovereign, i.e., by His sole will and pleasure, but as impartial Judge, guided in all things by invariable justice.[19] Thus, when he governs the eternal destiny of men, "it is clear that not sovereignty alone, but justice, mercy, and truth hold the reins."[20] Wesley was convinced that God would judge the world in righteousness and according to justice. There was no punishment for something an individual could not avoid doing, for punishment presupposes that the offender might have avoided the offense. "Otherwise, to punish him would be palpably unjust, and inconsistent with the character of God our Governor."[21]

Thus, for Wesley the sovereignty of God was not to be understood apart from his other attributes, "for the Scripture nowhere speaks of this single attribute, as separate from the rest." In particular, the sovereignty of God never superseded His justice.[22]

Wesley, then, felt two points to be crucial. He desired that the two ideas of God—God the sovereign Creator and God the just Governor—should be kept distinct and not be confused. Yet he insisted that a proper understanding of God meant that these two concepts must also be held together: one must not divorce one attribute, i.e., His sovereignty, from others, i.e., His justice and mercy. Thus, Wesley concluded: "So shall we give God the full glory of his sovereign grace without impeaching his inviolable justice."[23]

There was also a third role of God in relation to men that played a significant part in shaping Wesley's thought: the concept of God as Father. This was a category that described man's relationship to Him in terms of the metaphor of the home. Whereas sovereignty and righteousness were the attributes that correspond most closely to His role as Creator and Governor, it was the love of God that was most naturally associated with the idea of His Fatherhood. Just as it was the language of creation that described man's relation to a sovereign Creator, and the legal terminology that described his relation to a just Governor, so it was the figures of speech borrowed from the family analogy that characterized God as a loving Father.

This fresh understanding of the biblical data with respect to the fatherly role of God was in some measure related to the century in which Wesley lived. The great Reformers, Martin Luther and John Calvin, had been children of their age and, therefore, in some sense influenced by its thought forms. The Reformation era came at a time when men readily accepted Machiavelli's concept of the prince as the ideal ruler, and as a result the monarchs of the day ruled in splendor with almost absolute authority. No one questioned their "divine right" to exercise their authoritarian power, even when it appeared arbitrary or whimsical. They bestowed favors upon whomever they pleased, and they could execute cruel justice on those who crossed their fancy. Such a picture could not help but influence the Reformers' perception of God as a King, sitting on the throne of the universe and autocratically governing the fate of men on earth. This understanding of the nature of God makes it easier to see why they could picture God arbitrarily electing some to salvation while reprobating others to perdition purely on the basis of His good pleasure.[24]

It is not quite accurate to say that the political or intellectual climate of any age is determinative for the theology of a certain period. Yet the atmosphere of any given era appears to have an influence on how theologians perceive and emphasize certain aspects of the biblical data about God. The Reformers were quite right to observe that the Scripture describes God both as Creator and King, and their age made it easier to see God's relation to man in these categories.

The eighteenth century was quite another age altogether. It was a time when absolute despotism was becoming unfashionable, when there were leanings toward democracy both in Europe and America. This was the century in which an independent United States emerged as the first great experiment in democratic government, the era of the French Revolution, and the increasing influence of the constitutionalism of John Locke. In England, democratic tendencies were being felt in such areas as the increasing role of parliament in determining who was to occupy the throne. Under George I, authority to run the government was delegated to a prime minister and a cabinet. No longer was the divine right of kings unquestionably accepted. Absolute monarchs were quickly becoming obsolete. More just rule and more benevolent rule were being demanded in many places. So the temperament of the age was conducive to understanding that the Bible spoke of God as a just Judge and a loving Father, as well as a sovereign Creator and autocratic King. And it was precisely these roles of God that began to receive Wesley's fresh attention.

This is not to say that Wesley minimized any of the insights of the Reformation about God, but that his understanding was enlarged. This should not surprise us, for Wesley had the privilege of coming two centuries after the Reformers and building upon their rediscovery of the Bible as the primary source of theological truth. The Reformers came so close to a fresh recovery of the Scripture as normative for their understanding of God, man, and salvation. But we should not expect them to have seen every part of the biblical data as clearly as those who had the opportunity to build on their formulations in subsequent generations. Thus Wesley regarded himself as a true representative of the Reformation tradition, but also as one who has insights into additional aspects of scriptural truth, particularly the concept of God as Father who exercises His power in love.

This understanding of God's relation to men based on the analogy of the family made it possible for Wesley to preach as often about the new birth as he did on justification by faith. Salvation, he saw, was an inheritance that came to those who were regenerated in the image of God and who had become children of the Father. God's everlasting love was the motivating factor behind the whole of saving grace, as we have already seen in Charles Wesley's hymns on this theme.

Wesley's pastoral concern for new believers was also determined by this thought: fathers not only have children, they also nurture them and raise them to maturity. Wesley's whole scheme of societies, classes, bands, disciplined living, and corporate responsibility was designed for spiritual growth and presupposed this understanding of believers relating to God as children relate to their father. Further, it is this category that provided his favorite nomenclature for entire sanctification. For him, in its essence it was an experience of perfect love. Finally, as we shall see below, it influenced his thinking on almost every aspect of the doctrines related to predestination.

The Providence of God

Wesley's doctrine of providence was also closely bound up with his whole understanding of God. He believed that God's role as Governor, including His power to preserve, was intimately related to His omnipresence and omniscience. He held that God was everywhere present to know all, especially that which concerned the children of men. God's wisdom and goodness were also connected with his power to govern: "All his wisdom is continually employed in managing all the affairs of his creation for the good of all his creatures." Thus, Wesley concluded: "We cannot doubt of His exerting all his power, as in sustaining, so in governing, all that he has made."[25]

Although he believed in the general providence of God over all creation, Wesley strongly objected to those who limited God to a general oversight of the universe, excluding any particular providence:

> It is a self-contradiction, it is arrant nonsense. Either, therefore, allow a particular providence, or do not pretend to believe any providence at all. If you do not believe that the Governor of the world governs all things in it, . . . do not affect to believe that he governs anything, or has anything to do in the world. No; be consistent with yourself: Say that, as nature produced, so chance governs, all things.[26]

Closely related to this idea was Wesley's desire that a mature Christian be convinced that "there is no such thing as chance in the world," and he asserted that "so far as fortune or chance governs the world, God has no place in it."[27]

Wesley defined God's "particular" relations to men as a threefold circle of providence. The outermost circle included the whole of mankind: Jews, Muhammadans, heathens, as well as Christians; all these were objects of God's love and care, as evidenced by such universal blessings as the sun, rain, and fruitful seasons. The second, small circle included the whole visible Christian Church; for these God had a greater concern, especially in restraining the powers of darkness among them. The innermost circle contained only the "real Christians," who were the special objects of God's care: "Nothing relative to these is too great, nothing too little, for His attention. He has his eye continually as upon every individual person that is a member of this His family, so upon every circumstance that relates either to their inward or outward state; wherein either their present or eternal happiness is in any degree concerned."[28]

It was for these members of His family, Wesley believed, that God at times made exceptions to his general laws of nature and worked miracles, "either by suspending that law in favour of those that love him, or by employing his mighty angels."[29] In his description of the place of angels in providence, he wrote:

> In general we may be assured of that they are always ready to assist us when we need their assistance, always present, when their presence may be of service in every circumstance of life, wherein is danger of any sort, or would be if they were absent.[30]

God's work in particular providence, however, was not to be understood as counteracting His other work, especially the creation of man in His own image. Wesley held that this image included a capacity to understand, and a will and liberty to exercise that will. This liberty, he felt, was essential for the use of the understanding and the will, and without it a man would cease to be a moral agent.[31] Although this freedom made sin and suffering possible, Wesley affirmed that God could not abolish sin and pain without destroying the essence of mankind.

> Neither would it be kindness thus to exempt us from spiritual any more than from temporal danger; to deliver the soul from all pain. Were the angels of God enjoined to do this, as we should be without pain, so we must have been without virtue, seeing we should have no choice left and where there is no choice, there can be no virtue.[32]

Wesley declared his view to be far more to the glory of God:

> Whereas all the manifold wisdom of God (as well as all his power and goodness) is displayed in governing man as man; not as a stick or stone, but as an intelligent and free spirit, capable of choosing either good or evil; . . . in governing men so as not to destroy either their understanding, will, or liberty.[33]

Thus, he distinguished between God's government of the inanimate creation, which could make no opposition to His will, and His government of men who continually oppose Him:

> Here therefore is full scope for the exercise of all the riches both of the wisdom and knowledge of God, in counteracting all the wickedness and folly of men, and all the subtlety of Satan, to carry on his own glorious design, the salvation of lost mankind. Indeed were he to do this by an absolute Decree, by his own irresistible power, it would imply no wisdom at all.[34]

Sin was the only thing that Wesley excepted from the direct providence of God. Even here he allowed that God worked through the sins of others.[35] Although there was a mysterious element about this operation of divine providence, Wesley believed that it worked to extract good out of infirmities, follies, and sufferings. He declared that in all these things God's providence has purpose: "It disposes all things strongly and sweetly that befall them, perhaps through their own mistake, for their profit, that they may be the more largely partakers of His holiness."[36] Wesley had long seen this intimate connection between providence and sanctification. As early as the 1730s, he had written:

> Pleasures and pain, health and sickness, richness and poverty, honour and dishonour, friends and enemies, all are bestowed by his unerring wisdom and goodness with view to this one thing. The will of God in allotting us our several portions of all these, is solely our sanctification. All his providences, be they mild or severe, point at no other end than this.[37]

The Doctrines Related to Predestination

The Decree of God

The concepts of God as the sovereign Creator, the just providential Governor of the universe, and the loving Father of mankind overshadowed the rest of Wesley's understanding of the doctrines of predestination. The sovereignty of God related primarily to the eternal decree of God touching the destiny of men. Wesley believed that God as Creator established a basic principle by one unchangeable decree: "He that believeth shall be saved: He that believeth not shall be damned."[38] Thus, as Sovereign, God established the way of salvation. But He insisted that the doctrine of election should be understood, not in relation to the sovereignty of God, but primarily in relation to God as the just Governor of men. Hence, election of individuals to salvation was based not on an arbitrary, sovereign choice, but on God's judgment as a righteous Judge as to whether or not a man has met the condition of salvation, i.e., had he believed? By means of this twofold nature of God's relation to men, Wesley made a separation between the eternal decree of God and the election of individual men.

This distinction was an essential one for Wesley. It allowed him to recognize the place of God's sovereignty while at the same time not defining that sovereignty so absolutely as to ignore God's justice or minimize man's responsibility. God can be uniquely sovereign in determining the way of salvation, Wesley argued, but His justice and love may not be sacrificed. It was when the election of individuals related to God's sovereignty that the other aspects of God's character suffered. Wesley avoided the consequence of the latter by following the lead of Arminius and making election of individuals relate to God's just judgment as to whether or not they had met the condition of the way of salvation, i.e., had they trusted Christ for redemption. If so, they were predestined to eternal life; if not, to eternal separation from God. With this plan God had placed the responsibility for salvation or reprobation squarely on man's shoulders.

The Election of Individuals

When Wesley elaborated his position on personal election, he assigned to election two distinct meanings. First, he admitted that God did appoint some men to do a particular work in this world, and his examples included men such as Cyrus and Paul. This kind of election he viewed as unconditional, absolute, and personal.[39] For some years he felt this unconditional election could also refer to the salvation of some few men, while not excluding the possibility of a conditional election of all men. But from 1752 onward, he insisted that no one had been unconditionally elected to eternal glory.[40]

Second, Wesley believed that there was an election by divine appointment to salvation, but that this election was conditional, as was also the case with the corresponding reprobation. Wesley related this conditional election to the sovereign, eternal decree: "He that believeth shall be saved; he that believeth not shall be damned." "And this decree, without doubt, God will not change, and men cannot resist. According to this, all true believers are in Scripture termed elect, as all who continue in unbelief are so long properly reprobates."[41] By this position Wesley rejected any unconditional election to salvation as inconsistent with Scripture, and because it necessarily implied unconditional reprobation.

God's Foreknowledge of Faith

We turn now to the sequence of election in Wesley's thought. In this pattern, as he conceived it, the foreknowledge of God was of special importance for him. In the strict sense he felt there was no real foreknowledge or afterknowledge with God, since God exists outside of time as well as space. From this perspective God has only present knowledge, since He sees all things at once. The use of the term foreknowledge, Wesley thought, was God's accommodation to human language. Thus, in God's eternal present He knows who is going to believe and who is not. But Wesley was careful to distinguish between foreknowledge and foreordination; God knew who would believe, but He did not cause belief in some and not in others. "We must not think they are because He knows them. No; He knows them because they are."

This was one of the essential points where Wesley differed from the Calvinists, who made foreknowledge causative. With their Augustinian concept of the sovereignty of God, the Calvinists were forced to make God the direct cause of everything, and thus they could not conceive of His foreknowledge as being anything other than foreordination. If He knew something previous to its occurrence, then He could only have planned it to happen that way. Wesley's different view of God allowed Him to understand God as knowing beforehand what man would do with his God-given freedom of the will without predetermining the choice. This important distinction made it possible to let God "off the hook" of being directly responsible for all the actions of men, including sin. At the same time, His sovereign providential governance over the universe was maintained. Wesley summarized his position in this way:

God, looking on all ages from the creation to the consummation, as a moment, and seeing at once whatever is in the hearts of all the children of men, knows everyone that does or does not believe, in every age or nation. Yet what He knows, whether faith or unbelief, is in no wise caused by His knowledge. Men are free in believing or not believing as if He did not know it at all.[42]

God's Call to Saving Grace

On the basis of His foreknowledge, God calls those whom He knows will believe. Wesley divided this into an outward call, i.e., the word of His grace, that came primarily through proclamation, and an inward call, i.e., the working of the Spirit, what some term "effectual calling." Wesley does not often speak of a call in terms of predestination, but when he does it is clear that he is using a category more familiar to his opponents than to his own orientation. Usually he speaks of God's call to all men to respond to the gospel by faith, which is more characteristic of his Arminian perspective. But when he used the term predestination in describing the sequence of election, he used it in a more specified way.

Wesley said that God gives a special call to those whom in His foreknowledge He knows will believe, but he never spells out how this personal, more individualized call is related to the more general call that is to be given to all men. The lack of integration on this subject may be due to Wesley's own discomfort with using the term predestination as a description of the sequence of election at all. He does so because of the Calvinists' repeated use of Romans 8:29 as an outline of the various aspects of predestination, including the call, but apart from that specific structure he avoids using it in the same individualized sense.

As he rounded out his description of the plan of election, he referred to those whom God called as the ones he also justified. Wesley understood justification in the larger sense, i.e., as referring to the whole scheme of salvation. So he felt free to add an emphasis on holiness, which he believed he saw elsewhere in Scripture. For Wesley, therefore, those whom God justified, He sanctified; and those whom He sanctified, He glorified. These Wesley understood to be the logical connections between the various parts of the scheme of election.[43]

The Universal Atonement of Christ

An examination of Wesley's preaching during the early years of the revival, along with his hymns and early publications on predestination, has already demonstrated his strong commitment to the doctrine of universal redemption. This theological emphasis never ceased throughout Wesley's life. He was fully convinced that the Scripture taught an unlimited atonement—a fact he saw affirmed by such explicit testimony as "Christ died for all" (2 Cor. 5:14). The consequence of His dying for all was that "He is the propitiation for the sins of the whole world" (1 John 2:2). The design of Christ's death, Wesley felt, was defined in the passage "He died for all, that they which live should not live unto themselves, but unto Him which died for them" (2 Cor. 5:15).[44]

This witness from the Bible confirmed the teaching in Wesley's theology and made it central to his preaching. He could find no biblical warrant for an idea of limited atonement:

> Show me the Scriptures wherein God declares in equally express terms (1) "Christ" did not die "for all," but only for some. (2) Christ is not "the propitiation for the sins of the whole world," and (3) "He" did not die "for all . . . that they should live unto him who died for them."[45]

In addition to the express statements of Scripture, Wesley's view of universal grace was closely tied to how he understood the character of God as Governor of men. Because God was just, Wesley was certain that He would not punish a man for not accepting salvation if there had been no provision for it in the atonement. As God was sincere, Wesley felt He really meant what He said when He offered salvation to all men. "How can God or Christ be sincere in sending them (ministers) with his commission, to offer his grace to all men, if God has not provided such grace for all men, no, not so much as conditionally?" Further, the role of God as Father was bound up with his position, for Wesley felt that the love and goodness of God toward all men could be maintained only if God had provided eternal salvation for all. "How is God good or loving to a reprobate, or one that is not elected?" Rather, he believed that it was impossible to argue that a man was the object of the love and goodness of God if he were excluded from the possibility of redemption by limited atonement.[46]

Original Sin

The state of mankind as the object of God's saving grace played a central part in Wesley's understanding of predestination. Although frequently misunderstood by his Calvinistic opponents, Wesley declared himself one with Calvin on the doctrine of original sin. He was convinced of the total depravity of human nature. "Our nature is altogether corrupt, in every power and faculty. And our will, depraved equally with the rest, is wholly bent to indulge our natural corruption."[47] This doctrine Wesley perceived as "the first grand distinguishing point between Heathenism and Christianity." He repeatedly emphasized that "sin hath now effaced the image of God. Our nature is distempered, as well as enslaved; the whole head is faint, and the whole heart sick."[48]

The Effect of Prevenient Grace

However, in spite of Wesley's declared commitment to the idea of mankind's total depravity, his understanding of the actual state of sinful man was a significant modification of the position as held by the Calvinists. This was due to his views about the application of grace. Wesley was convinced that man in this fallen state could respond to God's offer of salvation only by means of God's gift of prevenient grace. This was the general grace given to all people that restores in them the ability to accept God's offer of redemption.[49] Yet Wesley's prevenient grace differed from the Calvinists' common grace. Though both provided a restraining influence on the evil in human beings so that society could exist, prevenient grace also restored the capacity of every man to accept salvation, whereas common grace did not. This prevenient grace Wesley saw as another evidence of how much God as Father "so loved the world." Wesley summarized the connection between his views of total depravity and prevenient grace in this way:

> I always did clearly assert the total fall of man and his utter inability to do any good of himself; the absolute necessity of the grace of the Spirit of God to raise even a good thought or desire in our hearts; the Lord's regarding no work and accepting of none but so far as they proceed from His preventing, convincing, and converting grace through the Beloved; the blood and righteousness of Christ being the sole meritorious cause of Our salvation.[50]

In spite of the frequent accusations that he was a Pelagian, Wesley's view of the depravity of the human race was so strong as to exclude any natural free will. Man was free to follow only his own desires, not to respond to any offer of salvation. Yet God, by His preventing grace, had restored a liberty to fallen man that allowed him to accept God's redemption in Christ.

> Natural free will, in the present state of mankind, I do not understand: I only assert, that there is a measure of free will supernaturally restored to every man, together with that supernatural light which "enlightens every man that cometh into the world."[51]

Wesley was careful to distinguish between these two understandings of free will: "Both Mr. Fletcher and Mr. Wesley absolutely deny natural free will. We both steadily assert that the will is by nature free only to evil. Yet we believe that every man has a measure of free will restored to him by grace."[52] As Wesley pointed out, his position on original sin, prevenient grace, and free will was essentially that of the Thirty-Nine Articles.[53]

This relationship between original sin and prevenient grace had a twofold impact on Wesley's doctrine of salvation. First, it made it possible for him to say that man in no way merits his own salvation; he is completely dependent on God for his redemption. Second, the concept of prevenient grace provided a basis for human responsibility. Since a man was enabled by this grace to turn to God, he became responsible for his decision about God's offer of salvation.[54] Thus, Wesley provided a balance between Calvinism on the one side, which emphasized that salvation was completely God's work, and the Pelagians on the other, who stressed the freedom of man and his attendant responsibility.

By means of a prevenient grace that is universally provided for all mankind, God receives all the glory for man's redemption, even his ability to exercise faith and receive salvation. At the same time, man is viewed as having some freedom of the will and therefore can be justly held responsible for his decisions. With this position the Gordian knot of God's sovereignty and human freedom is cut, and the positive side of each emphasis is preserved. The position that salvation is a free gift of God's sovereign grace and not something to be earned, was essential in Wesley's running debate over justification by faith with the leaders of the Church of England. In addition, the place of moral responsibility was of crucial importance in his struggles with antinomianism.

Resistible Grace

The doctrine of prevenient grace was also related to the question of whether or not saving grace was resistible. Although God worked in the life of an individual by prevenient grace to make it possible for him to "work out his own salvation," Wesley believed a man must avail himself of this grace and be a worker together with Him, or God "will cease working."[55] This meant that Wesley regarded part of the freedom restored by prevenient grace as a freedom to say "No" to God, or, in other words, God has given man the power to resist saving grace. He contrasted his own Arminian views with the Calvinistic position:

> The Calvinists hold that the saving grace of God is absolutely irresistible; that no man is any more able to resist it, than to resist the stroke of lightning. The Arminians hold, that although there may be some moments wherein the grace of God acts irresistibly, yet, in general, any man may resist, and that to his eternal ruin, the grace whereby it was the will of God he should have been eternally saved.[56]

His position was qualified by his allowance that God may at some times work irresistibly in some souls. Yet, even in these "exempt cases," where God works irresistibly for a time, Wesley declared: "I do not believe there is any human soul in which God works irresistibly *at all times*. . . . I am persuaded there are no men living that have not many times resisted the Holy Ghost." He believed that at some time, however, God set before every man eternal life and eternal death, and man "has in himself the casting voice." In support of this position he quoted Augustine: "He that made us without ourselves, will not save us without ourselves."[57]

Wesley further rejected as unscriptural the view that all are saved by irresistible grace. "Where, I pray, is it written, that none are saved but by irresistible grace? Show me any one plain scripture for this,—that all saving grace is irresistible." Further, Wesley felt it was more to the glory of God to save a man who could reject the offer than to save a man irresistibly. Irresistible grace, he felt, made "man a mere machine, and consequently, no more rewardable and punishable."[58]

Wesley's doctrine of God again stands in the background of this debate. For the Calvinists, with their emphasis on God as the sovereign Creator, irresistible grace was a natural outgrowth of their understanding of a God who acts solely on the basis of his arbitrary will. He who chooses to elect some and reprobate others without any reason other than His pleasure at the moment, is the same kind of God that would not give man any say about whether or not he will receive grace and be saved. But for Wesley, who held an understanding of God as not only sovereign Creator but also the just Governor and loving Father, an entirely different modus operandi was demanded for God. This kind of God desires that men respond to Him in two basic ways—in obedience and in love—and both of these presuppose some freedom of the will.

Obedience would be predetermined action only if freedom were not available to mankind, and love would not be a volitional commitment unless one were free not to love. As a righteous Governor, God looks for obedience, and as a loving Father, He desires that men love Him in return. Wesley thought both were possible, but only because of his understanding that genuine freedom to obey or disobey and to love or not to love was actually available to man through God's gift of prevenient grace.

The Final Perseverance of the Saints

The doctrine of the final perseverance of the saints was closely tied to the matter of resistible grace. Wesley realized that the basic question was whether any saint could fall totally and perish everlastingly. He was convinced that it was possible, and inevitably one of the bases for this position was his understanding of Scripture. "Whatever assurance God may give to particular souls, I find no general promise in holy writ, that none who once believes shall finally fall. . . . It wants one thing to recommend it,—plain cogent scripture proof."[59] To the assertion that many promises in Scripture are absolute and unconditional, Wesley responded that because there was no condition expressed, it did not mean that there was none implied. Thus for him those passages that seem to suggest an unconditional final perseverance must be understood in the light of those portions of Scripture that clearly made perseverance conditional.[60]

Wesley discussed two other principles of interpretation in relation to this doctrine. The first was the fallacy of begging the question "by applying to particular persons assertions, or prophecies, which relate only to the Church in general; and some of them only to the Jewish Church and nation, as distinguished from all other people."[61] This problem applied not only to the matter of perseverance, but also to many of the other doctrines related to predestination. Thus, Wesley vigorously objected to the application of passages such as Romans 9 to individuals when they referred, in fact, to the Jewish people. In his introduction to this chapter, he wrote that Paul "had not here the least thought of personal election or reprobation."[62]

In addition, Wesley challenged a second principle of interpretation. This was the assumption that whatever Jesus spoke to His apostles could be applied without qualification to all believers. John 17:11 was used by some to support an unconditional final perseverance, but Wesley objected that this part of the High Priestly Prayer referred only to the Twelve and could not automatically be applied to all Christians. Nor was he convinced that it supported infallible perseverance, as the case of Judas plainly revealed.

Wesley believed that the Bible taught a final perseverance conditioned upon a walk of faith and obedience.

> A child of God, that is, a true believer, while he continues a true believer, cannot go to hell. But if a believer makes a shipwreck of the faith, he is

no longer a child of God. And he may go to hell, yea, and certainly will, if he continues in unbelief.[63]

He considered Paul's declaration in 1 Corinthians 9:27 as illustrative of the general principle:

St. Paul was certainly an elect person if ever there was one; and yet he declares it was possible he himself might become a reprobate. Nay, he actually would have become such, if he had not thus kept his body under, even though he had been so long an elect person, a Christian, and an apostle.[64]

Wesley's belief in the importance of a walk of obedient faith was closely connected to his commitment to Christian holiness and was strongly reinforced by his fear of antinomianism.

Wesley recognized clearly that final perseverance was not to be separated from the other doctrines related to predestination, especially the questions of resistible versus irresistible grace, and conditional versus unconditional election. Irresistible grace and infallible perseverance must be understood as the natural consequence of unconditional election: "For if God has eternally and absolutely decreed to save such and such persons, it follows, both that they cannot resist his saving grace, and that they cannot finally fall from that grace which they cannot resist."[65]

Likewise, from Wesley's position, if election is conditional and therefore grace is resistible, then it follows naturally that perseverance would be conditional as well. While the logical connections of the Arminian view are not quite as "tight" as those of the Calvinist position, still Wesley was right when he declared, "In effect, the two questions come into one, 'Is predestination absolute or conditional?' "

An Assurance of Salvation

But though Wesley did not believe in unconditional final perseverance, neither was he insensitive to the human longing for some assurance concerning present as well as final salvation. He saw that without assurance the believer would have no security and would remain in a constant state of fear regarding his soul's salvation. "But if we can never have any certainty of our being in a state of salvation, good reason it is that every moment should be spent not in joy but fear and trembling; and then undoubtedly in this life we are of all men most miserable."[66] Yet he could never see this need for assurance of salvation as one of the things that made the whole Calvinistic understanding of predestination so attractive. As late as 1775 he asked, "What are the charms of Calvinism? *unde faces ardent*? How is it [that] so many fall in love with her?"[67]

The reason Wesley could not accept unconditional perseverance as conducive to assurance was twofold. The first reason was his conviction that willful, consistent sin would separate men from God after justification just as much as it had before justification. This was an outgrowth of his commitment to holiness of heart and life. Whenever some began to claim the doctrine of unconditional perseverance as a basis for living in open sin, Wesley felt they were rationalizing their theology in the face of the whole tenor and scope of Scripture that declared genuine faith to be manifested in holy living.

The second reason he could not connect the doctrine of unconditional perseverance with the assurance of salvation was because of the difficulty in answering the question "Who is elect?" If an individual knew that he was elect, then the doctrine would certainly provide assurance. But how could one know whether he was one of the elect rather than one of the reprobate? What if one had only appeared to be saved? And who could distinguish between genuine Christians and those who were only apparently so? If an individual had no way to know for sure that he was elect, then the doctrine would not provide assurance but only anxiety and despair. The decision regarding salvation would not be based on measurable phenomena, such as the exercise of faith or the fruits of the Spirit, but only on God's arbitrary election or reprobation. Hence, it was difficult for Wesley to understand how any of those committed to this view could have assurance of their salvation.

Wesley did believe, however, that assurance was not only possible, but was also the privilege of every Christian. "I believe a consciousness of being in the favour of God . . . is the common privilege of Christians fearing God and working righteousness."[68] This assurance had a twofold base: "There is in every believer, both a testimony of God's spirit, and the testimony of his own that he is a child of God." The witness of the believer's spirit was obtained by applying to himself those scriptural marks that reveal who is and who is not a child of God.

> This is no other than rational evidence, the witness of our spirit, our reason or understanding. It all resolves into this: Those who have these marks are children of God: but we have these marks: therefore, we are children of God.[69]

This was the objective, but indirect, side of assurance for Wesley.

The Scriptures again served as his standard: if a man saw in his own life what the Bible described as evidence of sonship, then he could rationally be assured that he was a son of God. The testimony of God's Spirit, on the other hand, was

> an inward impression on the soul, whereby the Spirit of God directly witnesses to my spirit, that I am a child of God; that Jesus Christ hath loved me, and given Himself for me; and that my sins are blotted out, and I, even I, am reconciled to God.[70]

This was the subjective, but not any less important, side of assurance for Wesley, and it gave a man a direct inward assurance of his salvation. Both the direct witness of God's Spirit and the indirect witness of man's spirit were necessary for Wesley. With this twofold witness to salvation, no one need be deceived regarding his salvation.

Wesley understood this combination of the direct and the indirect testimony as confirmation of the act of justification. "Everyone, therefore, who denies the existence of such a testimony, does in effect deny justification by faith."[71] In his early writings Wesley had gone a step further and made assurance inseparable from saving faith.[72] This was modified in later years, so that in 1768 he could write: "I have not for many years thought a consciousness of acceptance to be essential to justifying faith."[73] Though he felt some believers did not enjoy this assurance of their salvation, he was still convinced that many, if not most, had "the full assurance of faith, a full conviction of present pardon." However, only a very few had "a full assurance of hope, . . . a full conviction of their future perseverance."[74]

Thus, assurance for Wesley, was primarily related to present pardon, whereas the hope of final perseverance continued to be grounded in a life of faith and obedience. Although there is an important link between justification and assurance in Wesley's theology, there is nothing that corresponds to the interlocking connection that final perseverance has with the other doctrines of predestination in Calvinism.

The Question of Reprobation of the Non-Elect

After examining Wesley's views on the several doctrines related to predestination, we must stress again that the majority of his writings on these subjects were stated as a reaction to the Calvinistic view of unconditional reprobation. In the general structure of his major treatise, *Predestination Calmly Considered,* unconditional reprobation was the overarching question in dispute for seventy-one out of ninety sections. Wesley rejected unconditional election,

> because it necessarily implies unconditional reprobation. Find out any election which does not imply reprobation, and I will gladly agree to it. But reprobation I can never agree to while I believe the Scripture to be of God; as being utterly irreconcilable to the whole scope and tenor both of the Old and New Testament.[75]

Further, Wesley perceived the connection between this doctrine and other aspects of predestination:

> You are not to consider the doctrine of irresistible grace by itself, any more than that of unconditional election, or final perseverance; but as it stands in connection with unconditional reprobation: That millstone which hangs about the neck of your whole hypothesis.[76]

Wesley's objections to unconditional reprobation were legion, but they had a threefold basis. First, he was convinced that "if this were true, the whole scripture must be false." The Bible was his ultimate authority. Second, he objected to the practical effects it had on the spiritual life of Christians in their quest for holiness.

> I so earnestly oppose it . . . because it is an error of so pernicious consequences to the souls of men; because it directly and naturally tends to hinder the inward works of God in every stage of it.[77]

Wesley believed this, in fact, was the major difficulty in the whole Calvinistic scheme of predestination. "The very same observation may be made on every article of that doctrine. Every branch of it, as well as this, has a natural, genuine tendency, without any wrestling, either to prevent or obstruct holiness."[78]

Third, it was excluded by his understanding of God, the just Governor of the universe, and the loving Father of men. He repeatedly asked, "How can you possibly reconcile reprobation with those scriptures that declare the justice of God?" "How is God good or loving to a reprobate?"[79] Wesley could never harmonize reprobation with the character of God, i.e., His justice, truth, mercy, love, and goodness, and for him the biblical understanding of the nature of God was determinative.

7. The Controversy over Imputed Righteousness

O NE of the minor controversies in the eighteenth-century debates over pre destination was Wesley's literary exchange with his former student at Oxford, James Hervey. After discussing this exchange between Wesley and Hervey, we can provide a fresh summary of Wesley's doctrine of the righteousness of Christ. Finally, the chapter concludes with a discussion of the extent to which this particular controversy had a negative effect on Wesley's ministry in Scotland.

The Debate with James Hervey

Related to the larger predestination questions was Wesley's controversy with James Hervey over the doctrine of imputed righteousness. Hervey had been a struggling student at Lincoln College when Wesley first met him. He joined the Methodists, and Wesley began to give him considerable assistance with his studies, especially in Hebrew.[1] After ordination, he took a curacy in Dummer for another member of the Holy Club, Charles Kinchin, but this was interrupted by his feeble health and a prolonged retirement at Stoke Abbey in Devonshire. When Wesley and Whitefield summoned Hervey to join their labors during the early years of the revival, he declined on the grounds of poor health as well as objections to itinerant preaching.

Hervey's conversion to an evangelical faith culminated in 1740, about which time he accepted the curacy at Bideford, where he began his famous *Meditations among the Tombs*. After three years he became curate to his father, and later minister, at Weston Favel, Northamptonshire, where he remained until his death in 1759. The country parish made it possible for him to pursue a number of literary projects while still fulfilling his pastoral responsibilities.[2]

Although he refused to itinerate, Hervey described himself as being "at one with the Methodists." He also maintained a continuous correspondence with both Wesley and Whitefield. Wesley respected Hervey's ability with a pen and submitted to him his "Notes on the New Testament" for revision. Hervey observed: "You are too sparing of your remarks and improvements. Many expositions are too corpulent; yours are rather too lean."[3]

Although Wesley had been his tutor and spiritual guide at Oxford, Hervey's theology was Calvinistic. He described his position to Wesley:

> I am, what people would call, a moderate Calvinist; but I assure you, I can bear, I shall delight to have my notions sifted; nor am I so attached to any favourite scheme, but I can readily relinquish it, when Scripture and reason convince me it is wrong.[4]

While Hervey approached some aspects of the theology of predestination reluctantly, this was not the case with final perseverance, to which he had a strong commitment:

> The doctrine of the perseverance of Christ's servants: . . . I am thoroughly persuaded of. Predestination and reprobation I think of with fear and trembling. And if I would attempt to study them, I would study them on my knees.[5]

While Hervey probably leaned toward absolute election, he apparently reacted against reprobation. He was unprepared to press either doctrine too far, and when speaking of predestination, he noted "it is not necessary to faith and salvation either that we should embrace or that we should reject the doctrine."[6]

Hervey's major literary production was *Theron and Aspasio*, a three-volume work that dealt with the doctrines of Scripture, original sin, the atonement, and in particular, the imputed righteousness of Christ. The apologetic "dressing" of this theological work consisted of nineteen dialogues and twelve letters between two gentlemen of refinement and education. Each dialogue had a distinctive atmospheric setting, a garden, a meadow, or a library, in which Aspasio (Hervey) attempted in genteel conversation to influence Theron's views on certain theological issues.[7]

Theron and Aspasio was actually a presentation of Hervey's own theological position. He believed that man's will was bound by total depravity of human nature in matters that pertained to eternal salvation, although he was willing to grant a freedom of will in the ordinary affairs of life.[8] This total depravity he saw to be the result of the imputation of Adam's sin to all his posterity, and for this human problem God had provided the solution of justification:

> Justification is an act of God Almighty's grace, whereby He acquits His people from guilt, and accounts them righteous for the sake of Christ's righteousness, which was wrought out for them, and is imputed to them.

By Christ's righteousness, Hervey understood "all the various instances of His active and passive obedience." When he used the word "imputed," he meant that Christ's righteousness was "placed to our account, . . . reckoned or adjudged by God as our own."[9] There was in Hervey's view a reciprocal imputation in justification: Christ's righteousness was accredited to man, and man's sin and its consequences were imputed to Christ. He insisted that justification depended

> not on our own external duties, . . . not on the sincerity of our hearts, . . . not upon our faith, not upon our Lord's righteousness, considered only as passive, but upon his active and passive obedience united.[10]

Nor could a man appear before God on account of any native or acquired righteousness, but only through what was imputed.

There was for Hervey such a great stress on the objective aspect of the atonement that justification became unconditional:

> The gospel informs you, that whatever is necessary for your salvation is already done and obtained by Christ; that whatever is done and obtained by Christ is freely given you by the God of all grace. Consequently, that you are called only to receive a gift, not to perform a work[11]

Yet he insisted that this did not lead to antinomianism, discourage holiness, nor abrogate obedience.

In preparing his work, Hervey requested criticism from several friends, including Whitefield and Wesley. When Wesley returned the manuscript of the first three dialogues with only "a few inconsiderable corrections," Hervey complained: "You are not my friend, if you do not take more liberty with me."[12] When Wesley made more significant alterations, however, the wounded Hervey ceased to communicate, believing Wesley's judgment to be unworthy of comment. Somewhat hurt, he complained to a friend:

> Mr. John Wesley takes me very roundly to task, on the score of predestination; at which I am much surprised. Because a reader, ten times less penetrating than he is, may easily see, that this doctrine (be it true or false) makes not part of my scheme; never comes under consideration; is purposely and carefully avoided. I cannot but fear he has some sinister design. Put the wolf's skin on the sheep, and the flock will shun him, the dogs will worry him. I do not charge such an artifice, but sometimes I cannot help forming a suspicion.[13]

There were many things about *Theron and Aspasio* that Wesley approved. "Most of the grand truths of Christianity are herein explained and proved with great strength and clearness."[14] When in 1756 Wesley published his own treatise, *The Doctrine of Original Sin,* against the erroneous views of Dr. John Taylor, he wrote: "There are likewise many excellent remarks on this subject in Mr. Hervey's Dialogues."[15] And when an anonymous writer made an attack on Hervey, Wesley came to his defense with *A Sufficient Answer to "Letters to the Author of Theron and Aspasio."*[16]

Yet Wesley strongly objected to Hervey's use of the particular phrase "The imputed righteousness of Christ," which, he felt, was neither scriptural nor necessary, and which placed too much stress on the objective side of the atonement. Wesley advocated, instead, the scriptural phrase "faith reckoned for righteousness," a righteousness he saw as both inherent and imputed. God really did work righteousness and holiness in believers. Wesley did not agree that God counted men righteous without actually making them so. He concurred with Hervey that man could not be justified by works, and that it was the "satisfaction made by the death of Christ" that obtained pardon. But he objected that Christ did not fulfill the conditions of faith and repentance for initial justification, nor was His righteousness substituted for the Christian's walk of obedience after justification. If Christ fulfilled the whole law and therefore a believer need not fulfill it, this would make "the Holy One of God a minister of sin." Hervey claimed that "believers, who are notorious transgressors in themselves, have a sinless obedience in Christ," but Wesley viewed that assertion as leading directly to antinomianism.

Wesley's opposition centered on two factors. First, he felt Hervey's interpretation of righteousness and justification was not according to Scripture; and second, he believed that the whole emphasis on the imputed righteousness of Christ "instead of furthering men's progress in vital holiness, . . . made them satisfied without any holiness at all." "This is the grand, palpable objection to that whole scheme. It directly makes void the law. It makes thousands content to live and die transgressors of the law, because Christ fulfilled it for them."[17] Thus, Wesley could write: "Mr. Hervey is a deeply-rooted Antinomian—that is, a Calvinist consistent with himself (which Mr. Whitefield is not, nor Robert Bolton, nor any Calvinist who is not a Latitudinarian)."[18] The charge of antinomianism was sufficiently forceful to compel Hervey to begin another work on sanctification as a "Supplement to *Theron and Aspasio*."[19]

In order to assist those under his care, especially the young preachers, Wesley published in 1758 *A Preservative Against Unsettled Notions in Religion*. His design was not to convince "the perverted," but to "preserve" the faithful. Among the twelve shorter works he gathered together in the *Preservative* were "The Scripture Doctrine of Predestination, Election, and Reprobation," "An Extract from A Dialogue between an Antinomian and his friend," and a "Letter to the Rev. Mr. Hervey," which Wesley had written in 1756, giving his detailed criticisms of *Theron and Aspasio*.[20] Roughly a quarter of the *Preservative* was devoted to protecting his people against the Calvinistic view of predestination and the influence of antinomianism.

When the publication appeared, Hervey was offended at the inclusion of Wesley's "Letter" to him. While he contemplated a public reply to Wesley, he sought the counsel of his friend William Cudworth, who had served for a time with the Calvinistic Methodists at Whitefield's Tabernacle. The 1746 conference of the Tabernacle recorded that at

> this time a spirit of contention arose and antinomianism grew to a strong head and preachers, the brethren and conference were divided by means of Mr. Cudworth's and others introducing antinomianism that drunk into his spirit.[21]

Cudworth separated from Whitefield's connection and became pastor of an Independent congregation in Margaret Street, London. He declared that he abhorred Wesley "as much as he did the pope, and ten times more than he did the devil."[22] The feeling was mutual. After an interview in 1759, Wesley declared, "He is as incapable as a brute beast of being convinced even in the smallest point."[23] It was particularly at Cudworth that Wesley had directed *A Second Dialogue Between an Antinomian and His Friend*.[24]

Wesley wrote and asked that Hervey submit any complaint against him in private before publishing an attack abroad. This would be consistent with what Wesley had done for Hervey. Above all, he requested that Hervey "give no countenance to that insolent, scurrilous, virulent libel which bears the name of William Cudworth." Wesley expressed his concern that "an evil man has gained the ascendant over you, and has persuaded a dying man, who had shunned it all his life, to enter into controversy as he is stepping into eternity!"[25] Cudworth's encouragement, however, prevailed over Wesley's caution, and Hervey began to compose his answer to Wesley in a series of letters.

In addition to the counsel of his more Calvinistic friends, another factor that influenced the normally controversy-shy Hervey to enter into public debate was his declining health. Although he had never had a robust constitution, increasing frailty marked his last year of life. It was often with difficulty that he could even write a letter, and he was unable to attend church, much less preach, during the year preceding his death. Lawson cites a medical opinion on the relation between emotions and the effects of terminal illness to show that Hervey's tuberculosis probably heightened his feelings of sensitivity.[26] This may account in part for the fact that Hervey devoted his dying energies to the task of replying to Wesley.

But Hervey then had second thoughts about publishing against Wesley during the closing days of his life. He realized he was going to die without completing his "reply," and much of his work was still in his own shorthand, undecipherable to anyone but himself. On his deathbed he ordered his brother, William Hervey, not to publish the materials, a decision in keeping with the character shown throughout his life. Unfortunately, his last request was not honored. When a surreptitious edition of the work appeared, after his death, Hervey's brother felt compelled to print the genuine letters under the title *Eleven Letters From the Late Mr. Hervey, to the Rev. Mr. John Wesley; Containing An Answer to That Gentleman's Remarks Upon Theron and Aspasio*. The letters reveal that, among other things, Hervey had correctly understood Wesley's objection to the term "imputed righteousness of Christ as an actual opposition to the concept itself.[27]

Wesley always suspected that the *Eleven Letters* were more the work of Cudworth than James Hervey, and his affection for his former friend continued untarnished. Charles Wesley had more difficulty over this dispute, however, and refused to write an epitaph for Hervey:

> If they need a nobler trophy raise
> As long as Theron and Aspasio live,
> Let Madan or Romaine record his praise;
> Enough that Wesley's brother can forgive![28]

Wesley's Doctrine of the "Righteousness of Christ"

During this period Wesley published several works that dealt with the doctrines in question. In reply to the anonymous *A Seasonable Antidote Against Popery*, Wesley in 1758 wrote *A Letter to a Gentleman at Bristol*. In April 1762, he issued his *Thoughts Upon the Imputed Righteousness of Christ*. Later the same year he published *A Blow at the Root: Or, Christ stabbed in the House of His Friends*.[29] Wesley's reply to the *Eleven Letters* was in the form of an extract from John Goodwin's *Treatise on Justification*. He chose this method of defense in preference to an original composition partly because at the time he wrote the treatise the author was "a firm and zealous Calvinist." Wesley noted of Goodwin: "This enabled him to confirm what he advanced by such authorities, as well as from Calvin himself, as from his most eminent followers, as I could not have done."[30]

In 1765 Wesley preached a sermon on *The Lord our Righteousness*, and the following year he printed *Some Remarks on "A Defence of the Preface to the Edinburgh Edition of Aspasio Vindicated."*[31] With these publications it is possible to summarize Wesley's own views on the questions related to imputed righteousness.

The "righteousness of Christ" was a difficult expression for Wesley. He much preferred the "righteousness of God," which he found to be a more scriptural term, and which referred to (1) God's mercy, and (2) His method of justifying sinners.[32] When he used the term "righteousness of Christ," it had a twofold connotation: Christ's divine righteousness, and His human righteousness. The point at issue was Christ's human righteousness, which for Wesley was both internal and external. The internal righteousness was "the image of God, stamped on every power and faculty of his soul," and was, in fact, "a copy of his divine righteousness." Christ's external righteousness was further divided into two parts: His positive, outward obedience, usually termed active righteousness; and His submissive obedience, usually called His passive righteousness.

Yet, Wesley would allow no real division between these:

> As the active and passive righteousness of Christ were never, in fact, separated from each other, so we never need separate them at all, either in speaking or even in thinking. And it is with regard to both these conjointly, that Jesus is called "The Lord our righteousness."[33]

It was only through the righteousness of Christ "that a sinner is justified or accounted righteous before God." Wesley equated the righteousness of Christ with His merit, and thus he declared: "We are accounted righteous before God, justified only for the merit of Christ."[34] Next he faced the question "How is righteousness or merit imputed?" Wesley replied: "All believers are forgiven and accepted, not for the sake of anything in them, or of anything that was . . . done by them, but wholly and solely for the sake of what Christ hath done and suffered for them."[35]

Although Christ was seen as the meritorious cause of justification, this did not exclude faith as the instrumental cause in Wesley's eyes.[36] "Faith is the hand which apprehends, the instrument which applies, the merits of Christ for our justification." So faith, preceded by repentance, was "no part of the meritorious cause" of justification, but both were the conditions of it.[37] This accounts for Wesley's preference for the biblical statement, "Faith is imputed to us for righteousness." He believed that "faith is imputed to every believer, namely faith in the righteousness of Christ."[38]

While Wesley held that repentance and faith were gifts from God, he saw no reason why they should not be conditions as well: "Repentance and faith are privileges and free gifts. But this does not hinder their being conditions too. And neither Mr. Calvin himself, nor any of our Reformers, made any scruple of calling them so."[39] Yet, he strongly objected to the notion that Christ had fulfilled the conditions of repentance and faith.[40]

The righteousness of the believer was not only imputed; it was also inherent. He viewed inherent righteousness "not as the ground of our acceptance with

God, but as the fruit of it; not in place of imputed righteousness, but as consequent upon it. That is, I believe God implants righteousness in every one to whom he has imputed it."[41] This was linked with Wesley's emphasis on sanctification as a real change in believers. "You are really changed; you are not only accounted, but actually 'made righteous.'" He would have no part of the view that "Men are holy, without a grain of holiness in them! holy in Christ, however unholy in themselves." This position—allowing men to "be unrighteous still, seeing Christ has fulfilled all righteousness"—Wesley felt was a blow "at the root of all holiness, all true religion."[42]

The evidence that a man had been justified consisted in (1) the testimony of the Holy Spirit with his own spirit that he was a child of God, (2) the inward and then (3) the outward fruits of the Spirit. Wesley was quick to point out that "these fruits do not justify us, do not procure our justification, but prove us to be justified."[43] Thus it was holiness of life and the manifestation of the fruits of the Spirit that for Wesley gave evidence to the world that a man was justified.

Final justification, like initial justification, was also conditional for Wesley.[44] "We obey in order to [have] our final acceptance through his merits." This was related to his view of perseverance, i.e., that a man could fall from grace, a position which, in turn, rested on his conviction that sin always separated a man from God, either before or after an experience of conversion. "I testify unto you, that if you will continue in sin, Christ shall profit you nothing; that Christ is no Savior to you, unless he saves you from your sins."[45] To those who frequently used the phrase "imputed righteousness of Christ," he urged, "O warn them that if they remain unrighteous, the righteousness of Christ will profit them nothing."[46]

It was this disdain for holiness by proxy, i.e., men hiding their sins under "the righteousness of Christ," that made Wesley grow more and more reluctant to use that phrase. "I am myself [am] the more sparing in the use of it, because it has been so frequently and so dreadfully abused; and because the Antinomians use it at this day to justify the grossest abominations."[47] Wesley was convinced that the position represented by Hervey was a form of speculative or doctrinal antinomianism, which at the parish level often led men into practical antinomianism.

> What we are afraid of is this;—lest any should use the phrase, The Righteousness of Christ, or, the righteousness of Christ is imputed to me, as a cover for his unrighteousness. We have known this done a thousand times.[48]

Wesley exclaimed:

> For wherever this doctrine is cordially received, it leaves no place for holiness. Nay, it makes men afraid of personal holiness, . . . lest they deny the faith, and reject Christ and his righteousness: So that, instead of being zealous of good works, they are a stink in their nostrils.[49]

As in the free-grace controversy, it was the centrality of the doctrine of sanctification for Wesley that stood behind his reaction to Hervey's speculative antinomianism. At the 1765 Conference, in the midst of the controversy over Hervey's *Eleven Letters,* Wesley reiterated that God had thrust them out to raise up a holy people. But when "Satan could not otherwise prevent this, he threw Calvinism in our way; and then Antinomianism, which struck at the root of both inward and outward holiness."[50] Practical antinomianism, he feared, would be the outcome of an improper interpretation of the imputed righteousness of Christ. Thus it was his concern for holy living that caused him to react against Hervey's central emphasis.

The Influence of the Controversy in Scotland

Related to the Hervey controversy was the state of Wesley's work in Scotland. When he was first invited there in 1751, Whitefield had warned him: "Your principles are so well known, that if you spoke like an angel none would hear you," and if they did, it would only end in dispute. Wesley promised that he would "studiously avoid controverted points, and keep to the fundamental truths." In 1765 he recorded that he had kept his word, and was still convinced that to preach on predestination there would be a sin.[51]

Dr. John Erskine, pastor of Old Greyfriars Church, Edinburgh, republished in the mid-1760s Hervey's *Eleven Letters,* attacking Wesley in a preface with the accusation that he had concealed his real sentiments. Wesley replied that he had avoided predestination in order to promote harmony rather than division, but Erskine was not satisfied.[52] He printed a defense of his preface with an even stronger assault on the Methodists: "One is at the head of their Societies who has blended with some precious gospel truths a medley of Arminian, Antinomian, and enthusiastic errors." Erskine raised the accusation that while Wesley attacked predestination as subversive to all religion, he suffered his followers in Scotland to remain of that opinion, and he further objected to Wesley's views on "sinless perfection" and the imputation of Christ's active obedience.

Wesley clarified his position on the latter two charges, both in print and by a personal interview with Erskine, and he admitted some truth to the accusation about his conduct with regard to predestination. But he declared:

> I do not believe it is necessarily subversive of all religion. I think hot disputes are much more so; therefore I never willingly dispute with anyone about it; and I advise all my friends, not in Scotland only, but all over England and Ireland, to avoid all contention on the head, and let every man remain in his own opinion. Can any man of Candor blame me for this?[53]

But Erskine did blame him, and so effectively that Tyerman claimed it retarded Wesley's effectiveness in Scotland for the next twenty years.[54]

From 1765 it was clearly an uphill battle for Wesley's preachers in Scotland. Thomas Taylor claimed that the *Letters* carried such "gall and wormwood" that everyone kept their distance from him because of his connection with Wesley.[55] Thomas Hanby was even more disturbed:

> O the precious convictions those letters destroyed! They made me mourn in secret places. Mr. Erskine being much esteemed in the religious world, and recommending them through the whole kingdom, our enemies made their advantage of them. . . . Many were then brought to birth, but by those letters their convictions were stifled.[56]

The general Calvinistic climate, plus this heated exchange, were certainly major factors in Wesley's failure to establish Methodism as firmly in Scotland as he did in England.

8. The Relationship between Wesley and Whitefield

BECAUSE thus far our focus has been primarily on the controversies of the eigh teenth century, one could wrongly draw the conclusion that heated theological debate was the dominant atmosphere characterizing the relationships of the leaders of the revival. As a corrective to this, the cordial personal relations between John Wesley and George Whitefield from 1745 to 1770 will be examined. At the same time, a review is needed of the other side of their differences, i.e., the doctrine of Christian perfection. After a discussion of this doctrine and its place in Wesley's ministry, its effect on Wesley's relationship with the Calvinists will be evaluated.

Wesley, in an attempt at reconciliation, used the occasion of his delivery of Whitefield's funeral sermon as an opportunity to call for the laying aside of minor doctrinal differences. That sermon and the subsequent reaction to it by the Calvinists, lead to a discussion of the difference in Wesley's thinking between essential doctrine and opinion. The chapter concludes by showing how this understanding of the role of doctrine is related to Wesley's position on the "catholic spirit."

Cordial Friendship without Organizational Unity

From the separation in the 1740s until his death in 1770, mutual esteem and affection generally marked George Whitefield's relationship with the Wesleys. Although a formal connection was not possible, they continued to maintain close personal links. After Whitefield had called upon him in 1755, Wesley wrote: "Disputings are now no more; we love one another, and join hand in hand to promote the cause of our common Master."[1] Whitefield gave himself primarily to itinerant preaching among all groups, including Wesley's societies. "Though Mr. Wesley and I differ a little in some principles, yet brotherly love continues. I generally, when itinerating preach among his people, as freely as among those who are called our own."[2] John Wesley himself recorded Whitefield's contribution: "He is very affectionate and very lively, and his word seldom falls to the ground: though he does not frequently speak of the deep things of God or the height of the promises."[3]

While each preached among the other's societies, both apparently took care to avoid controversial issues. Wesley said in 1761: "I have preached 20 years in some of George Whitefield's Societies; yet to this day I never contradicted him among his people. I did not think it honest, neither necessary at all."[4]

Whitefield also moved toward a measure of his former intimacy with Charles Wesley. When he heard that Charles' wife, Sally, had survived a serious illness, he wrote:

I most sincerely rejoice and have given private and public thanks for the recovery of your dear yokefellow. My pleasure is increased by seeing your Brother so well as I found him on Tuesday at Lewisham. Oh that you may both spring afresh and your latter end increase more and more![5]

In like manner Charles responded in verse:

Come on, my Whitefield! (since tho' strife is past,
And friends at first are friends again at last)
Our hands, and hearts, and counsels let us join
In mutual league, t'advance the work Divine,
Our one contention now, our single aim,
To pluck poor souls as brands out of the flame.[6]

In 1747, John Wesley with four assistants attended the conference of the English Calvinist Methodist Association. Whitefield was in America, but Howel Harris recorded that they inquired together how they could remove any hindrances to brotherly love and prevent future contention. When that association feared that Wesley's preaching at Neath in Wales might separate their society, Wesley replied: "I don't design to erect at Neath or in any town in Wales where there is such a society already but to do all that in me lies to prevent any such separation."[7] They decided that one of Wesley's men should accompany Harris to Plymouth to endeavor to heal a breach there and "to insist on a spirit of love and its fruits among the people." They agreed to consult one another before accepting a call from a society belonging to the other side, and they promised to defend one another's characters. The occasion illustrates the attempt by the leadership of the Arminian and Calvinistic Methodists to prevent discord and overlapping activity, and to cooperate wherever possible.

An even closer alliance was formed in 1766 between the Wesleys and Whitefield, apparently at the instigation of the Countess of Huntingdon.[8] Charles Wesley described the relationship involved:

This morning I and my brother spent two blessed hours with George Whitefield. The threefold cord, we trust, will never be broken [Eccl. 4:12]. On Tuesday next, my brother is to preach in Lady Huntingdon's chapel in Bath. That and all her chapels are now put into the hands of us three.[9]

The following year when Whitefield and Howel Harris were present for Wesley's Conference in London, Christopher Hopper recorded that "all was love, all was harmony. It was a Pentecost indeed."[10]

Whitefield's friendly correspondence with several of Wesley's preachers is further indication of his desire to maintain fraternal relations. In 1766 Whitefield requested one of them, Joseph Crownley, to assist him for several weeks at the Tabernacle, claiming Wesley should readily consent, as "we are upon very good terms."[11]

While the relationship between Wesley's camp and Whitefield's was generally cordial, there were some troublesome moments. Wesley felt that certain Calvinistic preachers had adversely influenced members of his societies, and in 1753 the Conference decided to ban them from preaching among Wesley's people. They wrote a respectful letter to Whitefield, asking that he restrain his preachers from speaking against Wesley or his doctrines. The Conference carried their determination one step further when they forbade John Broseworth, one of their local preachers, to preach any longer among the societies, because he disputed continuously about predestination.[12] Similar treatment was later accorded William Darney, when the preachers declared: "Let him preach Calvinism elsewhere (we have no right to hinder him): but not among us." Wesley insisted, however, that this was not persecution. "I persecute no man on this account, or any other; and yet I cannot consent that any of our lay preachers should . . . preach predestination."[13]

The Debate over Perfection

The question of predestination was not the only dividing issue. In the early 1760s Wesley noted a revival of interest in Christian perfection, and he recorded that an increasing number of those in his societies were testifying to an experience of entire sanctification.[14] In the midst of this renewed emphasis on "evangelical perfection," two of Wesley's assistants in London began to press the doctrine to extremes. One of these, Thomas Maxfield, had been justified while praying with Wesley in Bristol in 1739 and had become one of his first lay preachers. He was later ordained by Bishop Barnard with a comment about Maxfield's relationship to Wesley: "Sir, I ordain you, to assist that good man, that he may not work himself to death." Maxfield served more than twenty years with Wesley. Though not always appreciated by some of the other preachers, he was defended consistently by Wesley.

In the early sixties Wesley had Maxfield meet in London with a select band of those who professed to be entirely sanctified. Parts of this group soon began to experience dreams, visions, and impressions. These Maxfield encouraged, and they grew contemptuous of the rest of the society. When some of Wesley's other preachers responded roughly, they reacted by refusing to hear them preach, claiming only to follow Maxfield. When Wesley returned to town in the autumn of 1762, the society was in an uproar, with Maxfield and his company meeting in a semidetached connection.[15]

George Bell, a native of Barningham, was the second assistant who began to divert scriptural perfection into perfectionism. Bell, who had been a corporal in the Life Guards before his conversion in 1758, claimed an experience of entire sanctification in March 1761. He began to hold meetings of his own, declaring that God no longer wanted preaching and sacraments. Some of his followers began to claim Adamic perfection, while others believed they could not fall from their state of grace. They became obsessed with miraculous healing, even attempting to restore sight to the blind and raise the dead, while at the same time becoming convinced that they were exempt from death. Bell declared that God was to be found only in his assemblies or those of his London friends, and he propagated the principle that "none could teach those who are renewed in love, unless they were in the state themselves."[16]

Wesley's response to these excesses was typically cautious. He wrote of his dealing with George Bell: "Being determined to hear for myself, I stood where I could hear and see, without being seen." After personal observation, Wesley noted that Bell had prayed nearly an hour. He then recorded what could be said positively for the fervency of Bell's spirit. Meanwhile, he also noted the things he could not admire, such as screaming, claiming a miraculous discernment of spirits, and condemning his opposers.[17]

The same basic approach was taken with Thomas Maxfield. John went with Charles to see Maxfield personally, and then he set down in a lengthy letter what he liked and disliked about their doctrine and behavior. He declared his appreciation of their doctrine of perfection, i.e., pure love excluding sin, their insistence that it comes by faith and, therefore, is instantaneous, their confidence in God and zeal for the salvation of souls, and their life devoted to God and spent doing good. But there were many things of which he disapproved, and the first listed was related to Wesley's own experience and teaching of entire sanctification:

> I disliked the saying, This was not known or taught among us till within two or three years. I grant you did not know it. You have over and over denied instantaneous sanctification to me; but I have known and taught it (and so has my brother, as our writings show) above these twenty years.

Wesley also disliked their depreciation of justification, the need for self-examination and private prayer, their unwillingness to be taught by anyone not in the same state as themselves, and the accusation that they had been persecuted by the Wesleys for the past two years. Further, he disapproved of the appearance of pride, overvaluing themselves, undervaluing others, not giving significance to tenderness of conscience, and regarding "faith rather as contradistinguished from holiness than as productive of it." He was especially disturbed at the appearance of enthusiasm (i.e., fanaticism) and antinomianism by "overvaluing feelings and inward impressions" and imaginations, while undervaluing reason, knowledge, and wisdom.

What Wesley disliked most of all was the lack of love for the other brethren in the society, and he objected to their appointing their own meetings at times that made it impossible to attend public preaching or their class or band. Last, he listed several aspects of disorder in worship that he felt were not appropriate. These included worshipers singing, praying, or speaking all at once; using improper expressions in prayer; using flat, bald hymns; never kneeling in prayer; screaming; affirming that people are justified or sanctified when they are not; bidding them say, "I believe"; and calling all who opposed them "hypocrites."[18]

In addition to his personal interviews and the letter of evaluation, Wesley moved to protect his people from these excesses by publishing a pamphlet entitled *Cautions and Directions Given to the Greatest Professors in the Methodist Societies*. The work is particularly significant for this study, because the counsel

Wesley gave was, in capsule form, his method for avoiding any form of antinomianism. He began with a caution to watch and pray continually against pride, for he was aware that this is always a temptation to those who are growing spiritually. He then warned about enthusiasm and urged that his people give no place to heated imagination or to things hastily ascribed to God. "Do not easily suppose dreams, voices, impressions, visions, or revelations to be from God. They may be from Him. They may be from nature. They may be from the devil." Wesley laid down this principle for evaluating all these subjective elements:

> Believe not every spirit, but try the spirits whether they be of God. Try all things by the written word, and let all bow down before it. You are in danger of enthusiasm every hour, if you depart ever so little from Scripture; yea, or from the plain literal meaning of any text, taken in connection with the context.[19]

The Word of God continued to be his standard of evaluation for all matters of truth. He further warned against expecting the end of godliness without the proper means: "Expecting knowledge, for instance, without searching the Scriptures and consulting the children of God; expecting spiritual strength without constant prayer, and steady watchfulness." Some, he felt, had been ignorant of this device of Satan and had left off searching the Scriptures to their detriment. So he cautioned them, "Beware of enthusiasm," such as imagining they had a gift of prophesying or discerning of spirits or of judging people by their own feelings. "This is no scriptural way of judging. O keep close to 'the law and to the testimony.' "

His third piece of advice followed naturally from this in a warning against antinomianism, i.e., "making void the law," or any part of it, "through faith."

> Even that great truth, that "Christ is the end of the law," may betray us in it, if we do not consider that he had adopted every point of the moral law, and grafted it into the law of love. Beware of thinking, "Because I am filled with love, I need not have so much holiness."[20]

He then carefully reinforced the disciplines of private prayer and self-examination. "Let us 'magnify the law,' the whole written word, and make it honourable." Wesley continued warning against books by antinomian authors, the problem of stillness, self-indulgence, and solifidianism, with people reciting "justification by faith alone,"

> crying nothing but, "Believe, believe!" and condemning those as ignorant or legal who speak in a more scriptural way. At certain seasons, indeed, it may be right to treat of nothing but repentance, or merely of faith, or altogether of holiness; but, in general, our call is to declare the whole counsel of God, and to prophesy according to the analogy of faith. The written word treats of the whole and every particular branch of righteousness.[21]

Wesley's fourth counsel was to beware of sins of omission; be zealous of good works; be always employed and not slothful. This was followed by the injunction to beware of desiring anything but God, and then a warning against schism or rending the church of Christ. This last prospect was to be avoided by observing every rule of the society and of the bands, never missing class or band meeting, or being absent from public preaching. His final advice was that they be exemplary in all things, especially in outward things such as dress, use of money, seriousness, and usefulness in conversation.[22]

In addition to publishing his "Cautions and Directions," Wesley went twice more to hear George Bell, after which he "was convinced he must not continue to pray at the Foundry. The reproach of Christ I am willing to bear, but not the reproach of enthusiasm, if I can help it." Yet Wesley's patience was long, and the last week of the year he gave Bell another chance:

> That I might do nothing hastily, I permitted George Bell to be once more at the chapel in West Street, and once more at the Foundry. But it was worse and worse; he now spoke as from God what I knew God had not spoken. I therefore desired that he would come thither no more.[23]

While the disturbance was creating confusion in the society, Wesley dealt with the problem with characteristic caution. "I move only a hair's breadth at a time. No sharpness will profit. There is need of a lady's hand, as well as a lion's heart."[24] Tyerman was convinced Wesley moved too slow: "We incline to think Wesley used the lady's hand too long, and that the lion's paw would have been far more useful."[25] Others apparently would have agreed. Charles Wesley wrote of the "sad havoc Satan has made of the flock" and indicated that for several years he had been warning of this "flood of enthusiasm which has now overflowed us." Another of the preachers described the situation in London:

> As to the follies of the enthusiasts, Mr. Charles hears every week less or more. Why his brother suffers them, we cannot tell. He threatens, but cannot find in his heart to put in execution. The consequence is, the talk of all the town, and entertainment for the newspapers.[26]

From a country parish in Madeley, John Fletcher wrote his evaluation to Charles Wesley:

> I have a particular regard for Mr. Maxfield and Mr. Bell; both of them are my correspondents. I am strongly prejudiced in favour of the wit- nesses, and do not willingly receive what is said against them; but allowing that what is reported is one half mere exaggeration, the tenth part of the rest shows that spiritual pride, presumption, arrogance, stubbornness, party spirit, uncharitableness, prophetic mistakes,—in short, every sinew of enthusiasm, is now at work among them. I do not credit any one's bare word; but I ground my sentiments on Bell's own letters.[27]

Apparently Fletcher's assessment was correct, for Bell finally consummated his fanaticism by prophesying that the world would come to an end on February 28, 1763. At this point Wesley disavowed all connection with Bell in private, in the society, and at last in the public newspaper. On the day before the predicted final catastrophe, Bell and some associates ascended a mound overlooking the city to have a last look at the doomed metropolis. While he was there, unfortunately, two constables arrested him for holding meetings in an unlicensed meetinghouse. Bell was then committed to prison by the magistrate, where he could await the fulfillment of his prediction in confinement. On the evening of what was to be the world's last day, Wesley preached on "Prepare to meet thy God," and endeavored to show the absurdity of Bell's prediction. Notwithstanding, many wandered in the fields all night, afraid to go to bed for fear of a great earthquake.[28]

Thomas Maxfield claimed not to have followed the same extremes as Bell. Though it is uncertain whether or not he believed the prediction, it is clear that he was promoting disunion within the London Society, telling people that Wesley was not capable of teaching them. At last he separated from Wesley on April 28, 1763, taking with him about 106 members of the society. Many of these later returned to Wesley. Maxfield himself, who lived about twenty years after the separation, later reestablished more friendly relations with the Wesleys. George Bell, however, turned away from any profession of faith. As Southy commented: "He recovered his senses to make deplorable use of them; passing from one extreme to another, the ignorant enthusiast became the ignorant infidel; turned fanatic in politics, as he had done in religion."[29]

In London, Wesley's cautious approach in handling fanaticism apparently paid off in spite of the impatience of some of his associates. On a tally of the members of the society, Wesley discovered that about "thirty of those who thought they were saved from sin had separated from their brethren; but above four hundred, who witnessed the same confession, seemed more united than ever."[30] The general effect of the controversy, however, was to bring discredit upon the Methodists in the eyes of the public, as well as to dampen interest in Christian perfection in some places. During the summer of 1763, when Wesley was on his yearly tour, he discovered the effects of the controversy in places like Yarm.

> I found the good doctrine of Christian perfection had not been heard of there for some time. The wildness of our poor brethren in London has put it out of countenance above two hundred miles off; so these strange advocates for perfection have given it a deeper wound than all its enemies together could do![31]

The following year Wesley wrote to his brother:

> The frightful stories wrote from London had made all our preachers in the North afraid even to mutter about perfection; and, of course, the people on all sides were grown good Calvinists in this point. 'Tis what I foresaw from the beginning—that the devil would strive by T. Maxfield and company to drive perfection out of the kingdom.[32]

Apparently Wesley was not willing for the devil to carry the day without a fight. He continued to preach on the subject and to record in his *Journal* the responses of those who experienced entire sanctification.[33] Wesley wanted to aid those who had thus been renewed in pure love, as well as to protect the doctrine from misunderstanding and abuse. So, throughout the remainder of the 1760s, he embarked on his most extensive publishing on the subject of Christian perfection. In 1763 he wrote his sermon on "Sin in Believers" and "Farther Thoughts upon Christian Perfection." This was followed by another sermon on "The Scripture Way of Salvation" in 1765, and then the next year a summary of his teaching to date in *A Plain Account of Christian Perfection*. In 1767 he published "Brief Thoughts on Christian Perfection," and in 1768 a sermon on "Repentance of Believers."

Many continued to respond to preaching on this subject, and clearly Wesley was not the only member of his connection promoting this experience. For example, on his first appointment under Wesley, George Story reported that when he discovered many "settled upon their leese [loss]" with "little expect[at]ion of being saved from inward sin til death," he began to speak "strongly of full salvation and God gave the word success. Several were stirred up to seek for purity of heart and others were convinced of sin." In one town where he reported "many were not a little prejudiced against me, as a setter forth of strange doctrines," he saw "the Power of God descend in a wonderful manner" so that people praised God for pardoning mercy and purifying grace. "And even those who could not yet understand this new doctrine were constrained to say, 'If we do not believe it, we will never speak against it any more.' " From that time, he recorded, "We seldom had any meeting . . . but some were either convinced, justified, or saved from all sin."[34]

In a review of the work during these years, Wesley described how many were convicted of sin, many justified, and many backsliders reclaimed. But "the peculiar work of this season" he described as "the perfecting of the saints." In various parts of both England and Ireland, many had experienced a deeper change that began with a "conviction of inbred sin" and led to being "so filled with faith and love (and generally in a moment) that sin vanished." Such a "glorious work of God," said Wesley, "considering both the depth and extent of it, we never saw in these kingdoms before." He did not, however, overlook the problems that arose with the blessings:

> It is possible [that] some who spoke in this manner were mistaken; and it is certain some have lost what they then received. A few (very few, compared to the whole number) first gave way to enthusiasm, then to pride, next to prejudice and offence, and at last separated from their brethren, but, although this laid a huge stumbling-block in the way, still the work of God went on. Nor has it ceased to this day in any of its branches. God still convinces, justifies, sanctifies. We have lost only the dross, the enthusiasm, the prejudice, and offence. The pure gold remains, faith working by love, and we have ground to believe increases daily.[35]

Wesley was disappointed that, in the midst of this debate over perfection within his own connection, the Calvinists took advantage of this "deluded fringe" to discredit his whole position on Christian perfection.

> Their voice seems rather, "Down with him, even to the ground." I mean (for I had used no ceremony on circumlocution) Mr. Madan, Mr. Haweis,

Mr. Berridge, and (I am sorry to say it) Mr. Whitefield. Only Mr. Romaine has shown a truly sympathizing spirit and acted the part of a brother.[36]

Wesley had great difficulty appreciating the Calvinistic abhorrence of perfection. As early as the free-grace controversy, they had pointed to select examples of extreme "perfectionists" as evidence of a latent antinomianism in Wesley's doctrine, and so they viewed the actions of Maxfield and Bell as confirmation of their worst fears.

Several factors lay behind the Calvinists' apprehension about perfection. One was the difference between Wesley and themselves over the application of grace in terms of righteousness. Wesley believed not only in imputed righteousness, but also in inherent righteousness, i.e., in being both declared righteous by God and actually being made righteous by Him. The first he saw as a relative change in one's relationship with God, while the second he believed to be a real change within the nature of the individual. One had to do with one's objective relation to God, while the other had to do with the subjective transformation of the person.

Because Wesley believed that a genuine change within the individual was a part of God's grace at work, he felt the concept of sanctification or perfection was an extension of that transforming power. God continued to remake man in His own image, and Wesley understood part of that activity in terms of a full renewal of the heart in love. The Calvinists of the eighteenth century, on the other hand, focused almost exclusively on imputed righteousness or a new positional standing before God. Any word about inherent or imparted righteousness smacked too much of a return to Catholicism for them and constituted a rejection of certain principles of the Reformation. Perfection, in particular, sounded too much like something earned or achieved, and therefore it was not compatible with salvation that was purely by grace. While this was not what Wesley was preaching, this is what the Calvinists heard through their own theological filter, and so they reacted accordingly.

A second factor behind the Calvinists' rejection of perfection had to do with a different definition of an act of sin. For the Calvinists, who basically took a legal definition of sin, any transgression of a law of God was classified as a sinful act. This included both willful disobedience and involuntary transgressions. Wesley had made a distinction, however, between voluntary and involuntary transgressions. The former he believed were sins "properly so called," while the latter he labeled as infirmities. He recognized the existence of the involuntary transgressions as a part of general depravity. But because they had nothing to do with the will, he felt they were covered by the general effects of the atonement and were not something for which man was held responsible. Therefore, man did not incur any guilt or punishment on account of these, and so, practically speaking, the only sins with which men could effectively deal were the voluntary transgressions.

It was this last category that related to the idea of perfection for Wesley. He believed it was possible to have consistent victory over willful disobedience, as well as to experience a cleansing of one's sinful nature. But even after such an experience of entire sanctification, Wesley recognized the continued existence of infirmities or involuntary transgressions. Therefore, he did not speak about an absolute or sinless perfection. When the Calvinists heard him, however, because of their different definition of sin, they took him to be teaching freedom from involuntary transgressions as well as voluntary ones. Whether they agreed that there could be freedom from willful disobedience or not, they certainly knew that there was no state of grace where men were free from involuntary transgressions such as mistakes, failures due to ignorance, and physical and emotional deficiencies.

As a result, the Calvinists saw Wesley setting an impossible standard, and accordingly they rejected the whole concept. They feared that some might even redefine their willful actions as "perfect" after an experience of entire sanctification, although their conduct was clearly at variance with biblical commands, i.e., a kind of philosophy that said, "I am perfect, and therefore, I can do no wrong." This was exactly their interpretation of Maxfield and Bell, which further reinforced their fears of Wesley's concept of imparted righteousness and actual holiness. And so they continued to grow increasingly uneasy with Wesley's effective promotion of perfection throughout the decade of the 1760s. This doctrinal issue then became one of the factors behind the serious rupture of relations in the 1770s.

However, in spite of these trouble spots, the overall tone of relationships was cordial during the last years of Whitefield's life.[37] Wesley wrote in his *Journal:* "Mr. Whitefield called upon me. He breathes nothing but peace and love. Bigotry cannot stand before him, but hides its head whenever he comes."[38] Since the *Journal* was primarily for contemporary consumption, Wesley's frequent mention of his cordial meetings with Whitefield must be understood as a deliberate attempt to remove any misgivings that may have been held by some of his more narrow-minded followers.

Wesley Preaches Whitefield's Funeral Sermon

On Sunday, September 30, 1770, Whitefield died in Newburyport, Massachusetts, and was buried two days later under the pulpit of the local Presbyterian meetinghouse. Long before that, it had been agreed that if Whitefield would die first, Wesley would preach his funeral discourse.[39] Accordingly, on Sunday, November 18, Wesley preached to an "immense multitude" in Whitefield's chapel at Tottenham Court Road. The service was to begin at half past five, but since the place was filled at three, Wesley started at four. He described the scene: "It was an awful season. All were still as night; most appeared to be deeply affected; and an impression was made on many, which one would hope will not speedily be effaced." He desired "to show all good respect to the memory of that great and good man."[40]

Wesley took his text from Numbers 23:10: "Let me die the death of the righteous, and let my last end be like his!" He began with a review of some of the particulars of Whitefield's life, chiefly extracted from the early *Journals.* Then, out of almost forty years of friendship with Whitefield, he proceeded to give a sketch of his character. He concluded:

> Have we read or heard of any person since the Apostles, who testified the gospel of the grace of God through so widely extended a space, through so large a part of the habitable world? Have we read or heard of any person who called so many thousands, so many myriads, of sinners to repentance? Above all, have we read or heard of any who has been a blessed instrument in His hand of bringing so many sinners from "darkness to light, and from the power of Satan unto God"?[41]

Wesley exhorted the assembly to improve the occasion "by keeping close to the grand doctrines which he delivered; and by drinking into his spirit." He reminded them that there were "many doctrines of a less essential nature, with regard to which even the sincere children of God" may disagree, but he called them to hold fast to what Whitefield believed were the essentials of the faith: the new birth and justification by faith. Because Wesley was in the midst of controversy with the Calvinistic Methodists over the 1770 Conference Minutes, he took the opportunity to remind Whitefield's followers that the two men both believed salvation was all of God, and that "there is no power (by nature) and no merit in man." He asserted his agreement with Whitefield that Christ's death was "the sole meritorious cause of . . . our pardon and acceptance with God, of our full and free justification." Justification for both men was "by faith alone." Further, he joined himself with Whitefield in subscribing to the inward change of the new birth: "His indwelling Spirit makes them both holy in heart, and 'holy in all manner of conversation.' "[42]

Wesley pointed out, however, that it would not suffice for one to "keep close to his doctrine" and not imbibe of Whitefield's "grateful, friendly, affectionate temper." He called upon the congregation to put on Whitefield's catholic spirit, and "let brother no more lift up sword against brother." Wesley closed with a prayer that the mantle of Whitefield should fall upon all that remained, entreating the Lord:

> Let his spirit rest upon these Thy servants! Show Thou art the God that answerest by fire! Let the fire of Thy love fall on every heart! And because we love Thee, let us love one another with a "love stronger than death."[43]

Wesley's sermon did not go unchallenged. William Romaine responded with a warm attack on Wesley's tribute in the *Gospel Magazine,* a publication of the Calvinistic Methodists. It began with an objection to Wesley's choice of a text from an oracle of Balaam: "How improper to apply the words of a mad prophet to so holy a man as Mr. Whitefield!" Wesley replied that he had not applied the words to Whitefield, but to himself! But a more serious charge was made against Wesley's understanding of Whitefield's essential theology: "The grand fundamental doctrines which he everywhere preached, were the everlasting covenant between the Father and the Son, and absolute predestination flowing therefrom."[44] This Wesley flatly rejected:

> Mr. Whitefield did not everywhere preach these. In all the times I myself heard him preach, I never heard him utter a sentence either on one or

the other. In all our chapels throughout England he did preach the necessity of the new birth, and justification by faith.[45]

Not all were pleased that Wesley had been asked to preach Whitefield's memorial sermon. On the same day that Wesley spoke in London, the Countess of Huntingdon requested Henry Venn to preach a sermon for Whitefield at her chapel in Bath. In describing Whitefield, Venn declared:

> His doctrine was the doctrine of the Reformers, of the Apostles, and of Christ: it was the doctrine of free grace, of God's everlasting love. Through Jesus he practiced the forgiveness of sins, the perseverance in holy living.
> . . . And the doctrines which he preached, he eminently adorned by his zeal and by his works.[46]

In still another funeral oration, Richard Elliot was even more explicit. He pointed out how Whitefield had avoided both the errors of the Antinomians and the Arminians by preaching on the central doctrines of original sin, the new birth, justification by faith, final perseverance, and unconditional election. In a defense of the central importance of the doctrine of election for Whitefield, Elliot repeated the substance of Whitefield's thirty-year-old *Answer to John Wesley*. Without mentioning Wesley by name, he warned Whitefield's followers: "Beware they do not beguile you with enticing words, by saying these are points of no great moment, mere opinions, circumstantials only."[47]

Wesley was correct in his assessment of Whitefield's doctrinal emphasis, but only within the context of his own experience. It is not surprising that Whitefield avoided the controversial points when Wesley was present. But neither is it surprising that Whitefield's followers reacted to Wesley's dismissal of Whitefield's Calvinism as being of marginal importance. They, in turn, overstated their case and claimed predestination to be at the heart of Whitefield's theology. While Wesley worked to minimize the doctrinal differences, when he undervalued the place of Whitefield's Calvinism, he succeeded in producing the opposite reaction. Whitefield's followers, out of supposed faithfulness to their fallen leader's theology, began to place even greater emphasis upon their distinctives. All of this only added fuel to the fire of the debate over the 1770 Conference Minutes. Moreover, Whitefield's death deprived the revival of his moderating influence. No one else possessed either his stature among the Calvinists or his unique relationship with Wesley. Whitefield's unique position in this regard had made possible almost thirty years of relatively cordial relations between the two theological camps.

Wesley's Catholic Spirit

When Whitefield and Wesley collaborated to steer around problem areas and stick to fundamentals, the, eighteenth-century evangelicals achieved a significant level of cooperation between 1745 and 1770. Since both the evangelical Anglican clergymen and the Methodists continued to live within the context of the established church, the parameters for theological discussion were clearly marked off by the authority of Scripture and, in a secondary sense, by the church's Articles of Religion. These the Anglicans viewed as a distillation of essential biblical truth. While the Thirty-Nine Articles delineated the outside limits, beyond which one was out of the doctrinal fold, there was still room for significant differences within the boundaries. This confessional context is essential for a proper understanding of Wesley's ecumenicity. No matter how ecclesiastically irregular he was in methodology, Wesley "never departed willingly or knowingly from the doctrines of the Church of England."[48]

Where there was room for divergent views, as there was with many of the Articles of Religion, Wesley classified the difference as "opinions." In 1765 he wrote to John Newton:

> You have admirably well expressed what I mean by an opinion contradistinguished from an essential doctrine. Whatever is "compatible with a love of Christ and a work of grace" I term opinion. And certainly the holding of Particular Election and Final Perseverance is compatible with these.[49]

Wesley regarded as an "opinion" that which was not "subversive of the very foundation of Christian experience." Thus, he could claim that he held Newton and other Calvinists in the highest esteem, "at whose feet I desire to be found in the day of the Lord Jesus."[50] This was in contrast to his differences over essential doctrine which he had experienced with the Moravians. The Moravian Brethren had undercut "the foundation" by rejecting the authority of Scripture and contradicting the theology of the Thirty-Nine Articles; the Calvinists had not. From the former, Wesley insisted on separation; with the latter, he was willing to pursue as close a cooperation as possible.[51]

Thus, Wesley had already expounded his views on fraternal collaboration in his 1749 sermon "Catholic Spirit," in which he stated: "Although a difference in opinions or modes of worship may present an entire external union, yet need it prevent our union in affection? Though we cannot think alike, may we not love alike?"[52]

In his exposition of the text, "Is thine heart right, as my heart is with thy heart?" (2 Kings 10:15), Wesley explained at length the essential doctrines that were necessary to have a heart right with God. In sermonic form, Wesley was clearly pointing out certain central emphases within the doctrinal framework of the Thirty-Nine Articles. Here he sought to discover whether his potential collaborator had applied this essential theology in his life.[53] If so, Wesley said, "give me thy hand." By this oft-misunderstood statement, Wesley meant that the two parties were to love one another, pray for one another, and provoke one another to love and good works. "So far as in conscience thou canst (retaining still thy own opinions, and thy own manner of worshipping God), join with me in the work of God; and let us go hand in hand."[54]

Although Wesley sought a measure of cooperation, there were certain limits to his tolerance, and he himself made this emphatically clear:

> A catholic spirit is not *speculative* latitudinarianism. It is not an indifference to all opinions: this is the spawn of hell, not the offspring of heaven.

> This unsettledness of thought, this being "driven to and fro, and tossed about with every wind of doctrine," is a great curse, not a blessing. . . . A man of a truly catholic spirit . . . is [as] fixed as the sun in his judgement concerning the main branches of Christian doctrine.[55]

Further, he declared no man was of a "catholic spirit" just because he had a "muddy understanding," his mind being "all in a mist." Nor did this catholic spirit include those who "have no settled, consistent principles, but are for jumbling all opinions together." These theological latitudinarians, he dismissed: "You think you are got into the very spirit of Christ; when, in truth, you are nearer the spirit of Antichrist. Go, first, and learn the first elements of the gospel of Christ, and then you shall learn to be of a truly catholic spirit."[56] Wesley's tolerance did not imply either doctrinal indifference or a theological pluralism that extended beyond the authority of Scripture or its essential truth as set down in the Articles of Religion.

The Calvinists with whom Wesley was associated, however, were as committed to the official theology of the Church of England as he was. In their several controversies, both sides continually appealed to the Thirty-Nine Articles as their ultimate source of authority next to the Scripture. Since they were both operating within this theological context, Wesley refused to categorize their differences as essential doctrine. He called upon the Calvinists "so far as in conscience thou canst (retaining still thy own opinion)" to join him in cooperative efforts wherever possible.

Charles Wesley took essentially the same approach. In his hymn "Catholic Love," which originally appeared at the close of his brother's sermon "Catholic Spirit," he declared:

> My Brethren, friends, and kinsmen these,
> Who do my heavenly Father's will;
> Who aim at perfect holiness,
> And all Thy counsels to fulfill
> A thirst to be whate'er Thou art,
> And love their God with all their Hearts.[57]

One concrete example of John Wesley's ecumenical spirit was his attempt in 1764 to improve collaboration among the evangelical clergy of the Church of England. In a printed letter he proposed a union based on three evangelical emphases: original sin, justification by faith, and holiness of heart and life. Among the some fifty clergy to whom Wesley sent his "eirenicon," or peaceful appeal, were Calvinist representatives: William Romaine, Walter Shirley, Thomas Haweis, Henry Venn, John Berridge, Martin Madan, and George Whitefield. Wesley insisted that he was not suggesting a union of opinions, expressions, or church order, and that there would be ample room for disagreement over the absolute decrees, perfection, imputed righteousness, and irregular preaching. He felt, however, that since within their larger common theological framework of the Thirty-Nine Articles, they were all preaching these three evangelical essentials (emphases named above), there were sufficient grounds for some positive accords.

He called upon them not to judge, envy, or speak critically of one another, but rather to love and respect each other, to believe only the good about each other, and to defend one another's character and influence wherever possible. While he admitted that humanly speaking such cooperation was unlikely, he affirmed his faith that "with God all things are possible."[58]

Although Wesley had solicited the support of Lord Dartmouth and Lady Huntingdon for the union, his proposals did not meet with a positive response. While only three recipients replied by correspondence,[59] a dozen attended Wesley's next Conference in Bristol. But instead of moving toward greater cooperation, they protested against the presence of the Methodist preachers in their parishes![60] Nevertheless, Wesley's desire for peace was still undeterred: "The great point I now labored for was a good understanding with all our brethren of the clergy who are heartily engaged in propagating vital religion."[61] By 1769, however, he had abandoned all hope of such a union outside his own connection of traveling preachers. After he reviewed his futile efforts among the clergy, he told the Conference: "I give this up. I can do no more. They are a rope of sand; and such they will continue."[62]

While he was unsuccessful, Wesley's efforts do indicate the theological framework within which he was willing to collaborate. It was a context that included a commitment to the ultimate authority of Scripture and to the theological formulations of the church's understanding of the Bible, as contained in the Articles of Religion. All the men with whom he desired a closer union were as committed to these as Wesley was. Further, there may even be hints that Wesley's "catholic spirit" was narrower than even the Thirty-Nine Articles. The fact that he sought closer cooperation only with those evangelicals who were emphasizing certain distinctives within the framework of the Articles, strongly suggests that limits of his ecclesiastical pluralism may have been much more restricted than has been thought.

What is clear, in any case, is that Wesley was committed only to a kind of theological pluralism that had distinctly marked parameters. And those parameters were not left to chance or vaguely defined as some "marrow of essential truth" without a specific spelling out of what was contained. For Wesley, commitment to the Church of England carried with it an intellectual integrity that meant he was also committed to the church's official position on the primary authority of Scripture and on the Articles of Religion as the essential core of biblical doctrine. Any attempt to use Wesley as a justification for a wider interpretation of pluralism, for a kind of theological latitudinarianism that extends beyond the Bible and a defined statement of scriptural truth like the Articles, must therefore be done without any historical foundation in Methodism. Wesley's comment on the use of the term "catholic spirit" seems unusually apropos to the twenty-first century. "There is scarce any expression which has been more grossly misunderstood, and more dangerously misapplied, than this."[63]

9. The Wesley–Toplady Controversy over Free Will

THE last of the minor controversies related to predestination was between John Wesley and Augustus Toplady. After a review of Toplady's life and the development of his Calvinistic theology, this chapter deals with how Wesley and one of his preachers, Walter Sellon, responded to Toplady's published views on predestination. This was the period when Wesley began openly to espouse the use of the label "Arminian." Then comes a review of the debate over God's sovereignty and human freedom, between Toplady on the one side, and Wesley, with the help of Thomas Olivers and John Fletcher, on the other. A résumé of Toplady's doctrine of predestination is followed by a discussion of his abusive treatment of Wesley in the debate. The Wesley-Toplady controversy must be understood as setting the stage for a proper understanding of the more explosive Minutes controversy of the 1770s.

Augustus Montague Toplady

In the late 1760s, Wesley entered another literary controversy over predestination, this time with the Anglican evangelical hymn writer Augustus Montague Toplady. The son of an army officer, Toplady was born in Farnham, Surrey, on November 4, 1740. After an early education at Westminster School, he moved to Ireland with his mother. At Codymain, County Wexford, in August 1756, he went by chance to a barn to hear the Methodist, James Morris, preach, and he was converted. Shortly thereafter he entered Trinity College, Dublin, and while there began to weigh the evidence between the Calvinistic and Arminian viewpoints.[1]

At first Toplady appeared to lean toward Arminianism. He wrote to Wesley, criticizing Hervey's failure to give proper attention to the passive obedience of Christ:

> I have long been convinced . . . that to insist on the imputation of Christ's righteousness, as alone requisite to salvation, is only strewing the way to hell with flowers. I have myself known some [to] make shipwreck of faith, and love, and a good conscience, on this specious quicksand.[2]

The balance for Toplady eventually tipped toward Calvinism, however, when in the same year he discovered Thomas Manton's "Discourses on John 17." Toplady's growing Calvinism was strongly reinforced by his reading of the hyper-Calvinist John Gill.

In 1762 Toplady was ordained and, after a time in Somersetshire, he became vicar of Broad-Hembury, Devonshire. Three years before his death in 1778, he removed to London for health reasons. There Toplady served as lecturer for the French Calvinistic chapel in Orange Street.[3]

In 1768 six Calvinistic Methodist students were expelled from St. Edmond Hall, Oxford; they were accused of such offenses as attending illicit conventicles, preaching without orders, praying extempore, and associating with known Methodists.[4] In a letter to the vice-chancellor, George Whitefield protested that whatever the pretended cause of the expulsion, it was clear that the actual reason was that "they were either real or reputed Methodists."[5] Richard Hill carried the accusation a step further in his *Pietas Oxoniensis,* charging that the students were dismissed for their Calvinistic views.[6]

When Hill supported this contention with the argument that the official theology of the Church of England was Calvinistic, he was answered by Dr. Thomas Nowell, principal of St. Mary's, Oxford, and a member of the committee that examined the six students. Nowell argued that the doctrines of the Church of England, especially the Thirty-Nine Articles, had been deliberately framed to steer a via media between the Calvinists and the Arminians.[7] The ensuing pamphlet controversy over this incident illustrates the fact that tension existed between the Calvinists and the Arminians, not only within the Methodist ranks, but also within the wider spectrum of Anglicanism.[8]

In 1769 Toplady entered this debate with *The Church of England Vindicated from the Charge of Arminianism.* In this pamphlet he joined issue with Thomas Nowell, not on whether the Calvinistic doctrines were right or wrong, but on whether they were the doctrines of the Church of England. Although Toplady had little interest in the six students, he was outraged at Nowell's assertion that "our Articles have been vindicated from the charge of Calvinism, by Bishop Bull, Dr. Waterland," and others. He labored at length to show that the Calvinistic interpretation of the disputed articles was the proper one, then concluded by asking how Arminians could, with a safe conscience, subscribe to the church's doctrines.[9]

The same year Toplady published *The Doctrine of Absolute Predestination Stated and Asserted,* which in large measure was a translation of a Latin work by Jerome Zanchius. He had received strong encouragement to issue this hyper-Calvinistic work by a personal visit from Dr. John Gill as early as 1760.[10]

Wesley and Arminianism

Wesley was not the only defender of his Arminian convictions. One of his preachers, Walter Sellon, was ordained and appointed to the parish of Ledstone, Yorkshire, by Lady Huntingdon's son.[11] Sellon was encouraged to support Wesley with his pen, and in 1769 he published his *Arguments against the Doctrine of General Redemption Considered.* It was his design to promote the Arminianism of John Goodwin's *Redemption Redeemed* and to defend that work from an attack by Dr. John Owen. Sellon then determined to prepare an answer to *A Practical Discourse on God's Sovereignty,* by Elisha Coles, a clerk of the East India Company.[12] When Wesley wrote to Sellon to encourage this project, he suggested: "Pray add a word to that lively coxcomb Mr. Toplady, not only with regard to Zanchius, but his slander on the Church of England. You would do well to give a reading to both his tracts. He does certainly believe himself to be the greatest genius in England."[13]

Sellon chose to deal with Toplady in a separate work, *The Church of England Vindicated from the Charge of Calvinism.* Toplady commented to a friend:

> The anonymous pamphlet . . . is the production of one Mr. W— S—;
> who was, originally, it seems, a baker by trade: he then became a lay-
> preacher of Mr. W's: and, in process of time, Lady Huntingdon got him
> into orders. She is now extremely sorry that she did so.[14]

Although he did not consider Sellon's "Low Libel" as a "real answer" to his
own "Vindication," Toplady nevertheless desired to make his case stronger. Thus,
he replied in 1774 with *Historic Proof of the Doctrinal Calvinism of the Church of
England,* his most scholarly work. He traced the Calvinistic doctrines through
the history of the church, with special attention to the early English Reformation. He identified Arminianism as "the central point wherein Popery and
Pelagianism meet,"[15] and he endeavored to show that it was not introduced to the
English church until the reign of James I. He supported his case by claiming that
none of the six archbishops that preceded Laud was an Arminian.[16] His sketch of
the Calvinistic tenets of the church down to the present was an elaboration on his
earlier thesis set out in *The Church of England Vindicated from the Charge of
Arminianism.*

While Sellon and Toplady were jousting, Wesley did not remain on the sidelines. Since his enemies had increasingly identified him in print as an Armenian,
Wesley moved to clarify the term with *The Question, What Is An Arminian? Answered.* He gave a short sketch of the life of Jacobus Arminius, professor of divinity at Leyden, in order to show the origin of the word "Arminian." Wesley rejected
the charges that Armenians were to be confused with Arians, or that they denied
original sin and justification by faith. "No man that ever lived, not John Calvin
himself, ever asserted either original or justification by faith in more strong, more
clear and express terms, than Arminius has done."[17]

On the differences between the Calvinists and the Arminians, Wesley pointed
out that the former held to absolute predestination, a limited atonement, irresistible grace, and infallible perseverance; while the latter, by contrast, believed
in conditional predestination, a universal atonement, resistible grace, and a
conditional perseverance. Wesley closed with a plea to preachers of both per-
suasions not to use the words "Calvinist" and "Arminian" as terms of reproach,
"a practice no more consistent with good sense or good manners, than it is with
Christianity."

The Wesley–Toplady Debate over God's Sovereignty and Human Freedom

While Wesley enjoined others to avoid name-calling, he did not on this account desert the field of battle regarding doctrinal issues. In 1770 he published
an abridgement of Toplady's *Absolute Predestination* with his own introductory
and closing paragraphs, designed to place the Calvinistic viewpoint in its most
extreme and unappealing form. Accordingly, he concluded the work:

> The sum of all is this: one in twenty (suppose) of mankind are elected;
> nineteen in twenty are reprobated. The elect shall be saved, do what they
> will; the reprobate shall be damned, do what they can. Reader, believe
> this, or be damned. Witness my hand, A— T—.[18]

Toplady believed Wesley had unfairly and maliciously misrepresented the Calvinistic position, and so he replied with *A Letter to the Rev. Mr. John Wesley: Relative to his Pretended Abridgement of Zanchius on Predestination.* He accused Wesley of not abridging faithfully, of adding interpretations, and of not permitting Zanchius to support his conclusions with evidence. He charged Wesley with falsely coloring the whole "by inserting a sentence or two, now and then, of your own foisting in." He continued his attack:

> You close the motley piece, with an entire paragraph, forged, every word of it, by yourself; and conclude all, as you began, with subjoining the initials of my name; to make the ignorant believe, that the whole, with your omissions, additions, and alterations, actually came from me.—An instance of audacity and falsehood, hardly to be paralleled![19]

After he warned Wesley that forgery was a criminal offense, he asked: "What would you think of me, were I infamous enough to abridge any treatise of yours, sprinkle it with interpolations, and conclude it thus: 'Reader, buy this book, or be damned, witness my hand, John Wesley'?"

Toplady then raised the old accusation that Wesley decided his theological convictions by chance:

> Remember, that it once depended on the toss of a shilling, whether you yourself should be a Calvinist or an Arminian. Tails fell uppermost, and you resolved to be a universalist. It was a happy throw, which consigned you to the tents of Arminius; for it saved us from the company of a man, who, by a kind of religious gambling, peculiarly his own, risked his faith on the most contemptible of all lots: and was capable of tossing up for his creed, as porters or chairmen, toss up for an half penny.[20]

In *The Consequences Proved,* Wesley defended his abridgment, and particularly his concluding paragraph. To the charge that he had unfairly stated the case, and "that no such consequence follows from the doctrine of absolute predestination," he responded: "I calmly affirm, it is a fair state of the case; this consequence does naturally and necessarily follow from the doctrine of absolute predestination, as here stated and defended by bold Mr. Augustus Toplady."[21]

Two extracts from Toplady's translation, Wesley felt, illustrated the whole question: "We assert, that the number of the elect, and also of the reprobate, is so fixed and determinate, that neither can be augmented or diminished." "That the decrees of election and reprobation are immutable and irreversible." He concluded: "From each of these assertions, the whole consequence follows, clear as the noon day sun,—Therefore, 'the elect shall be saved, do what they will; the reprobate shall be damned, do what they can.' "[22]

While Wesley argued the theological issue, he made no effort to defend himself from the accusation that it was both unlawful and unjust to publish his abridgment over Toplady's initials. It was Wesley's long-standing custom, however, to abridge authors so that they might be available at a price the poor could afford. He abridged fairly, at least in his own eyes, and never saw a reason to apologize for the practice. Lawton in his critique of Toplady declared Wesley's tract a bona-fide summary of Zanchius, and he interpreted it as "an attempt, well within the pamphleteering ethics of the period, to wither the young controversialist with ironical logic."[23]

This time Wesley was supported by Thomas Olivers, a Welshman who had been a shoemaker before his conversion under Whitefield.[24] A seasoned assistant who had been preaching for Wesley since 1753, Olivers came to his defense with *A Letter to the Rev. Mr. Toplady, Occasioned by his late Letter to the Rev. Mr. Wesley*. Wesley had published against Toplady, Olivers claimed, because Calvinistic "Antinomianism appears to him to be subversive to the whole power and practice of Religion." "It is certain," Olivers charged, "that your doctrine, and Antinomianism, are inseparable." "Consistent Predestination and Antinomianism are the very same thing."[25] Olivers contended that Wesley had abridged Toplady as he deserved: "He has summed up the whole as you *ought* to have done; but which, you were ashamed of doing." He called Toplady a "wilful liar" for asserting that Wesley decided his creed by the toss of a shilling, and he accused Toplady, not Wesley, of shifting his position:

> It was not many years since you were such an Universalist (yea, and Perfectionist too!) that a certain gentleman could scarce persuade you to give Mr. Whitefield so much as a single hearing. But by a fresh wind of doctrine the weather-cock is now turned from the east to the west.[26]

Toplady was not impressed. He responded in 1771 with *More Work for Mr. John Wesley: on a Vindication of The Decrees and Providence of God, from the Defamations of a Late Printed Paper, Entitled "The Consequence Proved."* He asserted that Wesley was trying "to thunder the Church out of her Calvinism," and he suggested that Wesley's motive for publishing *The Consequence Proved* was financial gain. Toplady dismissed Wesley's defenders: Olivers he described as a "journeyman shoemaker, now retained by Mr. Wesley, as a lay preacher, at the rate of ten pounds per annum." He styled Sellon as Wesley's "bully in chief."

In reply to Wesley's argument, Toplady insisted that the consequence was not proved, for the elect, he declared, "cannot be saved without sanctification and obedience." But there was no danger that the elect would not walk in the paths of holiness. "And why? because God's own decrees secure the means as well as the end, and accomplish the end by the means." Thus, he asserted, "it does not follow, from the doctrine of absolute predestination, that the elect shall be saved, do what they will. On the contrary, they are chosen as much to holiness, as to heaven." Reprobation, on the other hand, was "a thing purely negative: and consists in God not choosing some to glory, and not calling them by grace." Yet, he denied that God was the Author of sin, and then reversed the charge of antinomianism:

> The Arminian scheme, if probed to the bottom, opens, by necessary consequence, the floodgates of practical licentiousness; and with all its pretences to good works, is, in reality, but varnished Antinomianism! It

says, in effect, "Every man shall be saved, do what he will; no man shall be condemned, do what he can."[27]

No reply to Toplady was forthcoming until 1775, when John Fletcher responded on Wesley's behalf. Fletcher described his design: "Never did an Arminian go so near Calvinism: but it is, I hope to give it one of the deepest wounds it ever received. God direct my heart into truth and my pen unto the joints of Calvin's armour!"[28]

His work appeared as *An Answer to the Rev. Mr. Toplady's "Vindication of the Decrees" Etc.,* in which he supported Wesley's summary of Zanchius as the logical deduction for the Calvinistic scheme. Fletcher pointed out that though Toplady contended "that Calvinism insured the holiness of the elect, as the *necessary means* of their predestined salvation," he had failed to mention that this position also insured "the wickedness of the reprobate as the *necessary means* of their predestinated damnation."[29] Fletcher agreed that God was not a debtor to any man, but he insisted that He acted in accord with His own gracious and just nature, and thus He rewarded and punished men equitably. He rejected Toplady's endeavors to reconcile "Calvinian reprobation" with divine justice, for if men were not free agents, God could be neither Rewarder nor Judge.

Fletcher denied that reprobation could be reconciled with God's mercy. He accused Toplady of covering his argument by artfully substituting such phrases as "passing by, not electing, not owing salvation, limiting the display of goodness, not extending mercy infinitely, not enriching, etc.," instead of speaking about an "absolute unconditional dooming" of creatures to "necessary, remediless wickedness" before being consigned to everlasting fire. He argued that the doctrine of free will was more conducive to human sanctity than the concept of necessity because Calvinism confined holiness to the elect and insured "remediless wickedness to all the reprobate." Thus, Fletcher warned his readers not to be so drawn in admiration to "the right leg of Calvinism," i.e., unconditional election, that they overlook "the deformity of the left leg," i.e., unjust reprobation.[30]

Fletcher also cautioned his readers about the Calvinistic assertion, "Whatever is, is Right." Although Toplady called it "the first principle of the Bible and sound reason," Fletcher felt such a deterministic philosophy was a strong encouragement to antinomianism and made the "Calvinian decrees necessarily productive of sin and wickedness." "We desire Mr. T. to show how it could have been right in God to forbid sin by law, to necessitate man to sin by a decree, and to send them into eternal fire for not keeping a law which he had necessitated them to break."[31]

Toplady's Doctrine of Predestination

An important recent find for understanding Toplady's views on predestination is a personal copy of Wesley's *Explanatory Notes on the New Testament* containing marginal notes in Toplady's hand. On the title page he summarized his opinion of Wesley's work: "Oh the spurious word changes, false interpretations, tortured meanings, perverse blunders! . . . The manglings, alteration, distortions of the Word of Life!" Of Toplady's 131 notes in the margin, more than 50 percent were his objections to Wesley's views on predestination. He concluded with a description of Wesley as a "terrifying ogre" who "gives birth to unspeakable heresies and blasphemous conceits."[32] These marginal notes, together with Toplady's published works, make it possible to summarize his doctrine of predestination.

Although Toplady boasted "that from the very commencement of my unworthy ministrations, I have not had a single doctrine to retract, nor a single word to unsay,"[33] there had in fact been a shift in his early theology. Elsewhere he wrote that in 1758 "my Arminian Prejudices received an effectual Shock, in reading Dr. Manton's Sermons."[34] While he was delivered from the "Arminian Snare," he confessed concerning his view previous to this that "there was no more haughty and violent Free-Willer within the compass of the four Seas."[35] Toplady claimed that his new doctrines were based on the twofold authority of the Bible and the Thirty-Nine Articles, with a secondary place given to the Homilies and Liturgy.[36]

Toplady's understanding of God's sovereignty convinced him that the entire work of conversion was of God,[37] and he rejected any conditional election as grounding "the purpose of God on the precarious will of apostate men." The order of salvation he believed to be the following:

1. The eternal sovereignty of God, on which His decrees are founded.

2. Election; or designation of those He pleased to receive life.

3. Effectual calling, whereby the elect sinner is made to see his lost state by nature, and becomes desirous of redemption by Christ.

4. Faith, whereby God enables one to lay hold on Christ's righteousness in order to justification.

5. Holiness, whereby the sinner, so justified, runs the way of God's commandments with joy, diligence, and zeal.

6. Perseverance in faith, love, and holiness: and which is the crown of all.

7. Everlasting glory in the kingdom of the blessed God.[38]

Toplady vacillated between the supralapsarian and the sublapsarian view of election. Although he claimed to be a sublapsarian, he maintained that the Fall of man had been positively decreed by God.[39] By the same divine decrees, the elect were eternally secured: "Grace was given with them in Christ, before the world began: they were in the Divine Purposes, Sons from Eternity." He emphasized that "they are not Sons because they have the Spirit, but have the Spirit because they are Sons."[40] He agreed that his view of eternal election required a corresponding position on reprobation: "Election, without reprobation, cannot stand: it must have the other leg, or it will tumble down."[41] Accordingly, he maintained that unbelief was "not the *cause,* but one of the effects of reprobation. They were not endued with faith because . . . they were not by divine decree given to him from eternity."[42]

Though Toplady believed that Christ's death was the perfect satisfaction for sin, he limited its efficacy to the elect.[43] Any effort by men to obtain their salvation, he dismissed as an attempt at justification by works, and he rejected the Arminian proposal of an election grounded on God's foreknowledge of faith and/or good works. "The elect are not ordained to eternal life because they believed, but believed because they were ordained to eternal life."[44] Salvation involved a reciprocal imputation of Christ's righteousness for man's sins. "All that Christ is, is His people's. There is a happy exchange of interests: their debts, with the consequences thereof, are devolved on Him, and all that is His is *imputed* and *communicated* to them."[45]

Toplady tried to guard against antinomianism by asserting that absolute election destroyed the "merit of our works and obedience, but not the performance of them."[46] He contended that since there was "an *inviolable,* indissoluble connection between the means and the end," there could be no divorce of unconditional election and obedience to the moral law. This view rested on his conviction that faith and holiness were not conditions but the fruits of election."[47] Antinomianism, he maintained, was "as contrary to sound doctrine, as it is to sound morals."[48]

While he allowed that listeners could reject the "gospel of grace," he insisted that the "grace of the gospel" was irresistible. Effectual grace was not only irresistible; there was no possibility of falling from it.[49] It is as impossible for a true believer not to persevere in the ways of God, as for Christ Himself to come down and bleed again. Toplady grounded this position on the changelessness of the divine decree, the immutability of the divine promises, and the efficacy of regenerating grace. He summarized his commitment to unconditional perseverance:

> From whence we may infallibly conclude, that not a single person, who was ever, by true faith, united to Christ, can possibly by making shipwreck of faith draw back into perdition; and that all whom Christ will condemn at the last day, *never* had a saving interest in Him.[50]

In the earlier years of his ministry, Toplady had concentrated his preaching upon justification by faith and personal holiness, believing these were sufficient to convey a clear idea of salvation by grace. He discovered, however, that while many hearers were pleased, few were converted. When he began to emphasize predestination, on the other hand, he found that although many grew very angry, three people were converted to every one under the earlier plan.[51] While this provides some explanation for Toplady's major emphasis upon predestination in both his preaching and writing, it does little to justify the temper in which he advocated his cause.

Toplady's Treatment of Wesley in the Debate

Two factors in particular make it difficult to account for Toplady's abusive treatment of Wesley throughout their controversy. First, as a university student Toplady apparently had a warm and congenial relationship with Wesley.[52] This may have owed something to his conversion under one of Wesley's preachers. Second, his diary reveals a conscientious endeavor to fulfill the calling of an evangelical pastor.[53] Yet his language and temper in debate were frequently scurrilous and at times vitriolic. Even his remarks outside the direct controversy expressed a heated spirit on his part. He wrote of Wesley to a friend in 1773:

> Abstracted from all warmth, and from all prejudice, I believe him to be the most rancorous hater of the gospel-system, that ever appeared in this island. I except not Pelagius himself. The latter had some remains of modesty; and preserved . . . some appearances of decency: but the former has outlived all pre tension to both.[54]

Tyerman evaluated Toplady's controversial writings, as well as his work as editor of the *Gospel Magazine*. He concluded that Toplady's "abuse of Wesley is rancorous to a degree almost without parallel, and is expressed in terms far more nearly allied to the slang of Billingsgate than to the language of a Christian and a gentleman."[55] Even his biographer admitted that most of Toplady's writings had "a controversial air, calculated, in the first instance, to repel, rather than to attract the attention of those readers, who wish to be followers equally of peace and truth."[56] Nor were his attacks on Wesley confined to the question of predestination. He accused Wesley of unethical conduct in his requests that the Greek bishop Erasmus ordain certain of his lay preachers,[57] and he also published a tract to refute Wesley's views on perception.[58] Lastly, in *An Old Fox Tarred and Feathered,* he challenged Wesley's honesty, calling him a plagiarist because Wesley had borrowed almost the whole of Dr. Samuel Johnson's *Taxation No Tyranny* and republished it under his own name as *A Calm Address to Our American Colonies.*[59] Toplady explained his behavior:

> Mr. John Wesley is the only opponent I ever had, whom I chastised with a studious disregard to ceremony. Nor do I, in the least, repent of the manner in which I treated him. To have refuted the forgeries and perversion of such an assailant, tenderly, and with meekness falsely so called, would have been like shooting at an highwayman with a pop-gun, or like repelling the sword of an assassin with a straw. I rather blame myself, on a review, for handling Mr. Wesley too gently; . . . I only gave him the whip, when he deserved a scorpion.[60]

Apparently, it was Toplady's excessive zeal for what he believed to be essential Christian truth that caused him to overstep the bounds of Christian courtesy. Another aspect of his character is seen, however, in the publication of his *Scheme of Philosophical Necessity*. While this work was at the printers, Toplady heard a rumor that Wesley had died in Ireland, and he immediately requested his London publishers to suppress the work until he could recast it so as to leave out all references to his old antagonist.[61] Toplady's conduct must also be interpreted in the light of his chronic poor health, which most certainly aggravated his already sensitive feelings, as well as his long-standing grudge against Wesley for his abridgment of Zanchius.

On the other side, Charles Wesley confided to James Hutton in 1778 that he had never heard his brother "speak one unkind word of Mr. Hill or Mr. Toplady."[62] This was probably an overstatement in light of Wesley's comments to George Merryweather: "Mr. Augustus Toplady I know well. But I do not fight with chimney-sweepers. He is too dirty a writer for me to meddle with. I should only foul my fingers."[63] Yet, a comparison of the language and attitudes in the two men's writings unquestionably reveals Wesley to be far more gracious and charitable than his adversary.

While Toplady lay dying in London in 1778, a rumor circulated that he had renounced his Calvinistic views and wished to apologize personally to Wesley for some of his harsher writings. Against the advice of his doctors, he dragged himself for the last time into the pulpit to deny the assertions:

> So certain and so satisfied am I, of the truth of all that I have written; that, were I now sitting up in my dying bed, with pen and ink in my hand, and all the religious and controversial writing I ever published (more especially those relating to Mr. John Wesley, and the Arminian Controversy), whether respecting facts or doctrines, could at once be displayed to view, I should not strike out a single line relative to him or them.[64]

Thus, to the very end of his life, Toplady held to his doctrinal convictions, and he declined to show regret for the manner in which he had propagated them.

After the initial outbreak of controversy over election and final perseverance in 1739–41, Wesley proceeded over the next dozen years to produce his major written contributions to the debate. With his *Predestination Calmly Considered,* Wesley summarized his own position, a position that remained basically the same thereafter. In this work he concentrated his attack on the interconnected doctrines of election, reprobation, limited atonement, irresistible grace, and final perseverance. The center of controversy shifted somewhat in Wesley's exchange with James Hervey, focusing upon the issue of imputed righteousness. The question of whether the theology of the Church of England was Calvinistic or Arminian was raised by the expulsion of the six students from Oxford.

Last, in the somewhat melodramatic confrontation between Toplady and Wesley, the subject of God's sovereignty and man's free will occupied the center of the stage. All of these issues produced a permanent tension between the two theological camps of the revival that finally erupted in the Minutes controversy (see part 3, below) of the 1770s. Yet Wesley's differences with Toplady over free will served in a special way as a preview of the longer Minutes conflict.

Toplady accepted the necessity of all events. Still, he believed that predestination did not destroy, but rather coincided with, the free will of man. By contrast, Wesley felt that human liberty was essential to maintain moral accountability and to avoid a fatalistic antinomianism. Toplady attempted to disclaim antinomian tendencies by positing the predestination of "secondary causes." But Wesley insisted, as he had since 1739, that the inevitable practical consequences of unconditional election and final perseverance was antinomianism.

Conversely, Toplady believed that Wesley's universal free will, coupled with conditional salvation, was the essence of Pelagianism. He failed to recognize how the concept of prevenient grace rescued Wesley from the charge of giving God's glory to man.[65] This conflict with Toplady, perhaps more than any of the other doctrinal conflicts, sharpened Wesley's theological sensitivities to the deterministic aspect of Calvinism. It strengthened his resolve to combat any antinomian tendencies that might arise from that theological system.

PART III:

THE MINUTE CONTROVERSY, 1770–1778

Wesley and Fletcher
vs.
the Countess of Huntingdon

10. The Attack on Wesley's 1770 Conference Minutes

THE last and most disruptive of the controversies over predestination arose in conjunction with the Minutes of Wesley's 1770 Conference with his preachers. To properly understand the context as well as the controversy itself, we must examine the role of several key leaders in the revival. Two of the most important leaders were the Countess of Huntingdon and John Fletcher. Of particular significance was Fletcher's willingness to serve as the first president of the Countess' training College for preachers at Trevecka.

The intertwining of these lives with the Wesleys, and with the whole eighteenth-century revival, sets the stage for what happened at the 1770 Conference. The reaction to the Conference Minutes over the following year is reviewed in some detail, as is the Calvinists' confrontation of Wesley and his preachers at the 1771 Conference. The literary side of the controversy then springs up with Wesley's publication of John Fletcher's *Vindication of Mr. Wesley's Minutes*, later known as *The First Check to Antinomianism*. Finally, after having walked through the various events related to the controversy, attention will be given to its underlying causes.

The Countess of Huntingdon's Role in the Revival

The most prominent controversy of the eighteenth-century revival was over the Minutes of Wesley's 1770 Conference. In this conflict the fierce winds of contention blew across the smoldering coals of theological disagreement and fanned them into a blazing bonfire, scorching both the Calvinists and the Arminians. One historian wrote: "Over Whitefield's ashes the fire of the great Calvinistic controversy was rekindled, and burned more fiercely even than at first; perhaps for the reason that this time there was a woman in it!"[1] The woman was Selina, Countess of Huntingdon, whose lifetime spanned most of the eighteenth century (1707–92), almost half of which she served as a leader of the Calvinistic Methodists.[2]

Selina Shirley was born into the family of Washington Shirley, second Earl Ferrers. In June 1728 she married Theophilus, the ninth Earl of Huntingdon. Her sister-in-law, Lady Margaret Hastings, had been influenced by the preaching of Benjamin Ingham, whom she later married. Lady Margaret was the one who first brought Selina into contact with the Methodists. Apparently, Lady Huntingdon's conversion took place around 1738, when she joined the society at Fetter Lane.[3] Although her husband did not fully share her views, he attended meetings with her and opened their drawing rooms to Methodist preaching for the upper classes. The Earl died in 1746, leaving the bulk of his fortune to his widow, who during her lifetime reputedly spent more than $100,000 promoting the cause of the revival.[4]

From the earliest days of the revival, Lady Huntingdon was associated with the Wesleys. She accompanied John Wesley when he separated from the Moravian society at Fetter Lane in 1740, and then helped to guard Charles Wesley from their doctrine of "stillness." At Wesley's first Conference, the Countess entertained the preachers at her London home, No. 13 Downing Street. She also corrected early extracts of Wesley's Journal, dispatched her servants John and David Taylor as Wesley's traveling companions, and attended his mother, Susannah, on her deathbed.[5] Throughout her lifetime, her relations with Charles Wesley were even closer than those with his brother.[6] She nursed his wife, Sally, through an illness of smallpox, and in 1765 the Charles Wesleys, out of respect for the Countess, named their third daughter Selina.[7]

Lady Huntingdon's early views on the issues that divided the Calvinists and the Arminians are not clear. Apparently she was initially committed to Christian perfection. Thus she wrote to Wesley that by this doctrine "I hope to live and die," and she warmly recommended his sermon on the subject.[8] In light of her later hostility to the doctrine, however, one may question whether her understanding of the subject was the same as Wesley's. Her commitment to the particular doctrines of Calvinism probably occurred about 1748. In that year she made George Whitefield one of her chaplains, and the increased contacts may have heightened her interest in Whitefield's Calvinism. On the other hand, she had earlier experienced ample contact with Whitefield, and perhaps she appointed him partly because of his theological emphasis.[9] Another factor points to the late forties, however, as the time when the Countess more strongly embraced Calvinism. During that period she became personally acquainted with the hyper-Calvinist Dr. John Gill and was impressed by his three-volume *Commentary on the New Testament*.[10]

To further the work of the revival, Lady Huntingdon exercised the prerogative of nobility and appointed a number of domestic chaplains to preach to elite congregations in her private apartments.[11] In the 1760s the Countess extended this outreach by building a number of proprietary chapels throughout the country. Since Lady Huntingdon heavily subsidized both the chapels and their preachers, it became natural for her to retain oversight of the work. The result was the formation of the Countess of Huntingdon's Connection. At first it was largely staffed by Anglican clergymen, but later it contained a high proportion of lay preachers and students. Although the Countess' Connection remained distinct from both Whitefield's Connection and the Welsh Calvinistic Methodists, the three Connections maintained close relationships, and there was a considerable interchange of preachers among them.[12]

The relations between the Countess' circle and the Wesleys remained cordial throughout the 1750s and 1760s. At Wesley's 1762 Conference at Leeds, Lady Huntingdon and Whitefield were present, as were Romaine, Madan, and Venn.

At the close of the decade, Wesley could write to the Countess, rejoicing that she held to the "plain, old simple, unfashionable gospel."[13] In 1768 the Wesleys moved into a closer alliance with Lady Huntingdon and George Whitefield, which gave them access to her chapels. Wesley reciprocated by offering to share his meetinghouses with the Countess' preachers.[14]

In spite of this collaboration, there was a distance between them. To Howel Harris, the Countess spoke of Wesley "as an Eel, no hold of him and not come to the truth."[15] Wesley expostulated that though Whitefield, Romaine, Madan, Berridge, and Haweis preached numerous times at Lady Huntingdon's home, no more notice was "taken of my brother and me, as of a couple of postilions." Wesley attributed this to his style of preaching as well as its content:

> It only confirmed me in the Judgement I had formed for many years, I am too rough a Preacher for tender Ears. "No, that is not it: but you preach Perfection." What! Without why or wherefore? Among the unawakened? Among Babes in Christ? No. To these I say not a word about it. I have two or three grains of Common Sense. If I do not know how to suit my Discourse to my Audience at these years, I ought never to preach more.[16]

The central point of contention before 1770 was clearly Wesley's doctrine of Christian perfection. In spite of the Countess' early interest in the doctrine, she accused Wesley of preaching perfection instead of Christ because the Moravian concentration on Christ had forced him to find a distinctive doctrine of his own.[17] Her opposition was so strong that Wesley warned Joseph Benson:

> I assure you [that] you must not even mutter before her anything of *deliverance from all sin. Error Errorum*, as Count Zinzendorf says; "heresy of heresies." "I will suffer no one in my Society that even *thinks* of perfection."[18]

If John was hesitant to broach the subject, Charles Wesley was bolder and pressed the Countess to go on to perfection:

> For though our extravagances and blunders have almost frightened many serious Christians out of the use of that scriptural word Perfection, you cannot help longing and following *hard* after *the thing*. Nay you carry your hopes much farther and higher than our Perfectionists.[19]

To further the work of revival in winter 1767, Lady Huntingdon began planning a theological College to train candidates for the Christian ministry.[20] As early as 1763, Howel Harris had dreamed of such an academy for young preachers.[21] From his brother, Thomas Harris, the Countess acquired property for the College at Trevecka in Talgarth, South Wales.[22] She proposed to admit only converted young men who had dedicated themselves to Christian service. These might study for three years before they entered the ministry of either the Church of England or another Protestant denomination. So long as they remained at Trevecka, they gratuitously received their education plus board, lodging, and clothes.[23] On Lady Huntingdon's birthday, August 24, 1768, the College, with about sixteen students, was opened under the preaching of George Whitefield. John Wesley was also invited to attend the dedication and promised to do so along with his brother. Apparently affairs at the Conference meeting in Bristol earlier in the month forced him to change his plans and travel to Cornwall.[24]

John Fletcher and the First Methodist Training College

Lady Huntingdon chose John Fletcher to be head of the new College.[25] Born at Nyon, Switzerland, in 1729, Fletcher, whose original Swiss name was Jean Guillaume de la Flechere, came from a prominent upper-class family. Although as a boy he had experienced the forgiveness of God, it was not until he was about sixteen that he began "to strive in earnest to grow in holiness," and he recalled that "for eight months I walked as became a follower of Christ."[26] On being admitted to the University of Geneva to study classics, philosophy, and theology, he sought to find other Christians with whom he could have fellowship:

> I at last met with three students who formed with me a religious society: we met as often as we could to confess to one another our sins, to exhort, read and pray, and we would perhaps have been what the Methodists were at Oxford, had not one of us been led away by a Deist.[27]

From Geneva, Fletcher moved to Lentzbourg so he could learn German and study the art of military fortification. When he returned home to master Hebrew and work on mathematics,[28] his parents pressed him to become a clergyman. Although from childhood he had desired to serve God, he objected that he was unworthy of the task. He felt disgusted that he would have to subscribe to the doctrine of predestination in order to secure ordination by the Swiss Church.[29] When the Swiss laughed at him because he had no interest in "diversions of the world," he set out for Lisbon. There, in spite of certain doubts in his conscience, he accepted a captain's commission to serve with the Portuguese army in Brazil. While he was waiting to sail, a maid who brought his breakfast dropped a teakettle and so scalded his leg that he was confined to bed. During his convalescence his ship sailed and was never heard of again. Fletcher remarked: "He that will not turn at a check from God's Spirit must turn at the stroke of his rod."[30]

After abandoning his hopes for a military career, Fletcher traveled to Britain to learn English and soon became tutor to the sons of Thomas Hill, a member of Parliament for Shropshire. On a journey to London, while the Hills were drinking tea in an inn, Fletcher wandered about the village and met an old woman whose conversation was so pleasant that he forgot the hour and was left behind by the Hills. Taking a horse, he soon rejoined the family and explained his absence, whereupon Mrs. Hill remarked: "Don't go talking so to old women: people will say that we have got a Methodist preacher with us." Fletcher recalled: "I asked her what she meant by a Methodist, and when she told me I said that I would be one of them if there was such a people in England."[31]

On another visit to London the following winter, he inquired about the Methodists and came to the West Street Chapel, where he began to meet with Richard Edward's class regularly when in town. While searching for saving faith, Fletcher revealed in his diary that he was already convinced of the universal atonement of Christ: "Christ died for *all*, thought I; then he died for *me*; and, as I sincerely desire to be His, He will surely take me to Himself. He will surely let me know before I die that He died for me."[32] Within a few weeks he recorded his conversion experience: "As I was in prayer at one o'clock in the morning I was enabled to cast myself upon Christ so as to have peace, assurance, and power over sin."[33]

After consultation with Wesley, Fletcher was ordained in March 1757. He immediately hastened to Snowfields Chapel in order to aid Wesley in a great sacramental service, and for the next three years he continued to assist Wesley when he was in London with the Hill family for the sitting of Parliament. Fletcher spent the remainder of his time at Tern Hall, Shropshire, where he continued as tutor with the Hill family. When Thomas Hill's sons went up to Cambridge, Hill offered to name Fletcher to the parish church at Dunham at a stipend of £400 per annum. Fletcher declined on the grounds that it was too much money and too little labor. A smaller appointment in the village of Madeley was then suggested (with less than half the income of Dunham), and Fletcher accepted the more difficult parish. On the Shrewsbury racecourse, Hill arranged for his nephew to appoint Fletcher. Thus, over the strong objections of Wesley, Fletcher commenced his ministry at Madeley in October 1760. It lasted for twenty-five years.[34]

After both Whitefield and Charles Wesley had highly recommended Fletcher to Lady Huntingdon, John Wesley introduced him to her in 1758. The following year she invited him to preach and administer the sacrament in her home. Later she joined him at Everton to witness the beginning of revival under the ministry of John Berridge.[35] Over the following decade their mutual esteem and frequent correspondence made it no surprise that Lady Huntingdon should ask Fletcher to assume the leadership of her new College in 1767.

Before the College opened, Fletcher actively participated in the preparation by recommending candidates, selecting titles for the library, and planning the courses to be offered with Howel Harris.[36] Though he was not permanently in residence because of his parish responsibilities in Madeley, he frequently visited Trevecka and was received by students as "an angel of God, like Elijah in the schools of the prophets." Joseph Benson declared that when Fletcher appeared, the students laid aside all other pursuits while he spoke to them and "they seldom harkened long, before they were all in tears, and every heart catched fire from the flame that burned in his soul."[37] He was convinced that to be filled with the Holy Spirit was a far better qualification for the ministry than any classical learning. After preaching, Fletcher would often say: "As many of you as are athirst for this fulness of the Spirit, follow me into my room." Upon that invitation, the students often crowded into his quarters for two or three hours of prayer and waiting upon God.

Another indicator of Fletcher's influence is seen in his direction of an outbreak of revival in the early days of the College. Less than three months after the College opened, Fletcher arrived on a visit to find the spiritual life of the students at a very low level. He complained about this to the Countess:

> All here wore a melancholy aspect as to spiritual things. A round of duties and a form of godliness distinguish'd us from a worldly academy, and that was all. A spirit of levity, irony and trifling sat in the temple of God, and the humble broken wrestling spirit of prayer had disappeared. I was almost carried away by the force of the stream, & wish'd myself away.[38]

Fletcher told the students that if things continued at such a "poor trifling formal rate," he would recommend that Lady Huntingdon pick out a half dozen of the most earnest, and send the rest about their business. The students responded with genuine sorrow and, at their request, the following Wednesday was set apart as a day of fasting and humiliation. On Monday, however, while Fletcher was at his noonday hour of prayer, a student named Hull came to his room in anguish over his sins. Fletcher said, "I put him upon praying and believing, and after complaining to the Lord he could do neither and attempting to do both with great agony for about an hour, the Lord set him at liberty." After a time of praise, Hull cried out, "Lord, send me to the ends of the world or to the stake, if thou wilt, but give me to bring one soul unto thee."[39]

After a further hour of praise and intercession for the College, they went to the other students, some of whom were soon on their knees and praying. Later in the afternoon, Fletcher stood at the foot of a staircase with a group who overheard Hull and another student, on the floor above them, entreating God to awaken other hearts. Fletcher described the occasion:

> We could hear Joshua and Caleb thus praying for their prayerless Brethren. When shame had covered their faces I took them to my room and we began to pray also. By and by one and another of the students came in and to us. About 8 o'clock our hearts were greatly enlarged and we found *Power Power* coming upon us and loosing us from earth & self.[40]

After other students had joined them, they prayed what Fletcher felt was a prayer of humiliation and faith. "We were in the dark," he recalled, "but we needed no candle not so much as to give out hymns, admirably proper verses being given to one or another of the young men to give out in the interest of prayer."[41] In the midst of this, the maid stole into the room, and when the others departed, "she began to pour out her complaints of being tempted, dry and forgotten in the midst of the general shower." Fletcher prayed with her "for about an hour more when the Lord set her at liberty also and turned her mourning into the greatest transports of joy & love."

Tuesday morning the hymns and prayers of students awakened Fletcher, and that evening they met with Howel Harris for two or three hours of prayer. Wednesday was to be a fast day, but Fletcher described it as rather a day of feast! At six in the morning, they met with Howel Harris' people for two hours of prayer and singing. From nine to eleven-thirty, they gathered by themselves to hear one student preach, and many shared a word of exhortation. Then at noon they solemnly dedicated themselves afresh to the Lord. By early afternoon some had experienced "as much devotion as their fasting bodies could bear, and those who chose it went to get some refreshment." Because Fletcher feared breaking "old bottles with new wine," he determined to avoid further afternoon devotions, but the sound of two students at prayer drew all the rest together:

> We had a good time thanks be to our good Lord. He took off weariness from the young men & gave them to feel the service of God may be

perfect freedom. The door of intercession was open to us, and strength was given to pray round and enter in at the opening.[42]

Fletcher felt that, throughout the time, "enthusiasm" or fanaticism was kept down, and he feared the students would "fall rather by carelessness than by too much warmth." He concluded his evaluation to Lady Huntingdon by saying:

> We have often prayed that this might not be a flash but a spark before a fire, and I hope that he who quenches not the smoking flax will not quench us. This little revival hath been wrought without any preaching and at a time when a violent cold disabled me from speaking and striking in with the Holy Spirit's influences. The effects of it are a love to prayer, an end of divisions, a degree of zeal for God, brotherly kindness and watchfulness, and an apparent concern for souls & victory over flesh and blood.[43]

Apprehensive about Fletcher's close relations with the Countess of Huntingdon's circle, Wesley wrote Fletcher a long letter in March 1768 about his comment that he was "sick" of conversation with many who professed religion:

> I do not wonder at it at all, especially considering with whom you have chiefly conversed for some time past—namely, the hearers of Mr. Madan and Mr. Romaine (perhaps I might add of Mr. Whitefield). The conversing with these I have rarely found to be profitable to my soul.[44]

Wesley complained that the fruits of self-denial, patience, love, and inward and outward devotion to God could not be expected from either antinomian views or the doctrines of absolute decrees, irresistible grace, or infallible perseverance. He believed a strong emphasis on holiness and perfection was needed to protect the doctrine of salvation by faith from antinomianism:

> I seldom find it profitable for *me* to converse with any who are not athirst for perfection and who are not big with earnest expectation of receiving it every moment. Now, you find none of these among those we are speaking of, but many, on the contrary, who are in various ways directly or indirectly opposing the whole work of God.[45]

These "genteel Methodists," he wrote, "are (almost all) salt that has lost its savour, if ever they had any. They are thoroughly conformed to the maxims, the spirit, the fashions and the customs of the world." Yet he grudgingly admitted of some Calvinists: "It is undeniable these quacks cure whom we cannot cure. . . . God works by them, and has done so, for near thirty years. Therefore the opposing them is neither better nor worse than fighting against God."

Unfortunately, Fletcher communicated the contents of the letter to Lady Huntingdon, who reacted to a friend:

> You will not be much surprised to hear that dear Mr. Fletcher has been severely reprimanded for endeavoring to maintain peace and unanimity

in the household of God. His preaching so frequently for me and dear Mr. Whitefield, and mixing so much with those who have been sneeringly and contemptuously termed "the genteel Methodists," are considered great offences, and highly injurious to the cultivation of the life and spirit of the soul.[46]

Although she commended Fletcher for resisting the "violent attack," her personal relationship with Wesley clearly suffered over the incident.

Wesley also feared for the future of the College, and he asked in a letter to Charles: "Did you ever see anything more queer than their plan of institution? Pray who penned it, man or woman?"[47] The problem, he felt, was too much involvement on the part of the Countess. He declared, "Trevecka is much more to Lady Huntingdon than Kingswood is to me. It mixes with everything. It is *my* College, *my* masters, *my* students."[48] Clearly, the rupture between the Calvinists and the Arminians in 1770 must be understood against this background of serious personal conflicts.

Wesley's apprehension about the College did not prevent him from contributing to the enterprise. On the first anniversary of the College, Lady Huntingdon planned the celebration as a spiritual retreat, and Wesley attended with Fletcher, Howel Harris, Daniel Rowlands, William Williams, Howell Davies, Peter Williams, and Walter Shirley. Wesley and the other clergymen shared the preaching, the administration of the sacrament, and a love feast. Lady Huntingdon remembered this retreat as a time of "copious showers of Divine blessing."[49]

The first Master of the College was a young man named Williams. Williams' amorous involvement with the College housekeeper, Hannah Bowen, and with Howel Harris' daughter Betty, led to Fletcher's recommendation that he be replaced. Thus, in September 1769, the Countess discharged him along with the housekeeper. Upon learning that the College lacked its principal teacher, Wesley recommended that Joseph Benson be appointed.[50] Benson, only twenty-two years of age, had served four years as a classical master at Wesley's school at Kingswood, and he was currently studying at Oxford.[51] After a short visit in January 1770, he took up residence in the spring and was at first described by Howel Harris as "simple." After he heard Benson preach, however, Harris changed his mind and declared the sermon to be "one of the best discourses I ever heard."[52]

Although Wesley had warned him against doing so, Benson wrote a paper on the baptism of the Holy Ghost. Following Fletcher, he connected it with Wesley's doctrine of Christian perfection.[53] Benson also objected to some of Howel Harris' views and opposed him on perseverance. All of the agitation, however, did not come from one side. Fletcher noted that in numbers of students, the Calvinists held a three-to-one edge at the College. He wrote to Walter Sellon that while these led some disputes, "when the power of God comes they drop them."[54]

The Outbreak of the Controversy over the 1770 Conference Minutes

Wesley was concerned about the loss of momentum in the Evangelical revival. When he met with his preachers in August 1770, they discussed what could be done to revive the work where it had decayed. They agreed upon ten methods to promote the work; one was the final proposal that greater care should be given to the matter of doctrine. This section of the Minutes of the Conference, which became the center of heated controversy over the next several years, began with the admonition, "Take heed to your doctrine," and continued:

> We said in 1744, "We have leaned too much toward Calvinism." Wherein?
>
> (1) With regard to man's faithfulness. Our Lord himself taught us to use the expression: Therefore we ought never to be ashamed of it. We ought steadily to assert upon his authority, that if a man is not "faithful in the unrighteous mammon, God will not give him the true riches."
>
> (2) With regard to "working for life," which our Lord expressly commands us to do. "Labour," ἐργάξεσθε, literally, "work, for the meat that endureth to everlasting life." And in fact, every believer, till he comes to glory, works for as well as from life.
>
> (3) We have received it as a maxim, that "a man is to do nothing in order to justification." Nothing can be more false. Whoever desires to find favour with God, should "cease from evil, and learn to do well." So God himself teaches by the Prophet Isaiah. Whoever repents, should "do works meet for repentance." And if this is not in order to find favour, what does he do them for?
>
> Once more review the whole affair:
>
> (1) Who of us is now accepted of God?
>
> He that now believes in Christ with a loving obedient heart.
>
> (2) But who among those that never heard of Christ?
>
> He that, according to the light he had, "feareth God and worketh righteousness."
>
> (3) Is this the same with "he that is sincere"?
>
> Nearly, if not quite.

(4)   Is not this salvation by works?

Not by the merit of works, but by works as a condition.

(5)   What have we then been disputing about for these thirty years?

I am afraid about words, namely, in some of the foregoing instances.

(6)   As to merit itself, of which we have been so dreadfully afraid: We are rewarded according to our works, yea, because of our works. How does this differ from, "for the sake of our works?" And how differs this from *secundum merita operum*? which is no more than, "as our works deserve." Can you split this hair? I doubt I cannot.

(7)   The grand objection to one of the preceding propositions is drawn from matter of fact. God does in fact justify those who, by their own confession, neither "feared God" nor "wrought righteousness." Is this an exception to the general rule?

It is a doubt whether God makes any exception at all. But how are we sure that the person in question never did fear God and work righteousness? His own thinking so is no proof. For we know how all that are convinced of sin undervalue themselves in every respect.

(8)   Does not talking, without proper caution, of a justified or sanctified state, tend to mislead men; almost naturally leading them to trust in what was done in one moment? Whereas we are every moment pleasing or displeasing to God, according to our works; according to the whole of our present inward tempers and outward behaviour.[55]

After thus motivating his preachers, Wesley set out for Bristol, where he expected to join Lady Huntingdon, Walter Shirley, and Henry Venn. He had planned on accompanying them to Trevecka for the second anniversary of the College. A copy of the Conference Minutes, however, reached the Countess before Wesley arrived, and her objections to their doctrinal content were so vigorous that she wrote, informing Wesley that he was to be excluded from her pulpits as long as he held these views. Wesley was unperturbed and calmly set off for Cornwall. Fletcher, however, was present for the anniversary celebration and enjoyed a rich time of fellowship among the Calvinistic leaders. Meanwhile, Charles Wesley had met Lady Huntingdon upon her return to

Bristol, and after journeying with her to Bath, preached several times in her chapel.[56]

In spite of this rebuff, John Wesley could still speak of Lady Huntingdon as one "much devoted to God" and with "a thousand valuable and admirable qualities." Yet, for some time he had felt the need of candidly expressing himself to Lady Huntingdon, and so wrote her a long letter. He described that epistle to Joseph Benson:

> For several years I had been deeply convinced that I had not done my duty with regard to that valuable woman; that I had not told her what I was thoroughly assured no one else would dare to do, and what I knew she would bear from no other person, but possibly might bear from me. . . . So I at once delivered my own soul, by telling her all that was in my heart. It was my business, my proper business, so to do, as none else could or would do. Neither did I take at all too much upon me; I know the office of a christian minister. If she is not profited, it is her own fault, not mine; I have done my duty. I do not know there is one charge in that letter which was either unjust, unimportant, or aggravated.[57]

The following month, after reviewing his remarks again, he still felt he had spoken the truth in love. But others evaluated Wesley's letter somewhat differently. Howel Harris described it as "very bitter, charging her with self and being fallen to pride from the Lord."[58] When the Countess' cousin, Walter Shirley, learned of it, he wrote: "Though I had before a too well-grounded conviction of Mr. Wesley's Pride and Self-sufficiency, I never could have conceived he would have carried it to so immoderate a Pitch as has appeared in the last letter he wrote your Ladyship."[59]

Apart from the personal element, opposition to the Minutes centered on the conviction that Wesley had espoused a doctrine of salvation by works. At Whitefield's memorial service in November, Wesley attempted to allay those fears. He reminded a predominantly Calvinist congregation that from the earliest days he and Whitefield had been one in their commitment to justification by faith alone, and that their "grand principle was, There is *no* power (by nature) and no *merit* in man." Wesley emphasized his point by declaring that he and Whitefield had insisted that "all power to think, speak, or act aright, is in and from the Spirit of Christ; and all merit is (not in man, how high soever in grace, but merely) in the blood of Christ." "There is no power in man," he reiterated, "till it is given him from above, to do one good work, to speak one good word, or to form one good desire."[60] It became apparent, however, that Wesley's effort to remove any misunderstandings was unsuccessful; the *Gospel Magazine*, edited by William Romaine, launched a series of attacks on him during the first half of 1771.[61]

With the publication of the Conference Minutes in the autumn of 1770, Joseph Benson found himself embroiled in a heated debate at Trevecka. His defense of Wesley and his strong commitment to perfection raised the accusation of legalism against him. Wesley encouraged him to speak his mind, but cautioned him to do it with "all tenderness and respect." He reinforced Benson's view of the intimate connection between perfect love and real Christian liberty. To the charge of legalism, Wesley replied: "I find no such sin as legality in the Bible: the very use of the term speaks an Antinomian. I defy all liberty but liberty to love and serve God, and fear no bondage but bondage to sin."[62]

Another figure who played an important part in the controversy was Lady Huntingdon's cousin, Walter Shirley. Shirley was rector in Loughrea, Ireland, where, as an unconverted clergyman, he kept a pack of hounds and was known as the promoter of every amusement in the parish. It was not uncommon for him to enter the pulpit booted and spurred, with the dogs waiting outside the town, so that at the close of the service the hunt could proceed. His conversion in May 1758 brought an end to this style of life. He sold his dogs and racehorses as he began the serious work of an evangelical pastor.[63] Shirley soon entered into a warm correspondence with both John and Charles Wesley[64] and rejoiced with them at the news of Fletcher's appointment to Madeley.[65] When they met in Bath, Shirley gratefully accepted Charles' counsel that he cease using a written discourse from the pulpit.[66] In 1760 Shirley wrote, hoping that both brothers would be present to encourage him while he was in London at the murder trial of his brother, Lord Ferrers.[67] On the death of Whitefield in 1770, Shirley became a chaplain to the Countess of Huntingdon.

Lady Huntingdon traveled with Shirley to Trevecka in January 1771. She quickly discharged Benson. Her certificate of dismissal revealed that he was not asked to leave because of any defects in character or diligence, but because of his adherence to Wesley's views. Wesley later admitted that Benson had been a "little warped" by the doctrines of the Minutes, although he excused it as a "right-hand error."[68]

Fletcher's first reaction was that a "false step" had been taken, and he feared that if the original design of the College to train both Calvinists and Arminians was overthrown, he could not continue as President. He was disappointed that "the blow that should have been struck at the *dead spirit*," was instead "struck at *dead* Arminius, or *absent* Mr. Wesley."[69]

He cautioned Benson, however, not to make matters worse, but to "cast a mantle of forgiving love over the circumstances that might injure the cause of God." Fletcher wrote immediately to Lady Huntingdon and declared that although he was not a "party-man," he could not give up his friendship with Wesley. Further, he added:

> Mr. Benson made a very just defence when he said, he did hold with me the possibility of salvation for all men; that mercy is offered to all, and yet may be received or rejected. If this be what your Ladyship calls Mr. Wesley's opinion, free-will, and Arminianism, and if "every Arminian must quit the College," I am actually discharged also. For in my present view of things, I must hold that sentiment.[70]

Fletcher immediately recognized that the question of the place of works in salvation was closely bound up with Wesley's whole position on predestination: "All the sentiments of Mr. Wesley obnoxious to the Calvinist, except perfection, are inseparably connected with general redemption."[71]

On February 20 Fletcher journeyed to Trevecka, somewhat disenchanted by the state of affairs. The following day he tried to preach but declared: "I found myself as much shackled as ever I was in my life." He first discovered that Walter Shirley had successfully undermined his teaching on the baptism of the Holy Spirit, and that perfection had been "turned out of the College" in ridicule.[72] The most heartbreaking aspect for Fletcher, however, came when he "tried to stir up those who appeared to be carnally secure, or spiritually asleep on their soft doctrinal pillows." The students feared he was trying to rob them of "one of their jewels, the doctrine of perseverance," and "they imagined," he wrote later, "I wanted to drive them to the brink of some horrible precipice, or into the jaws of some monster called Perfection."[73]

Fletcher attempted, in vain, to soften the Countess' conviction that Wesley had fallen into heresy and given up "the grand point of the Methodists, free justification." All the students were forced to write their sentiments on Wesley's views of "salvation by works, working for life, the merit of works, etc.," and Fletcher decided to write with the rest.

Fletcher's twelve-page essay serves as a useful introduction to the theological discussion that follows. Fletcher expressed his conviction that the Minutes appeared to be "intended to *guard against antinomianism*, and *at first sight* seems calculated to support the equally dangerous error of legalists." Yet, he solemnly disavowed any tenet maintained by Wesley that was inconsistent with the doctrine of salvation by grace through faith in Jesus Christ," a doctrine," he declared, "which I am determined to maintain unto blood." He wrote of his abhorrence to "pharisaic delusion which sets up the powers of fallen man, . . . supersedes the blood and righteousness of Christ, and does not freely and fully ascribe to God's grace every degree of faithfulness, every good work, word, and desire." Good works he described as only the fruits of "that faith that saves by receiving the saving power of the Mediator."

After he had clearly repudiated any doctrine of salvation by works, he stated:

> Nevertheless, as the College appears to me rather in danger of running into the Antinomian than the legal extreme, I am in conscience bound to declare, that, though I stand with abhorrence from the sense some persons, more influenced by prejudice or mistaken zeal than candour, do absolutely fix to Mr. Wesley's minutes, I cannot disavow the doctrines they fairly contain, any more than I dare reject some parts of St. James's Epistles, and our Lord's discourses which in my humble judgement contain the same sentiments.[74]

Fletcher then took up Wesley's points one by one:

I. On the first question of man's faithfulness, Fletcher insisted that since the Fall, God had given every man "some degree of convincing grace" with a sufficient power to be faithful in the use of it. If anyone buried his talents and quenched the spirit of conviction, then destruction would follow.

II. On the article that referred to working for life, he believed that persons spiritually quickened or convinced of sin should and may, by the power of the grace which convinced them, break off their outward sins, use abstinence, deny themselves, take up their cross, be workers of mercy, and seek Jesus in the means of grace, either not to obstruct life given, or to receive more abundant life.[75]

As everyone agreed that prayer was work, and Fletcher frequently heard Lady Huntingdon herself pray for life, he asked how she could deny the concept of working for life. He insisted Wesley maintained no more than this, and he reminded her Ladyship of Wesley's evangelical preaching at Trevecka on the text: "When they had nothing to pay, he frankly forgave them both." "How many thousands," exclaimed Fletcher, "can witness that when [Wesley] invited them to Christ, he put no words in their mouths but

I give up every plea beside,
Lord I am damn'd but thou has died?

III. 1. The third proposition was that "the man who believes in Christ with a loving and obedient heart is now accepted of God." This meant, according to Fletcher, that faith, which admitted a believer to divine favor, was necessarily productive of love and obedience, and it was not to be confounded with "the feigned, inactive faith of antinomians."

IV. 2. The question of the heathen fearing God and working righteousness according to the light they had, Fletcher believed depended on the definition of "light," and he insisted it only meant "a *light* received by *grace.*"

V. 3. If this were understood as a sincere heathen, then he must be one "following the light of grace which he hath through Christ." Fletcher confessed, "I dare not, though I studied at Geneva, doom all the poor heathen to perdition."[76]

VI. 4. The next focus was the assertion that works could be a condition of salvation. This meant a thing "without which God is not wont to bestow the knowledge of salvation through the forgiveness of sins." These works, Fletcher defined again, as the fruits and evidences of faith.

VII. 5. He agreed there had been disputings about words for the past thirty years, but he felt that to fix an odious sense to that article, whose meaning was so obvious, could only be due "to prejudice, or such fears as make children believe, that every harmless object they perceive in the dark, is a lion ready to devour them."[77]

VIII. 6. In the next subdivision Wesley had said that Christians are rewarded according to their works or for the sake of them. This referred, said Fletcher, not to salvation by works, but to the works done after salvation by grace, and the rewards were those given after a believer had reached heaven through the merits of Christ.

IX. 7. On the admittedly unguarded expression "undervaluing ourselves," he said:

I dare not therefore say that Mr. Wesley is a heretic for holding that those who are convinced of sin, yea and of righteousness, see neither their person, nor state, nor works, in the same favourably gracious and glorious light which God, and their fellow mortals behold them.[78]

X. 8. The last article based the continued pleasing of God on works. These Fletcher interpreted as works springing from God, and he concluded that in God's estimation, the one who did the best works was the one with the most faith.

Fletcher regretted that the extract of the Minutes was so short, the subject so delicate, and some expressions so unguarded, that "at first sight it carries a strong appearance of legality." Upon close examination, however, he found nothing in it incompatible with salvation by faith. He then concluded his essay with his resignation:

> As Lady Huntingdon declared to me last night, with the highest degree of positiveness, what whosoever did not fully and *absolutely* disavow and renounce the doctrine contained in Mr. Wesley's Minutes should not, upon any terms, stay in her college, etc., and as it appears by the proceeding observations, that after an exact revisal of their contents, I rather disapprove the unguarded and *not sufficiently explicit* manner in which the doctrine is worded, than the doctrine itself, I should not act the part of an honest man if I did not *absolutely* resign my charge, and take my leave of this seminary of pious learning.[79]

The following morning he sent a further note to Lady Huntingdon, listing his reasons for leaving the College. The first was his support of Wesley's views; the second was "want of freedom in the College" to press his emphasis on the baptism of the Holy Ghost; and the third was "his own complete insufficiency." To this he added his "fears lest party spirit, and rash censures of things not properly examined and understood, or persons not sufficiently known, began to take place in the college."[80]

Before he left Trevecka, Fletcher advised Lady Huntingdon to choose a "moderate Calvinist" as the new president. He recommended Rowland Hill, whom he described as a "young Whitefield," for the position. In his account of the events reported to Wesley, Fletcher indicated that the Countess had promised to write to Wesley and request an explanation of the Minutes. Fletcher urged Wesley to "give them all the satisfaction you can." He affirmed his regard for Lady Huntingdon as "an eminent servant of God, an honest, gracious person, but not above the reach of prejudice; and where prejudice misleads her, her warm heart makes her go rather too fast." He requested that Wesley do all that was possible to break the prejudice she had against him, and "to become all things to her, that you may not cause her to stumble in the greatness of her zeal for the Lord."[81]

Lady Huntingdon decided for the time being not to accept Fletcher's counsel to write to Wesley for an explanation of the Minutes. Wesley, however, gave the Minutes another careful consideration and decided: "The more I consider them, the more I like them, the more fully I am convinced, not only that they are true, agreeable both to Scripture and to sound experience, but that they contain certain truths of the deepest importance."[82]

Nevertheless, upon deliberation he wrote to the Countess and reviewed for her his past commitment to the doctrine of salvation by faith. He complained, however, that during this time

> well nigh all the religious works hath set themselves in array against me, and among the rest many of my own children, following the example of one of my eldest sons, Mr. Whitefield. Their general cry has been, "He is unsound in the faith; he preaches another gospel!" I answer, Whether it be the same which they preach or not, it is the same which I have preached for above thirty years.[83]

To the accusation that in the previous August he had printed "ten lines" contradicting all his other writings, Wesley responded that it was probable he understood his own writings as well as any other person. Hence, he proposed that people read those lines in the light of his published sermons, especially his declaration of sentiments at Whitefield's funeral. By that sermon, he wrote,

> interpret those ten lines, and you will understand them better; although I should think that anyone might see even without this help that the lines in question do not refer to the condition of obtaining, but of continuing in, the favour of God.[84]

He closed the letter with an expression of his continued regard for Lady Huntingdon; "Such as I am, I love you well. You have one of the first places in my esteem and affection."

As the controversy grew warmer, Wesley decided that some further explanation of the Minutes was in order. He wrote a general letter to several preachers and friends, adding some brief remarks to each of the sections of the Minutes. His comments, though short, basically substantiated Fletcher's interpretation of them and clearly pointed out that the emphasis on works referred, not to how justification was obtained initially, but to how a believer maintained his walk with God after conversion. Works were only to be seen as a condition of final salvation.[85]

The opposition was not satisfied. In early June, Walter Shirley, in collaboration with the Countess, circulated a letter that called all "real Protestants" to gather at Wesley's next Conference to protest the doctrines contained in the 1770 Minutes. Shirley proposed that they go in a body to the Conference and "insist upon a formal recantation" of the Minutes. The missive encouraged the recipients to bring others with them to oppose the "dreadful heresy." A copy of the offending Minutes was attached to the letter, which promised lodgings to all that attended.[86]

Lady Huntingdon sent a copy to Charles Wesley, to be forwarded to his brother. She spoke of the Minutes as "Popery Unmasked," and sympathized with Charles that he should have to "suffer equal disgrace, and universal distrust, from the supposed union" with John. If the Countess had hoped to separate the two men, she was disappointed. Charles endorsed the letter, "Lady Huntingdon's Last. Unanswered by John Wesley's Brother!" The following month he suggested that

John might publish an extract from Brandt's *History of the Synod of Dort* or Goodwin's *Redemption Redeemed*. "I verily think," he wrote, "you are *called* to drive reprobation back to its own place."[87]

In a letter to Lady Huntingdon, Walter Shirley discussed the proper method for dealing with theological disagreement and also revealed his theoretical proposals for dealing with discord in the church. In July 1770, Shirley had dealt with the problem of strong disagreements within a society of believers. He recommended that "if any have a quarrel against any, that they should not suffer it to canker in their breasts, but that they should go to the party concerned, and tell him first his fault between party and party alone." Only then were they to take other steps to correct the problem.[88]

Unfortunately, Shirley did not heed his own advice in his relations with Wesley, and Fletcher expostulated with him for failing to acquaint Wesley privately with his objections before he attacked him publicly.[89] Shirley replied that if the apparent error had not been such a fundamental issue, he would not have been so zealous in his opposition. Since Wesley was the leader of some thirty thousand people and had been closely linked with the revival for many years, Shirley declared that to maintain silence while Wesley deviated so widely from his former sentiments would be nothing less than treachery. But the strongest motivation was probably Shirley's admission that

> as the world too frequently confounds all the Friends to vital Christianity under the common Name of *Methodists*, we were so solicitous, that no imputation should be upon our Names, . . . as tacitly consenting to Doctrines which we apprehended were fundamentally erroneous.[90]

While Shirley defended his letter, he failed to respond adequately to Fletcher's accusation that he should first have corresponded privately with Wesley over the issue.

The responses to Shirley's Circular Letter were various. Fletcher wrote Wesley that he was "grieved to see zeal borrowing the horn of discord, and sounding the alarm throughout the religious world." He assured Wesley of his support and spoke of his design to answer Shirley and justify the Minutes publicly, if private correspondence did not first produce a recall of the letter.[91] By June 24, 1771, Fletcher had prepared his defense in a series of five letters to Walter Shirley, and he invited Wesley to visit Madeley to discuss his arguments.[92] Wesley accepted the invitation on his way to the Conference at Bristol and took Fletcher's manuscript with him.[93]

Another of Wesley's close friends, Vincent Perronet, vicar of Shoreham, also wrote and expressed his sympathy with Wesley's position. He apologized that he had not earlier remonstrated with Lady Huntingdon, and he said that

> if one, who had laboured in the vineyard, I believe, full as much as any person since the days of the apostles, was not thought worthy of the mantle of love, for any mistake he might have made;—yet surely he had a right to expect, that notice would be given him to explain his meaning, before his judge pronounced sentence.[94]

The dispute was not limited to England and Wales. In Edinburgh, Wesley's preachers had shared in the preaching at St. Mary's Chapel, which had been rented by Lady Glenorchy for the promotion of the revival in Scotland. When she desired a minister of her own, Wesley had secured for her the services of Richard De Courcy, a former curate of Walter Shirley, whose Calvinism harmonized well with the views of Lady Glenorchy.[95] Wesley's catholic spirit was again revealed in 1771 as he expressed disgust that one of his preachers, Alexander M'Nab, had preached on a controversial doctrine while stationed at Glasgow. Wesley exclaimed that M'Nab "must be lost to all common sense to preach against final perseverance in Scotland."[96]

In spite of Wesley's desire to avoid controversy, however, the doctrinal differences were never far below the surface. In June 1771, after Shirley's letter had circulated abroad, Lady Glenorchy dismissed Wesley's preachers from her chapel. She justified her action by citing theological differences over predestination and the refusal of the other preachers to cooperate any longer with Wesley's men.[97] The following year the effects of the Circular Letter were still being felt when Wesley visited the Kingdom of Scotland and found himself branded as an "heretic."[98]

Richard Hill had been present at Lady Huntingdon's place with Shirley, Mr. Powis, and James Ireland when the Circular Letter was planned. He described it as "highly improper" and strongly objected to the use of his own name on the letter, as well as to the insertion of Lady Huntingdon's name as the head of the opposition. When it was implied that Hill had supported the original design, he declared that he "by no means testified an approbation of the proposed plan." He later wrote: "The more I considered the matter, the more cause I saw to believe that the determination agreed on of going to Bristol would answer no good end."[99] Other Calvinists also declined to participate in the confrontation, including the trustees of Whitefield's chapels.[100]

Edward Spencer, Vicar of Combe Grove near Southstoke, wrote a twenty-page critique of the Minutes, concluding that they were injudicious and dangerous, because they tended to settle some upon "a legal Bottom." He suggested, however, that a formal protest might add weight to the Minutes, make Wesley more obstinate, and solidify his preachers behind him. "To the world," he felt, "it would look like *Conference* against *Conference*." He asked, "Would it not be more Christian to desire to *confer* upon the Minutes" before making a protest?[101] The consensus of opinion even among Calvinists and Dissenters was that however much they might object to Wesley's views, the method selected to protest was the wrong one. Even Lady Huntingdon's biographer, A. C. H. Seymour, admitted that many persons objected to the dictatorial tone of the protests.[102]

Both Shirley and Lady Huntingdon apparently recognized their indiscretion, perhaps as a result of the responses to the Circular Letter. On the eve of the Conference, they wrote to Wesley and apologized for such "an arbitrary way of proceeding." Since they did not wish to defend truth presumptuously, they offered "to retract what a more deliberate Consideration might have prevented." They insisted that they did not mean to imply any juridical right to interfere with the Conference or to pretend to exercise authority over Wesley as an inferior. They acknowledged that "the Circular Letter was too hastily drawn up, and improperly expressed," and they begged his pardon "for the *offensive expressions* in it."[103]

The Calvinists Confront Wesley at His 1771 Conference

Wesley's Conference met on August 6 with a larger attendance than usual, probably due to Shirley's Circular Letter. Wesley appointed the third day of the Conference for the interview, at which time Shirley appeared with two other ministers from the Countess' chapels, three laymen, and two students from Trevecka. The absence of men of stature like Venn, Romaine, Madan, Berridge, and the Welsh leaders is significant. Toplady excused himself on the grounds that he had a houseguest and shortly expected a visit from the bishop, but he promised to "be present in the spirit."[104]

After Wesley prayed, Shirley requested that his and the Countess' recent letters to Wesley be read to the Conference by way of apology for any offense given. Not all the preachers were satisfied with this, however. John Pawson, in his description of Shirley's delegation, claimed that "they had very little to say in defense of their conduct."[105] Wesley then reviewed his ministry in order to show that he had always maintained justification by faith and that nothing in the Minutes was contrary thereto. The real opposition, he felt, "was not to the Minutes, but to himself personally."

Shirley sought to assure Wesley that the protest was not personal but was directed against the doctrines "in the plain natural Import of the Minutes."[106] He then produced a Declaration, which he had drawn up, and suggested that something analogous to it might be adopted to correct the false impression left by the Minutes. The Conference agreed that the more obvious meaning of the Minutes was reprehensible, and after Wesley had made some minor alterations, fifty-three of them signed the following Declaration:

> Whereas the doctrinal Points in the Minutes of a Conference held in London, August 7, 1770, have been understood to favour Justification by Works: Now the Rev. John Wesley, and others assembled in Conference, do declare that we had no such Meaning; and that we abhor the Doctrine of Justification by Works as a most perilous and abominable Doctrine; and as the said Minutes are not sufficiently guarded in the Way they are express'd, we hereby solemnly declare in the Sight of God that we have no Trust or Confidence but in the alone Merits of our Lord and Saviour Jesus Christ, for Justification or Salvation either in Life, Death, or the Day of Judgement; and though no one is a real Christian Believer, (and consequently cannot be saved) who doth not good Works, where there is Time and Opportunity, yet our Works have no Part in meriting, or purchasing our Salvation from first to last, either in whole or in Part.[107]

Only Thomas Olivers refused to sign the document and argued with them at length that man's second justification, on Judgment Day, was indeed by works.[108]

Shirley, however, understood that Wesley and the rest did not agree to a second justification by works. When Shirley was publicly pressed to acknowledge that he had mistaken the meaning of the Minutes, he promised to do so.[109] They closed with prayer and, in Shirley's mind, "with all the warmest Indications of mutual Peace and Love." Wesley concluded: "I believe they were satisfied that we were not so dreadful heretics as they imagined, but were tolerably sound in the faith."[110]

Immediately after the Conference, Wesley wrote to Lady Huntingdon and denied that he had ever surrendered the great truths of justification by faith. For these truths "I have given up all my worldly hopes, my friends, my reputation—yea, for which I have so often hazarded my life." He stated that any who considered Fletcher's letters in defense of the Minutes would be convinced that the Minutes were in no way contrary to that central doctrine. He pleaded "not guilty" to the charge of establishing the faith upon another foundation and declared that until Fletcher's letters were answered, he must consider all further opposition to the Minutes a "palpable affront" to Christ and totally destructive of His honor.[111]

There is good indication, however, that Lady Huntingdon was not satisfied either with the results of the Conference or with Wesley's letter. Howel Harris had dinner with her and Shirley on August 21. After Shirley recounted the proceedings of the Conference, Harris recalled that Lady Huntingdon referred to John Wesley as a "Rogue" and declared that "he should not come to her house." Harris responded characteristically: "I declared he should come to mine, and I would preach in his places, and that it was the Old Man in her."[112]

When Wesley had acquired Fletcher's manuscript[113] in July, it was in the form of letters to Shirley. He revised it and, satisfied that it represented his own views, gave it to the printer William Pine before the Conference began. When Shirley and James Ireland learned the morning after the Conference that Wesley had resolved to continue publication, they felt the sword of contention had been drawn again. Although Wesley assured them that he had corrected all the tart expressions, Ireland entreated him to suppress the work until they could communicate the events of the Conference to Fletcher. Ireland assured Wesley that Fletcher would not consent to the publication when he learned how amiably matters had been settled at the Conference.

After consideration Wesley decided to allow the publication to proceed. Shortly after Wesley left Bristol, a letter from Fletcher reached Ireland, in which he urged that his letters be suppressed. In the light of the Conference settlement, Fletcher feared that he had treated Shirley too severely, and he offered, if necessary, to defray the whole expense of printing by selling his last shirt.[114] He added, however, that if his letters were published, it must be seen as a necessary misfortune, and that "whether my letters were suppressed or not, the Minutes *must* be vindicated."[115] Ireland carried Fletcher's letter to William Pine, who then recommended to Wesley's preachers that the work be suppressed. The preachers decided, however, that Wesley's instructions had been too explicit, and Fletcher's work was sent forth as *The First Check to Antinomianism; or A Vindication of the Rev. Mr. Wesley's Minutes.*[116]

The Reasons for the Minutes Controversy

The publication of Fletcher's *Vindication*, cast as his letters to Shirley, was the beginning of a fresh outbreak of controversy between the two camps of Methodists. The explanation for Wesley's decision to publish, even after the removal of misunderstandings at the Conference, can be properly understood only in terms of Wesley's earlier reasons for producing the 1770 Minutes. According to Fletcher, it had been Wesley's purpose "to guard his preachers and hearers against Antinomian principles and practices, which spread like wild-fire in some of his Societies." This antinomianism, he believed, was closely bound up with the Calvinist emphasis on finished or complete salvation.

Fletcher illustrated his point with a story from his own parish, in which a married man who professed both justification and sanctification fell into this Calvinian theology, despised his brethren as legalists, and then convinced a serious young woman of his new principles. "What was the consequence?" asked Fletcher: "Why, they talked about finished salvation in Christ, and the absurdity of perfection in the flesh, till a perfect child was conceived and born." Fletcher insisted that such dreadful practices made it high time that someone cried out, "Take heed to your doctrine."[117]

Wesley had long felt that his chief obstacles to raising up a holy people were Calvinism and antinomianism. He had reminded the 1765 Conference: "Holiness was our point,—inward and outward holiness. When Satan could no otherwise prevent this, he threw *Calvinism* in our way; and then *antinomianism*."[118] He wrote to Fletcher about his conviction that "even the precious doctrine of Salvation by Faith has need to be guarded with the utmost care, or those who hear it will slight both inward and outward holiness."[119] Wesley felt the Calvinists' emphasis on election and perseverance too often sapped the motivation to press on to holy living, as evidenced by good works. In 1770 it was the question, "What must be done to revive the work where it is decaying?" that caused him to place renewed emphasis on the place of good works. The same year he wrote to one of his preachers:

> This testimony was lodged with us forty years ago, Without Holiness none shall see the Lord. But then came the Calvinists saying, No! Not without Holiness. But without any Holiness *in ourselves*. And how many thousands have they turned back into the world?[120]

The evidence indicates that Wesley's fears of antinomianism were not exaggerated. Walter Sellon wrote to the Countess of Huntingdon to advise her that her name was being used to countenance the most ungodly practices. He told her of one who had been a believer for several years before he heard of final perseverance. Upon learning this doctrine, he gave way to drunkenness and immorality, and when asked if he was doing right, he replied: "No. Yet it cannot hurt me, for I know I have a finished salvation, a complete righteousness." After a serious person reproved him, he responded: "Don't preach your legal stuff to me. I am not in bondage. I am of my Lady's gospel." The result of this and other instances, Sellon notes, was that the phrase, "My Lady's Gospel," is spread about, and I have heard it laughed at in several places. Some use it through ignorance. Others by way of contrast to the gospel of Christ; and others to vilify all true religion.[121]

Some of the Countess' students apparently veered in a similar direction. When Wesley visited Howel Harris at Trevecka in 1772, Harris told him:

I have borne with those pert, ignorant young men, vulgarly called students, till I cannot in conscience bear any longer. They preach bare-faced Reprobation, and so broad Antinomianism that I have been constrained to oppose them to the face, even in the public congregation.[122]

Behind this practical antinomianism, Wesley saw the doctrinal antinomianism of men like Hervey and Toplady. Up through the late 1760s, he had crossed swords over Hervey's views. In 1771 he was in the midst of heated conflict with Toplady. The latter had asked Walter Shirley whether in a forthcoming publication he should add a note against Wesley's Minutes.[123] This fear of antinomianism as a threat to personal holiness was certainly behind Wesley's concerns at the 1770 Conference. One further factor, as Jackson points out, was that Wesley had originally intended the Minutes for his preachers. They certainly understood them in light of the larger Conference discussions, as well as in the context of Wesley's whole theology. If the Minutes had been directed to the general public, Wesley probably would have been more circumspect in his presentation.[124]

These reasons behind the formulation of the 1770 Minutes were still much in Wesley's mind when he authorized the publication of Fletcher's *First Check to Antinomianism,* or *Vindication.* Although the misunderstanding over the wording of the Minutes was resolved in 1771 to the satisfaction of all, the real problems to which the Minutes were directed still remained. With Fletcher's work, Wesley clearly hoped to deal a heavy blow, at least to doctrinal antinomianism. He therefore declared that it "could not be suppressed without betraying the honour of our Lord."[125] Further justification of the decision to publish is contained in a letter to Fletcher, probably from Charles Wesley. This letter outlined the damage done by the Circular Letter and asked, Was Shirley's apology at the 1771 Conference "a remedy adequate to the evil done . . . to Mr. Wesley?"

Charles further noted three consequences: Wesley's reputation had been tarnished by letters sent to every serious churchman and Dissenter in three kingdoms. A lady "in her mistaken zeal, had represented him as a *Papist unmasked, a heretic, an apostate.*" Even a poem on Wesley's apostasy was forthcoming. Hence, the cry among Wesley's opponents was, "Now that he lieth, let him rise not more." As a consequence, he continued, "his dearest friends and children are staggered, and scarce know what to think. You, in your corner, cannot conceive the mischief that has been done, and is still doing." He assured Fletcher that his own letters were serving a useful purpose and observed that he had not been "too severe to dear Mr. Shirley, moderate Calvinists themselves being judges."[126]

John Wesley may well have felt that his own reputation was inseparably bound up with the doctrinal issues, and that both needed defense. This would account for his publication of Fletcher's *Vindication* in the form of personal letters to Shirley, rather than to have them sent forth simply as a doctrinal treatise. In any case, Wesley hoped to "quench the flame kindled over the three kingdoms," with Fletcher's letters, but he feared "the antidote cannot spread so fast as the poison."[127] The letters in the *Vindication*, however, proved more potent than Wesley had anticipated. Two and a half months later, he claimed that they had "given a deadly wound to Antinomianism."[128]

One may legitimately ask why Lady Huntingdon and Walter Shirley felt compelled to oppose Wesley and the Minutes so forcefully. It cannot be denied that they were zealous for theological purity, and this interest in doctrinal truth was clearly their stated reason for intervening in the affairs of Wesley's Connection. The 1771 Conference Declaration, however, seemed to clarify obvious misunderstandings over the doctrines of the Minutes. If Shirley was as readily satisfied with the resolution of apparent theological differences as he claimed to be, it is difficult to escape the conclusion that one doctrinal issue did not account for the whole of the opposition. There are multiple opportunities for an explanation of apparent difficulties.

When Wesley traveled to Bristol immediately after the 1770 Conference, why did Lady Huntingdon not allow him to join her party for the journey to the College and use the opportunity to clarify the meaning of the Minutes? If doctrine was the only major issue, why did not Fletcher's written and verbal explanations of the unguarded wording of the Minutes at Trevecka in February and March 1771 dissolve the sharp opposition of either the Countess or Shirley? Why was there no correspondence or request for an interpretation of the offending propositions for almost a year after the 1770 Conference? One may ask further, Why was no attempt made to understand the statements on works both in the immediate context of the Minutes and in the larger context of Wesley's overall preaching and publication? These questions seem to indicate that factors other than the theology of good works played a part in the controversy.

Wesley felt that the theological issue was heavily laden with antagonism to him personally. He argued this, not only at the 1771 Conference, but also in a letter to Fletcher: "These gentlemen do not love *Me*, and do love particular redemption."[129] This charge had considerable substance to it and was not just the outraged cry of the persecuted. Such personal opposition was probably overlaid with a tinge of envy at Wesley's larger sphere of influence. This was certainly Joseph Benson's conviction when he wrote that the Calvinists were "jealous of their authority."[130] A fear of undue personal influence by Wesley over the College would account for the rapid dismissal of Benson and the willing acceptance of Fletcher's resignation.

Within the area of doctrinal disagreement, however, the question of the relation between good works and salvation was not the only dividing issue. The Calvinists' strong abhorrence to Wesley's views on perfection had long been an area of contention. In December 1770 Shirley heard about a shift in the views of a Mr. Mead, and he exclaimed to the Countess: "Unspeakable is my satisfaction in hearing that that blessed Man of God is totally delivered from the Error of Perfection."[131] Shirley feared the doctrine would "necessarily lead seekers into a miserable bondage and the professors of it into Enthusiasm and spiritual pride," and he therefore determined "to oppose Perfection with my utmost might."[132]

Shirley's concern for the views of the students at Trevecka led him to pray that the Lord would preserve them "from every error and delusion, and especially that of Perfection."[133] His concern, however, was not limited to prayer, and when he resided at the College during the winter of 1771, he used all his influence to undermine Fletcher's emphasis on the doctrine. Yet, Wesley believed that this theological point was also a subterfuge for personal opposition. Thus he wrote in February 1771: "If he could find any other doctrine which he thought was particularly mine, Mr. Shirley would be as angry at it as he is at Christian Perfection."[134]

11. Wesley's Defense against the Calvinists' Attack

THE unusually close relationship between John Fletcher and both the Wesleys made it possible for Fletcher to be the principal spokesman for the Wesleyan party in the controversy with the Calvinists in 1770s. This chapter commences with a discussion of the bond of friendship between these three, then describes Fletcher's ongoing debate with Walter Shirley over Wesley's 1770 Conference Minutes. About this time, two new champions joined the Calvinist team—the brothers Richard and Rowland Hill. Their concerted attack upon Wesley, along with both Wesley's and Fletcher's responses, widened the debate from a discussion of Wesley's Minutes to include all the doctrines related to predestination. Finally, the chapter examines the Calvinists' countercharge against the Wesleyans' views on Christian perfection.

The Special Relationship between Fletcher and the Wesleys

Wesley held no man in higher esteem than John Fletcher. When he preached Fletcher's funeral sermon in 1785, Wesley chose for his text, "Mark the perfect man." He declared Fletcher to be the only man in Britain who could be compared with Gregory Lopez or Monsieur De Renty in their experience of the deep things of God:

> Many exemplary men I have known, holy in heart and life, within four-score years, but one equal to him I have not known,—one so inwardly and outwardly devoted to God. So unblameable a character in every respect I have not found either in Europe or America; and I scarce expect to find another such on this side of eternity.[1]

The supreme expression of Wesley's approbation of Fletcher was his repeated proposal that Fletcher should succeed him in directing the Methodists.[2]

Wesley's appreciation of Fletcher was not limited to his character. He had the greatest admiration for his literary talents and referred to him as "one of the finest writers of the age."[3] He especially commended Fletcher's responses to the Calvinists in his several *Checks to Antinomianism*, "in which one knows not which to admire most, the purity of the language, . . . the strength and clearness of the argument, or the mildness and sweetness of the spirit which breathes throughout the whole."[4] The fact that Wesley revised most of the *Checks* is strong evidence that what Fletcher wrote largely represented Wesley's own position.[5] As Wesley was "in no want of employment," he left much of the theological articulation in the 1770s to the less hurried Fletcher.

The other person who corrected Fletcher's manuscripts was Charles Wesley. Among the numerous manuscript letters to Charles, almost all from 1770 to

1775 have some request for Charles to prune, correct, or assist some work through the press.[6] This tends to substantiate Jackson's claim that nearly everything Fletcher published passed under the critical hand of Charles Wesley.[7] At one point Fletcher wrote: "I give you *carte blanche* to add, or lop off; but to *none but you.*"[8] Fletcher's works, then, represent not only his own theological views, but also those of both the Wesleys. He thus assumes a critical place in any analysis of Wesley's theology.

Fletcher Debates Shirley over Wesley's Minutes

Fletcher began his letters or *First Check* with a general review of Wesley's doctrine. Wesley held, he declared, the total fall of man, his inability to do any good of himself apart from the preventing (prevenient) grace of God, and the blood and righteousness of Christ as the sole meritorious cause of salvation. Wesley emphasized the doctrine of holiness of heart and life, represented Christ as the complete Savior from sin, and by Christian perfection meant nothing more than the rich cluster of all the spiritual blessings promised to believers.

As a consequence of his belief in general redemption and unlimited atonement, Wesley laid down two axioms: *First,* that all our salvation is of God in Christ, and therefore, by grace; and *second,* that all our damnation is of ourselves by obstinate unbelief. The former advanced the glory of God by ascribing all the salvation of the elect to His mercy and grace, and the latter presupposed the moral agency of man, while it freed God from the blame of "hanging the millstone of damnation about the neck of the reprobate." Moreover, Fletcher pointed out, none of Wesley's peculiar sentiments affected such fundamental Christian doctrines as the fall of man, justification by the merits of Christ, sanctification by the agency of the Holy Spirit, or the Trinity.[9]

Insisting that the Minutes were designed to combat "Antinomian principles and practices," Fletcher endeavored to vindicate them with arguments from Scripture, reason, experience, and the Calvinistic divines themselves. This interpretation of the Minutes was essentially that contained in his March essay for Lady Huntingdon. Fletcher then closed his *First Check* with some strong expostulations to Shirley over his high-handed treatment of a man of Wesley's stature, without prior consultation. He asked, What could be more cutting to an

> old general in the armies of Emmanuel . . . [than] to be traduced as "a dreadful heretic," in printed letters sent to the best men in the land . . . and signed by a person of your rank and piety; to have things that he know not, that he never meant, laid to his charge, and dispersed far and near? While he is gone to a neighbouring kingdom to preach Jesus Christ, to have his friends prejudiced, his foes elevated, and the fruit of his extensive ministry at the point of being blasted![10]

Although Fletcher had given Wesley permission to alter his letters, he was not altogether satisfied with the finished product after it had passed through the hands of both the reviser and the printer. He wrote to Charles Wesley: "I am surprised to see so many blunders in my letters. I saw a copy last week and find your brother hath added nothing, only in some places shortened them, sometimes a little for the worse (as I think) but in general for the better."[11]

He immediately sent word to the printer that a second edition was not to be issued without his corrections and additions. He also explained to Charles that, in his description of the antinomian preachers and hearers, he had hoped to be "more explicit upon the consequences of both: but their hurry in reprinting without consulting me *will prevent the blow I meditated for the wolf* in Lamb's clothing."

Although Wesley felt justified in allowing Fletcher's *First Check* to be printed, Walter Shirley believed he had been betrayed. He thought that the agreements at the 1771 Conference had ended the controversy. However, in the light of Fletcher's letter to Ireland, apologizing for the personal references to Shirley in his letters, Shirley felt that some public response was necessary. When he consulted with Lady Huntingdon, she not only recommended a narrative of the facts as a defense of their actions; she also wrote the introduction and conclusion.[12] Shirley also corresponded about the proposed publications with Fletcher, who thought it proper and necessary that an account of Shirley's behavior be made public.[13] Yet Fletcher expressed his fear to Charles Wesley that Shirley was "printing a narrative to turn off the eyes of the public upon the publishing of my letters," as much as to explain his own conduct. Nevertheless, with characteristic generosity, he wrote to Shirley and offered to bind some copies of the proposed narrative with his own letters, to show the world that they pursued a loving war. Shirley did not reply.[14]

Though Shirley had requested Fletcher's permission to quote him in the narrative, Shirley confessed to Lady Huntingdon that he intended to be selective in his use of the material:

> I only inserted such parts of Mr. Fletcher's letter to Mr. Ireland as indicated the earnest desire he had to have his book suppressed, but could not prevail on myself to publish to the world the humble manner in which he *begs my Pardon.*[15]

Shirley felt that a detailed theological reply was unnecessary. Yet he did respond to Fletcher's accusations that he had put a forced construction on the Minutes in order to find Wesley guilty, and that his own previously published sermons more strongly supported a doctrine of salvation by works than did the Minutes.[16] In his *Narrative*, Shirley declared the sincerity of his interpretation: "Nothing but the Declaration could ever convince me that Justification by Works was not maintained and supported by the Minutes." He recalled that even Fletcher at first sight had expressed his abhorrence of them to Lady Huntingdon, and had only later seen them in a different light. In reply to the second accusation, Shirley relegated his early sermons to "a time when I had more zeal than Light." Since his present thinking was quite different, he was taking this opportunity to disavow them publicly.[17]

All the attack upon Shirley did not come from the Wesleyan camp. The *Gospel Magazine*, in connection with its September assault upon Wesley and the ambiguity of the Conference Declaration, also expressed disappointment that Shirley's delegation had not been "more upon their guard than to have been put off by such an unmeaning confession." In comparison with Wesley and Fletcher, however, Shirley received gentle treatment when the magazine further argued:

> However these gentlemen may abhor the doctrine of justification by the merit of works, as most perilous and abominable, they are determined to abide by the doctrine of justification by works as a condition, which is all that is clearly expressed in the Minutes.[18]

Fletcher prepared a *Second Check to Antinomianism* as a reply to Shirley's *Narrative*. Since the *Gospel Magazine* had charged him with "scattering firebrands, arrows, and deaths" in his previous work, he sent Charles Wesley the fresh manuscript and entreated him: "Pray quench *my brands* in holy oil, and leave no death but that I meditate against Antinomianism."[19] Fletcher objected to Shirley's insinuation that Wesley and his preachers had abandoned the doctrine of justification by works on Judgment Day:

> Certainly so many judicious and good men could never so betray the cause of practical religion, as tamely to renounce a truth of that importance. If they had, one step more would have carried them full into Dr. Crise's eternal justification, which is the very centre of Antinomianism.[20]

He feared that "if faith alone [would] turn the scale of justifying evidence at the bar of God, how many bold Antinomians will claim relation to Christ, and boast they are interested in his imputed righteousness." Fletcher tried to show that a doctrine of a second justification by works was taught in Scripture, held by Calvinists like Whitefield and Matthew Henry, and supported by reasonable argument. Then he enumerated its advantages for the church: "It will rouse Antinomians out of their carnal security, stir up believers to follow hard after holiness, and reconcile fatal differences among Christians, and seeming contradictions in the Scripture."[21] Furthermore, he stated that there was no contradiction between that doctrine and the 1771 Conference Declaration, and he admonished Shirley for his recantation of some of his own early sermons.

Wesley and Fletcher Continue the Debate with Richard and Rowland Hill

At this juncture Richard Hill entered the fray. On a visit to Paris the previous July, Hill had discussed the Minutes with Martin Madan and a Catholic monk, Father Walsh, who had described them as "too near Pelagianism." At the same time, Walsh characterized Catholicism as about midway between Protestantism and Wesley.[22] Hill originally intended his *Conversation* to be printed with Shirley's *Narrative*, but at James Ireland's request, Shirley wisely decided to leave it out.[23] It appeared as a separate publication just when Fletcher was completing his *Second Check*. On the advice of John Wesley, Fletcher added a postscript noting the irony of the "real Protestants" calling for support from the Church of Rome. He remained unimpressed by a Calvinistic monk who supported Augustine against Paul, closing with a declaration: "So long as Christ, the prophets, and the apostles are for us, together with the multitude of the Puritan divines of the last century, we shall smile at an army of Popish friars."[24]

Fletcher's work was beginning to make itself felt. In December 1771, a reader who had been "much refreshed by reading Mr. Fletcher's Letters" commented on the conduct of the Calvinists: "Many in this age, who think they are the *Only Builders,* pull down the work of God because they were not the hewers of the stones."[25] The response of Fletcher's adversaries, however, was somewhat different. Walter Shirley declared: "Everything Mr. Fletcher writes makes me more a Calvinist. 0 the bitterness of a legal Arminian Spirit!"[26] He believed Fletcher had insinuated that all who disapproved of Wesley's Minutes were Antinomians, and he feared this charge would seriously weaken them as ministers of God. Although he felt that the *Second Check* abounded with "unfair misrepresentations," he was glad it was out because it laid bare hitherto disguised tenets. He also suspected it would appear so grossly erroneous as to disgust many even in Wesley's Connection.[27]

While Shirley was not convinced, neither was he anxious to continue the contest. Thus, he resigned his commission to Lady Huntingdon:

> I am ready to sink with shame at the additional weight we must have laid upon you from our idle wrangles. . . . I feel myself such a Blunderer throughout this whole affair that if your Ladyship can forgive me this once, I trust I shall keep clear of everything of the like nature for the future.[28]

At the same time he was candid enough to observe that the Countess' original catholic plan for Trevecka would never do. "In short," he stated, "you must never expect peace there unless the College consists wholly of Arminians, or wholly of Calvinists."

With Shirley's retirement from the field of battle, Richard Hill donned his mantle as champion of the Calvinists. In February 1772 he published an answer to the *First Check* in *Five Letters to the Rev. Mr. Fletcher.* While Shirley described Hill's work as "serious, sensible, and polite," he admitted "that there are some very high strokes of Calvinism in it, which are (at least) too strong Meat for the weak and I fear will generally disgust the outward readers."[29] Because Hill's objections to Fletcher were stated from a thoroughgoing Calvinistic perspective, a new dimension was added to the whole controversy, and the debate broadened into a much more general theological duel between Calvinists and Arminians.

As a result of the fall of Adam and the total depravity of his posterity, Hill believed that human beings were incompetent to perform any good thing previous to justification. Therefore, he thought it was ludicrous to expect "living actions from a dead corpse" or to look for repentance or any good work from anyone who had not been quickened by the Holy Ghost or accepted into God's favor. Further, he argued that "believing cannot possibly be previous to justification; and you must maintain the same, unless you will adopt the phrase of *an unjustified believer;* whereas the Holy Ghost teaches that *all who believe are justified.*"[30]

Hill maintained that since the reception of grace implied a state of pardon and acceptance, any works performed by prevenient grace could only be "from life," not "for life." He felt that repentance and faith followed justification and, while he allowed for sin subsequent to justification, he insisted that it did not annul God's covenant with man.

Hill alleged that Wesley's concept of merit was identical to the Roman view in that both attributed merit to good works accomplished under the power of divine grace. He attempted to "split the hair" between being rewarded "according to" works and "for the sake of" works by understanding the former to mean gracious reward. He refused, however, to "split the hair" between meritorious works and the works of supererogation.[31]

In his discussion of the place of works after justification, Hill distinguished between the sinner and the act of sin, as illustrated by David's sin with Bathsheba: "Though I believe that David's *sin* displeased the Lord, must I therefore believe that David's *person* came under the curse of the Law? Surely No. David was still a son, though a perverse one." Hill believed that the failure to differentiate between a believer and his actions was one of Wesley's capital errors:

> The former always stands absolved, always complete in the everlasting Righteousness of the Redeemer; whilst the latter are certainly pleasing or displeasing to God, every hour and every minute, according to the nature of them.[32]

Fletcher concluded that Hill's *Letters* were "calculated to quicken the Calvinists and *fix the odium*" that they deserved upon an alleged legalism of the Arminian position. Thus, early in 1772, he began his response as a *Third Check to Antinomianism*.[33] Although he was no lover of discord, Fletcher considered that controversy "properly managed, has a hundred times rescued truth, groaning under the lash of triumphant error." This literary exchange was justified in his eyes because he felt that his day stood "as much in need of a reformation from Antinomianism as our ancestors did of a reformation from Popery."[34] His original purpose had been "to oppose Antinomianism alone," but because Hill had defended his position primarily on Calvinist principles, Fletcher felt obliged to encounter him on that ground.

He argued that the free preventing (prevenient) grace of God to all of fallen men made it possible for them to repent and believe. This combination of total depravity and prevenient grace exonerated him from Hill's charge of Pelagianism. The failure to recognize the place of prevenient grace, Fletcher thought, was the reason Calvinists feared Wesley's emphasis on repentance and faith as a form of works righteousness. Fletcher's own position, he felt, reserved all the credit for salvation to God, while a universal offer of redemption made reprobation the responsibility of an obstinate moral agent, not out of any partiality on God's part. Yet he could agree that "our salvation or damnation turns upon the good or bad use which we make of the manifold grace of God." Fletcher rejected irresistible grace as inconsistent with God's invitations to salvation, which were extended to all men. He believed that although concurrence with grace was necessary, yet no one was accepted but through the meritorious blood of Christ.[35]

Fletcher then posited four degrees or aspects of justification. The first was a universal justification of all infants from original sin and a provision for the future justification of all men, conditioned upon repentance and faith. The second aspect was the actualization of this offer whereby faith was imputed for righteousness and was generally known as the experience of justification by faith. The third aspect was a justification consequent upon a genuine faith that bore fruit according to the believer's dispensation. The fourth aspect designated a final justification that referred to the Judgment Day. Fletcher believed that every aspect of justification was based upon the merit of Christ, but only in the first instance did man do nothing. For the second aspect, the penitent were given the power to believe by prevenient grace, and the last two aspects involved continued belief and working by faith together with God, as there was opportunity.[36]

He explained that Wesley's concept of merit was identical with that of Scotus, Bucer, and Baxter, and he held that works performed by faith were rewardable, but only because reward had been previously merited by Christ. Fletcher criticized Hill's distinction between God's displeasure at David's sin but not his person. He reminded his opponent that "a word spoken *for* sin generally goes farther than ten thousand spoken *against* it." He believed that Hill's position "drags after it all the absurdities of eternal, absolute justification." It "bears hard upon the equity of the Divine conduct, and strikes a fatal blow at the root of all diligence and faithfulness so strongly recommended in the oracles of God." Fletcher closed with a note of approbation that his opponents' doctrinal principles had not led them personally into practical antinomianism. Yet he added that he feared the consequences in others who were more "consistent Antinomians."[37]

Wesley was not all displeased at the effects of the controversy, although he remarked that "it is easier to loose our love in that rough field than to find truth." He was exceedingly grateful that he had a personal respite from polemical labors. "I am glad He has given to others both the power and the will to answer them that trouble me; so that I may not always be forced to hold my weapons in one hand while I am building with the other." Wesley believed that Fletcher's second work had given a considerable check to those who taught that "without holiness any man may see the Lord."[38] After he revised the *Third Check*, he told Charles approvingly that Fletcher had "drawn the sword and thrown away the scabbard."[39] He rejoiced at both Fletcher's ability and temper:

> He writes as he lives, I cannot say that I know such another clergyman in England or Ireland. He is all fire; but it is the fire of love. His writings, like his constant conversation, breathe nothing else to those who read him with an impartial eye.[40]

Predictably, there was also a different reaction. From Dublin, Walter Shirley wrote to the Countess that, while Wesley's people there had sent a letter of thanks to Fletcher, Lady Huntingdon's society had sent a protest.[41] His correspondence revealed, however, that although he had not slackened his opposition to Arminianism, Shirley was becoming increasingly careful about his presentation of the distinctive doctrines of Calvinism: "For my own part I preach free Grace in a Calvinistical view of things, without preaching systematically, or using any of the Cant Calvinistical Phraseology."[42] He continued, for example, to hold the Calvinistic position on final perseverance, but now he recognized more clearly its dangers: "There is no end to the fatal consequences to the Cause of truth by our setting any one down a believer, till the Lord has made that matter clear."[43]

The Countess of Huntingdon's reaction to the *Second Check* was expressed in a letter to Richard Hill: "It is most awful to see how this mighty man is fallen. . . . My heart has been made heavy on account of this publication, by a man whom I once revered as an Angel of God. . . . He now seems turned aside unto vain janglings."[44]

While Fletcher was composing his *Third Check,* Hill was preparing *A Review of all the Doctrines taught by the Rev. John Wesley.* Hill attacked a second justification by works as being non-Protestant, a view in which "Mr. Wesley and Mr. Fletcher have the whole Council of Trent on their side." The Reformers and Puritans, by contrast, professed "one complete, final everlasting justification of sinners by faith only in Jesus Christ."[45] Hill admitted that good works were "declarative evidence" of justification for the present, as well as at the final judgment, but he insisted that this did not constitute a second justification. He feared that Fletcher's emphasis upon the indispensability of works to sustain God's favor tended to nullify the mediatorial works of Christ and come perilously close to Socinianism. The doctrines of finished salvation and infallible perseverance, he grounded upon God's eternal decrees and the objective work of Christ. Hill further believed that God's promises to the elect had been ratified, communicated, and secured by Christ's atonement.[46]

He labeled Wesley's position on Christian perfection as "sinless perfection," endeavoring to connect it with the Pelagians, Jesuits, Anabaptists, and Count Zinzendorf. Hill accused the advocates of perfection of retreating into the Roman distinction between sin and infirmity, where they could claim conformity to the perfect law of love while admitting certain transgressions of infirmity. This doctrine, he asserted, was far closer to antinomianism than was any aspect of Calvinism. He called upon "all who reverence the sanctions of the moral law" to "protest against such licentious Antinomian tenets: which are by far the more dangerous as they come disguised under the specious garb of Christian perfection."[47]

Hill reserved the last forty pages of his *Review* for a "Farrago of Hot and Cold Medicines, by the Rev. Mr. John Wesley, extracted from his own Publications." In the *Review* he attempted to expose Wesley's supposed inconsistencies. A quotation from Bishop Hall characterized Hill's design on Wesley:

> I would I knew where to find you; then I could take direct aim. Where as now I must rove and conjecture. Today you are in the tents of the Romanists; tomorrow, in ours; next day, between both, against both. Our adversaries think you ours, we theirs; your conscience finds you with both and neither. . . . Will you be a Church alone? Alas! how full are you of contradictions to yourself![48]

He then juxtaposed apparently contradictory quotations from Wesley's writings on final perseverance, perfection, imputed righteousness, justification, a twofold justification, and works as a condition for salvation. Hill concluded with his acknowledgment that, although justification was by the instrumentality of faith alone, good works were evidence of justification. "Neither Mr. Shirley, nor I, nor any Calvinist that I ever heard of, deny, that though a sinner be justified of God by Christ alone, he is declaratively justified by works, both here and at the day of judgement."[49]

Fletcher believed that Wesley would suffer if Hill were not answered. Although he began a reply, he told Charles Wesley: "I think you and your brother *should interpose,* they are so *hot.*"[50] He especially felt that John should answer Hill's "farrago."[51] When John Wesley acquired a copy of Hill's work, he characterized it as having "nothing to do either with good nature or good manners, for he is writing to an Arminian."[52] Wesley justified his response:

> When Mr. Hill so violently attacked me in the famous Paris *Conversation*, I was as a man that heard not and in whose mouth were no reproofs. When he fell upon me again in his *Five Letters*, I still made no reply; nay, I chose not to read it, for fear I should be tempted to return evil for evil. When he assaulted me a third time more vehemently than ever in his *Review*, I still determined to answer nothing. But it was not long before one of my friends sent me word that I could no longer be silent and be innocent.[53]

Wesley was convinced that it was his "bounden duty as a public person" to answer Hill's objections. Nevertheless, he still desired to maintain a proper spirit in the controversy and to respond "with the inimitable sweetness and gentleness that Mr. Fletcher has done."

After he noted Fletcher's futile efforts to soften the spirits of the Calvinists, Wesley opened his *Remarks* on Hill's *Review* with the declaration: "I have done, therefore, with humbling myself to these men, to Mr. H. and his associates. I have humbled myself to them for these thirty years; but I will do it no more."[54]

Wesley believed that the source of his antagonist's "implacable hatred" was the supposition that no man can love God or his neighbor who is not clear in the belief of absolute predestination. As a consequence, Wesley saw that "if the doctrine of the decrees stands, then that of the Minutes must fall; for we willingly allow, that the one is incompatible with the other."[55]

Turning to the charge of inconsistency, Wesley noted that much of Hill's evidence came from passages out of the *Christian Library* (edited by Wesley; see chap. 6, above). Although he stood by his conviction that every tract in the *Library* was "true and agreeable to the oracles of God," Wesley protested that this did not mean he affirmed "every sentence contained in the fifty volumes." While it was probable that he had overlooked some passages unsuitable to his principles, Wesley insisted that it was primarily the carelessness of the printers that caused many citations to be included that he had intended to omit.

Nor did he feel it necessary to defend every expression of the extracts he had published from John Goodwin, Richard Baxter, and John Bunyan. The sense of them, he declared, "I generally approve, the language many times I do not."[56] Wesley concluded, therefore, that quotations from these sources against his other writings proved nothing. Further, Wesley did not attempt to defend every phrase in his brother's hymns, and while he admitted one or two of the accusations, he generally acquitted himself from the charge of self-contradiction by enlarging the context of his words or with further explanation of his meaning.

Without adding much to the discussion, Hill and Wesley rehashed the same questions in the winter of 1773. Hill published his *Logica Wesleiensis, or Farrago Double-Distilled,*[57] and Wesley responded with *Some Remarks on Mr. Hill's "Farrago Double-Distilled."*[58] In both of Wesley's *Remarks* to Hill, however, he attempted to reinforce his presentation of Christian holiness by defending the doctrine of perfection. He carefully distinguished between "sins" as voluntary transgressions of a known law, and "infirmities" as transgressions of the perfect law but without the volitional element. Wesley asserted that adult believers could be saved from the former.

He admitted that there were some "sins of surprise" which were difficult to categorize, but proposed that the key of interpretation should be the extent of the concurrence of the will.[59] Perfection he defined as "neither more nor less, than what St. John terms perfect love; and loving the Lord our God with all our heart, and mind, and soul, and strength." While he granted that he had once believed that those perfected in love would infallibly persevere, he insisted that for the past ten years he had been convinced that they too could fall.[60]

Rowland Hill, younger brother of Richard, joined the fracas in the middle of 1772 with his *Friendly Remarks* upon Fletcher's *Checks.* Hill had been in Bristol at the commencement of the 1771 Conference, but had left the city to avoid Shirley's protest, although he later expressed his concern over the Minutes to Wesley. It was Fletcher's *Second Check* that convinced him he could no longer remain neutral. "Our enemies," he claimed, were pointing to Fletcher, along with others, who

> has been among the Calvinists, has found out their hypocrisy, and are now publishing against them. Numbers of them, to my knowledge, carry about your book in ill-natured triumph, and cast in our teeth, as certain truth, the *dreadful slanders* you have invented. In short, Sir, you have brought over us such a day of *blasphemy* and *rebuke* as we never felt before.[61]

After he reviewed the Minutes, the Declaration, and Fletcher's *Vindication* in parallel columns, Hill asked: "Does it not appear that Mr. Wesley, according to custom, contradicts himself; that you contradict the Declaration, and that the Declaration contradicts you both?" He contended that the Minutes taught salvation by the merit of works, and that the Declaration repudiated this position, but that Fletcher had resurrected meritorious grace in man. Hill further charged that Wesley's and Fletcher's denial of man's total apostasy and of the absolute holiness of God's law, were closely joined with the doctrine of perfection on the high road to antinomianism. Thus, Hill could argue that it was the Arminians, not the Calvinists, who traversed a dangerous trail:

Believe me then, Sir, that it is out of no desire of pleading for sin, that we thus oppose your doctrine, however unkindly you charge it upon us. No; we are convinced in ourselves that we are utterly undone; and we are certainly assured, that if we are not saved at the final day only by Christ, we never shall be saved at all.[62]

Fletcher's error on "sinless perfection" arose, Hill felt, because he posited two laws of God: one law of Sinai and a second, milder, law of love. He objected, however, that man's inability to obey did not imply God's inability to command, nor did it mean He "bends the law" to accommodate man's "innocent infirmities."[63]

Hill rejected the accusation that a "finished salvation" dispensed with the necessity of repentance, faith, and obedience. These he regarded as evidence of justification, nonetheless infallibly secured by the eternal decrees. He conceded that after salvation by grace alone, the Lord would permit "obedience to appear in the day of judgment as *declarative proof* of the reality of their faith." But he charged Fletcher with excluding faith on the last day. Hill ridiculed Fletcher for his shift from one justification to two, and then to four, and queried: "May we not expect that as you proceed in your checks, these *four* justifications may be *doubled* and *doubled,* till they amount to fourscore."[64] He concluded with a defense against Fletcher's accusation:

Believe me, I hate Antinomianism from my inmost soul; but still dare not part with the glorious truths of free, sovereign, and everlasting love, for a thousand worlds; however they may be abused by some that pretend to hold them.[65]

At this stage of the controversy, the combatants appeared to be drawing closer on the place of works in the scheme of justification, while in actuality they moved further apart due to other issues. Wesley stoutly maintained with the Calvinists that initial justification was by faith alone, but he contended for good works as a condition of final salvation. The Hill brothers agreed that some place needed to be made for good works and were willing to admit them as declarative or evidential proof of faith on Judgment Day. At the same time, they were continuing to emphasize that all of justification was by faith.

While both parties were still not in agreement, they were both maintaining the importance of good works against antinomianism. By the time this "smoking brand" had begun to cool, however, other doctrinal logs had been added to the fire, and fierce rhetoric had blown up the flames of disagreement into red-hot contention. Wesley and Fletcher were now more certain than ever that all of the distinctives of Calvinism stood behind both the doctrinal and practical antinomianism that they opposed. On the other hand, the Calvinists charged that it was Wesley's perfectionism that encouraged those evils. Both sides made their case public, and the rift between the two wings of Methodism continued to grow ever wider.

12. A Wider Separation between the Wesleyans and the Calvinists

AFTER the Minutes debate between the Calvinists and the Wesleyans expanded to include the larger questions relating to predestination, an even greater gulf appeared between them during the mid-1770s. What Wesley felt were false accusations against him by the Hill brothers led to his own counterattack, spearheaded by John Fletcher. In his *Fourth Check to Antinomianism*, Fletcher attempted to demonstrate a direct connection between Calvinism and antinomianism, a connection that was becoming more apparent to many who had been affected by the eighteenth-century revival. The present chapter then proceeds with a summary of the disruptive effects of the continuing Calvinist controversy on Wesley's Societies. One major purpose of such a summary is to show the practical effects of doctrine on the lives of Christians.

The chapter concludes with the controversy carried on in more moderate tones between John Berridge for the Calvinists and John Fletcher for the Wesleyans. Fletcher's *Fifth Check* and his *Equal Check* pretty much carried the day in the overall theological debate. His last *Check to Antinomianism* was a description of his own position on Christian perfection and came as a response to the Calvinistic accusations regarding the Wesleyan views on perfection.

Wesley's Counterattack against Calvinism

By autumn 1772, Wesley was convinced that he had labored too long to sustain a truce with the Calvinists. He clearly saw that there was no way of preserving peace with his "contentious brethren" except by carrying the war into their camp. As long as he was on the defensive, he reasoned,

> they will never be afraid of us; for they have nothing to lose. But when with gentleness and yet with rigour and firmness we show all the horror of their opinions, while with calmness and yet with all earnestness we point [out] the whole absurdity and blasphemy of Reprobation; yet pinning them down, whether they will or no, to that point, they will soon be sick of war.[1]

Accordingly, Wesley called all Arminians to take the offensive:

> Chase the fiend, Reprobations, to his own hell, and every doctrine with it. Let none pity or spare one limb of either speculative or practical Antinomianism; or of any doctrine that naturally tends thereto, however veiled under the specious name of free grace.

Admitting that neither he nor Charles had borne sufficient testimony to their convictions for some years, he blamed this upon "a well-meant, but ill judged, tenderness" which had allowed "the reprobation Preachers to spread their poison almost without opposition." But now that they were awakened to the danger, he declared: "We look for neither peace nor truce with any who do not openly and expressly renounce this diabolical sentiment."[2]

Since his determination was positive as well as negative, Wesley began that November to preach more explicitly on the universal love of God. He noted:

> Perhaps in times past from an earnest desire of living peaceably with all men, we have not declared, in this respect, the whole counsel of God. But since Mr. Hill and his allies have cut us off from this hope, and pro claimed an inexpiable war, we see it is our calling to go straight forward, declaring to all mankind that Christ tasted death for all, to cleanse them from all sin.[3]

Fletcher, agreeing with Wesley, drafted a response to the Calvinists that "might under the appearance of a defence carry war into the enemies' territories, and either shame the Calvinical Clergy, or prevent some from following them into their peculiarities."[4] With his eye on Richard Hill, he described his intention:

> I may kill three birds with one stone by answering his review, his reply, and that letter of his brother. . . . My plan is to attack antinomianism and Calvinism with the weapon Mr. Hill granted, second justification by the evidence of works in the day of judgment, and to show upon his own confession the Minutes and our legality are fully established.[5]

In November 1771 his work appeared as *Logica Gevenensis: or, A Fourth Check to Antinomianism.* Fletcher called himself "a student from Geneva" and addressed his book to all candid Calvinists in the Church of England.[6]

Since he had dealt with the scriptural data earlier, Fletcher now turned to citations from the Thirty-Nine Articles, the Liturgy, Homilies, and many Puritan divines. Fletcher hoped to convince his opponents that their doctrinal tradition in the Reformed Church contended for "St. James' evangelical legality" by pleading for the divine rewarding of works far more strongly than Wesley did. He insisted even further that the Church of England, by making justification turn upon the instrumentality of "a lively faith, and the evidence of good works as there is opportunity to do them, tears up Calvinian and Antinomian delusions by the very roots." Fletcher argued that if works had no part in man's justification, they had no part in his condemnation; this view inevitably led to a doctrine of "absolute reprobation, free wrath, and finished damnation."[7]

In accordance with his original design, Fletcher asked why Hill was contending against Wesley, since Hill himself granted works as declarative evidence of justification at the judgment. By now, they had presumably agreed on the expression "a second justification" and on its meaning as "by the evidence of works." So Fletcher declared that the logical consequence of that agreement should be a proper interpretation, and therefore a vindication, of Wesley's Minutes. When Wesley spoke of salvation by works as a condition, Fletcher asserted, he meant works as evidence of faith. Yet he conceded that Wesley regarded faith as being an instrumental work at conversion.[8] He contended further that Paul had not set faith and free grace in absolute opposition to every work, especially the works meet for repentance and the work of faith. Instead, he had juxtaposed them against the ceremonial law, the hypocritical performance of the moral law, and the works of impious moralists.

A second consequence of Hill's concession, Fletcher believed, was an undercutting of the Calvinist position on imputed righteousness and the eternal decrees. Using the example of backsliders, he showed the contradiction between the Father, who justified by the imputation of eternally decreed righteousness, and the Son, who condemned at the judgment by the evidence of works.[9] Fletcher believed that too much zeal for God's sovereignty had caused the Calvinists to undervalue the role of Jesus:

> Never shall you be able to do justice to the Scripture, and our Lord's kingly office, till you allow that, agreeably to his evangelical law, He will one day "reward every man according to his works;" and the moment you allow this, you give up what you unhappily call your foundation, that is, unconditional election and finished salvation, . . . and are as heretical (should I say as orthodox?) as ourselves.[10]

Although Wesley believed that Fletcher had beautifully explained all this, he added his own comments on the doctrine of salvation, emphasizing the essential theological unity of the two men:

> None of us talk of being accepted for our works; that is the Calvinist slander. But we all maintain [that] we are not saved without works, that works are a condition (though not the meritorious cause) of final salvation. It is by faith in the righteousness and blood of Christ that we are enabled to do all good works; and it is for the sake of these that all who fear God and work righteousness are accepted of Him.[11]

He reasserted that man was not "entirely passive" in salvation, and that a man must "endeavour" to do good works because faith did not "necessarily" produce them.[12]

Wesley was especially delighted with the *Fourth Check* and with the connection Fletcher had tried to prove between Calvinism and antinomianism. While he felt that it settled many who were wavering, and convinced some who were just falling into strong delusion, he recognized its limits in a letter to a friend: "You must not think anything will convince a *warm Calvinist*—no, not an angel coming down from heaven."[13] But Wesley may have underestimated the influence of the *Checks*.

James Ireland, who had been among Shirley's delegation at the 1771 Conference, told Fletcher he had begun to see "the evil tendency of Calvinism." He encouraged Fletcher to fight on until he had won the field or was beat out of it.[14] Another important figure who was heavily influenced by the first four *Checks* was Dr. Thomas Coke. Later, after he had become Wesley's chief lieutenant, Coke recalled that Fletcher's works had been "the blessed means of bringing me among that despised people called Methodists, with whom, God being my helper, I am determined to live and die."[15] In 1775 he thanked Fletcher for his influence upon his own theology and declared: "Your excellent checks to Antinomianism have rivetted me in an abhorrence and detestation of the peculiar Tenets of Calvin."[16]

Wesley now felt that the *Checks to Antinomianism* had so favorably identified Fletcher with himself in the Methodists' eyes, as well as showing the author's spiritual and intellectual stature, that he wanted to designate him as his successor.[17] After Fletcher declined in January 1773, Wesley pressed the proposal in July: "Just now the minds of the people in general are on account of the *Checks* greatly prejudiced in your favour."[18] Even Charles Wesley's hopes that Fletcher would succeed his brother had no effect.[19] Claiming that such a prospect "would make me take my horse and gallop away," Fletcher defended his refusals after Wesley made a further offer at the close of 1775:

> Such a step would at this juncture be (I think) peculiarly improper, and would cast upon my vindication of your minutes and address such an odium as the Calvinists have endeavoured to cast upon your address. It would make people suspect that what I had done for truth and conscience sake, I had done it with a view of being what Mr. T——— calls the Bishop of Moorfields. We ought to give as little hold to the evil surmisings and rash judgements of our opponents as may be.[20]

Fletcher's caution was not unfounded. When Toplady heard of Wesley's first proposal, he wrote to a friend:

> Mr. Shirley told me . . . that Fletcher is to succeed Pope Wesley, as commander-in-chief of the Societies, if he should survive his holiness. No wonder, therefore, that the Cardinal of Madeley is such a zealous stickler for the cause. One would think that the Swiss were universally fated to fight for pay.[21]

The Disruptive Effects of the Controversy

Richard Hill, hoping to have the last word in the controversy, in January 1773 published *The Finishing Stroke*, in which he protested that Fletcher had caricatured the Calvinist position:

> You know in your own conscience that we detest and abhor that damnable doctrine and position of real Antinomianism, *let us sin that grace may abound,* and that we constantly affirm that all who live and die in the practice of any one allowed sin, and who do not *follow after* inward holiness and conformity to the image of Christ, should assuredly be damned forever, what ever their doctrinal notions of opinions may be.[22]

Hill agreed that men were freely justified by the instrumentality of faith, maintained that genuine faith was manifested by good works and holy living, and granted those works as evidence of justification. He contended, however, that all this did not constitute a new act of justification at the last judgment.

Further, he detested the notion that the works of a believer were in any way meritorious, and argued that the confounding of reward and merit opened the door to works of supererogation. His doctrine of finished salvation, he declared, referred only to Christ's personal work as complete, not to its application to believers, and he rejected any middle way between law and gospel by denying any

> third covenant made up of grace and works mixed. Whoever will trace Arminianism up to the fountain head, will always perceive that it is the twin sister of Pelagianism; and that slight notions of the fall, of the extent of the law, and of the demerit of sin, be ranking at the bottom of that system.[23]

He quoted some paragraphs from a sermon Fletcher had preached in 1764, which Hill believed to be "the best confutation of Mr. Wesley's Minutes, and of all Four Checks written in vindication of them."[24]

After Hill reported rumors from Worcester "of the shocking behavior of some that professed to be perfect," he repeated his assertion that perfectionists were the worst sort of Antinomians, because they called "sins by the soft appellation of infirmities and some transgressions as sins of surprise."[25] Wesley investigated Hill's charges when he visited Worcester in March. He reported: "The truth is, one of the society, after having left it, behaved extremely ill; but none who professed to love God with all their heart have done anything contrary to that profession."[26]

Wesley's societies, however, were now feeling the practical effects of the controversy. Some students from Trevecka visited Wesley's society at Dover, but he observed that "though they have left no stone unturned, they have not been able to tear away one single member from our society."[27] When the Calvinists were more successful in capturing a society meeting room in Yorkshire, Wesley wrote one member:

> The point they aim at is this—to make Calvinists. Our point is to make Christians. They endeavour to convert men to the dear Decrees; we to convert men to God. In every place they have used their whole strength in opposition to us. But you and many more will not be tossed to and fro with every wind of doctrine.[28]

One illustration of the divisive effects of the controversy was at Frome, where a local preacher led thirty members in a separation over predestination.[29] Since Wesley believed that the opposition "have everywhere done our Societies all the harm they could," he professed to see more and more the "mischievousness" of Calvinism:[30] "I am afraid Lady Huntingdon's preachers will do little good wherever they go. They are wholly swallowed up in that detestable doctrine of Predestination, and can talk of nothing else."[31]

The controversy also produced a number of disruptions among Wesley's societies in Ireland. A Mrs. Paul, wife of the Dean of Cashel, wrote to the Countess of Huntingdon that "great dissatisfaction prevails among Mr. Wesley's people," and that Fletcher's works had "unsettled the minds of many" and caused some to leave the society. Wesley also received word of divisions at Waterford and Limerick caused by the Calvinistic preaching of Mr. Hawksworth, from the Countess'

Connection. Hawksworth even acknowledged his desire to draw Wesley's people over to himself.[32] As early as March 1772, in a letter to Lady Huntingdon, Walter Shirley described this competition among the Calvinists and the Arminians:

> The spite of Mr. Wesley's people has been most amazingly wicked; however, they are all falling to pieces. Their congregations I hear are frequently not more than 18 or 20 persons. Your Ladyship's society here consists of about 150. . . . I am persuaded, if your Lordship has once a Chapel built, you would have an immense society, and Mr. Wesley's would most probably be entirely broke up.[33]

These disruptions made Wesley more convinced than ever that he should raise a standard against Antinomians and Calvinists. Thus, he lamented: "By our long silence we have done much hurt both to them and the cause of God."[34] He moved to redress the balance by preaching and printing his sermon on "Predestination" in June 1773.[35] This was essentially the same message on Romans 8:29–30 that he had first preached in 1741, but had not published due to the earlier uproar over his sermon on "Free Grace."

If differences in doctrine troubled Wesley, the way in which his opponents contended for their views disturbed him even more. He was dismayed that the preachers at Whitefield's Tabernacle "flatly maintain all who do not believe as they believe are in a state of damnation, all who do not believe that absolute decree of election, which necessarily infers absolute reprobation." In contrast to this "bigotry," he contended that he and Charles had begun with the broad principles:

(1)   None go to heaven without holiness of heart and life;

(2)   whosoever follows after this (whatever his opinions be) is my "brother and sister and mother."

And we have not swerved a hair's breadth from either one or the other of these to this day.[36]

In spite of his more open opposition to the Calvinist views on predestination, Wesley continued to believe that, compared with central doctrines, they were only peripheral opinion, "feathers, trifles not worth naming." Practical evidence of Wesley's generous spirit was revealed in his gracious letter to Lady Huntingdon in September 1773. Whitefield's Orphan House in Georgia, which he had left to the Countess on his death, had been destroyed by fire in June, and Wesley wrote to assure her of his frequent prayers during her time of difficulty over this loss.[37]

More Moderate Tones from John Berridge and Fletcher

In general, the participation of Calvinist clergymen in the Minutes controversy was limited. William Romaine expressed his views as editor of the *Gospel Magazine*, and Martin Madan corrected the manuscripts of Rowland and Richard Hill.[38] Yet the only moderate Calvinist Anglican really to venture into the contest was John Berridge, vicar of Everton. As a graduate, and then Fellow of Clare Hall, Cambridge, Berridge regularly studied fifteen hours a day. While at the University, he had no use for the Methodists or their fundamental doctrine of justification by faith.[39] He had remained unconverted during his first years as rector at Everton. After his conversion in 1758, however, his preaching took on a different note. He was soon associated with Whitefield, Lady Huntingdon, and Wesley, among other Methodists. Berridge then formed an evangelistic team with William Hicks, vicar of the neighboring parish of Wrestlingworth, and began preaching throughout the surrounding countryside in barns and farmhouses, sparking an outbreak of revival in East Anglia.[40]

In 1773, Berridge published *The Christian World Unmasked* as an evangelistic tract. Although he mentioned neither Wesley nor Fletcher by name, he clearly discounted many of their views, rejecting any covenant of grace and works, the free will of man, a remedial law of love, and a twofold or fourfold justification. At the same time, he maintained a traditional Calvinistic position on the doctrines of total depravity, imputed righteousness, eternal election, and final persever-ance.[41] Berridge cleverly had a non-Christian to observe:

> We are told that some very honest folks, who are cast in the gospel-foundry, often ring a fire-bell to quench these very doctrines. And . . . it makes us titter when we hear a cry of fire, and see some engines from the Foundry playing on the tabernacle-pulpit. It is pretty sport for us, when Gospel-men pull noses, and the gospel dames pull caps.[42]

Rumor reached Fletcher in remote Madeley that Berridge had represented the Arminians as "foxes." Distance made it difficult for him to obtain a copy of Berridge's works. So he asked Charles Wesley to send to him, by post from London, the publications concerning the controversy as they appeared, including his own. He also requested another kind of assistance:

> Propose to the leaders and other members of the society who have clear heads and humble hearts to gather together the most subtle objections of Calvinism which have been suggested to them by the enemy, or by Calvinists; that we might try to trace them to the fountain head and detect the fallacies whence they spring.[43]

While Fletcher was preparing his response, Richard Hill wrote three letters to him, announcing his resolve to publish no more and to stop the sale of his pamphlets. Hill admitted that the controversy had done him no good and apolo-gized for his actions: "For whatever may have savoured too much of my own spirit, either in my answers to you, or to Mr. Wesley, I sincerely crave the for-giveness of you both."[44] Since Fletcher had already prepared part of his answer to Hill's *Finishing Stroke*, he was now in a quandary about how to proceed. He explained his dilemma to Charles Wesley: "As I have fought for what I am persuaded is the *truth*, *I* shall wrong the truth and myself if I suppressed my *honest* pleas for it, which can alone vindicate my injured character before im-partial readers."[45] Accordingly, he declared that he would not leave the subject "explained by halves." So, early in 1774, he sent forth his *Fifth Check to Antinomianism.*

Unfortunately, the first half of this new work was less a plea for the truth than a vindication of Fletcher's "injured character." Accordingly, the result was not up to the standard of the first four *Checks*. Nevertheless, Fletcher did sharpen the issues by insisting that it was the question of eternal election and infallible perseverance that divided them.[46] On these two doctrines, he maintained, it was impossible consistently to uphold the necessity of good works. He further rejected as "Geneva Logic" the Calvinists' attempt to allow a justification by works before men and angels at the last day, but deny it before God, in whose sight men are justified only by Christ's righteousness.[47]

In the part 2 of his *Fifth Check*, Fletcher turned his attention to *The Christian World Unmasked*, carefully prefacing his work with an indication of his esteem for Berridge: "His conduct as a Christian is exemplary, his labours as a minister are great; and I am persuaded that the wrong touches which he gives to the ark of godliness are not only undesigned, but intended to do God service."[48] It was just Berridge's piety that Fletcher feared would carry some people from the doctrinal antinomianism of Everton into practical antinomianism. Thus, he branded Berridge's solifidianism as antinomianism unmasked, because it excluded works as a condition of final salvation and granted a finished salvation to backsliders. He chided Berridge for terming the law of liberty a "cobweb" and sincere obedience as a "Jack o' Lantern": "What! thousands lost by following sincere obedience to God's commands! Impossible! . . . Nobody was ever lost, but for not following after, or for starting from sincere obedience."[49]

Human redemption, he asserted, made it possible to obey "the law of faith." Although this "law of liberty" did not allow willful sin or require perfect innocence, neither did it reject imperfect obedience. He defined obedience as "doing with uprightness what we know God requires of us, according to the dispensation of grace which we are under." While he granted Berridge's assertion that sincere obedience unavoidably led to perfect obedience, he asked: "Why then should the world be driven from sincere, by the fear of perfect, obedience?"[50]

To the argument that works as an evidence of justification encouraged boasting, Fletcher replied that there was as much danger of being proud of one's faith, as of one's works of faith. He argued that Berridge's admission that damnation was wholly of man undermined the very foundations of the Calvinists' position:

> Now, if my damnation is neither from any unconditional decree of reprobation, . . . what becomes of absolute reprobation, and its inseparable companion, unconditional election? . . . If "my damnation is wholly from myself," the Just Judge of all the earth must damn me personally for something which he had put it in my power personally to do or leave undone. My damnation, then, and consequently my salvation, is necessarily suspended on some term or condition, the performance or nonperformance of which is at my option.[51]

He concluded by showing that the base of Calvinism was further weakened by Berridge's acknowledgement of a conditional element in final perseverance.

Berridge had earlier warned Fletcher that he would not respond to the *Fifth Check*: "I dare not trust my own wicked heart in a controversy. If my pamphlet is faulty, let it be overthrown; if sound, it will rise above any learned rubbish that is cast upon it."[52] Richard Hill, however, retired more reluctantly. Although he had repeatedly declared that he would print no more, when word spread abroad that he had changed his views, he felt compelled to publish three personal letters to Fletcher to dispel this rumor. To these he added in an appendix "A Creed for Arminians and Perfectionists" as a caricature of Wesley's and Fletcher's position.[53] "What! more finishing strokes!" cried the *Monthly Review*. "This retiring champion, however, like the Parthians of old, is not less formidable in his retreat than in a direct attack."[54]

Although Fletcher felt called to defend Wesley's theological position, his heart longed for peace. He had confided to Charles Wesley in 1771: "I hope the time will come when all our breaches will be made up."[55] The gulf was widened later that year, however, when the Countess of Huntingdon excluded Fletcher from preaching in her chapels, causing him to lament:

> The breach between her and me in point of outward connection is inseparable, but I should be glad . . . that we might live upon terms of civil friendship with her, and indeed with all. With some people we must be *very near*, or *quite off.* I doubt whether this is not a little the case with our great friend.[56]

Though he had literally dreamed of reconciliation with the Countess,[57] when he had the opportunity to meet her personally, he postponed the interview and told Charles Wesley:

> Lady H. (entre nous) gave me *leave* to see her privately. I declined as not conscious to have done anything to make her ashamed of giving me leave to wait upon her openly. She then consented I should see her before all the world, but I declined doing it till she had seen my *Scriptural essay* (which the Calvinists will call *popery unmasked*) and my scales.[58]

For some time Fletcher had planned to publish *An Equal Check to Pharisaism and Antinomianism,* which he hoped would "be of a reconciling nature, and a scriptural plan of union upon which the candid on both sides of the question will readily agree."[59] Yet in honesty he expected a mixed reaction. "I fear it will gall some touchy Calvinists. But when they try to gall us by false accusations we may be permitted to return *true* observations."[60] On the other side, however, he had added a rational essay on the doctrine of salvation by faith, "lest the *Check* appear unequal," and he was afraid this would offend some Arminians.[61]

Part 1 of the *Equal Check* began with "An Historical Essay on the Danger of Parting Faith and Works," in which Fletcher sketched the tension between Pharisaism and antinomianism from Adam to Wesley. He noted that whereas the medieval church and the Council of Trent represented a fall into Pharisaism; Luther's solifidianism, coupled with Calvin's predestination and the Synod of Dort, symbolized the overbalance into antinomianism. He pictured the intrusion of the maid "Antinomianism" into the English revival:

> A foolish virgin, who assumes the name free grace, walks before her, and cries, "Bend the knee, bow the heart, and entertain the old, the pure, the only Gospel." An ugly black boy, called free wrath, bears her enormous train, and with wonderful art hides himself behind it. While thousands are taken with smiles and cheerfulness of *wanton free grace*, . . . a grey-headed seer passes by, fixes his keen eyes upon the admired family, sees through their disguise, and warns his friends. Mr. H. and Mr. T., two of her champions, fall upon the aged monitor; and to the great entertainment of the Pharisaic and Antinomian world do the best to tread down his honour in the dust.[62]

Because Fletcher believed that the "high Predestinarians" had on the left hand embraced the fatalism of Hobbes and Voltaire, while falling prey to the mystics and the Quietists on the right,[63] he desired to help restore the evangelical balance. He thus included an earlier sermon on "Salvation by the Covenant of Grace." It was from this sermon, first preached in 1762, that Hill had printed some extracts in his *Finishing Stroke*. Fletcher had earlier complained to Wesley that Hill had mangled his message, but he admitted that when he republished it whole, it would "exactly show where I (for one) leaned too much toward Antinomianism till the minutes brought me to the equilibrium of gospel truth."[64] His revised sermon, Fletcher believed, was both a fuller check to Pharisaism and a finishing check to antinomianism.

The sermon was followed by "A Scriptural Essay on the Astonishing Rewardableness of Works, according to the Covenant of Grace." Fletcher endeavored to secure a place for works within the covenant of grace with his reflection upon the pride and prejudice of those who worked "*from* life and not *for* life." It was this specious error, he believed, that had quenched the seventeenth-century revival and was striking a fatal blow at the current movement toward godliness. He argued instead that godly fear was a legitimate "spring of action and preservative of holiness in all free agents." If man did not labor for rewards, there was no meaning to the biblical concept of hope or the promises of good things to come. Since God had revealed that man's proximity to the throne and enjoyment of Himself were proportional to his holiness and obedience, Fletcher contended that to neglect the pursuit of holiness through good works was to overlook God Himself.[65]

Fletcher believed his arguments would raise more "dust of prejudice" against him than any of his previous publications.[66] Therefore, as a balance to the emphasis on works in the "Scriptural Essay," he desired to give faith its proper weight with "An Essay on Truth; Being a Rational Vindication of the Doctrine of Salvation by Faith." Fletcher defined "saving faith" as "believing the saving truth with the heart unto internal and external righteousness, according to our light and dispensation." He explained that faith was only a gift from God in the sense of a capacity to believe, and not an irresistible compulsion.[67] To allow for redemption among those who had not lived in the Christian dispensation, Fletcher made "saving truth," rather than the historical Christ, the object of faith. But he coupled the word and the truth so closely to the person of Christ that he could claim: "To receive them is to receive him and to reject them is to reject him and his salvation."[68] Fletcher concluded with his belief that saving faith does not differ in species under any dispensation but only in degrees.

Part 2 of Fletcher's longest work appeared as *Zelotes and Honestus Reconciled: or, the Second Part of an Equal Check to Pharisaism and Antinomianism: Being the First Part of the Scripture Scales*. In it he tried to show that true Protestant faith, rooted in Scripture and reason, held together the apparently conflicting biblical data on free grace and free will.[69] In parallel columns he weighed passages of the Bible to show the tensions between the work of Christ and the place of obedience, primary and secondary causes, original merit and derived worthiness, as well as other concepts illustrating the doctrines of free grace and free will.

Honestus and Zelotes personified the contending positions of the Pharisee and the Antinomian. Honestus, a "sedate moralist," overvalued the Ten Commandments, underrated the atonement, and hoped his free will, best endeavors, and good works would save him without any reference to justification by faith. Zelotes, the "warm Solifidian," insinuated that the commandments were unrelated to perseverance, pressed home unconditional election, finished salvation, limited atonement, and absolute reprobation, while decrying free will and sincere obedience. While each of these imaginary characters attempted to tip the biblical "scale" in favor of his convictions, Fletcher insisted that the balance of the "*Scripture Scales*" required equal emphasis upon faith and works for salvation.[70]

Thus he balanced the Scripture verses and rational arguments on such questions as the origin of evil, the moral law, and responsibility for salvation and damnation. Then Fletcher recommended to Zelotes and Honestus that the former send "back to Geneva the false, intoxicating election recommended by Calvin." The latter was to bring "over from Ephesus the true, comfortable election maintained by St. Paul."[71]

In 1775 Fletcher followed with the second part of the *Scripture Scales* as a third part of *An Equal Check*, using the same plan to weigh the evidence on the issues of perseverance and freedom of the will. To perseverance, Fletcher's "balance" gave equal weight to "merciful free grace" and "faithful free will," and as his own "plan of reconciliation" between these two viewpoints, Fletcher astutely proposed Wesley's Declaration of the 1771 Conference, "guarded and strengthened by some additions."[72]

When he turned to the larger philosophical issue of natural freedom versus absolute necessity, Fletcher again argued for a "balanced truth." He rejected inherent free will on the one hand. On the other, he objected to the fatalistic determinism of Jonathan Edwards and Voltaire, charging that they confounded moral necessity with necessity in the natural world.[73] Fletcher believed that to be human implied the use of reason and conscience to make moral decisions. He insisted that this meant some degree of free will: "For the moment souls have lost their power of thinking and willing *freely*, they are no longer accountable."[74] Although Fletcher had contended throughout the *Equal Check* that he was maintaining a balanced position, he expressed his real hope to Charles Wesley: "I trust I have treated the subject in such a manner as to give a push to Calvin's ark without touching that of our Lord."[75]

While Fletcher now commanded the field on the literary front, he was attacked in Madeley from the rear. Describing the skirmishes, he wrote:

> Lady Huntingdon's preachers track us round. They come to the next parish and to three places where we preach; being called in by the baptists whose hands they strengthen. But no matter, if these strengthen people's hearts in the Lord.[76]

Because he felt as strongly as Wesley did about the importance of holiness, as early as November 1771 Fletcher had begun to write on Christian perfection. He declared that "one of the strange proofs that Antinomianism reigns among us, is the *abhorrence* or *neglect* of the doctrine of Christian perfection."[77] It was originally intended as a part of the *Third Check*, but was left out because of its length. On three other occasions, Fletcher laid it aside so he could answer Hill's challenges.[78] Although the treatise had been completed by January 1773, Fletcher still delayed its publication because of some questions about his own experience of the doctrine.[79] At last it appeared in 1775 as *The Last Check to Antinomianism: A Polemical Essay on the Twin Doctrines of Christian Imperfection and a Death Purgatory.*

By "Christian perfection," Fletcher meant "that maturity of grace and holiness which established adult believers attain to understand the Christian dispensation." This, he argued, was distinct from a perfection of grace in either the dispensation of the Jews or that of saints in heaven. Perfection was, he declared, "nothing but the cluster and maturity of the graces which compose the Christian character in the church militant." It could be described as a spiritual constellation made up of the stars of perfect repentance, perfect faith, perfect humility, perfect meekness, perfect self-denial, perfect resignation, and perfect hope. All of these, Fletcher believed, were satellites of the chief star, "perfect love," a phrase he often used to characterize the whole concept.[80]

In response to the Calvinistic outcry against "sinless perfection," Fletcher distinguished between an Adamic law with its paradisiacal perfection, and the law of Christ with its evangelical perfection. With respect to the former, he utterly renounced "sinless perfection."[81] The transgression of this Adamic law he identified with Wesley's definition of "sin, improperly so called, that is, an *involuntary* transgression of a Divine law." He fully agreed with Wesley that there was no perfection in this life free from these involuntary transgressions of ignorance and mistake.[82]

Fletcher insisted, however, that Christians now lived under a milder "law of Christ," and that this evangelical "law of liberty" could be fulfilled by loving faith. Therefore, he believed, since love was the fulfilling of the evangelical law, "fulfilling the law of Christ, and sinning (in the evangelical sense of the word)," were "as diametrically opposite to each other as obeying and disobeying, working righteousness and working iniquity." Only in this sense, he said, was it possible to guard the concept sufficiently and speak of an "evangelically" sinless perfection. He summarized:

> We believe that although adult, established believers or perfect Christians, may admit of many involuntary improprieties of speech and behaviour; yet so long as their will is bent upon doing God's will, so long as they fulfill the law of liberty by pure love, they do not sin according to the Gospel: because (evangelically speaking) "sin is the transgression, and love is the fulfilling of that law."[83]

Fletcher believed the objections of the Calvinists arose because they confounded the law of innocence with the law of Christ, the power to sin with actual use of that power, and Adamic with Christian perfection. In particular, he explained that Adamic perfection came before any trial of obedience and extended to the whole man. On the other hand, Christian perfection came only after a trial of obedience of faith, and extended chiefly to the will, not to the mind or the body. The capital objection of the Calvinists, however, was that Wesley's perfection excluded growth. This supposition Fletcher flatly denied.[84]

In turn he rejected the Calvinistic argument for permanent indwelling sin, an imputed perfection, and a perfection at death, styled as "death purgatory." Because he felt that these only added fuel to the fires of the Antinomians, he spelled out the alternatives:

> If you choose imputed righteousness and imputed perfection without any conditions, it will "unavoidably" lead thee down into a death purgatory, through the chamber of indwelling sin, if thou art an *elect person*, . . . or to eternal damnation through the chambers of necessary sin if thou art one of those whom our opponents call *reprobates*. But if thou cordially choose the sincere, voluntary, evangelical obedience of faith, which we preach both as a condition and as a privilege, it will "unavoidably lead thee up to perfect obedience." There is absolutely no medium between these two Gospels.[85]

Since the 1774 publication of his "Essay on Truth," Fletcher had been equating Wesley's doctrine of entire sanctification on perfection with the Pentecostal language of the fullness of the Spirit. Lawrence Wood has shown that Wesley's identification of entire sanctification with the dispensation of the Spirit and his occasional correlation of perfect love with the fullness of the Spirit served as the basis for Fletcher's equation. What was implicit in Wesley becomes explicit in Fletcher.[86] Fletcher was convinced that one of the beauties of Wesley's doctrine of entire sanctification was that it, like conversion, could be described by so many different terms or phrases. He believed that one of the ways it could be described was with the Pentecostal language regarding the work of the Holy Spirit. Fletcher felt that this was one further piece of the biblical evidence for the experience and would therefore strengthen the doctrine. Thus, he wrote to Charles Wesley about including this more fully in his *Last Check:*

> I shall introduce my, why not your doctrine of the Holy Ghost, and make it one with your brother's perfection. He holds the truth, but this will be an improvement upon it, if I am not mistaken. In some of your pentecostal hymns you paint my light wonderfully. If you do not recant them we should perfectly agree.[87]

When Wesley saw the *Last Check*, he expressed his approval to Fletcher:

> I know not whether your last tract was not as convincing as anything you have written. That method of untwisting the truth and falsehood which had been so artfully woven together has enabled many to distinguish one from the other more clearly than ever they did before.[88]

Wesley's strong approbation would certainly appear to include Fletcher's use of the baptism or the fullness of the Spirit as identical with entire sanctitification.[89] The only place Wesley had reservations regarding the terminology from Acts about the Spirit was with the use of the phrase "receiving the Holy Ghost." He had expressed these earlier in a letter to Joseph Benson:

> With all zeal and diligence confirm the brethren, (1) in holding fast that whereto they have attained—namely, the remission of all their sins by faith in a bleeding Lord; (2) in expecting a second change, whereby they shall be saved from all sin and perfected in love. If they like to call this 'receiving the Holy Ghost,' they may: only the phrase in that sense is not scriptural and not quite proper; for they all 'received the Holy Ghost' when they were justified.[90]

Wesley was apparently anxious not to give the impression that justified believers had no relationship with the Holy Spirit. Fletcher would have agreed that everyone who is justified is born of the Spirit and thus has the Holy Spirit in his life. But Fletcher felt that the phrase "receiving the Holy Ghost" carried a technical meaning in Scripture that referred to the same experience as being filled or baptized with the Holy Ghost, and thus he believed it to be identical with entire sanctification. It is significant that while Wesley desired to maintain that all believers have "received the Holy Ghost" in some sense, he does not object to Fletcher's use of such phrases as the baptism or the infilling of the Holy Ghost as being identical with entire sanctification. This was certainly due to his own equation of Pentecostal language with Christian perfection.

In another letter to Benson, Wesley wrote: "I believe one that is *perfected in love,* or *filled with the Holy Ghost,* may be properly termed a *father.* This we must press both babes and young men to aspire after."[91] Thus, after a further evaluation of Fletcher's *Last Check* in August 1775, Wesley could write, "I do not perceive that you have granted too much, or that there is any difference between us."[92]

While the more philosophical arguments over necessity versus human freedom were still under discussion, Fletcher's *Last Check* concluded the theological aspect of the Minutes controversy. The debate that began over the place of works in the Christian life, had quickly spread to the whole concept of justification, and then moved to the question of election, perseverance, and perfection. While Richard Hill carried the largest share of the weight for the Calvinists, Wesley was singularly fortunate to secure John Fletcher to shoulder the literary responsibilities for the Arminians.

Within the larger scope of our study, it has been precisely because Fletcher seems to have been almost a theological alter ego for Wesley that so much attention has been given to his work. By the end of the theological part of the debate, Fletcher clearly had carried the day. This may have been partly due to his perseverance in polemics, as opposed to Hill's lack of staying power. But literary stamina was not the only factor that made Fletcher appear as the reigning champion on the doctrinal battlefield. In contrast to the harsher language and acrimonious temper of the Hill brothers and Toplady, Fletcher's softer tones and courteous manner certainly gave him a psychological advantage with readers.

Further, Fletcher's intellectual capacity made his arguments clearer and more persuasive than those of his opponents. With relentless logic he pressed the Calvinist position until its back was up against the wall of reprobation. At the same time, he made a reasonable case for demonstrating that Calvinism was theologically behind much of the current antinomianism. His success at making Calvinism appear in its worst light, along with his ability to connect that position with antinomianism, made his case for Wesley's views very appealing indeed. The resulting overall picture was that Arminianism became much more firmly entrenched as the dominant theological ethos of the revival.

13. The Last Phase of the Minutes Controversy

THE final part of the controversy between the Wesleyans and the Calvinists came in another round of debate over human freedom, with Wesley and Fletcher on one side and Augustus Toplady on the other. After a survey of the debate, this chapter turns to look at the last minor pamphlet exchange in relationship to the larger debates over predestination. Movements toward reconciliation and an end of the public controversy came with John Fletcher's publications in 1777. Following a review of these olive branches extended toward the Calvinists, the chapter gives a summary of the personal reconciliations that took place between the many adversaries in the debate. Finally, a word is added about the ongoing effects of the Minutes controversy upon Wesley's work.

The Debate over Necessity

In 1774, Wesley joined the debate over the larger, more philosophical, questions about human freedom and published his *Thoughts Upon Necessity*. Since he wanted to avoid a return to personal controversy, he omitted all references to his immediate opponents and began with the basic question, "Is man a free agent?"[1] Yet his purpose was clearly to preserve a personal sense of responsibility against the antinomianism that he saw latent in Calvinism. He surveyed a list of those who held that man was not self-determined: Adam, the Manichaeans, the Stoics, the Westminster Assembly, and several contemporary writers, including Dr. Harley, Lord Kames, and Jonathan Edwards. The systems of each, Wesley believed, implied a "universal necessity of human actions" because they concluded that human beings were absolutely determined by a principle external to themselves. Wesley attributed to Edwards the responsibility for connecting the fatalistic scheme of the Stoics with contemporary Calvinism.[2]

Wesley objected that all necessitarian views led to the logical conclusion that God was the Author of sin. Without some liberty of choice, Wesley could find no place in human nature for moral good or evil that, in turn, excluded rewards and punishment as well as future judgment. Wesley held that "no being can be accountable for its action, which has not liberty, as well as will and understanding." Consequently, he rejected "the doctrine of necessity" because "it destroys all morality of human actions, making man a mere machine."[3] Though he granted that sensations, reflections, and judgments, along with the will and passions, depended on the brain, he denied that this connection implied the total necessity of all human actions. Even if the strongest possible connections between these existed, Wesley believed that God had intervened to give man the power of choice,[4] a view that was directly related to his understanding of prevenient grace.

Toplady declared Wesley's *Thoughts Upon Necessity* to be "an equal portion of gross Heathenism, Pelagianism, Mahometism, Popery, Manichaeism, Ranterism, and Antinomianism; culled, dried, and pulverized." He published in reply *The Scheme of Christian and Philosophical Necessity In Opposition to Mr. John Wesley's*

Tract on that Subject.[5] By his definition that "free" agency equaled voluntary agency, Toplady could assert that whatever was done by preference or desire was a free action. He divided necessity into the "necessity of compulsion," referring primarily to inanimate bodies; and the "necessity of infallible certainty," which only rendered an event inevitably future, without any compulsory force on the will of the human agent.

Although Toplady tried to show that a man's actions might be both free and necessary at the same time, he held simultaneously that, strictly speaking, no one was ever "self-determined to only one action."[6] Instead, those actions were "determined by the views with which an infinity of surrounding objects necessarily, and almost incessantly, impress his intellect." Further, those external objects are "solely dependent on God himself." This he saw as one of the many arguments for "the great doctrine of philosophical necessity," which governed every individual atom and spirit according to the wisdom and love of God.[7]

Contrary to Wesley, Toplady affirmed that moral good and evil could exist with necessity. If necessary virtue were not moral, then God, who was necessarily good, would be an immoral being. He further insisted that there was no contradiction between necessity and rewards, punishments or future judgments. This was true because God had established that certain causes would produce certain results, such as the connection between virtue and happiness, vice and misery. Moreover, Toplady held that without "universal necessitation, . . . all things would be, in a moment, unhinged, disjoined, and reversed," which would lead to endless confusion in the natural and moral world. Finally, he concluded that the Arminians themselves ultimately took refuge in necessity: "It is necessary, they say, that man's will should be free: for, without freedom, the will were no will at all."[8]

Fletcher responded for Wesley in *A Reply to the Principle Arguments, by which the Calvinists and the Fatalists Support the Doctrine of Absolute Necessity: Being Remarks on the Rev. Mr. Toplady's "Scheme of Christian and Philosophical Necessity."* He argued not only against Toplady, but also against Voltaire, Jonathan Edwards, Hartley, Priestley, and David Hume. These writers, he charged, had joined forces to bind mankind with an invisible chain of absolute necessity:

> If their scheme be true, God and nature inevitably bind upon us all our thoughts and actions; so that no good man can absolutely think or do worse—no wicked man can at any time think or do better than he does, each exactly filling up the measure of unavoidable virtue or vice which God, as the first cause, or the predestinating and necessitating author of all things, has allotted him from all eternity.[9]

Fletcher pointed out that Toplady's Calvinistic chain—God, God's will, God's decree, Creation, necessity, providence, and sin—unavoidably led to the conclusion that God was the Author of sin. He labeled as contradictory the contention that human action could at the same time be both free and necessary.[10]

He believed that God did not have to determine every event that should come to pass, but that He had a thousand ways to curb and manage free agents in order to accomplish His ultimate purposes. Fletcher held that free agents had received both their life and freedom from God, that they depended on God to preserve these, and that they would ultimately be rewarded or punished by God for the way in which they had used their freedom. He felt that the doctrine of necessity was "the capital error of the Calvinists," and he would only admit its validity in the case of the salvation of infants.[11] Fletcher besought his opponents not to consider his challenge to their doctrine as arising from any prejudice against their persons, much less against God's free grace. He testified that both he and Wesley were willing to go as far as they could toward reconciliation:

> We go so far as to allow there is a partial, gratuitous election and repro-
> bation. By this election, Christians are admitted to the enjoyment of
> privileges far superior to those of the Jews: and, according to this repro-
> bation myriads of heathens are absolutely cut off from all the prerogatives
> which accompany God's covenants of peculiar grace. In a word, we grant
> to the Calvinists everything they contend for, except the doctrine of
> absolute necessity: nay, we even grant the necessary, unavoidable salva-
> tion of all that die in their infancy.[12]

The Final Aspects of the Minutes Controversy

Although the serious theological debate was waning, the personal attacks upon Wesley continued.[13] Jackson claims that Mrs. Wesley pieced together extracts from Wesley's correspondence in order to defame his character.[14] She then placed them at the disposal of certain Calvinists, who assailed him in the public press.[15] Wesley triggered another pamphlet volley when the foundation stone of the City Road Chapel was laid. In his sermon on the occasion, Wesley mentioned that early in the revival Whitefield had conversed much with Dissenters, contracted prejudices against the Church of England, and separated from the Wesleys.[16]

In his *Imposture Detected, and the Dead Vindicated*, Rowland Hill immediately assaulted Wesley for blackening Whitefield as a Nonconformist, while Wesley professed fidelity to the Church of England on the occasion of building a new Dissenting meetinghouse![17]

After he saw the pamphlet, Wesley observed: "I stood amazed. Compared to him Mr. Toplady himself is a very civil, fair-spoken gentleman!"[18] Charles Wesley more vividly described the renewed attacks on his brother:

> A Popish and Geneva trick,
> "Throw dirt enough, and some will stick,
> Will choke the reprobate Arminian,
> And damn him in the world's opinion."[19]

Since he was still convinced that "the main flood in England seems to be Antinomianism," Wesley moved to strengthen his defenses at the 1776 Conference. He urged all his preachers to read the works of Fletcher, Sellon, and himself,[20] to preach universal redemption "frequently, explicitly and lovingly," and not to imitate the Calvinistic preachers by screaming, allegorizing, or boasting.

He advised all Methodists to avoid hearing the opposition and to pray earnestly that "God would stop the plague."[21] In 1777 Wesley added his own final protest against the Calvinistic view of predestination with the publication of *Thoughts Upon God's Sovereignty*. In a description of this work, he pointed to the key of his own interpretation:

> To a cool man, I think the whole matter will appear to rest on a single point: as Creator, He could not but act according to His own sovereign will; but as Governor He acts, not as a mere sovereign, but according to justice and mercy.[22]

A Movement toward Reconciliation between the Leaders of the Debate

Fletcher began to grow hopeful about a termination of his own polemical labors:

> I see the end of my controversial race, and I have such courage to run it out, that I think it is my bounden duty to run and strike my blow and fire my gun, before the water of discouragement has quite wetted the gunpowder of my activity.[23]

In a step toward reconciliation with the Calvinists in 1777, Fletcher published *The Doctrines of Grace and Justice*. This work he hoped would "reconcile all the candid Calvinists and Arminians, and will be a means of pointing out the way in which peace and harmony might be easily restored in the Church."[24] He defined the gospel as "an assemblage of holy doctrines of Grace, and gracious doctrines of Justice," which pointed out for "sinners the way of eternal salvation, agreeable to the mercy and justice of a holy God." Fletcher summed up the whole controversy as an effort to maintain these two gospel axioms of grace and justice. It was Wesley, he declared, who followed Thomas Cranmer and Jacob Arminius in representing the balanced middle position between the extremes of Pelagianism and Calvinism.[25]

Grace and Justice served as Fletcher's introduction to *The Reconciliation or An Easy Method to Unite the Professing People of God*.[26] The *Reconciliation* was based on the admission that the gospel contained doctrines of partial grace and unconditional election, as well as doctrines of impartial justice and conditional election. Fletcher believed it was the confounding of these two elections that had produced the divisions.

Fletcher proposed that the Arminians grant the Calvinists that there was a partial election of grace taught in Scripture. By such partial election God bestowed, without regard to merit or demerit, more favors and natural talents upon some than others; so that while God was gracious to all, he was not equally gracious. According to this election, when God freely, but discriminately, elected a man to receive one talent, he also reprobated him with respect to receiving two or more talents.[27]

In turn, Fletcher asked the Calvinists to allow with the Arminians that there was also an impartial election of justice, whereby God administered rewards or punishments irrespective of persons. By this election God impartially rewards, "according to their works," the faithful servants with eternal glory and the wicked with the punishment of reprobation. This admission, Fletcher claimed, would also deny any "proper merit," or merit of condignity. Yet it would grant evangelical worthiness, or the merit of congruity, as the basis of God's justice, the Bible's promises and threatenings, and rewards and punishments.[28]

Though this was Fletcher's best attempt at reconciliation, it was not altogether convincing to the Calvinists.[29] It was based on his attempt to place Wesley's doctrine between the Calvinists and a position labeled "rigid Arminian" or Pelagian. But Fletcher in reality had only refined and elaborated, not substantially altered, the views he originally propounded in the *First Check*. When he offered to grant his opponents a highly qualified partial election in exchange for their surrender of Calvinistic absolute election and reprobation, he was in fact giving up nothing of consequence from his own position. At the same time, he was asking the other side to abandon the heart of their theology on predestination.

While Fletcher's efforts did not produce a theological or organizational reconciliation, a measure of rapprochement was achieved among some of the disputants. The Countess of Huntingdon had never totally lost her respect or concern for the Wesley brothers. At the height of the controversy in 1773, she renewed her correspondence with Charles: "It has been a sore trial your *Brother's sufferings* but I see the power and glory of Christ rests upon him. *I can never pray for either of you* but I have you before me as Moses and Ellias in the mount above all."[30]

In June 1775, when John Wesley was close to death in Ireland, she wrote again:

> I do grieve to think his faithful labours are to cease here on earth. How does an hour of loving sorrow swallow up the *just* differences our various judgements make. . . . *I have loved him this five and thirty years* and it is with pleasure I find he remains in my heart as a friend as a laborious and beloved servant of Jesus Christ. I will hope that the Lord may spare him.[31]

From the other side, Joseph Benson reported a conversation in which Wesley had given him "a very good account of the loving and catholic spirit of Lady Huntingdon."[32] During 1776, in an exchange of cordial letters with John Wesley, Lady Huntingdon explained why her students had accepted an invitation to preach in Cornwall, near Wesley's work. "All cannot believe with either you or us from the remoteness of our principles to each other. So the liberty of chusing every honest and sensible man justly claims." She insisted, however, that she did not wish to give offense: "Many have been the interpositions made by me to prevent any attack unkind or severe upon you or upon any who serve with you in the gospel, believing many to be worthy and excellent men."[33] Accordingly, she proposed: "Let it be our mutual business to love one another and serve those severally who will be helped by either."

Wesley agreed: "Your Ladyship observes extremely well that all human creatures have a right to think for themselves: and I have no right to blame another for not being of the same judgement with me."[34]

Although quite pleased with the Countess' letter, Wesley did request her to caution the Trevecka students about their abusive treatment of him. In spite of his clashes with the students, Wesley endeavored to be fair. In 1779 he had some reservations about the honesty of a young man who claimed to have been at Trevecka, but he wrote to Lady Huntingdon for a character reference before dealing with him.[35]

When the Countess read an account of John Wesley's death, she was apparently surprised to learn that at the end he acknowledged his sole dependence upon the meritorious sacrifice of Christ for salvation. She called for Joseph Bradford, who had been Wesley's traveling companion for many years, and he confirmed the fact, assuring her that this invariably had been the subject of Wesley's ministry. Lady Huntingdon then confessed her earlier belief that Wesley had grievously departed from the truth and, bursting into tears, she expressed her deep regret at the separation between them.[36]

In 1776, when Fletcher returned to Everton after a twenty-year absence, his traveling companion recorded the cordial meeting with John Berridge.

> The instant we entered the room the good old Vicar rose, and ran up to Mr. Fletcher, embracing him with folded arms; and then, with looks of delight and tears of affection, exclaimed, "My dear brother this is indeed a satisfaction I never expected. How could we write against each other, when we both aim at the same thing, the glory of God, and the good of souls! But my book lies very quietly on the shelf;—and there let it lie."[37]

In 1777, the year he published his *Reconciliation,* Fletcher lay very ill at Stoke Newington. During this time he renewed his cordial correspondence with the Countess, and received a friendly call from Walter Shirley and Rowland Hill.[38] In later life, Rowland Hill lamented that the controversy had not been pursued in a different spirit, and confessed that "a softer style and spirit would have better become me."[39]

Richard Hill had earlier acknowledged his harshness in his *Three letters* to Fletcher. In these, he had requested pardon "for whatsoever has appeared to savour too strongly of my own spirit." Wesley responded with a "short and civil" letter, in which he hoped "that all would be peace for the time to come, and that they should think and let think, bear and forebear with one another." The next time he was in London, Hill took the opportunity to visit the West-Street Chapel, and personally thanked Wesley for his letter. After he expressed his hope that the controversy might be dropped, Hill recorded: "Mr. Wesley took me by the hand, assured me of his loving pacific disposition, and we parted very good friends."[40]

Although personal differences were becoming less acrimonious, Wesley determined that his theological position would not be as quietly passed over as it had been prior to the recent controversy. To ensure a positive and continued presentation of his convictions, he launched the *Arminian Magazine.* Although it had the immediate appearance of a counterbalance to the Calvinistic publications, *The Spiritual Magazine* and *The Gospel Magazine,* Wesley had, in fact, contemplated such a periodical for nearly forty years.[41] Immediately after the 1777 Conference, Wesley drew up specific proposals for the magazine.[42]

The first issue was published in January 1778. He intended that it should "contain no news, no politics, no personal invectives," but "by speaking the truth in love," he desired to maintain that "God willeth all men to be saved." Wesley promised that each issue would contain some defense of the doctrines of general redemption, an extract from the life of a godly man, accounts and letters of contemporary experiences of spiritual persons, and poetry that supported his theological convictions. Appropriate for its title, the first volume began with a "Life of Jacob Arminius" and contained an "Account of the Synod of Dort."[43]

When Thomas Taylor, one of his preachers, complained that the magazine would foster further controversy, Wesley granted only that it was intended as an antidote to the "poison" of the Calvinistic publications, but he insisted that its design was not polemical:

> This Magazine not only contains no railing, but (properly speaking) *no controversy.* It proves one point: "God willeth all men to be saved and to come to the knowledge of the truth." It goes straight forward, taking notice of no opponent but invariably pursuing the one point.[44]

Wesley assured Taylor that he planned the periodical, not for Calvinists, but for his own people: "I publish it not to convince but preserve."[45]

Though Wesley may not have intended the *Arminian Magazine* to be polemical in a strict sense, its publication clearly signaled his intention to keep his own views openly before the Methodists.[46] In contrast to the years of 1742 to 1770, he now abandoned his attempts to smooth over the doctrinal differences between the two theological positions. The title of the new magazine made it clear to all concerned that he had adopted a less tolerant stance within the Protestant tradition. Wesley did not surrender his conviction that the Church of England and her Thirty-Nine Articles were broad enough to encompass both the Calvinist and Arminian positions. Theoretically, he continued to place the doctrines of predestination in the category of "opinion," although, practically, they had assumed a position of much greater pastoral significance. And while he was not ready to reclassify predestination as an "essential" doctrine, he clearly intended it to occupy a larger role in his own ministry.

Although the Minutes controversy caused a certain amount of disruption in some of Wesley's societies, its general effect was to confirm his Connection in a solid Arminian position. Wesley himself said little that he had not said previously, but Fletcher, speaking for Wesley, had convincingly reiterated the Arminian views. In one sense his *Checks* served as the vehicle that popularized Wesley's theology among the Methodists. At the same time, though, the *Checks* anathematized Calvinism in the eyes of many. No one could have asked for a more effective standard-bearer than Wesley found in John Fletcher.

If the Minutes controversy solidified the majority of Methodists into an Arminian viewpoint, its effect upon their relations with Anglican evangelicals was somewhat different. Many evangelical clergymen were moderate Calvinists and, although they did not always approve of the defense of their cause by the Hills and Toplady, neither were they convinced by the arguments of Wesley and Fletcher. For the most part these evangelical preachers stood aloof from the debate. Yet the controversy itself, by its emphasis on differences rather than areas of agreement, generally had the effect of widening the gap between themselves and Wesley. Hence, Wesley's attempts at fraternal unity with the evangelical clergy had not produced the close links he desired, and yet there was still a measure of fellowship and tolerance. After the 1770s, however, all hope of closer cooperation disappeared. This could be interpreted as yet another element in the widening breach between the Methodists and the Church of England.

PART IV:

CONCLUSIONS

14. Evaluations of the Controversies

JOHN Wesley's understanding of predestination was primarily determined by the character of God that he found in Scripture. Looking to the Bible as his ultimate source of authority, Wesley could not discard its presentation of a just, merciful, and loving God. But neither could he reconcile these characteristics with the Calvinistic view of predestination. Unconditional reprobation was the stumbling block.[1] Wesley could never disconnect absolute election from its logical corollary, absolute reprobation, and he was unable to harmonize eternal reprobation with a God of justice, mercy, and love. "Find out any election which does not imply reprobation," challenged Wesley, "and I will gladly agree to it."[2] While still at Oxford, he first saw this "millstone" around the neck of the whole Calvinistic hypothesis, and the impression remained with him throughout his life.

Yet, as George Croft Cell and Roger Ireson have convincingly shown, Wesley's rejection of the Calvinistic position on predestination did not carry with it a corresponding repudiation of the larger Reformed tradition. These two studies have substantiated Wesley's claim that his theology came within a "hair's breadth" of Calvinism. Wesley had very early established this commitment to mainstream Protestant orthodoxy in the 1745 Conference for his preachers:

> Q. Does not the truth of the Gospel lie very near both to Calvinism and Antinomianism?

> A. Indeed it does, as it were within a hair's breadth, so that it is altogether foolish and sinful, because we do not quite agree either with one or the other, to run from them as far as ever we can.

> Q. Wherein may we come to the very edge of Calvinism?

> A. 1. In ascribing all the good to the free grace of God;
> 2. In denying all natural free will, and all power, antecedent to grace; and,
> 3. In excluding all merit from man, even for what he has or does by the grace of God.[3]

By thus placing himself within the Augustinian framework of grace, Wesley attempted to protect his position from the charges of Pelagianism or semi-Pelagianism. These accusations were made against his theology because of his emphasis on man's accountability. Nevertheless, Wesley repeatedly insisted that it was the doctrine of prevenient grace that allowed him to give all the glory to God while at the same time emphasizing moral responsibility.

Wesley's somewhat unique position in this regard has made it difficult for the systematicians to classify him. Cell and Ireson, for example, see his theology as monergistic,[4] while others, such as Cannon and Lindström, believed him to be synergistic.[5] The point of departure will determine one's conclusion on this matter. If one begins with Wesley's doctrine of God, who is responsible for all of salvation, including man's ability to respond to grace, then Wesley will be viewed as a monergist. However, if one begins with Wesley's doctrine of man, who is responsible before God for his moral choices, then Wesley will be perceived as a synergist. The fact that Wesley's doctrine of prevenient grace allowed him to hold both views simultaneously means that Wesley would be more accurately described as a synergist within a monergistic framework. Man can act responsibly and with freedom because God has already acted in the atonement to provide him with the grace that makes his choices possible.

The real problem may lie not with Wesley's views, but with the categories within which Wesley's theology—like the scriptural data—does not always readily fit. Certainly, in his desire to be faithful to all the biblical materials, Wesley has provided the church with a significant synthesis of the relation between God's sovereignty and human freedom.

While the overall framework of Wesley's theology maintained this balance, different circumstances throughout his ministry forced him at different times to emphasize either sovereign grace or human liberty. The clashes with the Calvinists came, of course, when the latter received undue attention in the societies. Unfortunately, Wesley did not always speak as circumspectly as he might have, perhaps at times even giving needless offense. The unguarded manner of the 1770 Minutes is a classic example. Clearly, Wesley had been "disputing about" more than "words" for the past thirty years in his struggle to call the moralistically inclined preachers of the Church of England back to a more biblical position on justification by faith. And it only tended to confirm the Calvinists' worst fears when he uncritically observed of Pelagius in 1781: "I doubt whether he was more a Heretic than Castellio or Arminius."[6] Yet, however much Wesley's fears of antinomianism caused him to emphasize good works and moral responsibility, his theology was neither Pelagian nor semi-Pelagian.

If his views on the justice, mercy, and love of God were what determined Wesley's separation from Calvin over predestination, then it was his concept of the holiness of God that heavily influenced his separation from the eighteenth-century Calvinist evangelicals. From his early days at Oxford, Wesley was convinced that because God was holy, it followed that "without holiness no man shall see" Him. Therefore he designed his ministry to promote holiness of heart and life both in himself and others. It was for the encouragement of holy living that Wesley emphasized the importance of the fellowship meetings, societies, bands, and classes; the systematic exposition of Scripture; private devotions of prayer and Bible reading; attendance at divine service and participation in Holy Communion; fasting, the love feast, and watch-night services; and reading significant Christian literature.

Since all these "methods" were for the spiritual support of the Methodists in their desire for godliness, Wesley perceived anything that undercut these disciplines as a threat to the sanctification of the believer, and for that reason to be strenuously resisted. Thus the Moravian doctrine of "stillness," which recommended setting aside these scriptural "means of grace," was in Wesley's eyes a dangerous menace to the spiritual lives of Christians. It was so perilous, in fact, that this was one of the major reasons he judged separation from such views to be essential for the preservation of his societies.

It has been alleged that this kind of reaction to antinomianism was a significant force in shaping Wesley's theology. In reality, it was the centrality of sanctification in Wesley's thought that shaped his reaction to antinomianism, or anything else that tended to undermine godly living. Wesley's struggle with the Antinomians was only the negative side of his positive, unremitting commitment to scriptural holiness. His reaction to unholy conduct in "Christians" must be viewed in the light of his concrete efforts to strengthen the spiritual lives of believers. Since holiness was not a "given" but something to be pursued, he concluded that the quest for it was intimately bound up with good works and the "means of grace."

Wesley's relation to Calvinism and the Calvinist evangelicals can be properly understood only in this context. In spite of the fact that many Calvinists of his acquaintance—such as Venn, Grimshaw and Whitefield—were godly men who stressed holiness in their preaching, Wesley believed that Calvinism contained a latent antinomianism. He felt that there was a doctrinaire rigidity about the Calvinist plan of salvation that undermined the pursuit of godliness. All the Calvinists' insistence upon "making their calling sure" and their stress on good works as "evidence of election" never shook Wesley's conviction that something within Calvinism dampened the believer's ardor for holy living.

As long as this element of doctrinal or speculative antinomianism remained primarily on the level of intellectual understanding, Wesley was anxious to pursue all the cooperation possible with the Calvinists. But as Semmel points out, Wesley believed that doctrinal antinomianism ultimately "had the effect of increasing man's presumption while defeating his holiness."[7] Thus, when doctrinal antinomianism turned into practical antinomianism, Wesley felt compelled to attack what he saw as the root of the problem, i.e., the fundamental theological questions. Consequently, he found his personal relations with the Calvinists strained. Although Wesley carefully designed his publications on predestination to be doctrinal discussions rather than personal attacks, his opponents were not always so circumspect. The inevitable result was the clash of personalities and the disruption of cooperative endeavors.

Another aspect of Wesley's accent on holiness was the doctrine of Christian perfection or entire sanctification. This was a central part of his preaching from the earliest days of the revival. Wesley was convinced that this truth was inseparably bound up with personal spiritual growth, and he repeatedly exhorted his preachers to concentrate on the doctrine: "If you press all the believers to go on to perfection and to expect deliverance from sin every moment, they will grow in grace. But if ever they loose that expectation they will grow flat and cold."[8]

Wesley tried to guard the concept of Christian perfection from antinomian abuse by insisting that the experience could be lost and by placing a high degree of moral responsibility upon the believer. Christian perfection might be attained by faith in a moment, but it was maintained by spiritual accountability and the use of the means of grace.

He professed not to understand why the Calvinists were so afraid of this doctrine. Wesley asked, Why is it "that the very name of perfection has been cast out of the mouths of Christians; yea, exploded and abhorred, as if it contained the most pernicious heresy?"[9] It was obviously the prominent place of human responsibility in the scheme, as well as what was regarded as an overly optimistic view of human nature, that caused the Calvinists to react. They believed that Wesley had a deficient view of sin[10] and that he robbed God of His glory by placing too much emphasis on what man could do. They were also quick to point out the fall of certain perfectionists, such as Maxfield and Bell, as evidence that the doctrine led to antinomianism. They further charged that those who were "saved from sin say they have no need of the merits of Christ."

Wesley countered that such abuse was "no reason for giving up this or any other scriptural doctrine." He also insisted that those who had experienced entire sanctification "never before had so deep, so unspeakable a conviction of the need of Christ in all his office as they have now."[11] But it was to no avail. The Calvinists continued to object to Christian perfection as strongly as Wesley objected to Calvinistic predestination. Cell is not quite accurate when he claims that Wesley substituted perfection for predestination in his theology. But he is very close to the truth when he quotes Wesley's "laconic remark" that "the real issue between me and extreme Calvinism is in the doctrine of holiness or Christian Perfection."[12]

After beginning with the doctrine of God's holiness, Wesley moved to the resultant demand by God for personal sanctity among Christians. His concern was the remaking of God's image in the souls of men. From a practical point of view, however, this stress upon the cultivation of personal holiness appeared to some Calvinists as very man-centered. Failing to understand the place of prevenient grace in Wesley's theology, they accused him of preaching natural free will and justification by works. They felt that man was receiving the glory that belonged only to God, and that Wesley, having abandoned the orthodox Protestant tradition with its emphasis on sovereign grace, had conformed to the spirit of the age, with its optimistic view of human nature. Wesley's views on imparted righteousness and Christian perfection were viewed simply as an extension of this anthropologically centered theology.

Coupled with this concern about an overemphasis on man growing out of the Age of Reason, was the defensive position of the Calvinists in Wesley's day. After the Restoration of the monarchy in 1660, the fortunes of Calvinism declined so rapidly that by the early 1700s the only significant writer to defend that position was Dr. John Edwards of Cambridge.[13] Thus, the eighteenth-century Calvinists operated with a kind of minority mentality that regarded itself as under attack from every side. When Wesley began preaching justification by faith against the current moralistic theology that dominated the Church of England, he was welcomed by Calvinistic Evangelicals as another voice to call the nation back to the first principles of orthodoxy. But when he began to speak against predestination and for perfection, they soon began to ask whether he was not an ally of the Age of Reason rather than of the Reformation. Toplady's fears went even further. He viewed Wesley's Arminianism as a "return to popery."[14]

If the concept of Christian holiness was one determining factor in Wesley's relationship with the Calvinists, a second was the basis of his distinction between essential doctrine and opinion. All theology for Wesley was to be measured by the touchstone of Scripture. On the question of ultimate authority, Wesley clearly placed himself within the orthodox Reformed commitment to *sola scriptura;* any doctrine that was not biblical was not to be received. Within the confines of Scripture, though, Wesley allowed that there was room for significant latitude in interpretation. Indeed, he used a rather narrower set of boundaries to establish the parameter for "essential doctrine." This more restricted standard for judging theological views was the Thirty-Nine Articles of Religion.[15] These, for him, determined the outside limits of essential doctrine.[16]

Thus, as in the case of the Moravians, when certain people advanced a doctrine clearly at variance with both the Scripture and the Articles, Wesley could no longer cooperate and fellowship with them. But, as he attempted to do with the Calvinists, where doctrinal disagreement was within the confines of the Church of England's official theology, Wesley sought collaboration as well as fellowship wherever possible. This was true for him even when there was strong divergence of views over the interpretation of certain points, such as article 17, on predestination. From Wesley's standpoint, that doctrine was to be debated inside the established church's theological boundaries, where there was ample room for different "opinions."[17] While he was conscious that even these differences of "opinion" made a certain distance inevitable between the various parties, he conscientiously strove to minimize these, endeavoring to emphasize areas of agreement. Even after the Minutes Controversy of the 1770s, Wesley continued to maintain this distinction between essentials and opinions.

This catholic spirit was not only characteristic of Wesley, but also of many Calvinists. Although the subject matter of this book has necessarily concentrated on the essential differences between the two groups, one needs to remember that an attitude of fraternal collaboration was, in fact, the norm during the eighteenth-century evangelical revival. Controversy occupied a secondary place. When this generous temper prevailed, church leaders could achieve a remarkable degree of cooperation. Such was evidenced, for example, by Wesley's close working relationship with William Grimshaw of Haworth, and by the collaboration between Arminians and Calvinists during the first two years at Trevecka.

Wesley's cooperative attitude, based on his distinction between essential doctrine and opinions, met its severest tests when he felt that a doctrine labeled "opinion" began to undermine his emphasis on holy living. When the Calvinistic position on predestination gave rise to practical antinomianism, Wesley's catholic spirit was stretched to the limit. Intellectually, Wesley stood his ground; even during the 1770s he continued, at least theoretically, to classify Calvinistic predestination as "opinion." But the assault upon personal holiness by what Wesley believed to be a latent antinomianism in Calvinism produced another response. Emotionally as well as rationally, Wesley was committed to the promotion of godliness; he always stood ready to oppose anything that hindered personal spiritual growth.

At certain times in the 1740s and 1770s, Wesley believed the dangers of practical antinomianism to be increasing, so his reaction to the Calvinistic position, i.e., the doctrinal antinomianism behind the problem, grew stronger. During these two periods, his anti-Calvinistic publications appear somewhat inconsistent with a tolerant catholic spirit. But these struggles represent Wesley's attempt to maintain the centrality of Christian holiness, while preserving the distinction between crucial doctrine and nonessentials. Where a choice had to be made, Wesley clearly opted for Christian holiness. But even then he never wanted to surrender his intellectual convictions about the classification of doctrines, nor his genuine desire for fraternal relations with those whom he knew to be genuine spiritual leaders. This tension is reflected in the character of Wesley's publications on predestination; they are theological arguments against Calvinism rather than personal attacks against Calvinists. Wesley was even ready to debate "opinions," but he had no desire for this to eclipse cordial fellowship with other evangelicals.

Both the theological and the spiritual kinship of the combatants heightened the emotional aspects of the discussion. Because they lived within the same doctrinal framework of the Church of England, Wesley could admit that "the true gospel touches the very edge of both Calvinism and Antinomianism."[18] Similarly, his close personal relationship with men like George Whitefield and James Hervey made any disagreement quite painful for Wesley. The controversy was much like a family quarrel, where because mutual affection is so strong, dissension is often very intense; yet members keep striving for accord wherever possible out of emotional attachment to each other.

Wesley's dispute with the Calvinists was not a static one or a constant one. The free-grace controversy with Whitefield concentrated on election, perseverance, and perfection; then in the late 1750s and early 1760s, Wesley argued with Hervey over imputed righteousness. In the clash with Toplady, the focus of debate was on free will. Though the Minutes controversy began over the question of how faith and works related to justification, its center shifted in midstream, converging on election and perfection. The wheel had come full circle. Many points were discussed and rediscussed, but the hub of disagreement was centered on tension between predestination and holiness.

Notes

Introduction

1. In this book and in the period under study, "man" (in the generic sense) or "mankind" means "human beings" and thus includes all of humanity.

2. John Wesley, *Works*, ed. Thomas Jackson, 3d ed. (London: Wesleyan-Methodist Book Room, 1831), 3:340 (emphasis added). Cited as *Works*.

1. Early Development of Wesley's Views

1. For seventeenth-century England, see Holden Hutton, *The English Church from the Accession of Charles I to the Death of Anne* (London: Macmillan, 1903); Gerald R. Cragg, *The Church and the Age of Reason, 1648-1789* (Harmondsworth, England: Penguin Books, 1960); J. R. Green, *History of England*, vol. 3 (New York: Harper and Row, 1902); Christopher Hill, *Puritanism and Revolution* (New York: Schocken Books, 1958); Godfrey Davies, *The Early Stuarts* (Oxford: Clarendon, 1937); J. W. Bready, *England: Before and after Wesley* (London: Holden and Stoughton, N.d.); Martin Schmidt, *John Wesley: A Theological Biography*, vol. 1 (Nashville, Tenn.: Abingdon, n.d.); Geoffrey F. Nuttall, *The Puritan Spirit* (London: Epworth, 1967).

2. Adam Clark, *Memoirs of the Wesley Family* (London: J. T. Clarke, 1823), 60–61.

3. Ibid.

4. Three volumes were published in 1703 as *The Athenian Oracle; or Casuistical Mercury Resolving All the Nice and Curious Questions Proposed by the Ingenious*. In 1710 a fourth volume was published; Clark, *Memoirs*, 69–70. Also George J. Stevenson, *Memorials of the Wesley Family* (London: S. W. Patridge and Co., 1876), 63.

5. *Athenian Oracle*, 1:178; cf. Luke Tyerman, *The Life of Samuel Wesley* (London: Simkin and Marshall, 1866), 144, for a discussion of Samuel Wesley's theology.

6. *Athenian Oracle*, 2:111.

7. Ibid, 1:58.

8. Ibid, 2:101.

9. Ibid, 3:531.

10. Ibid, 3:260.

11. Ibid, Supplement, 141–42.

12. Tyerman, *Samuel Wesley*, 143.

13. Clark, *Memoirs*, 225; and Stevenson, *Memorials*, 160.

14. *Arminian Magazine* 1 (1778): 37, July 18, 1725.

15. "Articles of Religion," *The Book of Common Prayer* (Cambridge University Press, n.d.), 693.

16. John Wesley, *Works*, 10:245. Wesley did not record his reading of Burnet, however, until August 1730; Richard Heitzenrater, "John Wesley and the Oxford Methodists, 1725–1735" (Ph.D. diss., Duke University, 1972), 499.

17. Gilbert Burnet, *An Exposition of the XXXIX Articles of the Church of England*, 2nd ed. (Oxford: Oxford University Press, 1796), 195.

18. Wesley, *Letters*, 2:70; cf. 2:57–58.

19. Heitzenrater, "Oxford Methodists," 503, 524. The latter was from Isaac Watts, *Essay on the Ruin and Recovery of Mankind*. In 1740 Wesley published an extract from this as *Serious Considerations of the Doctrines of Election and Reprobation*; cf. infra.

20. MS: Wesley, First Oxford Diary, vol. 1, Methodist Archives, London. On September 27, 1725, he wrote on the subject morning and afternoon. The author is indebted to Richard Heitzenrater for calling this to his attention.

21. William R. Cannon, *The Theology of John Wesley* (New York: Abingdon, 1946), 54–64; and Martin Schmidt, *Wesley*, 1:73–89, 106–12.

22. Works, 5:203.

23. John Wesley, *A Collection of Forms of Prayer for Every Day in the Week*, 3d ed. (London: Printed for James Hutton, 1738), iv; cited in Heitzenrater, "Oxford Methodists," 247.

24. MS: Charles Wesley Sermonbook, Methodist Archives: The Johns Rylands Library, Manchester, 50–51.

25. Heitzenrater, "Oxford Methodists," 44–45.

26. Schmidt, *Wesley*, 115.

27. *Letters*, 5:258–59; cf. *Journal*, 2:159f., in 1734; and *Works*, 6:281.

28. Cf. Samuel Wesley, *The Life of our Blessed Lord and Savior Jesus Christ: An Heroic Poem, The History of the Old and New Testaments*; and in Latin, his *Dissertations on the Book of Job*.

29. *Arminian Magazine* 13 (1790): 214.

30. Schmidt, *Wesley*, 1:76–77.

31. Burnet, *XXXIX Articles*, 92.

32. Ibid, 29.

33. John Wesley, *A Plain Account of Christian Perfection* (London: Epworth, 1952), 6.

34. Heitzenrater, "Oxford Methodists," 289.

35. Robert Tuttle Jr., *John Wesley: His Life and Theology* (Grand Rapids: Zondervan, 1978), 150.

36. *Letters*, 1:207–8.

37. *Journal*, 1:420

38. John Wesley, *The Standard Sermons of John Wesley* (London: Epworth, 1921), 1:245.

39. Ibid.

40. Heitzenrater, "Oxford Methodists," 161. Wesley also read William Cave, *Primitive Christianity*, in Georgia (*Journal*, 1:264–68).

41. Howard Snyder comments, "This meant Scripture and tradition were not an unbroken line, but that the two were sometimes in conflict. And, in the case of conflict, tradition must give way." *The Radical Wesley* (Downers Grove, Ill.: InterVarsity, 1980), 69.

42. *Journal*, 1:419, on Jan. 24, 1738. Baker thinks Wesley became convinced that "uncorrupted antiquity was the coordinate with reason in interpreting and supplementing Scripture." Frank Baker, *John Wesley and the Church of England* (London: Epworth, 1970), 139.

43. John Wesley, *The Works of John Wesley* (Oxford: Clarendon, 1980), 25:533. Cited as *Works* (Oxford).

44. Ibid, 615. Cf. Snyder's evaluation that Wesley "was always clear as to the priority of Scripture, especially from 1738 on." *Radical Wesley*, 71.

45. *Journal*, 1:447, on Mar. 23, 1738.

46. Ibid, 454, on Apr. 22, 1738. Bohler also brought living witnesses to testify to their conversion in this manner. For Wesley's time, testimony from experience served to confirm Scripture, but not to supersede it as final authority. Cf. *Journal*, 1:471–72.

47. *Sermons*, 1:32–33.

48. Snyder, *Radical Wesley*, 71.

49. Cohn Williams, *John Wesley's Theology Today* (Nashville: Abingdon, 1960), 23.

50. *Works*, 7:198–99.

51. *Works*, 8:340.

Excursus:
Arminianism and Calvinism in the Eighteenth Century

1. For the Arminianism of the Church of England, see G. R. Cragg, *From Puritanism to the Age of Reason: A Study of Changes in Religious Thought within the Church of England, 1660–1700* (Cambridge: Cambridge University Press, 1966), 13–36; T. M. Parker, "Arminianism and Laudianism in Seventeenth-Century England," *Studies in Church History*, vol. 1, ed. C. W.

Dugmore and C. Duggan (London: Nelson, 1964), 20–34; R. N. Stromberg, "Arminianism," *Religious Liberalism in Eighteenth-Century England* (Oxford: Oxford University Press, 1954), 88–109; Gordon S. Wakefield, "Armianism in the Seventeenth and Eighteenth Centuries," *London Quarterly and Holborn Review*, 185 (1960): 253–58; O. W. Howe, "Decline of Calvinism," *Comparative Studies in Society and History* (Cambridge: Cambridge University Press, 1972), 14:306–27. Bernard Semmel, *The Methodist Revolution* (London: Heinemann, 1973), 23–109; A. W. Harrison, *Arminianism* (London: Duckworth, 1973), 122–222; and Otto W. Heick, "Arminianism in England," *A History of Christian Thought*, vol. 2 (Philadelphia: Fortress, 1966), 79–92.

2. John Tulloch, Rational Theology and Christian Philosophy in England in the Seventeenth Century, vol. 1 (Edinburgh: Blockwood and Sons, 1874), 124.

3. Cragg, *From Puritanism*, 16, 29–30.

4. Cf. N. R. N. Tyacke, "Arminianism in England, in Religion and Politics, 1604 to 1640" (D.Phil. diss., Oxford University, 1968). Also Cragg, *From Puritanism*, 15.

5. Heick, *Arminianism*, 82, 85–90.

6. Cragg, *From Puritanism*, 33–34; Heick, *Arminianism*, 90–92.

7. Harrison, *Arminianism*, 179; Cragg, *From Puritanism*, 29–30. In the eighteenth century, Unitarianism was called Socinianism (from Faustus Socinus, 1539–1604).

8. Stromberg, "Arminianism," 111, 116, 119, 121; Cragg, *From Puritanism*, 30.

9. For Wesley's relationship to Arminius, see Alfred H. Pask, "The Influence of Arminius on John Wesley," *London Quarterly and Holborn Review* 185 (1960): 258–63; and Frank Baker, "Wesley and Arminius," *Proceedings of the Wesley Historical Society* 22 (1939–40): 118–19 (hereafter, *Proceedings WHS*).

10. For the theology of Arminius, see Carl Bangs, *Arminius* (New York: Abingdon, 1960);

F. Stuart Clark, "The Theology of Arminius," *The London Quarterly and Holborn Review* 185 (1960): 248–53; and H. A. Slaate, *The Arminian Arm of Theology* (Washington, D.C.: The University Press, 1980).

11. Pask, "Influence of Arminius," 262.

12. Wesley, "The Question 'What Is an Arminian?' Answered," *Works*, 10:359, in 1770. The only evidence that Wesley read Arminius is indirect. He asked: "How can any man know what Arminius held, who has never read one page of his writings?" Ibid, 360. He was better acquainted with other Remonstrant writings. On July 6,1741, in the midst of his controversy with George Whitefield, Wesley read the works of Episcopius, successor to Anninius as professor at Leyden and leader of the Remonstrants at the Synod of Dort; *Journal*, 2:473. Since his Oxford days, Wesley had known the writings of another leading Dutch Arminian, Grotius; *Letters*, 1:48. Cf. Pask, "Influence of Arminius," 261.

13. Pask, "Influence of Arminius," 259; Wakefield, "Arminianism," 258; Semmel, *Methodist Revolution*, 105.

14. John Ryland, ed., *The Works of the Rev. Andrew Fuller*, 8 vols. (London: B. J. Holdsworth, 1924), 2:189. The position here termed as "High Calvinism" was designated by some in the eighteenth century as "Strict Calvinism."

15. The supralapsarians believed that God's decree of election should be placed *before* His decrees of Creation, the Fall, and the Atonement. The infralapsarians and sublapsarians placed the decree of election *after* the decrees of Creation and the Fall.

16. Peter Toon, The Emergence of Hyper-Calvinism in English Nonconformity, 1689–1765 (London: The Olive Tree, 1967), 143–44.

17. For discussion of "Fullerism" as representative of High Calvinism, see E. F. Chipsham, "Andrew Fuller and Fullerism: A Study in Evangelical Calvinism," *The Baptist Quarterly* 20 (1963–64): 99–114, 146–54, 214–25, 268–76; and Toon, *Emergence of Hyper-Calvinism*, 150–52.

18. What is here described as Hyper-Calvinism was called by some in the eighteenth century "False Calvinism" or "High Calvinism." The term Hyper-Calvinism did not come into general use until the nineteenth century. Toon, *Emergence of Hyper-Calvinism*, 144.

19. Ibid, 144–45.

20. Chipsham, *Andrew Fuller*, 102–4.

21. Toon, Emergence of Hyper-Calvinism, 93–103, 144.

22. Bernard Manning, *Essays in Orthodox Dissent* (London: Independent, 1939), 192.

23. J. D. Walsh, "Yorkshire Evangelicals in the Eighteenth Century, with Special Reference to Methodism" (Ph.D. diss., Cambridge University, 1957), 3–10; see chap. 1, "Moderate Calvinism," 1–49.

24. Ibid, 27–30.

25. For the theology of Amyraut, see Brian C. Armstrong, *Calvin and Amyraut Hershey* (Madison: University of Wisconsin Press, 1969), 158–221; and Walter Rox, *Essays on Pierre Bayle and Religious Controversy* (The Hague: Martinus Nijhoff, 1965), 99–108.

26. For the theology of Baxter, see James I. Packer, "The Redemption and Restoration of Man in the Thought of Richard Baxter" (D.Phil. diss, Oxford University, 1954), 195–270.

27. Walsh, Yorkshire Evangelicals, 30–32.

28. Ibid, 18–20.

29. Ibid, 24–25.

30. Ibid, 35–38; cf. his description of Henry Venn as one who "says little on Calvinistical points, but insists much on the Doctrine of Assurance." MS: Shirley to Huntingdon, ND (1770), Cheshunt College Archives FL/1567, Cambridge.

2. Controversy on Predestination

1. In 1731 Wesley briefly touched the subject while reading William King, *Divine Predes-* *tination and Foreknowledge Consistent with the Freedom of Man's Will*. The same year he read Thomas Bennet, *The Thirty-Nine Articles of Religion;* and Edward Welchman, *The Thirty-Nine Articles of the Church of England*, which he used as a study book with the Holy Club. Heitzenrater, "Oxford Methodists," 509, 496, 524.

2. *Journal*, 2:31–32.

3. Thomas Jackson, *The Life of Charles Wesley*, vol. 1 (London: Mason, 1841), 247.

4. George Whitefield, *George Whitefield's Journals*, 193.

5. *Journal*, 2:289.

6. For a discussion of Whitefield and Wesley's open-air preaching, see J. S. Simon, "Whitefield and Bristol," *Proceedings WHS* 10 (1915): 1, 10, at the time of his departure.

7. MS: Whitefield to Wesley, Apr. 3, 1739, Methodist Archives, Manchester. Also *Journal*, 2:171n.

8. *Whitefield's Journals*, 261.

9. Arnold Dallimore argues for a restoration of Whitefield to his rightful place of influence in the eighteenth-century revival. He believes the way to do this is to show how Whitefield was originally the leader of the movement rather than Wesley. Accordingly, he takes great pains to show how Wesley usurped the leadership role while Whitefield ministered in America, and then would not relinquish that position when Whitefield returned to England in 1741. By deprecating Wesley's position in the early years of the revival, Dallimore hopes to make his case for Whitefield's primacy on the leadership issue. This false presupposition unfortunately mars what is otherwise an excellent book, and it forces Dallimore to argue that it was really Wesley who separated from Whitefield by stealing away his converts, rather than Whitefield separating from Wesley because of differences over predestination. Dallimore, *George Whitefield* (London: Banner of Truth Trust, 1970 and 1980), 1:278–79, 313–14, 381–83, 385–86, 389; 2:5–78, passim.

10. MS: Mary Thomas to Charles Wesley, Early Methodist Volume, Methodist Archives, Manchester.

11. MS: Eliz. Sayce to Charles Wesley, Early Methodist Volume, Methodist Archives, Manchester.

12. *Journal*, 2:173–76.

13. Ibid, 175; cf. other texts from this period that may have been used to support this doctrinal position, e.g., Isaiah 55:1, "Ho, *everyone* that thirsteth, come ye to the waters," and John 7:37, "If *any man* thirst, let him come unto me and drink" (emphasis added).

14. Ibid, 183.

15. *Letters*, 1:302–3.

16. *Journal*, 2:184; *Letters*, 1:303–4.

17. *Letters*, 1:302–3.

18. "Extracts from the Diaries of Howel Harris," *Bathafarn* 9 (1954): 31, on Mar. 10, 1739.

19. *Letters*, 1:302. A third letter that Wesley did not see until May 2, described him as a deceiver of the people because he taught that God wills all men to be saved; *Journal*, 2:1–8.

20. *Journal*, 2:184.

21. *Letters*, 1:308–9.

22. Toon, *Hyper-Calvinism*, 96–100. John Gill, *The Doctrine of God's Everlasting Love* (1732).

23. *Journal*, 2:206 n. Wesley later republished Whitby's *Discourse* in the *Arminian Magazine* 8–12 (1785–89).

24. John Gill, *The Cause of God and Truth*, vol. 1 (New Edition; London: Printed by E. Justian, 1860).

25. Ibid, vol. 2. The fact that his presentation began with reprobation and centered almost exclusively on the distinctives of Calvinism supports Toon's evaluation of Gill as a Hyper-Calvinist.

26. Ibid, 1:v.

27. Luke Tyerman, *The Life of the Rev. George Whitefield*, 2 vols. (London: Hodder and Stoughton, 1876), 1:277.

28. Ibid, 312.

29. *Whitefield's Journals*, 299.

30. It is interesting to observe that John Wesley and Whitefield always refer to one another as "Mr. Whitefield" and "the Rev. Mr. John Wesley," whereas Charles Wesley usually calls Whitefield by his first name, "George."

31. MS: Whitefield to Charles Wesley, Dec. 10, 1737, no. 81, Letters to Charles Wesley, vol. VI, Methodist Archives, Manchester.

32. John Wesley and Charles Wesley, *The Poetical Works of John and Charles Wesley*, 13 vols. Ed. G. Osborn (London: Wesleyan-Methodist Conference Office, 1868), 227–31.

33. *Journal of Charles Wesley*, 1:159, 163.

34. MS: Benjamin Seward to Charles Wesley, Sept. 8, 1739, Letters to Charles Wesley, vol. 6, Methodist Archives, Manchester.

35. *Journal of Charles Wesley*, 1:176, 179.

36. MS: John Edmonds to Charles Wesley, Early Methodist Volume, Methodist Archives, Manchester.

37. *Journal of Charles Wesley*, 1:188.

38. *Whitefield's Journals*, 62.

39. Arnold Dallimore, *George Whitefield*, 1:84–85.

40. There seems to be a lack of clarity in the use of the term "Calvinism." Dallimore at times uses the designation to refer to the whole system of Christian theology as seen by Calvin. The problem is that in large measure this theological position is shared by other Protestants. Wesley's own agreement with the Reformers on major doctrines has been well demonstrated: cf. George Croft Cell, *The Rediscovery of John Wesley* (New York: Henry Holt, 1935); and Roger W. Ireson, "The Doctrine of Faith in John Wesley and the Protestant Tradition" (Ph.D. diss., University of Manchester, 1973). This particularly applies to views that make God completely responsible for salvation and to the doctrine of justification by faith alone. Tyerman, on the other hand, gener-

ally restricts the word "Calvinism" to those doctrines that distinguish the theology of Calvin and subsequent Calvinist theologians from the views of others within the Protestant tradition; this usually has special reference to predestination and related doctrines. In this study, these are termed the distinctive doctrines of Calvinism.

41. This conclusion is supported by Tyerman, *Whitefield*, 1:305; and Earl P. Crow, "John Wesley's Conflict with Antinomianism in Relation to the Moravians and Calvinists" (Ph.D. diss., University of Manchester, 1964), 119. Dallimore lists two sermons as indications of Whitefield's commitment to the Calvinistic distinctives during this period: *A Farewell Sermon*, 1737 (London: Simkin, Marshall, 1842); and "Justification by Christ," 1738 (George Whitefield, *Works*, 6:214–25). The evidence of the sermons, however, does not support his contention. Cf. Tyerman's discussion, *Whitefield*, 1:274–75, and Roland Austin, "Bibliography of the Works of George Whitefield," *Proceedings WHS* 10 (1915): 169–84, 211–223.

42. Tyerman, *Whitefield*, 1:273; and Whitefield, *Works*, 1:58.

43. *Arminian Magazine* 1 (1778): 178–79.

44. Tyerman, *Whitefield*, 1:310.

45. *Whitefield's Journals*, 335.

46. Ibid, 335, 586.

47. John Edwards, *The Preacher* (London: F. Robison, F. Lawrence, and F. Wyat, 1705–09), 1:186.

48. Ibid, 1:v.

49. Ibid, 2:132.

50. Ibid, 1:ix.

51. *Whitefield's Journals*, 559.

52. Tyerman, *Whitefield*, 1:314.

53. *The Weekly History*, no. 4 (May 2, 1741), on Nov. 1739.

54. Whitefield, *Works*, 1:101, from Nov. 10, 1739. Cf. "Trevecka *MSS* Supplement, No. 7," *CCH* 19 (1933): 241.

55. Some have felt Whitefield was not a Calvinist before he arrived in America. E.g., Edwin Sidney, *The Life of Sir Richard Hill, Bart* (London: R. B. Seeley and W. Burnside, 1839), 171; and Thomas Coke and Henry Moore, *The Life of the Rev. John Wesley, A.M.* (London: 1792), 222. As shown above, this judgment is not accurate.

56. Moore indicates they recommended to him the Puritan divines. *The Life of the Rev. John Wesley, A.M.*, 494.

57. Cf. Tyerman's discussion of William Tennet Sr., pastor at Neshaminy, Pennsylvania, and his four sons, who were also Presbyterian ministers; in *Whitefield*, 1:315–28.

58. In June, Whitefield had read Erskine's sermons; *Whitefield's Journals*, 287. Tyerman, followed by Crow, suggests that these Calvinistic sermons heavily influenced Whitefield's thinking. Since it is unclear which sermons Whitefield read, and what their content was, this remains only conjecture. See Tyerman, *Whitefield*, 1:274; and Crow, "Wesley's Conflict with Antinomianism," 143.

59. Tyerman, *Whitefield*, 1:333–34.

60. Cf. Sidney, *Life of Richard Hill*, 171: "He caught the tone and imbibed the opinions of the great, the searching, but too gloomy Jonathan Edwards. His *Treatise on the Will* was too deep a book for Whitefield, and the probability is, that the author himself was somewhat out of his own depth when he wrote it. No wonder that when Whitefield first came into contact with Edwards, he 'winced a little under his metaphysical probe'; but, at last, he adapted his Calvinistic views, though it may be fairly doubted if he ever fully understood them." Crow, "Wesley's Conflict with Antinomianism," also discusses Edwards' theology at length to show his influence over Whitefield.

61. John Gillies, *The Life of the Reverend George Whitefield, M.A.* (London: Dilly, 1772), 61.

62. Joseph Tracey, *The Great Awakening*, 225–26; cited in Dallimore, *Whitefield*, 1:540.

3. Storm over Predestination

1. *Journal*, 2:332, 370, 379, 387, 390, 391, 393, 407.

2. *Journal of Charles Wesley*, 1:211.

3. MS: Ian Mason to Howel Harris, July 26, 1740, no. 56, Letters to Charles Wesley, vol. 6, Methodist Archives, Manchester.

4. *Journal*, 2:353.

5. *Letters*, 1:343.

6. *Journal*, 2:312.

7. Ibid, 312 n. Also Luke Tyerman, *The Life and Times of the Rev. John Wesley, M.A., Founder of the Methodists*, 2d ed., 3 vols. (London: Hodder and Stoughton, 1872–75), 1:297–98. Cited as Tyerman, *Wesley.*

8. MS: Martha Jones to Charles Wesley, Early Methodist Volume, Methodist Archives, Manchester.

9. MS: T. Cowper to Charles Wesley, Early Methodist Volume, Methodist Archives, Manchester. Others resisted the "stillness" doctrine; cf. "Account of Jane Muncy," *Arminian Magazine* 4 (1781): 153.

10. *Journal*, 2:328–31, 333, 335.

11. Ibid, 331, 345. Cf. Wesley's disagreement with a Bristol man on Jan. 25, 1740: "I cannot approve of your terms, because they are not scriptural. I find no such phrase as either 'faith of assurance' or 'faith of adherence' in the Bible." Ibid, 333.

12. Ibid, 359–60.

13. Ibid, 354–56.

14. Ibid, 369–70.

15. Seymour, *Huntingdon*, 1:36. Also Snyder, *The Radical Wesley*, 39–40.

16. MS: Ian Mason to Howel Harris, July 26, 1740, no. 56, Letters to Charles Wesley, vol. 6, Methodist Archives, Manchester.

17. *Letters*, 1:350, in Aug. 1740.

18. Ibid, 353; cf. 354, his earlier statement to James Hutton: "I think the Brethren wrong in a few things . . . because I believe the Bible. The chief thing wherein I think them wrong is in mixing human wisdom with divine."

19. After the division Wesley detailed his theological differences with the Moravians in a letter to the church at Herrnhut. The chief points of controversy were over Christian salvation, saving faith, the way of faith, the ordinances of God, the church, the Scriptures and tradition, and good works; *Letters*, 2:345.

20. In August, Wesley had read Elisha Coles, *A Practical Discourse on God's Sovereignty* (London: Ben Griffin, 1673). *Journal*, 2:380.

21. *Serious Considerations of the Doctrines of Election and Reprobation* (London: 1740), p. 3.

22. Ibid, p.11.

23. *The Poetical Works*, 1:308–14.

24. Cf. one Calvinist reaction: "Mr. Wesley had published another large collection of hymns of his own and his brother's making in which he has as strong expressions against Election as in his sermon on Free-Grace." MS: Ian Mason to Howel Harris, July 26, 1740, no. 56, Letters to Charles Wesley, vol. 6, Methodist Archives, Manchester.

25. Geoffrey L. Fairs, "The Death of William Seward at Hay, 22 October, 1740," *Proceedings WHS* 29 (Feb. 1973), 2; cf. Tyerman's discussion of the Seward family, *Whitefield*, 1:164–68.

26. "William Seward to Thomas Seward," on June 16, 1739; cited in Tyerman, *Whitefield*, 1:251.

27. "William Seward to Mrs. Martha Beecher, Nov. 8, 1739," "The Trevecka MSS, Supplement, No. 7," *CCH* 19 (Feb. 1934), 238.

28. For a discussion of Seward's several Journals, see Hilda Lofthouse, "The Journal of William Seward 6th September to 15 October 1740," *Proceedings WHS* 34 (Mar. 1963), 17–20.

29. MS: Ian Mason to Howel Harris, July 26, 1740, no. 26, Letters to Charles Wesley, vol. VI, Methodist Archives, Manchester.

30. William Seward, *Journal of a Voyage from Savannah to Philadelphia and from Philadelphia*

to *England, MDCCXL* (London: J. Oswald's, 1740), May 16, 1740, 33. He later described Coles' book as "worth its weight in gold" (35).

31. Ibid, 19–20, on Apr. 27, 1740; cf. Crow's discussion of Seward's theology, in "Wesley's Conflict with Antinomianism," 131–33.

32. Ibid, 33–34, on May 16, 1740.

33. Tyerman, *Whitefield,* 1:251, "Letter to Thomas Seward," on June 16, 1739; and Seward, *Journal,* 24, on May, 1740.

34. *Journal,* 42–43, on May 17, 1740.

35. William Seward, MS: "Journal for Sept. 6–Oct. 15, 1740." MS: MUN: A.2.116, Chetham's Library, Manchester, 96, on Sept. 16, 1740.

36. *Journal,* 34, on May 17, 1740.

37. MS: Journal, MS: MUN: A.2.116, 67–69, on Sept. 16, 1740; Seward, *Journal,* 54–56, on May 29, 1740; and 20, in Apr. 1740.

38. William Seward, "MS Journal for July 20–Sept. 6, 1740," Bangor MS 34, University College of North Wales, Welsh Library; Photostat copy, Chetham's Library, Manchester; Aug 3 and 12,1740. Also, *Journal,* 37, May 20, 1740; and Crow, "Wesley's Conflict with Antinomianism," 133.

39. Crow incorrectly identifies this with a yet-undiscovered Journal of June 20–July 19, 1740; "Wesley's Conflict with Antinomianism," 134.

40. *Journal of Charles Wesley,* 2:169.

41. MS: Eliz. Downs to Charles Wesley, Early Methodist Volume, Methodist Archives, Manchester.

42. MS: Journal, MS: MUN: A.2.116, Chetham's Library, Manchester, Sept. 7, 1740. See also Sept. 19, 1740.

43. *Journal of Charles Wesley,* 1:250.

44. MS: Journal, Sept. 24, 1740.

45. MS: Journal, Sept. 24–25, 1740.

46. Ibid.

47. *Journal of Charles Wesley,* 1:250.

48. MS: Journal, Sept. 25–26, 1740.

49. MS: Journal, Sept. 26 and 28, 1740; Oct. 2–3, 5, 9–10, and 12, 1740.

50. William Parlby, "The First Methodist Martyr: William Seward, His Grave at Cusop, 1702–1740," *Proceedings WHS* XVII (1929–30): 187–91. Seward's martyrdom has traditionally been located at Hay on Oct. 22, 1740. This view has now been questioned by Geoffrey L. Fairs in "The Death of William Seward at Hay, 22 October 1740," *Proceedings WHS* 39 (Feb. 1973), 2–5. Fairs also suggests that his death may have been due to his earlier injuries received at Caerleon, and not a second stoning at Hay. If so, it would be further evidence of the severity of Seward's illness during his break with Charles Wesley.

51. *Journal of Charles Wesley,* 1:254, on Oct. 28, 1740.

52. Howel Harris, *Brief Account of the Life of Howel Harris, Esq.* ed. B[enjamin] La T[robe] (Trevecka: 1791), 13–14. Cited in Eifion Evans, *Howel Harris, Evangelist, 1714–1773* (Cardiff: University of Wales Press, 1974), 6, 23–24; and Griffith I. Roberts, *Howel Harris* (London: Epworth, 1951), 19–25. Cf. Richard Bennett, *The Early Life of Howel Harris* (1962), 79. 53. In a letter from Bristol dated Mar. 10, 1739. *CCH* 6 (Mar. 1921): 153–54. For an introduction to the various published extracts from Harris' manuscripts, see Griffith I. Roberts, "The Trevecka Manuscripts," *Proceedings WHS* 27 (1950): 178–80.

54. "Extracts from the Diaries of Howel Harris," *Barthafarn* 9 (1954): 31, in Mar. 1739. On Harris and Whitefield, see R. W. Evans, "The Relations of George Whitefield and Howel Harris," *Church History* 30 (June 1961): 170–90. Cf. Harris, *Brief Account,* 110; and Edward Morgan, *Life and Times of Howel Harris* (1852), 30. 55. *Whitefield's Journals,* 229–30.

56. "Extracts," *Bathafarn* 9 (1954): 32, on June 19, 1739.

57. *Letters,* 2:323; *Journal,* 2:342, 292.

58. "Trevecka Letters, No. 349," on July 1, 1741; cited by Griffith T. Roberts, "Wesley's First Society in Wales," *Proceedings WHS* 27 (Mar. 1950): 112.

59. "Trevecka Letters, No. 280," *Journal of CMHS*, Trevecka Supplement, no. 10, 400B; cited by Roberts, ibid.

60. *Letters*, 2:342; *Journal of Charles Wesley*, 1:226.

61. *Howel Harris, Reformer and Soldier (1714–1773)*, ed. Tom Beynon, 125; cf. Evans, *Harris*, 16.

62. Evans, *Harris*, 15–18; and "Rev. Thomas Jones to Mr. Whitefield" ("Trevecka MSS Supplement," no. 5), *CCH* 9, no. 2 (Nov. 1924): 165.

63. Evans, *Harris*, 18; cf. Geoffrey F. Nuttall, *Howel Harris, 1714–1773, The Last Enthusiast* (Cardiff: University of Wales Press, 1965), 63–64; *Selected Trevecka Letters (1742–1747)*, ed. Gomer M. Roberts, 166; and *Howel Harris's Visits to London*, transcribed from his diaries and ed. Tom Beynon (Aberystwyth, 1960), 247; http://www.bautz.de/bbkl/h/harris_h.shtml cf. Evans, *Harris*, 18; Nuttall, *Harris*, p.63.

64. "Extracts," *Bathafarn* 6 (1951): 54–55; cf. Wesley's account of the conversation, *Journal*, 2:507.

65. Ibid.

66. Richard Bennett, *The Early Life of Howel Harris*, 134; cf. Evans, *Harris*, 16.

67. "Extracts," *Bathafarn* 9 (1954): 32–33. Also, *Howel Harris's Visits to London*, 28–29, 33.

68. *The Weekly History*, no. 13, on July 4, 1741.

69. Ibid, no. 13 (July 4, 1741); and no. 14 (July 11, 1741).

70. *Journal of Charles Wesley*, 1:259.

71. "Trevecka Letters, No. 238," July 1, 1741; and "Trevecka Diaries, No. 65," Nov. 19, 1740; cited in Roberts, *Proceedings WHS* 27 (Mar. 1950): 114–15.

72. "Trevecka Letters: Howel Harris to Charles Wesley," Feb. 1741, *Proceedings WHS* 17 (1929–30): 63–65.

73. John Cennick, *The Life of Mr. J. Cennick: With an Account of the Trials and Temptations which he endured till it pleased our Saviour to show him his love, and send him into his Vineyard* (Bristol: 1745), 12, 22–26, 28–33.

74. Ibid, 34–36. Also, *Letters*, 1:355. Cf. Cennick-Wesley Correspondence, *Arminian Magazine* 20 (1797): 29–31.

75. *Journal of Charles Wesley*, 2:246, on July 27, 1740; and 254–55, on Nov. 4, 1740.

76. MS: Joseph Humphreys to John Wesley, Feb. 26, 1741, Methodist Archives, Manchester.

77. *The Weekly History*, no. 13 (July 4, 1741); and no. 14 (July 11, 1741).

78. Compare Cennick's return correspondence, which Harris described as "very strong and very clear and very sweet on Election and Perseverance"; in "Extracts," *Bathafarn* 4 (1949): 56.

79. John Cennick, "An Account of the most remarkable occurrences in the awakenings at Bristol and Kingswood till the Brethren's labours began there in 1746," *Morarian Messenger* (Mar.–June 1906); reprinted in *Proceedings of WHS* 6 (1908): 135; written by Cennick in Apr. 1750.

80. *Journal of Charles Wesley*, 1:263, for Nov. 30, 1740; Dec. 2 and 6, 1740.

81. *Journal*, 11:407–8, for Dec. 15, 16, and 20, 1740.

82. MS: Elizabeth Downs to Charles Wesley, Early Methodist Volume, Methodist Archives, Manchester.

83. Cennick, "An Account of remarkable occurrences," *Proceedings of MHS* 6 (1908): 11, n. 79; cf. Cennick's request on December 21 for Harris to come "as quickly as possible" because of the "great Confusion" at Kingswood; "Letter to Howel Harris," *Proceedings of MHS* 6 (1908): 11, n. 79; and Cennick, *Life*, 22.

84. "A Short Narrative of the Life of Cennick," extracted from his autobiography, English MS 1065, John Rylands Library, Manchester.

85. Cennick, "An Account of remarkable occurrences," *Proceedings of MHS* 6 (1908): 11, n. 79.

86. John Cennick, MS: Diary Memorable Passages relating to the Awakening in Wiltshire, which began in the year 1740. Also several such like matters relating to Kingswood, Dublin, etc., Moravian Church House, London.

87. "A Short Narrative," English MS 1065, John Rylands Library, Manchester.

88. *Journal*, 2: 427–28, on Feb. 22, 1741.

89. MS: Elizabeth Halfpenny to Charles Wesley, Early Methodist Volume, Methodist Archives, Manchester.

90. *Journal*, 2:430, on Feb. 28, 1741.

91. Ibid, 433, on Mar. 6, 1741.

92. Ibid. Of the total Society, 52 joined Cennick while 90 remained with Wesley. The following morning Wesley had tea with Cennick, but apparently no agreement was reached.

93. Ibid, 415, on Oct. 12, 1760; cf. Jackson, *Charles Wesley*, 1:251.

94. Ibid, 411.

95. Ibid, 435–36. His texts were Gen. 18:25; Ezek. 18 and 33.

96. From March to November 1740, John Wesley wrote five times to Whitefield, and Charles Wesley wrote at least once. Whitefield replied with at least seven letters.

97. Whitefield, *Works*, 1:156, in Mar. 1740.

98. Ibid, 181–82, on May 24, 1740.

99. *Letters*, 1:351, on Aug. 9, 1740.

100. Whitefield, *Works*, 1:, on June 25, 1740; 1:205, on Aug. 25, 1740.

101. *Journal of Charles Wesley*, 2:169–70, on Sept. 1, 1740; endorsed by Charles Wesley: "Mine to Whitefield, labouring for peace."

102. *Journal*, 1:314. This sermon was not published until 1741. Cf. also 1:275, 283–84, 289.

103. Whitefield, *Works*, 1:211, on Sept. 25, 1740.

104. Ibid, 219, on Nov. 9, 1740.

105. Ibid, 205, on Aug. 25, 1740.

106. *Whitefield's Journals*, 491, on Nov. 9, 1740.

107. Whitefield, *Works*, 1:205, on Aug. 25, 1740; and 212, on Sept. 25, 1740.

108. *Whitefield's Journals*, 491, on Nov. 9, 1740.

109. Whitefield, *Works*, 1:219, on Nov. 9, 1740; and 225, on Nov. 24, 1740.

4. Division of Methodist Societies

1. *Journal*, 421, on Feb. 1, 1741.

2. E.g., the reaction of Joseph Humphreys: "I heard that you publicly tore Mr. Whitefield's letter. Indeed I think it was not right." MS: Humphreys to John Wesley, Feb. 26, 1741, Methodist Archives, Manchester.

3. *Journal*, 2:422, on Feb. 3, 1741.

4. *Life and Diary of Ralph Erskine*, 320. Cited in Tyerman, *Whitefield*, 1:465.

5. Whitehead, *Life of Wesley*, vol. 2 (London: Stephen Couchman, 1796), 133.

6. Whitefield, *Works*, 1:256, on Mar. 25, 1741.

7. William Holland's Account of the Beginning of the Brethren's work in England, 1732–1741, English MS 1076, John Rylands Library, Manchester; written in 1745. This view was shared by others; see MS: Congregation Diary (1742), 12, Moravian Church House, London.

8. *Works,* 7:373.

9. Ibid, 2:373–75.

10. Ibid, 7:376–83.

11. Ibid, 7:381,385.

12. Tyerman, *Wesley,* 1:318.

13. *Letters,* 6:304.

14. "A Letter to the Rev. Mr. John Wesley, in Answer to his sermon, entitled 'Free Grace,' " *George Whitefield's Journals,* 569, on Dec. 24, 1740. Hereafter abbreviated "Answer."

15. Ibid, 563, title page. Cf. the influence of Dr. John Edwards of Cambridge on Whitefield; supra.

16. Ibid, 571, 574–75.

17. Ibid, 574–75.

18. Ibid, 575–87.

19. Ibid, 588.

20. *Journal,* 2:441, on Apr. 4, 1741. Cf. Irwin W. Reist, "John Wesley and George Whitefield: A Study in the Integrity of Two Theologies of Grace," *The Evangelical Quarterly,* 47 (Jan.–Mar. 1975), 26–40, for a discussion of Wesley's sermon on "Free Grace" and Whitefield's "Answer."

21. "Answer," *Whitefield's Journals,* 588; cf. "Letter to J. W.," *Works,* 1:211, on Sept. 25, 1740; and *Works,* 1:204, 219.

22. *Works,* 6:5–6, 19.

23. Ibid, 5:11; preached at Oxford, June 18, 1738.

24. "Principles of a Methodist," *Works,* 8:363–64, in 1741.

25. "Brief Thoughts on Christian Perfection," *Works,* 11:446, on Jan. 27, 1767.

26. *Works,* 11:379–80.

27. Thomas Olivers, *A Rod for a Reviler* (London: J. Fry and Co., 1777), 9–10.

28. Whitefield, *Works,* 4:48, on Nov. 1, 1740. Cf. his approbation of lots in "Letter to John Wesley," Mar. 22, 1739; *Proceedings WHS* 10 (1915): 123.

29. Ibid, 1:331, on Oct. 10, 1741. Cf. Whitefield's public apology, *Works,* 4:244, on June 24, 1748.

30. *Journal,* 2:439–40, on Mar. 28–29, 1741; and 441, in Apr. 1741.

31. Gilles, *Life of Whitefield.* Cited in Tyerman, *Whitefield,* 1:475–76. Unfortunately, Whitefield chose just this time to discontinue his Journal.

32. [Thomas Maxfield], *A Short Account of God's Dealings with Mrs. Elizabeth Maxfield, Wife of the Rev. Thomas Maxfield; from the Time of her being awakened at the Beginning of Mr. Whitefield's Preaching till her Death* (London: J. W. Pasharn, 1778), 17.

33. "Letter to Thomas Maxfield," *Letters,* 6:304, on Feb. 14, 1778.

34. Ibid, 305.

35. Whitefield, *Works,* 1:257; and 4:45–49, on Nov. 1, 1740.

36. Dallimore, *Whitefield,* 1:402, 467–73.

37. Whitefield, "A Letter to the Inhabitants of Maryland, Virginia, and North and South Carolina Concerning their Negros," *Works,* 4:35–41, on Jan. 23, 1740.

38. *Works,* 4:244, on June 24, 1748.

39. *Letters,* 1:358.

40. *Letters,* 5:339, on Sept. 18, 1772.

41. Photostat of the Viney Diary for 1744, English MS 965, John Rylands Library, Manchester, on May 27, 1744. Cf. M. Riggal, "Diary of Richard Viney 1744," *Proceedings WHS* 4 (1904): 194.

42. Seymour, *Huntingdon,* 1:198.

43. Whitefield, *Works,* 1:277, on July 13, 1741; and 268–69, on June 6, 1741.

44. Seward said Whitefield had been encouraged to begin the *Christian's Weekly Journal*, for the purpose of giving "an account of conversions and other Affairs relating to the progress of the Gospel." MS: Letter from William Seward to James Hutton, Box A3, Moravian Church House, London. Cf. *Proceedings WHS*, 11 (1917): 39.

45. *CCH* 2 (Dec. 1916): 47–54. After the first fourteen issues, the phrase "By the encouragement of the Rev. Mr. Whitefield" was omitted; cf. *Proceedings WHS* 11 (1917): 39.

46. Printer John Lewis wrote: "The Rev. Mr. Whitefield intends to supply me with fresh Matter every week"; *The Weekly History*, no. 8 (May 30, 1741). Both Tyerman and Nehemiah Curnock refer to *The Weekly History* as the first Methodist newspaper. Apparently neither was aware of the earlier paper, *The Christian's Amusement;* Tyerman, *Whitefield*, 1:495; and Curnock, ed., *Journal of John Wesley*, 2:421; cf. *CCH* 2 (Dec. 1968): 48.

47. M. H. Jones, "References to the Wesleys in the first Calvinistic Methodist Newspaper," *Proceedings WHS* 12 (1920): 158–63.

48. "James Hutton's Account of the Beginning of the Lord's work in England to 1744," English MS 1976, John Rylands Library, Manchester. Cf. a similar, earlier description of the "sorts" of Methodists; MS: Ian Mason to Howel Harris, July 16, 1740, no. 56, Letters to Charles Wesley, vol. 6, Methodist Archives, Manchester.

49. *The Gentleman's Magazine* 11 (June 1741): 321–23; cited in Crow, "Wesley's Conflict with Antinomianism," 163.

50. *Letters*, 1:352, on Apr. 12, 1741. The controversy was continued by correspondence; *Letters*, 1:355–56, on Apr. 27, 1741.

51. "Sermon LVIII," *Works*, 6:225–30. Because of the uproar over the publication of "Free Grace," Wesley did not print this sermon until the midst of the controversy in the 1770s. Cf. Green, *Wesley Bibliography*, 168.

52. On April 17, 1741, Wesley preached in London on Romans 8:29–30, and again on April 27 he used the same text; *Journal* 2:446, 450. On May 21, 1741 at Bristol he preached again from the same text and declared: "In the evening I published the great decree of God, eternal, unchangeable; 'He that believeth shall be saved; he that believeth not shall be damned.' " This basic point to the whole presentation confirms that the sermon preached in 1741 was essentially the same as that published in the 1770s. On May 24, 1741, he spoke a fourth time on this text; *Journal*, 2:458–59.

53. *Journal*, 2:449, 451, 469; on Apr. 25, May 2, and June 19, 1741.

54. Ibid, 473–74, on July 6 and 9, 1741.

55. Bull, 1634–1709, was bishop of St. David's Parish in South Wales. Samuel Wesley described him as a "strong and nervous writer, whose discourses and directions to his clergy can scarce be too often read"; *Journal*, 2:470. Note Wesley's rejection of Bull on justification; "Sermon CXXXIV," *Works*, 7:455; MS dated June 24, 1741, but not published in Wesley's lifetime.

56. Harrison, *Arminianism*, 163; *Journal*, 2:473–77.

57. *Journal*, 2:474–81.

58. "A Dialogue," *Works*, 10:259–66.

59. Ibid, 10:260.

60. *The Works of the Rev. John Wesley*, ed. Joseph Benson, vol. 14 (London: John Jones, 1809), 382–96. Wesley reprinted this work in *A Preservative against Unsettled Notions in Religion*, and in *The Arminian Magazine* 11 (1779): 105ff.

61. *Letters*, 1:352.

62. *Journal of Charles Wesley*, 1:272, on May 4, 1741.

63. Ibid, 280, on June 8, 1741; cf. 272, 278–79.

64. Ibid, 276–77, on May 19, 1741.

65. Jackson, *Charles Wesley*, 1:261.

66. Tyerman, *Whitefield*, 1:482.

67. Ibid.

68. MS: Eliz. Sayre to Charles Wesley, Early Methodist Volume, Methodist Archives, Manchester.

69. J. E. Rattenbury, *The Evangelical Doctrines of Charles Wesley's Hymns* (London: Epworth, 1941), 118.

70. Ibid, 121.

71. "Free Grace," *Poetical Works*, 3:94.

72. Rattenbury, *Evangelical Doctrines*, 125–29.

73. "Hymns on God's Everlasting Love," *Poetical Works*, 3:2.

74. Ibid, 3:34–36, 94.

75. *Journal of Charles Wesley*, 1:267, 274.

76. Ibid, 278–79, 295.

77. Ibid, 296, on Aug. 31, 1741.

78. Ibid, 291, on July 28, 1741.

79. MS: Hannah Hancock to Charles Wesley, Early Methodist Volume, Methodist Archives, Manchester.

80. *Journal of Charles Wesley*, 1:282–83, on June 19 and 26, 1741.

81. "Extracts," *Bathafarn* 10 (1955): 20.

82. Ibid, 20–21, 25–26; also *Howel Harris's Visits to London*, 22.

83. Ibid, 38.

84. "Trevecka Diaries, No. 86"; cited by Roberts, "Wesley's First Society in Wales," *Proceedings WHS* 27 (Mar. 1950): 116.

85. "Trevecka Letters: Howel Harris to Charles Wesley," *Proceedings WHS* 17 (1929–30): 66, on Aug. 28, 1742.

86. *An Account of Joseph Humphreys' Experience of the Work of Grace upon his Heart* (Bristol: Feliz Farley, 1742); also cited in Tyerman, *Whitefield*, 1:223–24.

87. *Journal*, 8:93, on Sept. 9, 1790.

88. MS: Humphreys to John Wesley, Jan. 17, 1741, Methodist Archives, Manchester.

89. MS: Humphreys to John Wesley, 26 Feb. 1741, Methodist Archives, Manchester.

90. "Humphreys to John Wesley, April 5, 1741," *The Weekly History*, no. 11 (June 30, 1741).

91. *Journal*, 2:441–45, on April 5 and 8–10, 1741.

92. "Humphreys to Charles Wesley April 11, 1741," *The Weekly History*, no. 12 (1741).

93. *The Weekly History*, no. 4 (May 2,1741).

94. *Letters*, 1:354, on Apr. 27, 1741.

95. *Journal*, 8:93, on Sept. 9, 1770.

5. Limited Reconciliation

1. "Extracts," *Bathafarn* 10 (1955): 36, on Sept. 20, 1741. Cf. the Cennick-Wesley correspondence, 1751, *Arminian Magazine* 11(1779): 260.

2. Ibid, 40–41, 36.

3. *Journal*, 2:598, on Oct. 10, 1841.

4. MS: Joseph Humphreys to Charles Wesley, Dec. 3, 1741. Early Methodist Volume, Methodist Archives, Manchester.

5. Bissicks was described as one who "preached with blessing 'till falling into the most rigid Doctrines of Reprobation he became dry in his heart and at last few or none would hear him." For a time he joined the Baptists, but he soon separated from them, was unsuccessful at setting himself up, and at last returned to being a collier. John Cennick, MS: Diary, Memorable Passages relative to the Awakening in Wiltshire, Moravian Church House, London. Cf. Bissicks' role in the Cennick controversy, supra.

6. "Extracts," *Bathafarn* 10 (1955): 43, on Oct. 16 and 17, 1741; and Griffeth T. Roberts, "John Wesley Visits Wales (October 15th–21st, 1741)," *Bathafarn* 13 (1958): 47–49.

7. *Journal*, 2:509, on Oct. 17, 1741.

8. Whitefield, *Works*, 1:331, on Oct. 10, 1741. See Morgan, *The Life and Times of Howel Harris*, 93.

9. "Letter to Howell Harris," on Oct. 28, 1741, *Proceedings WHS* 10 (1915): 24; correct date, Nov. 28, 1741, editor.

10. MS: Huntingdon to Wesley, Feb. 19, 1724, Letters of the Countess of Huntingdon, Methodist Archives, Manchester.

11. *Journal*, 2:487.

12. Whitefield, *Works*, 1:359, on Jan. 2, 1742.

13. *Journal*, 3:4, on Apr. 3, 1742.

14. Ibid, 9, on May 12, 1742.

15. Whitefield, *Works*, 1:448–49, on Oct. 11, 1742.

16. Ibid, 438, on Sept. 22, 1742.

17. *Letters*, 2:25, on Aug. 22, 1744.

18. R. A. Knox, *Enthusiasm* (Oxford: Clarendon, 1950), 496.

19. "Fifth Visit to London, 1743," *Howel Harris, Reformer and Soldier*, 48–49, 51–52.

20. *Journal*, 3:84–85, on Aug. 24, 1743.

21. *Journal*, 3:85–86, on Aug. 24, 1743.

22. Photostat of Diary of Richard Viney, May–June 1744, English MS 965, John Rylands Library, Manchester. Cf. *Journal of Charles Wesley*, 1:367–68.

23. *John Bennet's Copy of the Minutes* (London: *WHS* Publication no. 1 [1896]), 18. The fact that the official *Minutes* makes no mention of this proposal probably means Whitefield declined.

24. "Minutes of Some Late Conversations between the Rev. Mr. Wesley and Others, 1744," *Works*, 8:278, on June 25, 1744.

25. The main pillars of antinomianism were the following: (1) That Christ abolished the moral law; (2) that therefore Christians are not obliged to observe it; (3) that one branch of Christian liberty is liberty from obeying the commandments of God; (4) that it is bondage to do a thing because it is commanded, or forbear it because it is forbidden; (5) that a believer is not obliged to use the ordinances of God, or to do good works; and (6) that a Preacher ought not to exhort to good works; not unbelievers, because it is hurtful; not believers, because it is needless; *Conference Minutes*, 1744, 3–4.

26. *Works*, 8:278–79, 284–86, 293–98.

27. Cf. Crow, "Wesley's Conflict with Antinomianism."

28. *Journal*, 2:451, 456; 3:154.

29. *Conference Minutes*, 1744, 4–5; 1745, 8–11; 1746, 14–15; 1747, 17–21.

30. "True Christianity Defended," *Works*, 7:456.

31. "The Wedding Garment," *Works*, 7:316.

32. "Difference between the Moravians and Methodists," *Works*, 10:203.

33. "True Christianity Defended," *Works*, 7:456.

34. *Journal*, 5:284; also, *Works*, 7:317.

35. *Works*, 8:349, in 1765.

36. *Letters*, 5:115.

6. Wesley's Theology of Predestination

1. Wesley had a project of this nature in view while still in Georgia; *Journal*, 1:425. The idea received strong encouragement from Calvinist Philip Doddridge, principal of a Dissenting academy in Northampton; "Letter to Wesley, June 18, 1746: A Scheme of Study for a Clergyman," *Arminian Magazine* 1 (1778): 419–25.

2. Wesley, *A Christian Library: Consisting of Extracts from, and Abridgements of, the Choicest Pieces of Practical Divinity which have been published in the English Tongue* (Bristol: Felix Fancy, 1749–55; quotations from 2d ed., in 30 volumes: London: T. Cordeux, 1819–26). Hereafter cited as *CL*.

3. Robert C. Monk, *John Wesley: His Puritan Heritage* (London: Epworth, 1966), 45–61.

4. Tyerman, *Wesley*, 2:65.

5. *CL*, 28:261–378; 1:v–x; *Works*, 10:405.

6. "The Shorter Catechism," *The Confession of Faith* (Blackwood and Sons, 1959), 117–26. Cf. James A. MacDonald, *Wesley's Revision of the Shorter Catechism* (Edinburgh: George A. Morton, 1906).

7. Ibid, 117–19; *CL*, 14:393, 398.

8. Monk, *John Wesley*, 55–57.

9. John Wesley, *Explanatory Notes Upon the Old Testament* (Bristol: William Pine, 1765), 1:iv–v.

10. Green, *Wesley Bibliography*, 39.

11. John Wesley, *Explanatory Notes Upon the New Testament* (1st ed., 1755; London: Epworth, 1950); cf. Romans, introduction and chaps. 8–11; 1 Cor. 9:27; Eph. 1:5ff.; 1 Pet. 1:2.

12. Cf. Gill's response, *Doctrine of Predestination stated and set in the Scripture Light; in Opposition to Mr. Wesley's Predestination Calmly Considered* (London: G. Keith, 1752).

13. *Letters*, 3:96; cf. *Journal*, 3:85.

14. "Unofficial Minutes by Jacob Rowell," *Conference Minutes*, 714.

15. Cf. the influence of this work on Thomas Taylor's conversion from Calvinism, *The Lives of Early Methodist Preachers*, ed. Thomas Jackson, 4th ed. (London: Wesleyan Conference Office, 1873), 5:53–54.

16. For the early development of Wesley's views on Scripture and the nature of God, see Schmidt, *Wesley*, 1:73–78, 83–89.

17. "Serious Thoughts on God's Sovereignty," *Works*, 10:361; cf. 11:159.

18. "Predestination Calmly Considered," *Works*, 10:235.

19. "Serious Thoughts on God's Sovereignty," *Works* 10:362.

20. "Predestination Calmly Considered," *Works*, 10:235.

21. "Serious Thoughts on God's Sovereignty," *Works*, 10:363.

22. "Predestination Calmly Considered," *Works*, 10:220–21.

23. "Serious Thoughts on God's Sovereignty," *Works*, 10:363.

24. Maldwyn Edwards, *Sons to Samuel* (London: Epworth, 1961), 85–91.

25. "Divine Providence," *Works*, 6:315–17; "The Unity of the Divine Being," *Works*, 7:265–66, 271; and an extract from a late author, "Of Eternal Providence," *Arminian Magazine* 8 (1785): 210–13.

26. "An Estimate of the Manners of the Present Times," *Works*, 11:160. Cf. MS: Sermon IV, "Guardian Angels," Ps. 91:11, p. 100; transcribed by Charles Wesley from his brother's copy, Sept. 1736, no. 68, Charles Wesley MSS, Box III, Methodist Archives, Manchester.

27. *Letters*, 6: 45; *Journal*, 6:326.

28. "Divine Providence," *Works*, 6:319–20; also, "Spiritual Worship," *Works*, 6:428–29.

29. *Works*, 6:322; also, "A Farther Appeal to Men of Reason and Religion," *Works*, 8:159.

30. "Guardian Angels," 84.

31. "The General Spread of the Gospel," *Works*, 6:280.

32. "Guardian Angels," 87. For these reasons, Wesley believed, "the blessed Angels may not always prevent sin or affliction from assaulting the soul or body; yet when either has taken hold upon us, they may prevent our being totally overthrown."

33. *Works*, 6:218; also, "God's Omnipresence," *Works*, 7:240.

34. "Sermon on Wisdom and Knowledge of God," *Arminian Magazine* 7 (1784): 347–48.

35. "The Nature of Enthusiasm," *Works*, 5:475.

36. *Letters*, 6:329, 345.

37. MS: Sermon II: "One Thing Is Needful," Luke 10:42, 46, Charles Wesley MSS, Box III, Methodist Archives, Manchester.

38. "Predestination Calmly Considered," *Works*, 10:235.

39. Ibid, 210.

40. *Letters*, 3:96.

41. "Predestination Calmly Considered," *Works*, 10:210.

42. "On Predestination," *Works*, 6:226–27. Also, *Notes on the N. T.*, 872.

43. *Works*, 6:226–27; also, *Notes on the N. T.*, 551.

44. "Predestination Calmly Considered," *Works*, 10:225. These are only representative of the large number of Scripture passages that Wesley listed as evidence for a universal offer of salvation.

45. Ibid.

46. Ibid, 224–228.

47. "Original Sin," *Works*, 6:63.

48. "Self Denial," *Works*, 6:107; MS: Sermon II, "One Thing Is Needful," 41.

49. Baxter insisted upon the universality of "common grace." *Richard Baxter's Confession of His Faith*, vi. According to David Shipley, "Baxter's description of common grace is a striking precursor of what is found in Wesley's conception of an efficacious prevenient grace." See "Wesley and some Calvinistic Controversies," *The Drew Gateway*, 25 (1955): 208; cited in Monk, *John Wesley*, 103.

50. *Letters*, 5:231; cf. *Poetical Works*, 13:15.

51. "Predestination Calmly Considered," *Works*, 10:229–30; cf. Harald Gustaf Åke Lindström, *Wesley and Sanctification* (Stockholm: Nya Bokförlags aktiebolaget, Almqvist & Wiksells Boktryckeri A.B., 1946), 44–50; cf. new ed. (Nappanee, Ind.: Francis Asbury Press, 1996).

52. *Works*, 5:392; cf. also "Remarks On a Defence of Aspasio Vindicated," *Works*, 10:350.

53. "A Further Appeal to Man of Reason and Religion," *Works*, 8:52–53.

54. "Working Out Our Own Salvation," *Works*, 6:508–9; cf. Lindström, *Wesley and Sanctification*, 49–50.

55. Ibid, 511–13.

56. "What Is an Arminian?" *Works*, 10:360.

57. "The General Spread of the Gospel," *Works*, 6:281; also, "Working Out Our Own Salvation," *Works*, 6:513.

58. "Predestination Calmly Considered," *Works*, 10:254, 232.

59. Ibid, 242.

60. "Serious Thoughts Upon the Perseverance of the Saints," *Works*, 10:290.

61. Ibid, 287.

62. *Notes on the N. T.*, 554; cf. Wesley's outline of Romans, with special reference to chap. 9, in "Predestination Calmly Considered," *Works*, 10:218–19.

63. "Serious Thoughts Upon the Perseverance of the Saints," *Works*, 10:292–97.

64. *Notes on the N. T.*, p.613.

65. "What Is an Arminian?" *Works*, 10:134.

66. *Letters*, 1:20.

67. *Letters*, 6:146.

68. Ibid, 358. Cf. *Letters*, 5:235; "The Witness of the Spirit II," *Works*, 5:134.

69. "The Witness of the Spirit I," *Works*, 5:113–14

70. Ibid, 115.

71. "The Witness of the Spirit II," *Works*, 5:129; Cf. Ireson's discussion of assurance, "The Doctrine of Faith in John Wesley," 366–69.

72. *Journal*, 2:333ff.; *Letters*, 1:274ff.; 2:59, 90; *Works*, 5:33.

73. *Letters*, 3:160; cf. *Letters*, 5:358; 7:61; A. S. Yates, *The Doctrine of Assurance, [with] Special Reference to John Wesley* (London: Epworth, 1952), 72–81; *Bibliotheca Sacra*, 132 (Apr.–June 1975): 161–77.

74. *Letters*, 3:305; 5:358; cf. A. S. Yates, *Doctrine of Assurance*, 77.

75. "Predestination Calmly Considered," *Works*, 10:211.

76. Ibid, 255.

77. Ibid, 256.

78. Ibid, 258.

79. Ibid, 216, 227.

7. The Controversy over Imputed Righteousness

1. *Arminian Magazine*, 1 (1778): 130, 134.

2. Tyerman, "Rev. James Hervey, M.A., The Literary Parish-Priest," Luke Tyerman, *The Oxford Methodists* (London: Hodder and Stoughton, 1882) 201–33. John Tyland, *The Character of the Rev. James Hervey*, M.A. (London: 1791); *Letters* 1:332–33; *Works*, 8:348; 10:316.

3. Tyerman, *Methodists*, 290. June, 1754.

4. Hervey, *Works*, 5:353ff.; cited in Tyerman, *Methodists*, 285.

5. Tyerman, *Methodists*, 270; cf. his letter to Wesley in which he professed to be attached neither to particular nor to universal redemption; *Arminian Magazine* 1 (1778): 135, on Dec. 30, 1747.

6. Ibid, 306.

7. James Hervey, *Theron and Aspasio*, 1st ed. (London: Hamilton Adams, 1755), Preface. For summaries, see Crow, "Wesley's Conflict with Antinomianism," 173–75; A. B. Lawson, "John Wesley and Some Anglican Evangelicals of the Eighteenth Century" (Ph.D. diss., University of Sheffield, 1974), 263–71.

8. Hervey, *Theron and Aspasio*, 1:544–51, in "Dialogue XIII."

9. Ibid, 1:62, "Dialogue II."

10. Ibid, 1:179, "Dialogue V"; 1:413–14, "Dialogue X."

11. Ibid, 2:421, "Dialogue XVI."

12. Simon, J. S., *John Wesley the Master Builder* (London: Epworth, 1927), 166. *Works*, 10:317.

13. Tyerman, *Methodists*, 290.

14. *Works*, 10:335.

15. "Original Sin," *Works*, 9:193. He further cites Hervey against Taylor, 197, 242, 286, 291, 300–301, 315. But cf. Harvey's objections to Wesley's quotations from *Theron and Aspasio*, in Tyerman, *Methodists*, 315.

16. *Works*, 10: 298–315, in Nov. 1757. Letters to the author of *Theron and Aspasio* appeared over the nom de plume "Palaemon." The author was either the Scotsman John Glass, as Wesley supposed (*Works*, 10:298), or his son-in-law Robert Sandeman; *Letters*, 3:231 n; cf. Tyerman, *Wesley*, 2:293; J. T. Hornsay, "Wesley, Hervey, Sandeman," *Proceedings WHS*, 20 (1935–36), 112–13.

17. *Letters*, 3:372–84; *Works*, 10:318–31.

18. Ibid, 229–30.

19. Whitefield, *Works*, 3:136.

20. *A Preservative Against Unsettled Notions in Religion* (Bristol: E. Farley, 1758); cf. "Preface," *Works*, 14:239.

21. "London Tabernacle Minutes, 1742–47 (Trevecka MS. 2946)," *Two Calvinistic Methodist Chapels, 1743–1811*, ed. Edwin Welch ([Leicester]: London Records Society, 1975), 11. The minutes were taken by Howel Harris. Cf. Wesley, *Works*, 7:429; 11:349.

22. *Letters*, 4:144.

23. *Journal*, 4:303.

24. Tyerman, *Wesley*, 1:482. Cf. "Wesley and William Cudworth," *Proceedings WHS*, 12 (1920): 34–36.

25. *Letters*, 4:47; *Works*, 12:160–61.

26. Lawson, "Wesley and Some Anglican Evangelicals," 279; Tyerman, *Methodists*, 315.

27. Hervey, *Eleven Letters* (London: Charles Rivington, 1765), preface; "Letters I," 9. For further details of the Wesley-Hervey Controversy, see J. C. Whitebrook, "An Account of Tracts and Pamphlets on the Doctrines of Grace published by Hervey, Sandeman, Wesley, and others, from 1755 to 1773," *CCH* 10, no. 1 (May 1925); Crow, "Wesley's Conflict with Antinomianism," 172–84, n. 7; Lawson, "Wesley and Some Anglican Evangelicals," 272ff.

28. *Poetical Works*, 8:443; *Works* 10:346–80.

29. *Works*, 10:306–15, 364–69.

30. *Works*, 10:317. He later abridged Goodwin's "Exposition of the 9th Chapter of Romans," *Arminian Magazine* 3 (1780): 9ff. For a summary and evaluation of Goodwin on justification, see Thomas Jackson, *The Life of John Goodwin* (London: Longman, 1822), 38–51.

31. *Works*, 5:234–46; 10:346–57. This was Wesley's reply to a defense of *Theron and Aspasio* by Dr. John Erskine of Scotland.

32. "Thoughts on the Imputed Righteousness of Christ," *Works*, 10:312–15.

33. "The Lord Our Righteousness," *Works*, 5:236–37.

34. "A Letter to a Gentleman at Bristol," *Works*, 10:307–11.

35. "The Lord Our Righteousness," *Works*, 5:239; cf. *Treatise on Justification*, 3.

36. *Treatise on Justification*, 139–43.

37. "A Letter to a Gentleman at Bristol," *Works*, 10:307, 310, 326.

38. "The Lord Our Righteousness," *Works*, 5:241–42.

39. "A Letter to a Gentleman at Bristol," *Works*, 10:308; cf. *Works*, 5:242; 10:325.

40. "A Preface to a Treatise on Justification," *Works*, 10:326.

41. "The Lord Our Righteousness," *Works*, 5:241.

42. "A Blow at the Root," *Works*, 10:366–67.

43. "A Letter to a Gentleman at Bristol," *Works*, 10:307.

44. "A Preface to a Treatise on Justification," *Works*, 10:320.

45. "A Blow at the Root," *Works*, 10:367.

46. "The Lord Our Righteousness," *Works*, 5:244.

47. "Thoughts on Imputed Righteousness of Christ," *Works*, 10:315.

48. "The Lord Our Righteousness," *Works*, 5:244.

49. "A Blow at the Root," *Works*, 10:366.

50. *Conference Minutes*, 52.

51. *Letters*, 4:295–96.

52. *Journal*, 5:111; *Letters*, 4:294–96, on Apr. 24, 1765.

53. *Letters*, 5:89–90.

54. Tyerman, *Wesley*, 2:531.

55. *Lives*, 5:29.

56. *Lives*, 2:145.

8. The Relationship between Wesley and Whitehead

1. *Journal*, 4:139

2. Whitefield, *Works*, 3:229, in 1758.

3. *Letters*, 5:63, in 1767; cf. 5:69.

4. *Letters*, 4:158; cf. the letter to Wesley declaring that Whitefield "defended your doctrine and discipline and people under your care, both

in public and private." *Methodist Magazine* 21 (1798): 46; *Letters*, 4:69.

5. MS: Whitefield to Charles Wesley, Dec. 20, 1753, no. 83, Letter to Charles Wesley, vol. VI, Methodist Archives, Manchester.

6. Charles Wesley, *An Epistle to the Reverend Mr. George Whitefield* (written, 1755; London: J. and W. Oliver, 1771), 3.

7. "English Calvinistic Methodist Association Minutes, 1745–9 (Trevecka MS. 2946)," *Two Calvinistic Methodist Chapels*, 27–28; "Extracts from the Trevecca MSS: An Account of an Association held at Bristol, January 22, 1746/7," *Proceedings WHS* 15 (Mar. 1926), 120–21. Cf. M. H. Jones, "Attempts to Re-establish Union between Howel Harris, English and Welsh Methodists and the Moravians," *Proceedings WHS*, 16 (June 1928): 113–17.

8. "Huntingdon to John Wesley, September 14, 1766," *Arminian Magazine* 20 (1797): 304–5; *Journal*, 5:182.

9. *Journal of Charles Wesley*, 2:247, on Aug. 21, 1766. Both sides had long talked of the elusive "union." *Arminian Magazine* 1 (1778): 417, 478–79; Supplement, 20 (1797): 43.

10. Lives, 1:214; *Journal*, 5:227–28.

11. *Arminian Magazine* 17 (1794): 499, 525–27; *Lives*, 1:237–38; 2:30.

12. "Unofficial Minutes by Jacob Rowell," *Conference Minutes*, 717–18; *Letters*, 3:144.

13. *Letters*, 3:187, in 1756. This appears to be at variance with Wesley's 1765 statement to John Newton, *Letters*, 4:297; cf. John Walton's evaluation of Darney, in *Lives*, 6:43–44.

14. *Works*, 13:350–51; cf. Moore's discussion, *Life of Wesley* 2:218–31. Wesley used the terms *Christian perfection, entire sanctification, perfect love*, and *full salvation* interchangeably. See Lindström, *Wesley and Sanctification*, 127; W. E. Sangster, *The Path to Perfection* (Hodder and Stoughton, 1943), 27.

15. *Journal*, 5:10–13. See Charles Atmore, *Methodist Memorial* (Bristol: R. Edwards, 1801),

266–69; and Wesley's analysis of the situation to Charles, in *Letters*, 4:196.

16. Tyerman, *Wesley*, 2:433–34.

17. *Journal*, 4:539; cf. other contacts with Bell: 4:540–42; 5:4.

18. *Letters*, 4:191–94.

19. *Works*, 11:427–29.

20. Ibid, 429–31.

21. Ibid, 431–32.

22. Ibid, 432–35.

23. *Journal*, 4:542.

24. *Letters*, 4:200.

25. Tyerman, *Wesley*, 2:436.

26. *Lives*, 2:27–28.

27. *Arminian Magazine* 18 (1795): 50.

28. *Journal*, 5:9, 12; Tyerman, *Wesley*, 2:437–38.

29. Tyerman, *Wesley*, 2:437, 440–41.

30. *Journal*, 5:9. These were those who professed entire sanctification, whereas the 106 people Wesley mentions elsewhere (*Journal*, 5:40) would include some who did not claim this experience.

31. Ibid, 17.

32. *Letters*, 4:245.

33. For examples in 1763–66, see *Journal*, 5:16, 18–19, 35, 41, 56, 59, 66–67, 97, 100, 116, 130, 138, 140, 143, 148–49, 162, 169, 174, 194; for personal promotion of the doctrine, see *Letters*, 4:208, 212–13, 216, 225, 231, 241, 251, 265, 268, 299, 307, 313, 321; 5:3–7, 9, 16, 20, 25.

34. *Lives*, 5:238–39.

35. *Journal*, 5:41

36. "To the Countess of Huntingdon," *Letters*, 4:206. Wesley (*Letters*, 4:200) also wrote to Charles: "Mr. Whitefield has fallen upon me in

public open-mouthed, and only not named my name. So has Mr. Madan." See also *Howel Harris, Reformer and Soldier,* 161–62.

37. Cf. Whitefield's 1764 letter to Wesley on the need for itinerants in America; *Arminian Magazine* 5 (1780): 47–48. Note Wesley's request (*Letters,* 5:183–84) that Whitefield encourage his first preachers in America, in 1770.

38. *Journal,* 5: 154, in Jan. 1766. Cf. 5:297, in Jan. 1769; 5:303, in Mar. 1769. Note Whitefield's 1768 letter asking for Wesley to recommend a tutor for the Orphan House and requesting a set of Wesley's *Works* for the library there; *Arminian Magazine* 6 (1883): 684.

39. *Lloyd's Evening Post,* Nov. 16, 1770; cited in Tyerman, *Wesley,* 3:76.

40. *Journal,* 5:397, 399. Wesley also preached funeral sermons for Whitefield at Greenwich, Nov. 23, 1770; and at Deptford, Jan. 2, 1771.

41. *Works,* 6:167–77. Cf. Charles Wesley's description: "From strength to strength, our young Apostle goes, / Pours like a torrent, and the land o'erflows, / Resistless wins his way with rapid zeal, / Turns the world upside down, and shapes the gates of hell!" *An Elegy on the late Reverend George Whitefield* (Bristol: William Pine, 1771), 19.

42. Ibid, 177–79.

43. Ibid, 179–82.

44. *Gospel Magazine,* Feb. 1771. Cited in "A letter to the editor of 'Lloyd's Evening Post,' " *Letters,* 5:224.

45. *Letters,* 5:225.

46. Seymour, *Huntingdon,* 2: 44.

47. Richard Elliot, "A Summary of Gospel Doctrine Taught by Mr. Whitefield," *Select Sermons of George Whitefield* (London: Banner of Truth Trust, 1958), 35–43.

48. Robert Southy, *The Life of Wesley,* vol. 2 (London: Longman, 1846), 70.

49. *Letters,* 4:297.

50. Ibid, 298.

51. Cf. a June 22, 1763, letter to Henry Venn, in *Letters,* 4:217: "You are welcome to preach in any of those houses as I know we agree in the main points; and whereinsoever we differ you would not preach there contrary to me."

52. *Works,* 5:493.

53. Ibid, 497–99.

54. Ibid, 493.

55. Ibid, 502.

56. Ibid.

57. *Poetical Works,* 6:72.

58. *Journal,* 5:60–63, at Scarborough, on Apr. 19, 1764; *Letters,* 4:235–39. Wesley indicated that he had contemplated the proposal for some years, and had actually written the letter two and a half years earlier.

59. Richard Hart, W. S. [Walter Sellon], and Vincent Perronet; all favored the proposal; *Journal,* 5:63–66.

60. "Life of John Pawson," *Lives,* 4:28–29. One of the more moderate of the twelve was Martin Madan, whom Wesley invited to preach to the conference.

61. *Journal,* 5:91, on Aug. 6, 1764.

62. *Conference Minutes,* 87, on Aug. 4, 1769.

63. *Works,* 5:501.

9. The Wesley–Toplady Controversy over Free Will

1. "An Account of the Life and Writings of the Rev. Augustus Montague Toplady, A.B.," *The Works of Augustus M. Toplady, A.B.,* vol. 1 (London: William Baynes and Son, 1825), 1–10.

2. *Arminian Magazine* 3 (1780): 54, on Sept. 13, 1758.

3. Toplady, "An Account," *Works,* 1:10, 14, 24, 17: After reading Gill's work on predestination, against Wesley, Toplady recalled: "A few years ago, Mr. Wesley said to me, concerning Dr. Gill that 'he is a positive man, and fights for his opinions through thick and thin.' " Darby

Stafford, "A Dead Controversy and a Living Hymn: John Wesley and August Toplady," *The Methodist Recorder,* July 12, 1906, 9. Cf. Ibid, 10, 12, 108. See George A. Lawton, "Augustus Montague Toplady, A Critical Account with Special Reference to Hymnology" (B.D. thesis, University of Nottingham, 1964), 10–177.

4. *Lloyd's Evening Post,* Mar. 25, 1768; *The London Magazine,* 1768, 125; J. S. Reynolds, *The Evangelicals at Oxford, 1735–1871* (Oxford: Blackwell, 1953), 35–41; Charles Smyth, *Simeon and Church Order* (Cambridge: Cambridge University Press, 1940), 209–15; A. D. Godley, *Oxford in the Eighteenth Century* (London: Methuen and Co., 1908), 274f.; Seymour, *Huntingdon,* 1:422–27.

5. Whitefield, "A Letter to the Reverend Dr. Durell," *Works,* 4:314–27.

6. Hill was from Hawkstone and received his education at Westminster School and Oxford. He was earlier influenced by John Fletcher, but was not converted until 1759. See Sidney, *Life of Richard Hill.* Also, Richard Hill, *Pietas Oxoniensis: or, A Full and Impartial Account of the Expulsion of the Six Students from St. Edmond's Hall,* Oxford (London: G. Keith, 1768), 26–29.

7. Thomas Nowell, *Answer to A Pamphlet Entitled Pietas Oxoniensis* (Oxford: Clarendon, 1768), 94. Cf. Hill's response: *Goliath Slain* (London: G. Keith, 1768); and *A Letter to the Rev. Dr. Nowell* (London: G. Keith, 1769). See also Wesley's comment that Nowell "says quite enough to clear the Church of England from the charge of Predestination—a doctrine which he proves to be utterly inconsistent with the Common Prayer, the Communion Service, the Homilies, and the other writings of those that compiled them." *Journal,* 5:293.

8. For a list of publications produced over the incident, see S. L. Ollard, *The Six Students of St. Edmond Hall* (London: A. R. Mowbray and Co., 1911), 51–59.

9. Toplady, *Works,* 4:1–149.

10. Ibid, 5:151–312; 6:189. For Toplady's approbation of Gill, see MS: Toplady's Marginal

Notes in his personal copy of Wesley's *Notes on the N. T.;* Methodist Archives, Manchester. Notes on Mark 7:4; 1 Cor. 9:27; 2 Peter 2:1; and his eulogy of Gill, in John Gill, A *Collection of Sermons and Tracts,* 2 vols. (London: 1773).

11. Atmore, *Methodist Memorial,* 381–84.

12. See Toplady's response, "A Word to the Rev. Mr. Walter Sellon," *Works,* 5:344–45; and his esteem of Coles in MS: Toplady's Marginal Notes on Luke 22:62; John 6:40; 1 John 2:19; 5:12.

13. *Letters,* 5:167, on Dec. 30, 1769. Sellon's work appeared as A *Defence of God's Sovereignty, against the impious and horrible Aspersions cast upon it by Elisha Coles, in his practical treatise on that subject.* Tyerman, *Wesley,* 3:55. Cf. Wesley's comment on Coles: "so plausibly written that it is no wonder so many are deceived thereby"; *Journal,* 5:316.

14. Toplady, *Works,* 6:189–90.

15. Ibid, 1:244. Cf. Fletcher's criticism, in Wesley, *Works,* 2:220–31.

16. Ibid, 2:205–75, 278.

17. *Works,* 10:358–61, in 1770.

18. "The Doctrine of Absolute Predestination Stated and Asserted. By the Reverend Mr. A–T–," *Works,* 14:190–98; Seymour denied that Toplady's work was representative of the Lady Huntingdon and her preachers; *Huntingdon,* 2:247.

19. Toplady, *Works,* 5:319–20, on Jan. 9, 1771.

20. Ibid, 321–22.

21. *Works,* 10:370, in 1771.

22. Ibid, 10:371–72.

23. George, Lawton, *Shropshire Saint* (London: Epworth, 1960), 130.

24. *Lives,* 2:53–58, 73.

25. Thomas Olivers, A *Letter to the Rev. Mr. Toplady* (London: E. Cabe, 1771), 6, 43, 45.

26. Ibid, 2, 28, 54. Cf. the cordial interview between Olivers and Toplady, in *Lives*, 2:87; and Toplady, *Works*, 6:169–80.

27. Toplady, *Works*, 5:353, 355, 357, 361, 365–66, 382, 391.

28. MS: Fletcher to Charles Wesley, Dec. 1775, no. 90, Fletcher Volume, Methodist Archives, Manchester.

29. John Fletcher, *Works of the Reverend John Fletcher II* (1st ed., 1775; Salem, Ohio: Schmul Publishers, 1974), 417–20 (cited as Fletcher, *Works*). He believed, however, that the *Vindication* had more "show of argument" than any of Toplady's other works. MS: Fletcher to Charles Wesley, Dec. 4, 1775, no. 90, Fletcher Volume, Methodist Archives, Manchester.

30. Fletcher, *Works*, 432, 436, 441, 446, 470, 480.

31. Ibid, 476.

32. MS: Toplady's Marginal Notes, Title page and 757.

33. Toplady, "A Caveat," *Works*, 3:14; cf. "An Account," *Works*, 1:25.

34. *The Reverend Mr. Toplady's Dying Avowal of His Religious Sentiments* (London: James Matthews, 1778), 7.

35. Toplady, *Free-Will and Merit Fairly Examined* (London: James Mathews 1775), 12–13; cf. Toplady, *Works*, 6:175.

36. Toplady, "A Caveat," *Works*, 3:14–16.

37. MS: Toplady's Marginal Notes on John 6:65 and Acts 18:27.

38. MS: Toplady's Marginal Notes on Matt. 13:12; for a slightly variant order, cf. Toplady, "A Caveat," *Works*, 3:19–30.

39. Toplady, "More Work for John Wesley," *Works*, 5:377; "Observations on the Divine Attributes," 5:201–3.

40. MS: Toplady's Marginal Notes on Gal. 3:6; cf. also Notes on John 10:10; 10:26; 15:9; Acts 18:10; Eph. 5:25.

41. Toplady, "The Church of England Vindicated," *Works*, 5:102; also MS: Toplady's Marginal Note on Acts 19:9.

42. MS: Toplady's Marginal Note on John 10:26.

43. Toplady, "A Caveat," *Works*, 3:27–28; MS: Toplady's Marginal Note on John 17:9.

44. MS: Toplady's Marginal Note on Acts 13:48; cf. also Notes on Acts 19:9 and Rom. 11:6.

45. MS: Toplady's Marginal Note on 1 John 5:12; cf. Notes on Rom. 4:5; 4:7; 5:19; Rev. 12:1.

46. Toplady, "A Caveat," *Works*, 3:22.

47. MS: Toplady's Marginal Notes on 1 Pet. 1:4; Rom. 11:6.

48. Toplady, "A Caveat," *Works*, 3:37.

49. Ibid, 34, 47–49; also MS: Toplady's Marginal Note on 1 Pet. 1:14.

50. MS: Toplady's Marginal Notes on Matt. 13:12, 1 Pet. 1:5; Matt. 7:23.

51. Seymour, *Huntingdon*, 2:293.

52. *Letters*, 4:48; Tyerman, *Wesley*, 2:315–16; Toplady, "An Account," *Works*, 1:17.

53. Toplady's diary, "Short Memorials of God's Gracious Dealings with my soul in a Way of Spiritual Experience from Dec. 6, 1768," covers only one year. "An Account," *Works*, 1:13–89.

54. Toplady, *Works*, 6:188.

55. Tyerman, *Wesley*, 2:316.

56. Toplady, "An Account," *Works*, 1:102–3.

57. *Works*, 5:336–40.

58. Toplady, "A Dissertation Concerning the Sensible Qualities of Matter: More especially, Concerning Colors," *Works*, 5: 107–34.

59. "An Old Fox Tarred and Feathered. Occasioned by What is Called Mr. John Wesley's *Calm Address to our American Colonies*," *Works*, 5:441–59.

60. Toplady, *Works*, 3:53.

61. Lawton, *Shropshire Saint,* 147.

62. *Letters,* 8:267.

63. Ibid, 5:192, on June 24, 1770.

64. Toplady, "The Rev. Mr. Toplady's Dying Avowal of his Religious Sentiments," in "An Account," *Works,* 1:110–12. For Richard Hill's attack on Wesley at Toplady's death, see Tyerman, *Wesley,* 3:267.

65. Cf. Crow, "Wesley's Conflict with Antinomianism," 204.

10. The Attack on Wesley's 1770 Conference Minutes

1. Fitchett, W. H., *Wesley and His Century* (London: 1906), 378.

2. The Countess of Huntingdon has been unfortunate in the persons who have chosen to be her biographers. The standard work is the poorly written and undocumented account by A. C. H. Seymour, *The Life and Times of the Countess of Huntingdon,* 2 vols. (London: Painter, 1839). The two other full-length works are only abridgments of Seymour, albeit in more ordered form: A. H. New, *The Coronet and the Cross* (London: Patridge, 1847); and Sarah Tytler, *The Countess of Huntingdon and Her Circle* (London: Sir Isaac Pitman and Sons, 1907). Cf. the shorter treatment by F. F. Bretherton, *The Countess of Huntingdon* (Wesley Historical Society Lecture, no. 6; London: Epworth, 1940); and a review of Seymour by J. H. Newman, "Selina Countess of Huntingdon," in *Essays, Critical and Historical* (essay, 1840; reprint, London: Basil Montague Pickering, 1871), 386–424. Principal Victor Murray of Cheshunt College, Cambridge, was in the midst of preparing a new biography when he died. His notes and materials are preserved among the Murray Papers, Cheshunt College Archives, Westminster and Cheshunt Colleges, Cambridge. A work on the Countess is currently in process by Alan Harding, Oxford University. Two other books attempt to picture the Countess in her proper place of influence in the eighteenth-century revival: C. E. Vulliamy, "Lady Selina," *John Wesley* (London: Geoffrey Bles, 1931), 165–81; and A. S. Wood, "The Count-

ess and Her Connection," *The Inextinguishable Blaze* (Exeter: Paternoster, 1967), 189–204.

3. Seymour, *Huntingdon,* 1:1–16.

4. Wood, *The Inextinguishable Blaze,* 193–94.

5. *Methodist Magazine* 21 (1798): 489–90, 642; 22 (1799): 99; and *Journal,* 3:14, 24 n. For a full account of Lady Huntingdon's early relations with the Wesleys, see Bretherton, *The Countess,* 9–12, 20.

6. Cf. the ninety-nine letters to Charles Wesley, in MSS: Huntingdon to Wesley, Methodist Archives, London. Also, note the ministry of Charles Wesley to the Countess and her family during the trial and execution of her cousin, Lawrence, fourth Earl of Ferrers. Jackson, *Charles Wesley,* 2:171–78.

7. Seymour, *Life and Times,* 2:381; *Methodist Magazine* 49 (1846):43.

8. MS: *Huntingdon* to Wesley, Oct. 24, 1741, Methodist Archives, London; and *Methodist Magazine* 21 (1798): 489.

9. Vulliamy, *John Wesley,* 170; followed by Crow, "Wesley's Conflict with Antinomianism," 207. Both make too much of very scanty evidence. For her early contacts with Whitefield, cf. Wood, *The Inextinguishable Blaze,* 193.

10. Seymour, *Huntingdon,* 1:113. Unfortunately, Seymour is so vague about this contact that it is difficult properly to evaluate Gill's influence on Lady Huntingdon.

11. In addition to Whitefield, other evangelical leaders wore the Countess' scarf: William Romaine, Walter Shirley, Joseph Townsend, Martin Madan, Thomas Haweis, Cradock Glascott, and William Jesse. Others who acted in concert as close allies included Henry Venn and John Berridge. See Wood, *Inextinguishable Blaze,* 196–97.

12. Welch, *Two Calvinistic Methodist Chapels,* xii.

13. Seymour, *Huntingdon,* 1:281; and *Letters,* 5:74, on Jan. 4, 1768.

14. *Journal*, 5:304, on Mar. 5, 1769; and *Letters*, 5:153, on Nov. 5, 1769.

15. *Howel Harris' Visits to London*, 25, on Nov. 4, 1763.

16. MS: Wesley to Huntingdon, Jan. 8, 1764, Cheshunt College Archives, Cambridge; published in *Proceeding WHS* 27 (1949–50), 3–4.

17. *Howel Harris, Reformer and Soldier*, 206, on Nov. 4, 1763.

18. *Letters*, 5:166, on Dec. 26, 1769.

19. MS: Charles Wesley to Huntingdon, Mar. 9, 1769, Cheshunt College Archives, G2/1, Cambridge.

20. It is often mistakenly assumed that the College was conceived only as a response to the expulsion of the six students from St. Edmund's Hall, Oxford, in April 1768; e.g., Crow, "Wesley's Conflict on Antinomianism;" 208; and Bretherton, *The Countess*, 28. However, the diaries of Howel Harris reveal that he arranged the lease of Trevecka estate for the school in December 1765. See "The Itinerary of Howel Harris, 1765," *CCH* 12, no. 4 (Dec. 1927): 31–32; other early references to the College are Oct. 11–14 and Nov. 1–30, 1766; Jan. 12–17 and Feb. 1–3, 1767; ibid, 34, 36.

21. *Howel Harris, Reformer and Soldier*, 197, on Sept. 25, 1763. The College was close to Harris' Christian Community, also in Trevecka, and he supervised the early construction of buildings in addition to his contribution to the spiritual welfare of the students.

22. "The Itinerary of Howel Harris, 1767," *CCH* 12, no. 4 (Dec. 1927): 32, 36.

23. Joseph Benson, *The Life of the Rev. John William de la Flechere* (London: Thomas Cordeux, 1817), 138; and Wesley, "Life of Fletcher," *Works*, 11:294.

24. MS: John Wesley to Lady Huntingdon, Neath, Aug. 9, 1768, Cheshunt College Archives, G2/1, Cambridge.

25. Fletcher is variously called president, superintendent, principal, and visitor.

26. MS: Fletcher to Mr. Wesley, May 10, 1757, Methodist Archives, London. The fact that this autobiographical account is slightly different from that in Wesley's *Life of Fletcher*, and thus in subsequent biographies, led another hand to add a note at the end of the MS suggesting that Wesley, when writing the *Life*, could not lay his hands upon this letter and so quoted from memory. Frank Baker has shown, however, that the MS was originally written for Charles Wesley, and this explains why John did not make use of it. *Proceedings WHS* 33 (1961): 25–29.

27. MS: Fletcher to Wesley, May 10, 1757, Methodist Archives, Manchester.

28. Benson, *Flechere*, 1–2. Benson claimed to have incorporated all of the earliest biography by Wesley, "A Short Account of the Life and Death of the Reverend John Fletcher," *Works*, 1st ed. (1786), 11:273–365, plus some biographical notes of Joshua Gilpin. In turn, the standard work on Fletcher by Luke Tyerman, *Wesley's Designated Successor* (London: Hodder and Stoughton, 1882), claims to include all the biographical material of any importance from previous publications.

29. Ibid, 9; *Arminian Magazine* 17 (1794): 219.

30. MS: Fletcher to Wesley, May 10, 1757, Methodist Archives, Manchester.

31. Ibid.

32. Tyerman, *Successor*, 15, on Jan. 12, 1755; and Wesley, "Life of Fletcher," *Works*, 11:282.

33. MS: Fletcher to Wesley.

34. Tyerman, *Successor*, 54–55, 57; Fletcher, *Works*, 4:368, on Nov. 24, 1756.

35. Seymour, *Huntingdon*, 1:232; Wesley, *Journal*, 4: 199.

36. Seymour, *Huntingdon*, 2:81–86; Fletcher, "Letter to Lady Huntingdon," *Works*, 4:373–74, on Jan. 3, 1768; and "The Itinerary of Howel Harris, 1768," *CCH* 12, no. 4 (Dec. 1927), 37. Harris also purchased books and later exercised some oversight of the College in Fletcher's absence.

37. Benson, *Fletchere*, 139.

38. MS: Fletcher to the Countess of Huntingdon, Nov. 10, 1768, Cheshunt College Archives, FL/1449, Cambridge.

39. Ibid.

40. Ibid.

41. Ibid.

42. Ibid.

43. Ibid. Fletcher cautiously waited several days before sending his account to Lady Huntingdon. But as he prepared to leave the College, his hopes were high that the renewal would continue. His closing note was dated Nov. 15, 1768.

44. *Letters*, 5:83.

45. Ibid.

46. Seymour, *Huntingdon*, 1:235.

47. *Letters*, 5:88.

48. Seymour, *Huntingdon*, 2:235.

49. *Journal*, 5:334, 337; Tyerman, *Successor*, 148–50; "The Itinerary of Howel Harris, 1769," *CCH* 12, no. 4 (Dec. 1927): 41; and Benson, *Fletchere*, 138. Whitefield wrote to Wesley about his hopes that "such a pentecost season" would be an "earnest of good things to come." See *Arminian Magazine* 6 (1783): 273.

50. The first master was not Joseph Easter-brook (Seymour, *Huntingdon*, 2:83–84, 96–97; Tyerman, *Wesley*, 3:35), nor twelve-year-old John Henderson (Tyerman, *Successor*, 131f.), who declined because of his age (MS: Fletcher to Huntingdon, May 27, 1769, Cheshunt College Archives, Fl/1467, Cambridge), but a young man named Williams; MSS: Fletcher to Huntingdon, Cheshunt College Archives, FI/1449 (Nov. 10, 1768), Fl/1457 (Feb. 10, 1769), F1/1464 (Apr. 12, 1769), Fl/1467 (May 27, 1769); "The Itinerary of Howel Harris, 1769," *CCH* 12, no. 4 (Dec. 1927): 39–40; and *Howel Harris, Reformer and Soldier*, 219–20, 227–28.

51. James Macdonald, *Memoirs of the Rev. Joseph Benson* (London: T. Blanshard, 1822), 6–21; and Richard Treffry, *Memoirs of the Rev. Joseph Benson* (London: Mason, 1840), 26–32; cf. Benson, *Fletchere*, 137f., for Benson's account of Trevecka.

52. *Howel Harris, Reformer and Soldier*, 235, 239, 241.

53. Tyerman, *Successor*, 179.

54. Fletcher, *Works*, 4:342, on Oct. 7, 1769.

55. *Conference Minutes* (1770), 1:95–96.

56. Seymour, *Huntingdon*, 2:106–9.

57. *Letters*, 5:211, on Nov. 30, 1770; see also *Letters*, 5:202, 215.

58. *Howel Harris's Visits to London*, 26, on Oct. 12, 1770.

59. MSS: Shirley to Huntingdon, 1770, Cheshunt College Archives, FL/1565, Cambridge,

60. *Works*, 6:178.

61. Cf. Romaine's criticism in January of Wesley's memorial sermon for Whitefield, supra; also, in March, Walter Sellon's *Defence of God's Sovereignty* was censured; in May the Minutes were printed as "Popery Unmasked"; and in June a satirical review of the Minutes was published. See Tyerman, *Successor*, 187.

62. *Letters*, 5:202–3, on Oct. 5, 1770; and 211–12, on Nov. 30, 1770.

63. C. H. Crookshank, *History of Methodism in Ireland*, vol. 1 (Belfast: R. S. Allen, Son and Allen, 1885), 130; *Arminian Magazine* 3 (1780):106–7.

64. *Arminian Magazine* 3 (1780): 106–7, 168–69, 333–34, 560; 20 (1797): 407–8, 459; and Supplement, 50. The suggestion by Moore and Crookshank that Wesley was the instrument of his conversion is not supported by this correspondence; Crookshank, *History*, 1:130.

65. MS: Shirley to Charles Wesley, Dec. 10, 1760, no. 99, Letters to Charles Wesley, vol. VI,

Methodist Archives, Manchester. Endorsed by Charles, "Prospect for good."

66. MS: Shirley to Charles Wesley, Jan. 12, 1760, no. 69, Letters to Charles Wesley, vol. VI, Methodist Archives, Manchester.

67. MS: Shirley to Charles Wesley, Feb. 23, 1760, no. 70, Letters to Charles Wesley, vol. VI, Methodist Archives, Manchester.

68. Macdonald, *Benson*, 21; *Letters*, 6:40, on Sept. 10, 1773.

69. Macdonald, *Benson*, 17; cf. Wesley's response, *Letters*, 5:216–17.

70. Benson, *Fletchere*, 145.

71. Tyerman, *Successor*, 182.

72. Benson, *Fletchere*, 147–48.

73. Tyerman, *Successor*, 184–85.

74. MS: Essay of Fletcher to Lady Huntingdon, [Trevecka] College, Mar. 7, 1771, 1–2, Cheshunt College Archives, E4/7, Cambridge.

75. Ibid, 3.

76. Ibid, 4–5.

77. Ibid, 5–7.

78. Ibid, 7–9.

79. Ibid, 9–12.

80. MS: Note from Fletcher to Lady Huntingdon, Sat. Morning, Cheshunt College Archives, E4/7, Cambridge.

81. Tyerman, *Successor*, 178–79, on Mar. 18, 1771. Cf. Fletcher's account to Benson, Mar. 22, 1771; Benson, *Fletchere*, 147–49. Also, "An account of John Fletcher's case, with the reasons that have induced him to resign the superintendency of the Countess of Huntingdon's College in Wales," Tyerman, *Successor*, 180–86.

82. *Letters*, 5:252, on May 27, 1771; the Countess apparently wrote to Wesley in June or July after he had written to her; cf. Wesley's reference to two letters before the Conference; *Letters*, 5:274.

83. Ibid, 258–59, on June 19, 1771.

84. Ibid.

85. Ibid., 262–65, on July 10, 1771; John requested Charles to publish 1,500 copies immediately under the title *A Defence of the Minutes of Conference (1770) Relating to Calvinism*; Green, *Bibliography*, 154–55.

86. Walter Shirley, *A Narrative of the Principle Circumstances Relative to the Rev. Mr. Wesley's Late Conference* (Bath: W. Gye, 1771), 7–8.

87. Jackson, *Charles Wesley*, 2:255–57, on June 8, 1771.

88. MS: Shirley to Huntingdon, July 7, 1770, Cheshunt College Archives, F/1521, Cambridge.

89. Fletcher, *Works*, 1:61.

90. Shirley, *Narrative*, 5–6.

91. Tyerman, *Wesley*, 3:96, on June 24, 1771; and *Successor*, 188.

92. MS: Fletcher to John Wesley, June 24, 1771, Methodist Archives, Manchester. In his extract of the letter, Tyerman omits the section with this information; *Wesley*, 3:95–96.

93. *Journal*, 5:424, on July 26–28, 1771.

94. *Arminian Magazine* 20 (1797): 253–54.

95. *Arminian Magazine* 7 (1784): 278–79; and Tyerman, *Wesley*, 3:64–65, 86.

96. *Letters*, 5:219.

97. Tyerman, *Wesley*, 3:65; cf. Seymour, *Huntington*, 1:411.

98. *Journal*, 5:460–61.

99. MSS: Richard Hill to Walter Shirley, Jan. 4, 1771, 2, Cheshunt College Archives, F1/1385, Cambridge; and a second letter, Jan. 10, 1772, Cheshunt College Archives, FL/1386. Shirley had a very different impression and insisted that Hill had originally supported the Circular Letter; MS: Shirley to Richard Hill, Jan. 18, 1772, Cheshunt College Archives, FL/1387, Cambridge; and MS: Shirley to Mr.

Powis, Jan. 2, 1772, Cheshunt College Archives, Fl/1388.

100. Seymour, *Huntingdon*, 2:241.

101. MS: Edward Spencer to Shirley, June 20, 1771, Cheshunt College Archives, Er/7, Cambridge. Wesley preached in Spencer's Church, Sept. 21, 1769; *Letters*, 5:149.

102. Seymour, *Huntingdon*, 2:241.

103. Shirley, *Narrative*, 8–12.

104. MS: Toplady to Shirley, 1771, Cheshunt College Archives, Rl/1572, Cambridge. Cf. a different letter, in which Toplady explained the absence of himself, Romaine, and others as due to their desire to avoid fellowship with Wesley and his preachers; MS: Toplady to William Lunell, n.d., Methodist Archives, Manchester; cited in Crow, "Wesley's Conflict with Antinomianism," 228.

105. *Lives*, 4:43.

106. Shirley, *Narrative*, 12–13.

107. Ibid, 1–15. Apparently Wesley recopied the altered Declaration in his own hand before he and the preachers signed it. This would account for Seymour's statement that Wesley must have written the original draft, because Seymour had the original before him in Wesley's handwriting; Seymour, *Huntingdon*, 2:242.

108. Olivers reported his warning to the Conference "that if they signed it, they would repent of it another day. But Mr. Shirley's Entreaties and Tears so wrought on Mr. Wesley (whose charity thinketh no evil) that what I said was overruled." See Thomas Olivers, *A Scourge to Calumny* (London: R. Harris, 1774), 89.

109. Ibid, 16–17. Shirley fulfilled his promise, and also published in his *Narrative* both his and the Countess' initial letters of apology to Wesley and a note to Wesley signifying his satisfaction with the Declaration.

110. *Journal*, 5:425.

111. *Letters*, 5:274–75, on Aug. 14, 1771.

112. *Howel Harris' Visits to London*, 26. The Countess later wrote to Shirley that she could not explain Wesley's letter except by "attacking his integrity or suspecting that his judgement is impaired." See Seymour, *Huntingdon*, 2:244.

113. Variously called "Letters," or "Vindication," but published as *First Check to Antinomianism*.

114. Shirley, *Narrative*, 18–19.

115. Fletcher, "Preface to the Second Check," *Works*, 1:68. In his *Narrative*, Shirley failed to mention this.

116. Shirley, *Narrative*, 19–20. Seymour suggested that Thomas Olivers' influence lay behind the publication; Seymour, *Huntingdon*, 2:234. But against this, see Fletcher, *Works*, 1:69.

117. Fletcher, *Works*, 1:20.

118. *Conference Minutes*, 52. For practical examples of the problem, see *Journal*, 5:399; and *Lives*, 5:30, 178–79.

119. *Letters*, 5:83. Cf. discussion supra.

120. "Wesley to Daniel Bumstead, January 13, 1770," *Proceedings WHS* 2 (1935–36): 12.

121. MS: Walter Sellon to Huntingdon, Nov. 20, 1771, Cheshunt College Archives, E4/4, Cambridge. Fletcher also mentioned this phrase "My Lady's Gospel," in MS: Fletcher to Walter Sellon, Jan. 7, 1772, no. 71, Fletcher Volume, Methodist Archives, London.

122. *Journal*, 5:482, on Aug. 14, 1772.

123. MS: Toplady to Shirley, 1771, Cheshunt College Archives, Fl/1569, Cambridge.

124. Jackson, *Charles Wesley*, 2:251. Knox believed the 1770 Minutes were the result of a change in Wesley's views on December 1, 1767. Wesley's statements about the continuity of his convictions, however, makes this position difficult to support. See "Remarks on Character of Wesley by Alexander Knox," in Robert Southby, *Life of Wesley*, 2 (London: Longman, 1846), 478f.; *Journal*, 5:243–44.

125. "To the Countess of Huntingdon," *Letters*, 5:275. In this letter Wesley gives no hint that he ever really considered suppressing Fletcher's work.

126. Fletcher, "Preface to Second Check," *Works*, 1:68–69, Sept. 11, 1771; cf. Jackson, *Charles Wesley*, 2:269–70.

127. *Letters*, 5:276, on Sept. 1, 1771.

128. Ibid, 290, on Nov. 20, 1771.

129. Ibid, 84.

130. *Letters*, 5:202, on Oct. 5, 1770. Cf. Shirley's recognition of Wesley's influence; *Narrative*, 5–6.

131. MS: Shirley to Huntingdon, Dec. 10, 1770, Cheshunt College Archives, FI/1522, Cambridge.

132. MS: Shirley to Huntingdon, [Dec.] 19, 1770, Cheshunt College Archives, P1/1565, Cambridge.

133. MS: Shirley to Huntingdon, [1770], Cheshunt College Archives, Fl/1567, Cambridge.

134. *Letters*, 5:222, on Feb. 16, 1771.

11. Wesley's Defense against the Calvinists' Attack

1. *Works*, 7:448–49.

2. *Letters*, 6:10–12, on Jan. 15, 1773; and MS: Fletcher to John Wesley, Jan. 9, 1776, Methodist Archives, Manchester.

3. *Letters*, 6:76, on Mar. 1, 1774.

4. *Works*, 7:436.

5. "Preface to Second Check," *Works*, 1:68–69; Tyerman, *Successor*, 209; and MS: Fletcher to Charles Wesley, Sept. 21, 1771, no. 37, Fletcher Volume, Methodist Archives, Manchester, where Fletcher discusses Wesley's corrections of the *First Check* and the *Second Check*.

6. Among other references, see MS: Fletcher to Charles Wesley, Nov. 24, 1771, no. 38, Fletcher Volume; and MS: Fletcher to Charles

Wesley, May 31, 1772, no. 44, Fletcher Volume, Methodist Archives, Manchester.

7. Jackson, *Charles Wesley*, 2:293–94.

8. MS: Fletcher to Charles Wesley, May 21, 1775, no. 51, Fletcher Volume, Methodist Archives, Manchester.

9. Fletcher, *Works*, 1:12–19. Fletcher had received Wesley's reaffirmation of these sentiments as recently as March 22, 1771; cf. Wesley, *Letters*, 5:231.

10. Fletcher, *Works*, 1:61–62.

11. MS: Fletcher to Charles Wesley, Sept. 21, 1771, no. 37, Fletcher Volume, Methodist Archives, Manchester.

12. Seymour, *Huntingdon*, 2:244; and MS: Shirley to Huntingdon, [1771], Cheshunt College Archives, FL/1569, Cambridge.

13. Fletcher, *Works*, 1:67.

14. MS: Fletcher to Charles Wesley, Sept. 21, 1771, no. 37, Fletcher Volume, Methodist Archives, Manchester.

15. MS: Shirley to Huntingdon, [1771], Cheshunt College Archives, FL/1569, Cambridge.

16. Shirley, *Narrative*. Cf. Fletcher's evaluation; MS: Fletcher to Charles Wesley, Sept. 21, 1771, no. 37, Fletcher Volume, Methodist Archives, Manchester.

17. Ibid, 20–21.

18. *The Gospel Magazine*, Sept. 1771; cited in Tyerman, *Successor*, 207.

19. MS: Fletcher to Charles Wesley, Nov. 24, 1771, no. 38, Fletcher Volume, Methodist Archives, Manchester.

20. Fletcher, *Works*, 1:71–72.

21. Ibid., 72–80; see also 87, 89–93.

22. Richard Hill, *A Conversation Between Richard Hill, Esq.; The Rev. Mr. Madan, and Father Walsh* (London: E. and C. Dilly, 1771), 11, 13, 14.

23. Ms: Fletcher to Charles Wesley, Sept. 21, 1771, no. 37, Fletcher Volume, Methodist Ar-

chives, Manchester; cf. also MS: Fletcher to John Wesley, Dec. 1771, no. 40, Fletcher Volume, Methodist Archives, Manchester.

24. Fletcher, *Works*, 1:132.

25. MS: Michael Callenden to Charles Wesley, Dec. 12, 1771, no. 32, Early Methodist Volume, Methodist Archives, Manchester.

26. MS: Shirley to Huntingdon, Jan., 23, 1771, Cheshunt College Archives, FL/1580, Cambridge.

27. Ibid, Jan. 9, 1772, Cheshunt College Archives, FL/1576, Cambridge.

28. Ibid, Feb. 17, 1772, Cheshunt College Archives, F4/1, Cambridge.

29. Ibid, Jan. 23, 1772, Cheshunt College Archives, F1/1580, Cambridge.

30. Richard Hill, *Five Letters to the Rev. Mr. Fletcher* (London: E. and C. Dilly, 1772), 5–6, 11. For Fletcher's part in Hill's conversion, see Sidney, *Life of Richard Hill*, 23–24.

31. Ibid, 9, 17, 20–21.

32. Ibid, 24–25, 28–29.

33. MS: Fletcher to Charles Wesley, Jan. 1772, no. 41, Fletcher Volume, Methodist Archives, Manchester.

34. Fletcher, *Works*, 1:135.

35. Ibid, 137–46, 153–54, 161. Cf. Wesley's approbation of Fletcher on prevenient grace; *Letters*, 6:239.

36. Ibid, 161–62. In print, Wesley never supported four justifications. While preaching in Bristol on September 12, 1774, however, he tentatively touched on the subject. William Dyer reported: "Heard John Wesley's curious distinction of four justifications." See *Proceedings WHS* 18 (1931–32): 122.

37. Ibid, 173–83, 190, 194.

38. *Letters*, 6:304, on Feb. 8, 1772.

39. *Letters*, 5:311, on Mar. 17, 1772.

40. Ibid, 304. Others concurred with Wesley: *Lives*, 5:181; and *Arminian Magazine* 7 (1784): 557.

41. MS: Shirley to Huntingdon, Mar. 9, 1772, Cheshunt College Archives, E4/1, Cambridge. Fletcher responded to both parties in one letter, with his thanks for each.

42. Ibid, Mar, 14, 1772, Cheshunt College Archives, E4/1, Cambridge.

43. Ibid, Apr. 19, 1772, Cheshunt College Archives, E4/1, Cambridge.

44. Richard Hill, *A Review of all the Doctrines Taught by the Rev. John Wesley* (London: E. and C. Dilly, 1772), 2.

45. Ibid, 3–4.

46. Ibid, 11, 24–25, 64.

47. Ibid, 49–56.

48. Ibid, title page. Hill had hinted at this plan of attack earlier in his *Conversation*, 20.

49. Ibid, 148–49.

50. MS: Fletcher to Charles Wesley, May 31, 1772, no. 44, Fletcher Volume, Methodist Archives, Manchester.

51. Ibid, July 5, 1772, no. 72, Fletcher Volume, Methodist Archives, Manchester. Thomas Olivers also came to Wesley's defense in *A Scourge to Calumny*. Cf. Wesley's approval in *Letters*, 6:67, 73.

52. *Journal*, 5:476, on July 11, 1772.

53. *Letters*, 5:339–40, on Sept. 18, 1772.

54. Wesley, "Some Remarks on Mr. Hill's 'Review of All The Doctrines Taught by Mr. John Wesley,' " *Works*, 10:375–76, on Sept. 9, 1772.

55. Ibid, 379, 417–18.

56. *Works*, 10:381–82, 385, 418–19, 422.

57. Richard Hill, *Logica Wesleiensis, or Farrago Double-Distilled: With an Heroic Poem in Praise of Mr. John Wesley* (London: E. and C. Dilly,

1773). Cf. Charles Wesley's satirical response, in *Poetical Works*, 8:446.

58. *Works*, 10:415–46.

59. Ibid, 395–401.

60. Ibid, 407.

61. Rowland Hill, *Friendly Remarks Occasioned by the Spirit and Doctrines Contained in the Rev. Mr. Fletcher's Vindication* (London: Edward and Charles Dilly, 1772), 4–6, 15–16.

62. Ibid, 4–6, 27–29.

63. Ibid, 44–45.

64. Ibid, 31–33, 67.

65. Ibid, 61–63. In spite of his intention to retire from the battlefield, Richard Hill could not long remain on the sidelines. He sent forth *Some Remarks on a Pamphlet, Entitled, A Third Check to Antinomianism,* in which he endeavored to defend the doctrine of particular election from the allegation of divine inequity by employing the traditional Calvinistic assertion that the creature had no right to impugn the just character of the Creator. He rejected Fletcher's four degrees of justification as well as the concept of relative punishment, and maintained that the sole penalty for sin was eternal death. See *Some Remarks* (London: Edward and Charles Dilly, 1772), 4–5.

12. A Wider Separation between the Wesleyans and the Calvinists

1. *Letters*, 5:344, on Nov. 4, 1772.

2. *Works*, 10:413, on Sept. 9, 1772.

3. *Journal*, 5:488, on Nov. 8, 1771.

4. MS: Fletcher to Charles Wesley, Aug. 5, 1772, no. 45, Fletcher Volume, Methodist Archives, Manchester.

5. MS: Fletcher to Charles Wesley, July 5, 1772, no. 72, Fletcher Volume, Methodist Archives, Manchester.

6. Fletcher, *Works*, 1:203, 205, on Nov. 15, 1772. Of the thirteen letters that made up the *Fourth*

Check, no. IX was addressed to Rowland Hill, nos. X and XI to both men, and the rest to Richard Hill.

7. Fletcher, *Works*, 1:221, 277.

8. Ibid, 235–38. David Shipley declares that "every element in Wesley's answer . . . to theoretical Antinomianism, even to the precise detail of the concept of a double justification, had been set forth in the seventeenth century" in the works of Baxter and John Flavel; "Wesley and Some Calvinistic Controversies," *The Drew Gateway* 25 (1954): 205.

9. Ibid, 297–98, 242–43.

10. Ibid, 302–3.

11. *Letters*, 6:76–77, on Mar. 1, 1774; cf. Wesley's exasperation that this was not clear to his opponents: "Until Mr. Hill and his associates puzzled the cause, it was as plain as plain could be. The Methodists always held, and have declared a thousand times, the death of Christ is the meritorious cause of our salvation—that is, of pardon, holiness and glory; loving, obedient faith is the condition of glory." See *Letters*, 6:79–80, on May 2, 1774.

12. *Letters*, 6:28, on May 24, 1773.

13. Ibid, 8, on Jan. 12, 1773; cf. *Letters*, 6:345, on Nov. 4, 1772.

14. MS: Fletcher to Charles Wesley, Feb. 28, 1773, no. 47, Fletcher Volume, Methodist Archives, Manchester. But contrast the response of Cornelius Winter, another layman in Shirley's 1771 Delegation; *Arminian Magazine* 8 (1785): 336.

15. J. S. Drew, *Life, Character and Literacy Labours of Samuel Drew* (1834), 18; cited in John Vickers, *Thomas Coke, Apostle of Methodism* (London: Epworth, 1969), 23. A second influential assistant of Wesley to be established by the *Checks* was the Rev. James Creighton; *Methodist Magazine* 28 (1805): 24–28.

16. MS: Coke to Fletcher, Aug. 28, 1775, Methodist Missionary Society Archives; cited in Vickers, *Coke*, 24. After Coke became an Arminian, he made a public avowal of the change in his views; ibid, 25.

17. *Letters*, 6:10–12, on Jan. [15], 1773; and 6:33–34, on July 21, 1773; cf. Fletcher's response, Tyerman, *Successor*, 263–64.

18. Ibid, 6:34, on July 21, 1773; cf. *Journal*, 5:517.

19. MS: Copy, Charles Wesley to Mr. D., Jan. 1, 1773, no. 61, Letters to Charles Wesley, vol. II; and MS: Copy, Charles Wesley to John Wesley, Jan. 20, 1774, no. 63, Letters to Charles Wesley, vol. II, Methodist Archives, Manchester.

20. MS: Fletcher to John Wesley, Jan. 9, 1776, Methodist Archives, Manchester.

21. Toplady, "Letter to Ambrose Serle," *Works*, 6:209–10, on Jan. 11, 1774.

22. Richard Hill, *The Finishing Stroke* (London: Edward and Charles Dilly, 1773), 7.

23. Ibid, 12, 20, 23, 43.

24. Ibid, 44.

25. Ibid, 29.

26. *Journal*, 5:500, on Mar. 16, 1773.

27. Ibid, 491, Dec. 8, 1772.

28. *Letters*, 6:34–35, on July 30, 1773.

29. Stephen Tuck, *Wesleyan Methodism in Frome* (Frome: S. Tuck, 1837), 48–50. The leader and several others later rejoined the society.

30. *Letters*, 6:60, on Dec. 23, 1773. In Norfolk he visited a once-promising work and noted that "Calvinism, breaking in upon them, had torn the infant society in pieces." See *Journal*, 6:5, on Nov. 1, 1773; also at Yarmouth, noted in *Journal*, 6:49, on Nov. 15, 1774; and at Gravesend, reported in *Lives*, 11:185, for 1773.

31. Ibid, 52, on Oct. 22, 1773; cf. R. A. Knox, *Enthusiasm* (Oxford: Clarendon, 1950), 503.

32. Crookshank, *History*, 1:283–86;] cf. Wesley's reply, *Letters*, 6:76–77, on Mar. 1, 1774, where he advises the people not to hear Hawksworth.

33. MS: Shirley to Huntingdon, Mar. 14, 1772, Cheshunt College Archives, E4/1, Cambridge.

34. *Letters*, 6:35, on July 31, 1773.

35. Curnock says he preached it at the request of several clergymen; *Journal*, 5:511 n, on June 4, 1773. Cf. Green, *Bibliography*, no. 290.

36. *Letters*, 6:61, on Dec. 28, 1773.

37. Ibid, 41–42, on Sept. 16, 1773. Apparently Wesley was responding to a letter from Lady Huntingdon, which would indicate that not all of those with a "broad spirit" were on one side. Cf. also "Letter to Peter Bohler," *Letters*, 6:140–41, on Feb. 18, 1775.

38. MS: Fletcher to Charles Wesley, May 31, 1772, no. 44, Fletcher Volume; and ibid, Aug. 5, 1772, no. 45, Fletcher Volume, Methodist Archives, Manchester. Madan privately corresponded with Fletcher over the controversy; MS: Fletcher to Charles Wesley, Apr. 20, 1773, no. 87, Fletcher Volume; and ibid, Aug. 24, 1773, no. 48, Fletcher Volume, Methodist Archives, Manchester. In January 1772 Madan also published *A Scriptural Comment Upon the Thirty-nine Articles of the Church of England* (London: John and Francis Rivington, 1772), with an attack on Wesley's Arminianism in an appendix. Cf. Wesley's uncomplimentary evaluation of the preaching of Romaine and Madan; *Letters*, 7:60–61, Dec. 28, 1773.

39. Autobiographical letter of Berridge; *Arminian Magazine* 345 (1812): 457–65.

40. J. C. Ryle, *The Christian Leaders of the Eighteenth Century*, 216–35; Charles Smyth, *Simeon and Church Order*, 164–65.

41. John Berridge, *The Christian World Unmasked: Pray Come and Peep* (1st ed., 1773; London: W. Isbister, 1874), 29, 94, 35, 154–57, 22–28, 148–49, 178–88, 190–98. Berridge had not always been a Calvinist. In 1760 he rejected predestination and wrote to Wesley that his sentiments "differ the least from yours of any others." See *Arminian Magazine* 20 (1797): 303.

42. Ibid, 198.

43. MS: Fletcher to Charles Wesley, Aug. 24, 1773, no. 48, Fletcher Volume, Methodist Archives, Manchester.

44. Tyerman, *Successor*, 285–88.

45. MS: Fletcher to Charles Wesley, Aug. 24, 1773, no. 48, Fletcher Volume, Methodist Archives, Manchester.

46. Fletcher, *Works*, 1:337–38, completed Sept. 13, 1773, but not published until early 1774.

47. Ibid, 341–44, 358–59.

48. Ibid, 369.

49. Ibid, 369–71, 372, 375.

50. Ibid, 377–79.

51. Ibid, 383–84.

52. Berridge, *Works*, 384;] cited in Tyerman, *Successor*, 284, for Aug. 31, 1773.

53. Richard Hill, *Three Letters, Written by Richard Hill, Esq., to the Rev. J. Fletcher* (Shrewsbury, 1773). Fletcher responded with *The Fictitious and Genuine Creed: Being "A Creed for Arminians," Composed by Richard Hill Esq., to which is Opposed a Creed for Those who Believe That Christ Tasted Death for Every Man* (London: 1775).

54. *Monthly Review,* Jan. 1775; cited in Tyerman, *Successor,* 292.

55. MS: Fletcher to Charles Wesley, Mar. 12, 1772, no.42, Fletcher Volume, Methodist Archives, Manchester. He confessed: "I am tired of controversy. I do not see the least prospect of good from it now." See MS: Fletcher to John Wesley, Feb. 13, 1772, Methodist Archives, Manchester.

56. MS: Fletcher to Charles Wesley, Aug. 24, 1773, no. 48, Fletcher Volume, Methodist Archives, Manchester. Cf. also MS: Fletcher to Charles Wesley, Aug. 5, 1772, no. 45, Fletcher Volume, Methodist Archives, Manchester.

57. MS: Fletcher to Charles Wesley, Mar. 12, 1772, no. 42, Fletcher Volume, Methodist Archives, Manchester. Fletcher dreamed that he had embraced the Countess' knees and pleaded for peace, and that she had cast a mantle of forgiveness over all grievances, making him extremely happy. Upon waking, he declared, "I wish it might be an omen for future peace."

58. MS: Fletcher to Charles Wesley, Feb. 20, 1774, Methodist Archives, Manchester; cf. Fletcher, *Works*, 4:346, on Feb. 6, 1774.

59. MS: Fletcher to Charles Wesley, Apr. 20, 1773, no. 87, Fletcher Volume, Methodist Archives, Manchester. Fletcher's *Equal Check* did not appear until late 1774.

60. Ibid; Richard De Courcy confirmed Fletcher's fears and told him that the *Equal Check* would greatly offend Lady Huntingdon; MS: Fletcher to Charles Wesley, Aug. 14, 1774, no. 50, Fletcher Volume, Methodist Archives, Manchester.

61. MS: Fletcher to Charles Wesley, Feb. 20, 1774, Methodist Archives, Manchester. This was no afterthought with Fletcher. In 1773 he wrote to a friend: "There is such a thing as to go from one extreme to the other, while you avoid Antinomian dotages, go not over to pharisaic stiffness, by which I can see through your letter you do not make enough of *free-grace*." See MS: Letter of John Fletcher, Oct. 17, 1773, Methodist Archives, Manchester; also MS: Fletcher to Charles Wesley, July 4, 1774, no. 49, Fletcher Volume, Methodist Archives, Manchester.

62. Fletcher, *Works*, 1:435–40, 442–43.

63. Ibid, 444–45.

64. MS: Fletcher to John Wesley, Feb. 28, 1773, no. 47, Fletcher Volume, Methodist Archives, Manchester.

65. Fletcher, *Works*, 1:428, 507–8.

66. "Letter to James Ireland," *Works*, 4:346, on Feb. 6, 1774.

67. Fletcher, *Works*, 1:524–26.

68. Ibid, 529–31,575.

69. Ibid, 11, 12, 16.

70. Ibid, 24. Cf. Wesley's word of caution: "That expression 'the necessary union between faith and good works' must be taken with a grain

of allowance; otherwise it would infer irresistible grace and infallible perseverance." See "Letter to Fletcher," *Letters*, 6:75, on Feb. 26, 1774.

71. Ibid, 126.

72. Ibid, 137–46, 159–61.

73. Ibid, 186–90, 195.

74. Ibid, 172.

75. MS: Fletcher to Charles Wesley, Feb. 20, 1774, Methodist Archives, Manchester.

76. MS: Fletcher to Charles Wesley, July 4, 1774, no. 49, Fletcher Volume, Methodist Archives, Manchester. Cf. divisions created in other places: *Letters*, 6:76 n, Feb. 10, 1774; *Journal*, 6:49–50, on Nov. 15, 1774; and 6:87, on Dec. 6, 1775. Contrast *Journal*, 6:12, on Mar. 18, 1774.

77. MS: Fletcher to Charles Wesley, Nov. 24, 1771, no. 38; and MS: Fletcher to John Wesley [1771], no. 39, Fletcher Volume, Methodist Archives, Manchester.

78. MS: Fletcher to Charles Wesley, Jan. 1772, no. 41, Fletcher Volume; ibid, Feb. 28, 1773, no. 47, Fletcher Volume; and MS: Fletcher to Walter Sellon, Jan. 7, 1772, no. 71, Fletcher Volume, Methodist Archives, Manchester.

79. MS: Fletcher to Charles Wesley, Jan. 16, 1773, no. 46, Fletcher Volume, Methodist Archives, Manchester.

80. Fletcher, *Works*, 2:492–93.

81. Ibid, 495.

82. Ibid; Fletcher quotes Wesley, *A Plain Account of Christian Perfection*, 60.

83. Fletcher, *Works*, 2:492–93.

84. Ibid, 498–99.

85. Ibid, 505, 600. Cf. *Lives*, 4:255–57, reporting Matthias Joyce's experience of Christian perfection after reading the *Last Check*.

86. Lawrence W. Wood, *Pentecostal Grace* (Wilmore, Ky.: Francis Asbury Publishing Co., 1980), 177–239.

87. MS: Fletcher to Charles Wesley, Nov. 24, 1771, no. 38, Fletcher Volume, Methodist Archives, Manchester.

88. *Letters*, 6:146, on Mar. 22, 1775.

89. E.g., Fletcher, *Works*, 2:630–33, 645–48, 655–56. For the debate over Wesley and Fletcher's views on Pentecostal language, see *Wesleyan Theological Journal* 13 (1978); 14, nos. 1 (spring 1979) and 2 (fall 1979); 15, no. 1 (spring 1980).

90. *Letters*, 5:215, on Dec. 28, 1770. Cf. Wesley's comment: "It seems our views of Christian perfection are a little different, though not opposite. It *is* certain every babe in Christ has received the *Holy* Ghost, and the Spirit witnesses with his spirit that he is a Child of God. But he has not obtained Christian perfection." See "Letter to Fletcher," *Letters*, 6:146, on Mar. 22, 1775.

91. Ibid, 229, on Mar. 16, 1771.

92. Ibid, 175.

13. The Last Phase of the Minute Controversy

1. *Works*, 10:457, on May 14, 1774. Toplady had reentered the controversy this same year with *Historic Proof of the Doctrinal Calvinism of the Church of England.*

2. *Works*, 10:456–63. Cf. Wesley's observations on Kames, on May 24, 1774: "What good would it do to mankind if he could convince them that they are a mere piece of clockwork." See *Journal*, 6:21–22.

3. Ibid, 463–69.

4. Ibid, 470–74.

5. Toplady, *Works*, 6:v, on Jan. 22, 1775. Toplady stated that he wrote while he was so ill that he could hardly hold his pen; ibid, 6:260.

6. Ibid, 10, 12, 14.

7. Ibid, 12, 14, 27.

8. Ibid, 29, 31, 66–67, 102.

9. Fletcher, *Works*, 2:367. Cf. Semmel, *Methodist Revolution*, 90; and "Review of Priestley's

Doctrine of Philosophical Necessity," *Arminian Magazine* 11 (1788): 33ff.

10. Ibid, 369–76.

11. Ibid, 402, 405, 408.

12. Ibid, 410.

13. Cf. The satirical pamphlet *A Necessary Alarm and Most Earnest Caveto against Tabernacle Principles and Tabernacle Connections; containing the substance of an Extraordinary Harangue and Exhortation; on an Extraordinary Occasion. By J. W. Master of very Extraordinary Arts,* 1774; and Toplady in the *Gospel Magazine,* 1776, 475; also the poem "The Serpent and the Fox; or an interview between old Nick and Old John," *Gospel Magazine,* 1777, 337; cited in Tyerman, *Wesley,* 3:232–33, 257.

14. This much of the accusation is supported by Wesley's letter to his wife, Sept. 1, 1777, in *Letters,* 6:273.

15. He singled out Rowland Hill as the chief culprit, citing Hill's *Imposture Detected,* 22. Jackson, *Charles Wesley,* 2:279–82. Tyerman, claiming to have further documentation, supported this accusation; *Wesley,* 3:233; but Knox questioned whether the interpolated letters ever reached the newspapers; *Enthusiasm,* 502.

16. *Works,* 7:429, on Apr. 21, 1777.

17. Rowland Hill, *Imposture Detected, and the Dead Vindicated* (London: T. Vallance, 1777).

18. *Journal,* 6:157–58, on June 26, 1777. Wesley replied in "An Answer to Mr. Rowland Hill's Trace, entitled: 'Imposture Detected,' " *Works,* 10:446–54, on June 28, 1777. Thomas Olivers also came to his defense in *A Rod for a Reviler* (London: J. Fry, 1777). Cf. Hill's rejoinder, *A Full Answer to the Rev. J. Wesley's Remarks Upon a Late Pamphlet* (Bristol: T. Mills, 1777).

19. Jackson, *Charles Wesley,* 2:282.

20. *Letters,* 6:113, on Sept. 16, 1774. Thomas Paine wrote to Wesley: "By reading and considering yours, Mr. Fletcher's and Mr. Sellon's works, I was entirely delivered from the whole hypothesis of absolute predestination." See *Lives,* 2:288.

21. *Conference Minutes,* 1:126–27. The Calvinists continued, however, to trouble his societies for some years; *Journal,* 6:131, 217, 241, 286–87; and *Letters,* 6:331.

22. *Journal,* 6:155, on June 14, 1777.

23. MS: Fletcher to Charles Wesley, Dec. 4, 1775, no. 90, Fletcher Volume, Methodist Archives, Manchester. Fletcher mentioned that he was "greyheaded" at forty-six.

24. MS: Fletcher to Charles Wesley, May 11, 1776, no. 53, Fletcher Volume, Methodist Archives, Manchester.

25. Fletcher, *Works,* 2:261, 274–82.

26. Dedicated to James Ireland as the "Peacemaker." Tyerman, *Successor,* 378.

27. Fletcher, *Works,* 2:292, 296, 300.

28. Ibid, 321–22.

29. There is no doubt, however, about Fletcher's sincere desire for reconciliation. Cf. "Letter to C. Middleton," *Arminian Magazine* 11 (1788): 386–88, May 18, 1778.

30. MS: Huntingdon to Charles Wesley, Oct. 1773, no. 80, Huntingdon Letters, Methodist Archives, Manchester; copy in Cheshunt College Archives, G1/17, Cambridge.

31. MS: Huntingdon to Charles Wesley, June 28, 1775, no. 81, Huntingdon Letters, Methodist Archives, Manchester; copy in Cheshunt College Archives, GI/17, Cambridge. Charles Wesley in his reply observed: "We shall be *in our death not divided.*" See copy inscribed on letter from Countess; ibid, July 2, 1775.

32. *Wesleyan Methodist Magazine* 4 (1825): 385–87.

33. MS: Huntingdon to John Wesley, Sept. 8, 1776, Cheshunt College Archives, E4/3, Cambridge.

34. MS: John Wesley to Huntingdon, Sept. 15, 1776, Cheshunt College Archives, E4/3, Cambridge; and *Proceedings WHS* 27 (1949): 4. Cf. Wesley's later judgment on the Countess'

preachers in Cornwall; *Journal*, 6:208, on Aug. 28, 1778.

35. MS: John Wesley to Huntingdon, Aug. 19, 1779, Cheshunt College Archives, G2/1, Cambridge.

36. Jackson, *Charles Wesley*, 2:295–96.

37. *Wesleyan Methodist Magazine* 6 (1825): 604.

38. MS: Fletcher to Huntingdon, Mar. 18, 1777, Cheshunt College Archives, Cambridge; and Fletcher, *Works*, 4:380, on Jan. 29, 1777.

39. Sidney, *Life of Rowland Hill* (London: Baldwin & Cradock, 1835), 108–10.

40. Sidney, *Life of Richard Hill*, 198. In 1781 Wesley commended Hill for the spirit in which he wrote on a controversy with Martin Madan; *Journal*, 6:313.

41. *The Arminian Magazine: Consisting of Extracts and Original Treatises on Universal Redemption* 1 (1778): 111; *see Journal*, 6:176, on Nov. 24, 1777.

42. *Journal*, 6:169, on Aug. 14, 1777. Tyerman, *Wesley*, 3:281–82, includes original "Proposals."

43. *Arminian Magazine* 1 (1778): iv–vi, 9–28. Cf. Fletcher's approval; *Arminian Magazine* 5 (1782): 47–48.

44. *Letters*, 6:295, on Jan. 15, 1778.

45. Ibid; see A. W. Harrison, "The Arminian Magazine," *Proceedings WHS* 12 (1920): 150–52; and "The Methodist Magazine 1778–1969," *Proceedings WHS* 37 (1969): 72–76.

46. In 1780 Wesley admitted that the bulk of the first two volumes of the magazine had been devoted to the "best tracts" of the recent Arminian-Calvinist debate, but he hoped to limit "controversial matter" to fifteen pages in future editions. A survey of succeeding volumes indicates that he largely fulfilled his intention. See *Arminian Magazine* 3 (1780): iii–iv.

14. Evaluation of the Controversies

1. *Letters*, 1:22–23.

2. *Works*, 10:211.

3. *Conference Minutes*, 9, Aug. 2, 1745.

4. Cell, *Rediscovery of Wesley*, 270; and Ireson, "Doctrine of Faith in John Wesley," 413.

5. Cannon, *Theology*, 113–15, 138; Lindström, *Wesley and Sanctification*, 98, 215, more carefully refers to a "synergistic tendency."

6. Wesley, *Concise Ecclesiastical History*, vol. 1 (London: 1781), 248 n. Yet it was well after the Minutes controversy and in a private letter to Fletcher, rather than in a printed publication, that Wesley made his well-known remark about "predestinarianism" being "hatched by Augustine in spite to Pelagius (who very probably held no other heresy than you and I do now)." See *Letters*, 6:175.

7. Semmel, *Methodist Revolution*, 99.

8. *Letters*, 6:66; cf. also 6:54, 59, 74, 97, 103, 137, 240.

9. "Plain Account," *Works*, 11:443.

10. This charge is repeated by R. Newton Flew, *The Idea of Perfection in Christian Theology* (Oxford: Oxford University Press, 1934), 332–36.

11. "Plain Account," *Works*, 11:443.

12. Cell, *Rediscovery of Wesley*, 362.

13. Cf. G. R. Cragg, "The Eclipse of Calvinism," *From Puritanism to the Age of Reason*, 13–36.

14. Toplady, *Works*, 2:152–57; 5:156–58.

15. Cf. "Principles of a Methodist," *Works*, 8:363.

16. Cf. Wesley's appeal to the authority of the Thirty-Nine Articles, in *Works*, 8:52–53; and *Letters*, 1:279; 2:88, 192; 3:200; 4:18, 131, 295; 5:366; 6:28.

17. Wesley considerably strengthened the hand of the Arminians in the United States, however, when he omitted altogether the article "On Predestination" from the Twenty-Four Articles he intended to be one of the doctrinal standards of the newly established Methodist Church in America.

18. *Letters*, 4:208.

Bibliography

Primary Sources

Albin, Thomas A., and Oliver A. Beckerlegge, eds. *Charles Wesley's Earliest Sermons*. London: Wesley Historical Society, 1987. Six unpublished manuscript sermons.

The Arminian Magazine. 20 Vols., ed. successively by J. Wesley and G. Storey. London: Fry et al., 1778–97.

The Writings of James Arminius, D.D. 3 Vols., Grand Rapids: Baker Book House, 1956. Reprint of 1853 edition of *The Works of James Arminius.*

"Articles of Religion," *The Book of Common Prayer*. Cambridge: University Press, n.d.

Atmore, Charles. *The Methodist Memorial.* Bristol: Richard Edwards, 1801.

Berridge, John. *The Christian World Unmasked, Pray Come and Peep*. London: W. Isbister and Co., 1874; 1st ed. 1773.

Beynon, Tom, ed. "Extracts from the Diaries of Howel Harris," *Bathafarn* 4 (1949); 6 (1951); 9 (1954); 10 (1955).

_____. *Howel Harris, Reformer and Soldier*. Caernavon, 1958.

_____. *Howel Harris's Visits to London.* Aberystwyth: The Cambrian News Press, 1960.

_____. *Howel Harris's Visits to Pembrokeshire.* Aberystwyth: The Cambrian News Press, 1966.

Burnet, Gilbert. *An Exposition of the 39 Articles of The Church of England*. Oxford: University Press, 1796; 1st ed. 1699.

Calvin, John. *Institutes of the Christian Religion.* Translated by Henry Beveridge. London: James Clark & Co. Ltd., 1957.

Cennick, John. "Account of the Awakenings at Bristol and Kingswood, 1738, 1739," *Proceedings W.H.S.* 4 (1908), 101–10, 133–41.

_____. *The Life of Mr. J. Cennick*. Bristol: n.p., 1745.

_____. *Twenty Discourses*. 2 Vols. London: Trapp, 1777.

Coles, Elisha. *A Practical Discourse on God's Sovereignty*. London: Ben. Griffin, 1673.

Anonymous. *A Complete Account of the Conduct of that eminent Enthusiast Mr. Whitefield*. London: C. Corbett, 1739.

Edwards, John. *The Preacher*, 4 Vols. London: F. Lawrence & F. Wyat, 1705–09.

_____. *A Narrative of Surprising Conversions*. London: Banner of Truth Trust, 1965.

Elliot, Richard. "A Summary of Whitefield's Doctrine," *Select Sermons of George Whitefield*. London: Banner of Truth Trust, 1958.

Fletcher, John. "Early Life: MS to Wesley," *Proceedings W.H.S.* 33 (1961): 25–29.

_____. *The Works of the Reverend John Fletcher.* 4 Vols. Salem, Ohio: Schmul, 1974; 1st ed. 1804.

Fleetwood, William. *The Perfectionists Examined; or, Inherent Perfection in this Life, no Scripture Doctrine. To which is Affix'd, The Rev. Mr. Whitefield's Thoughts on this Subject, in a Letter to Mr. Wesley.* London: J. Roberts, 1741.

Gill, John. *The Cause of God and Truth: being an Examination of the Several Passages of Scripture made use of by the Arminians.* 4 Vols. London: E. Justin, 1816.

_____. *The Doctrine of Predestination stated and set in the Scriptural light; in opposition to Mr. Wesley's Predestination Calmly Considered. With a reply to the exceptions of the said writer to the Doctrine of the Perseverance of the Saints.* London: G. Keith et al., 1752.

_____. *Doctrine of the Saints' Final Perseverance, asserted and vindicated. In answer to a late pamphlet, called Serious Thoughts on that subject.* London: G. Keith, 1752.

Goodenough, Matthew. *The Snake in the Grass Discovered, in a Friendly Epistle, to the Vicar of Broad-Hembury, Devonshire: Alias, Mr. Augustus Montague Toplady.* London: Matthew Goodenough, 1777.

Henry, Matthew. *A Commentary on the Holy Bible.* 6 Vols. London: Marshall Brothers, n.d.

Hervey, James. *Eleven Letters from the Late Rev. Mr. Hervey, to the Rev. Mr. John Wesley; Containing An Answer to that Gentleman's Remarks on Theron and Aspasio.* London: Charles Rivington, 1765; 1st ed. 1765.

_____. *Theron and Aspasio.* 2 Vols. London: Hamilton Adams and Co., 1824; 1st ed. 1755.

Hill, Richard. *A Conversation Between Richard Hill, Esq.; The Rev. Mr. Madan, and Father Walsh, Superior of a Convent of English Benedictine Monks at Paris, Held at the said Convent, July 13, 1771; in the Presence of Thomas Powis, Esq.; and others, Relative to some Doctrinal Minutes, Advanced by the Rev. Mr. John Wesley and others at a Conference held in London, August 7, 1770.* London: E. and C. Dilly, 1771.

_____. *The Finishing Stroke: Containing Some Strictures on the Rev. Mr. Fletcher's Pamphlet, entitled* Logica Genevensis, *or, a Fourth Check to Antinomianism.* London: Edward and Charles Dilly, 1773.

_____. *Five Letters to the Reverend Mr. Fletcher, Relative to his Vindication of the Minutes of the Reverend Mr. John Wesley.* London: E. and C. Dilly, 1772.

_____. *Logica Wesleiensis, Farrago Double-Distilled. With an Heroic Poem In Praise of Mr. John Wesley.* London: E. and C. Dilly, 1773.

_____. *Pietas Oxoniensis: or, A Full and Impartial Account of the Expulsion of Six Students From St. Edmund Hall, Oxford.* London: G. Keith, 1768.

_____. *A Review of All the Doctrines Taught by The Rev. Mr. John Wesley; Containing a Dill and Particular Answer to a*

Book Entitled, "A Second Check to Antinomianism." London: E. and C. Dilly, 1772.

_____. *Some Remarks on a Pamphlet, Entitled, a Third Check to Antinomianism.* London: E. and C. Dilly, 1772.

_____. *Friendly Remarks Occasioned by the Spirit and Doctrines Contained in the Rev. Mr. Fletcher's Vindication, And More Particularly in His Second Check to Antinomianism to Which is Added a Postscript, Occasioned by His Third Check.* London: E. and C. Dilly, 1772.

Humphreys, Joseph. *An Account of Joseph Humphreys Experience.* Bristol: n.p., 1742.

"James Hutton's Account of 'The Beginning of the Lord's Work in England to 1741,'" *Proceedings W.H.S.* 15 (1926): 178–89.

"James Hutton's Second Account of the Beginnings of the Lord's Work in England down to the year 1747," *Proceedings W.H.S.* 15 (1926): 206–14.

Jackson, Thomas, ed. *The Journals of Rev. Charles Wesley.* 2 Vols. London: John Mason, 1949. Reprinted Grand Rapids, Michigan: Baker Books House, 1980.

_____. *The Lives of Early Methodist Preachers.* 6 Vols. London: Wesleyan Conference Office, 1875.

Kimbrough, S.T., Jr., *The Unpublished Poetical Writing of Charles Wesley.* 3 Vols. Nashville: Kingswood Books, 1988–1992.

Kimbrough, S.T., Jr. and Oliver A. Beckerlegge, eds. *The Unpublished Poetry of Charles Wesley.* Nashville: Abingdon Press, 1993.

Knox, Alexander. *Remains of Alexander Knox.* London: James Ducan, 1834.

L(aTrobe), B(enjamin), ed. *Brief Account of the Life of Howel Harris, Esq.* Trevecka: n.p., 1791.

Madan, Martin. *A Scriptural Comment upon the Thirty-Nine Articles of the Church of England.* London: John and Francis Rivington, 1772.

Minutes of the Methodist Conferences. London: John Mason, 1862.

(Maxfield, Thomas.) *A Short Account of God's Dealings with Mrs. Elizabeth Maxfield, Wife of the Rev. Thomas Maxfield.* London: J.W. Pasham, 1778.

The Methodist Magazine. 25 Vols. London: 1798–1821.

Nowell, Thomas. *Answer to a Pamphlet Entitled Pietas Oxoniensis.* Oxford: The Clarendon Press, 1769; 1st ed. 1768.

Olivers, Thomas. *Descriptive and Plaintive Elegy on the Death of the Late Rev. John Wesley.* London: G. Paramore, 1791.

_____. *A Letter to the Reverend Mr. Toplady, Occasioned by his Late Letter to the Reverend Mr. Wesley.* London: E. Cabe, 1771.

_____. *A Rod For a Reviler: or a Full Answer to Mr. Rowland Hill's Letter, Entitled, Imposter Detected, and the Dead Vindicated.* London: J. Fry and Co., 1777.

_____. *A Scourge to Calumny in Five Parts. Inscribed to Richard Hill, Esq.* London: R. Hawes, 1774.

Poole, Matthew. *A Commentary on The Holy Bible.* 3 Vols. London: Banner of Truth Trust, 1962; 1st ed. 1683, 1685.

Roberts, Gomer M., ed. *Selected Trevecca Letters.* Caernavon: The Calvinistic Methodist Bookroom, 1956.

Sellon, Walter. *The Arguements Against General Redemption Answered.* London: E. Cabe, 1769.

_____. *The Church of England Vindicated from the Charge of Absolute Predestination.* London: E. Cabe, 1771.

_____. *A Defence of God's Sovereignty against the Impious and Horrible Asperations cast upon it by Elisha Coles, in his Practical Treatise on that subject.* 2 Vols. London: E. Cabe, 1814.

Shirley, Walter. *A Narrative of the Principle Circumstances Relative to the Rev. Mr. Wesley's Late Conference, Bristol, 1771.* Bath: W. Gye for T. Mills, 1771.

"The Shorter Catechism, Agreed Upon By The Assembly of Divines at Westminster," *The Confession of Faith.* Edinburgh: William Blackwood & Sons, 1959.

Toplady, Augustus M. *A Caveat Against Unsound Doctrines.* London: J. Gurney, 1770.

_____. *The Church of England Vindicated from the Charge of Arminianism.* London: J. Gurney, 1769.

_____. *The Doctrine of Absolute Predestination Asserted with a Preliminary Discourse on the Divine Attribution.* London: Matthews, 1779; 1st ed. 1769.

_____. *The Doctrine of Absolute Predestination Stated and Asserted.* London: J. Gurney, 1769.

_____. *Free-Will and Merit Fairly Examined: or, Men Not Their Own Saviours.* London: J. Matthews, 1775.

_____. *Good News From Heaven: or, The Gospel a Joyful Sound.* London: J. Matthews, 1775.

_____. *Historic Proof of the Doctrinal Calvinism of the Church of England.* 2 Vols. London: George Keith, 1774; 1st ed. 1769.

_____. *Hymns and Sacred Poems.* London: Daniel Sedgwick, 1860; 1st ed. 1759.

_____. *Jesus Seen of Angels; and God's Mindfullness of Man.* London: J. Gurney, 1771.

_____. *A Letter to the Reverend Mr. John Wesley: Relative to His Pretended Abridgement of Zanchius on Predestination.* London: J. Gurney, 1770.

_____. *A Memoir of Some Principle Circumstances in the Life and Death of the Rev, and Learned Augustus Montague Toplady, B.A., To which is Added, Written by Himself, the Dying Believer's Address to His Soul, and His Own Last Will and Testament.* London: J. Matthews, 1778.

_____. *Moral and Political Moderation Recommended.* London: T. Vallance, 1776.

_____. *More Work for John Wesley.* London: J. 1772.

_____. *The Reverend Mr. Toplady's Dying Avowal of His Religious Sentiments.* London: J. Matthews, 1778.

_____. *The Scheme of Christian and Philosophical Necessity Asserted.* London: Vallance and Simmons, 1775.

_____. *The Works of Augustus Toplady, B.A.* London: B. Bensley, 1837; 1st ed. 1794.

Thickens, John. *Howel Harris yn Llundair.* N.c.: n.p., 1939.

"The Treveccan MSS Supplement," *Cylcligrawn Cymedeithas Hanes Eglwys Methodisliaid Clafinaidd Cymurm* 5 (1920); 6 (1921); 9 (1924); 11 (1926); 19 (1934); 20 (1935).

Anonymous. *A Vindication of the Proceedings Against the Six Members of E— Hall, Oxford.* London: M. Hingeston, 1768.

The Weekly History, or An Account of the most Remarkable Particulars relating to the present Progress of the Gospel. Vol. 1. From April 15, 1741 to November 6, 1742. London: J. Lewis, n.d.

Welch, Edwin, ed. *Five Calvinistic Chapels 1743–1811.* London: London Records Society, 1975.

Wesley, Charles. *An Elegy on the Late Reverend George Whitefield, M.A.* Bristol: William Pine, 1771.

_____. *An Epistle to the Reverend Mr. George Whitefield.* London: J. and W. Oliver, 1771.

_____. *The Journal of the Rev. Charles Wesley.* Ed. Thomas Jackson, 2 Vols. London: John Mason, 1849.

Wesley, John and Charles. *The Poetical Works of John and Charles Wesley.* 13 Vols. Ed. G. Osborn. London: Wesleyan-Methodist Conference Office, 1868.

Wesley, John, ed. *A Christian Library: Consisting of Extracts from, and Abridgements of the Choicest Pieces of Practical Divinity which have been published in the English Tongue.* 50 Vols. Bristol: Felix Farley, 1749–55; 2nd ed. 30 Vols., London: T. Cardeux, 1819–26.

_____. *A Concise Ecclesiastical History from the Birth of Christ to the Beginning of the Present Century.* 4 Vols. London: n.p., 1781.

_____. *Concise History of England.* 4 Vols. London: Robert Hawes, 1776.

_____. *Explanatory Notes Upon The New Testament.* London: Epworth Press, 1950; 1st ed. 1755.

_____. *Explanatory Notes Upon The Old Testament.* 3 Vols. Bristol: William Pine, 1765.

_____. *A Defence of the Minutes of Conference (1770) relating to Calvinism.* Dublin: n.p., 1771.

_____. *The Journal of the Rev. John Wesley, A.M.* 8 Vols. Ed. Nehemiah Curnock. London: Culley, 1909.

_____. "Letter to Daniel Bumstead, January 13, 1770," *Proceedings W.H.S.* 20 (1935– 36): 12.

_____. *The Letters of the Rev. John Wesley, A.M.* 8 Vols. Ed. John Telford. London: Epworth Press, 1931.

_____. *A Preservative Against Unsettled Notions in Religion.* Bristol: E. Farley, 1758.

_____. *The Standard Sermons of John Wesley.* 2 Vols. Ed. E. Sugden, London: Epworth Press, 1921.

_____. *The Scripture Doctrine Concerning Predestination, Election and Reprobation. Extracted from a late Author.* London: W. Strahn, 1741.

_____. *Serious Considerations on Absolute Predestination. Extracted from a late Author.* Bristol: S. and F. Farley, 1741.

_____. *Serious Considerations of the Doctrines of Election and Reprobation. Extracted from a late Author.* London: n.p., 1740.

_____. *A Treatise on Justification, extracted from Mr. John Goodwin.* London: Conference Office, 1807; 1st ed. 1764.

_____. *The Works of the Rev. John Wesley, A.M.* 14 Vols. Ed. T. Jackson. London: Wesleyan-Methodist Bookroom, 1829–31.

_____. *The Works of John Wesley: Vol. XI.* Ed. Gerald R. Cragg. Oxford: Clarendon Press, 1975.

Wesley, Samuel. *Advice to a Young Clergyman in a Letter to Him.* London: C. Rivington, 1735.

_____. *The Athenian Oracle: or Casistical Mercury, Resolving All the Nice and Curious Questions Proposed by the Ingenious.* 4 Vols. London: Andrew Bell, 1703, 1710.

_____. *The Young Student's Library.* London: John Dunton, 1692.

Whitefield, George. *A Letter to the Reverend Dr. Durell.* London: J. Millan, 1768.

_____. *Journals.* London: Banner of Truth Trust, 1960.

_____. *The Works of the Rev. George Whitefield, M.A.* 6 Vols., London: Dilly, 1771.

Secondary Sources: Books

Abbey, Charles J. and Overton, John H. *The English Church in the Eighteenth Century.* London: Longman, Green and Co., 1887.

Armstrong, Brian. *Calvin and the Amyraut Heresy.* London: University of Wisconsin Press, 1969.

Ayling, Stanley. *John Wesley.* New York: William Collins Publishers, 1979.

Baker, Eric W. *A Herald of the Evangelical Revival: A Critical Inquiry into the Relationship between William Law and John Wesley and the Beginnings of Methodism.* London: Epworth Press, 1948.

Baker, Frank. *Charles Wesley As Revealed In His Letters.* London: Epworth Press, 1948.

_____. *John Cennick (1718–55): A Hand List of His Writings.* Leicester: Alfred A. Taberer, 1958.

_____. *John Wesley and the Church of England*. London: Epworth Press, 1970.

_____. *Methodism and the Love-Feast*. London: Epworth Press, 1957.

Bangs, Carl. *Arminius*. Nashville: Abingdon, 1971.

Bennett, G.V. *The Tory Crisis in Church and State 1688–1730*. Oxford: Claren-don Press, 1975.

Bennett, Richard. *The Early Life of Howel Harris*. 1962.

Benson, Joseph. *The Holy Bible with Notes, Critical, Explanatory, and Practical*. London: Wesleyan Conference Office, 1815.

Bett, Henry. *The Early Methodist Preachers*. London: Epworth Press, 1935.

Bready, J. Wesley. *England: Before and After Wesley*. London: Hodder and Stoughton, 1939.

Bretherton, F.F. *The Countess of Huntingdon*. London: Epworth Press, 1940.

Brown, Robert. *John Wesley's Theology: The Principles of its Vitality and its Progressive Stages of Development*. London: E. Stock, 1965.

Brown-Lawson, Albert. *John Wesley and the Anglican Evangelicals of the Eighteenth Century a Study in Cooperation and Separation with Special Reference to the Calvinistic Controversies*. Edinburgh: Pentland Press, 1994.

Bulmer, John. *Memoirs of the Life and Religious Labours of Howel Harris*. N.c.: n.p., 1824.

Burtner, R.W. and Childes, R.E., eds. *A Compend of Wesley's Theology*. New York: Abingdon, 1954.

Callen, Barry L. *God as Loving Grace*. Nappanee, Indiana: Evangel Publishing House, 1996.

Campbell, Ted A. *John Wesley and Christian Antiquity: Religious Vision and Cultural Changes*. Nashville: Kingswood Books, 1991.

Cannon, William R. *The Theology of John Wesley*. New York: Abingdon, 1946.

Cell, George Croft. *The Rediscovery of John Wesley*. New York: Henry Holt, 1935.

Church, L.F. *The Early Methodist People*. London: Epworth Press, 1948.

_____. *More About the Early Methodist People*. London: Epworth Press, 1949.

Clark, Adam. *The Holy Bible with Commentary and Critical Notes*. 6 vols. London: William Tegg, 1859.

_____. *Memoirs of the Wesley Family*. London: J. and I. Clarke, 1823.

Coke, Thomas and Moore, Henry. *The Life of the Rev. John Wesley, A.M.* London: Paramore, 1792.

Coleman, Robert E. *"Nothing to do but to Save Souls": John Wesley's Charge to his Preachers*. Grand Rapids, Michigan: Zondervan, 1990.

Collins, Kenneth J. *A Faithful Witness: John Wesley's Homiletical Theology*. Wilmore, Kentucky: Wesley Heritage Press, 1993.

_____. *A Real Christian: The Life of John Wesley.* Nashville, Tennessee: Abingdon Press, 1999.

_____. *John Wesley: A Theological Journey.* Nashville, Tennessee: Abingdon Press, 2003.

_____. *The Scripture Way of Salvation: The Heart of John Wesley's Theology.* Nashville, Tennessee: Abingdon Press, 1997.

Collins, Kenneth J. and John H. Tyson. *Conversion in the Wesleyan Tradition.* Nashville, Tennessee: Abingdon Press, 2001.

Cox, L.G. *John Wesley's Concept of Perfection.* Kansas City: Beacon Hill Press, 1968.

Cragg, G.R. *The Church and the Age of Reason 1648–1789.* Harmondsworth: Penguin, 1960.

_____. *From Puritanism to the Age of Reason.* Cambridge: University Press, 1966.

Crookshank, C.H. *History of Methodism in Ireland: Vol. 1.* London: T. Woolmer, 1885.

Dallimore, Arnold. *George Whitefield, Vol. 1.* London: Banner of Truth Trust, 1970.

_____. *Susanna Wesley: The Mother of John and Charles Wesley.* Grand Rapids, Michigan: Baker Book House, 1993.

Davies, Horton. *Worship and Theology in England from Watts and Wesley to Maurice, 1690–1850.* London: Oxford University Press, 1961.

Davies, R. and Rupp, G. A *History of the Methodist Church in Great Britain, Vol. 1.* London: Epworth Press, 1965.

Deschner, John. *Wesley's Christology: An Interpretation.* Dallas: Southern Methodist University Press, 1960.

Doughty, W.L. *John Wesley, His Conference and His Preachers.* London: Epworth Press, 1944.

Drew, J.H. *The Life, Character, and Literary Labours of Samuel Drew, A.M.* London: Longman et al., 1834.

Eayrs, George. *John Wesley, Christian Philosopher and Church Founder.* London: Epworth Press, 1926.

Edwards, Maldwyn. *Sons to Samuel.* London: Epworth Press, 1961.

Elliot-Binns, L.E. *The Early Evangelicals.* London: Lutterworth Press, 1953.

Evens, Eifion. *Howel Harris, Evangelist, 1714–1773.* Cardiff: University of Wales Press, 1974.

Fawcett, Arthur. *The Cambusland Revival: The Scottish Evangelical Revival of the Eighteenth Century.* London: Banner of Truth Trust, 1971.

Fisher, G.P. *History of Christian Doctrine.* Edinburgh: T. & T. Clark, 1896.

Fitchett, W.H. *Wesley and His Century: A Study in Spiritual Forces.* New York: Eaton and Mains, 1906.

Flew, R.N. *The Idea of Perfection in Christian Theology.* Oxford: University Press, 1934).

Fuller, Andrew. *The Complete Works of the Rev. Andrew Fuller.* Ed. by A. G. Fuller, London: Henry G. Bohn, 1866.

_____. *The Works of the Rev. Andrew Fuller.* 8 Vols. Ed. by John Ryland. London: B. J. Holdsworth, 1824.

Gillies, John. *The Life of the Reverend George Whitefield, M.A.* London: Dilly, 1772.

Godley, A.D. *Oxford in the Eighteenth Century.* London: Methuen & Co., 1908.

Gradin, Arvid. *A Short History of the Bohemian-Moravian Protestant Church of the United Brethren.* London: James Hutton, 1743.

Green, Richard. *Anti-Methodist Publications.* London: Kelly, 1902.

_____. *The Conversion of John Wesley.* London: Francis Griffiths, 1909.

_____. *The Works of John and Charles Wesley. A Bibliography.* London: Kelly, 1896.

Green, V.H.H. *The Young Mr. Wesley.* London: Edward Arnold, 1941.

Gunter, W. Stephen. *The Limits of "Love Devine": John Wesley's Response to Antinomianism and Enthusiasm.* Nashville: Kingswood Books, 1989.

Hall, Basil. "Calvin Against the Calvinists," *John Calvin.* Ed. by G. Duffield. Appleford, Berkshire: Sutton Courtenay Press, 1966.

Harrison, A.W. *Arminianism.* London: Duckworth, 1937.

Harrison, G. Elsie. *Son to Susanna.* London: Nicholson and Watson, 1937.

Heitzenrater, Richard P. *Diary of an Oxford Methodist: Benjamin Ingham.* Durham, N.C.: Duke University Press, 1985.

_____. *The Elusive Mr. Wesley.* 2 Vols. Nashville: Abingdon Press, 1984.

_____. *Mirror and Memory: Reflections on Early Method-ism.* Nashville: Kingswood Books, 1989.

_____. *Wesley and the People Called Methodists.* Nashville: Abingdon Press, 1995.

Howe, D.W. "Decline of Calvinism," *Comparative Studies in Society and History.* Cambridge: University Press, 1972.

Huehns, Gertrude. *Antinomianism in English History.* London: Cresset Press, 1951.

Hughes, Hugh Joshua. *Life of Howel Harris.* London: Bisbet, 1892.

Hutton, J.E., M.A. *John Cennick. A Sketch.* London: Moravian Publication Office, n.d.

_____. *A History of the Moravian Church.* London: Moravian Publication Office, 1909.

Jackson, Thomas. *The Life of the Rev. Charles Wesley, M.A.* 2 Vols. London: John Mason, 1841.

_____. *The Life of John Goodwin, A.M.* London: Longwan et al., 1822.

Kay, J.A., ed. *Wesley's Prayers and Praises.* London: Epworth Press, 1958.

Knight, Henry H. *The Presence of God in the Christian Life: John Wesley and the*

Means of Grace. Metuchen, New Jersey: Scarecrow Press, 1992.

Knox, R.B. "The Wesleys and Howel Harris," *Studies in Church History.* Vol. 3. Edited by G. J. Cuming. Leiden: Brill, 1966.

Knox, Ronald. *Enthusiasm: A Chapter in the History of Religion with special reference to the XVII and XVIII Centuries.* Oxford: Clarendon Press, 1950.

Lawson, John. *Notes on Wesley's Fourty-four Sermons.* London: Epworth Press, 1946.

Lawton, George. *Shropshire Saint.* London: Epworth Press, 1960.

Lean, Garth. *John Wesley, Anglican.* London: Blandford Press, 1964.

Lee, U. *The Lord's Horseman.* London: Hodder and Stoughton, 1956.

Lindström, Harald. *Wesley and Sanctification.* Stockholm: Nya Bokförlags Aktiebolaget, 1946.

MacDonald, James. *Memoirs of the Rev. Joseph Benson.* London: T. Cordeux, 1822.

MacDonald, James A. *Wesley's Revision of the Shorter Chatechism.* Edinburgh: George A. Morton, 1906.

McGonigle, Herbert. *The Arminianism of John Wesley.* Derby's, England: Moorley's Bookshop, 1988.

_____. *John Wesley's Doctrine of Prevenient Grace.* Derby's, London: Moorley's Bookshop, 1995.

McNeil, John. *The History and Character of Calvinism.* New York: Oxford University Press, 1954.

Maddox, Randy L. *Responsible Grace: John Wesley's Practical Theology.* Nashville, Tennessee: Kingswood Books, 1994.

Manning, Bernard. *Essays in Orthodox Dissent.* London: Independent Press, 1939.

Miller, Perry. *The New England Mind.* New York: Macmillan, 1939.

Monk, Robert. *John Wesley, His Puritan Heritage.* London: Epworth Press, 1966.

Moore, Henry. *The Life of the Rev. John Wesley, A.M.* 2 Vols. London: John Kershaw, 1824.

Morgan, Edward. *Life and Times of Howel Harris.* N.c.: n.p., 1852.

Morris, J.W. *Memoirs of the Life and Writings of the Rev. Andrew Fuller.* London: J.W. Morris, 1815.

New, A.H. *The Coronet and the Cross.* London: Partridge and Co., 1857.

Newton, John A. *Methodism and The Puritans.* London: Dr. William's Trust, 1964.

Nichols, James. *Calvinism and Arminianism Compared in Their Principles and Tendency.* 2 Vols. London: Longman, et al., 1824.

Niesel, Wilhelm. *The Theology of Calvin.* Translated by Harold Knight. London: Lutterworth Press, 1956; 1st German ed., Munich: 1938.

Nuttall, G.F. *Howel Harris, 1714–1773, The Last Enthusiast.* Cardiff: University of Wales Press, 1965.

_____. *The Puritan Spirit.* London: Epworth Press, 1967.

Oden, Thomas C. *John Wesley's Scriptural Christianity: A Plain Exposition of His Teaching on Christian Doctrine.* Grand Rapids, Michigan: Zondervan Publishing House, 1994.

Ollard, S.L. *The Six Students of St. Edmund Hall Expelled from the University of Oxford in 1768.* London: A. R. Mowbray & Co., 1911.

Overton, John H. and Relton, Frederic. *The English Church from the Accession of George I to the End of the Eighteenth Century (1714–1800).* London: Macmillan & Co., Ltd., 1906.

_____. *John Wesley.* London: Methuen & Co., 1891.

Outler, Albert C., ed. *John Wesley.* New York: Oxford University Press, 1964.

Philip, Robert. *The Life and Times of the Rev. George Whitefield.* London: George Virtue, 1838.

Piette, Maximin. *John Wesley in the Evolution of Protestantism.* London: Sheed & Ward, 1938.

Plumb, J.H. *The Pelican History of England, Vol. VII: England in the Eighteenth Century.* Middlesex, England: Penguin Books, 1938.

Plummer, Alfred. *The Church of England in the Eighteenth Century.* London: Methuen & Co., 1910.

Pollock, John. *George Whitefield and the Great Awakening.* London: Hodder, 1972.

Pope, W.B. *A Compendium of Christian Theology.* 3 Vols. London: Wesleyan Conference Office, 1879.

_____. *A Higher Catechism of Theology.* London: T. Woolmer, 1883.

Rack, Henry D. *Reasonable Enthusiast: John Wesley and the Rise of Methodism.* 2nd Ed. Nashville: Abingdon Press, 1993.

Rattenbury, J.E. *The Evangelical Doctrines of Charles Wesley's Hymns.* London: Epworth Press, 1941.

_____. *Wesley's Legacy to the World.* London: Epworth Press, 1928.

Reynolds, John. *Anecdotes of Wesley.* Leeds: n.p., 1828.

Reynolds, J.S. *The Evangelicals at Oxford 1735–1871.* Oxford: Basil Black-well, 1953.

Rex, Walter. *Essays on Pierre Bayle and Religious Controversy.* The Hague: Martinus Nyhoff, 1965.

Roberts, Griffith T. *Howel Harris.* London: Epworth Press, 1951.

Rowe, Kenneth E., ed. *The Place of Wesley in the Christian Tradition.* Revised Ed. Metuchen, New Jersey: Scarecrow Press, 1980. Reissue of 1976 edition with updated bibliography.

Ryland, John. *The Character of the Rev. James Hervey, M.A.* London: 1791.

Ryle, J.C. *The Christian Leaders of England in the Eighteenth Century.* London: Thynne & Jarvis, 1868.

Rupp, E.G. *Principalities and Powers.* London: Epworth Press, 1952.

Sangster, W.E. *The Path to Perfection.* London: Hodder and Stoughton, 1943.

Schmidt, Martin. *John Wesley: A Theological Biography.* 3 Vols. Nashville: Abingdon Press, 1972, 1973; 1st German ed., 1966.

(Seymour, A.C.H.) *The Life and Times of Selina Countess of Huntingdon.* London: Painter, 1840.

Semmel, Bernard. *The Methodist Revolution.* London: Heinemann, 1974.

Sykes, Norman. *Church and State in England in the Eighteenth Century.* Cambridge: University Press, 1934.

Simon, John. *John Wesley and the Religious Societies.* London: Epworth Press, 1921.

_____. *John Wesley and the Methodist Societies.* London: Epworth Press, 1923.

_____. *John Wesley and the Advance of Methodism.* London: Epworth Press, 1925.

_____. *John Wesley the Master Builder.* London: Epworth Press, 1927.

_____. *John Wesley the Last Phase.* London: Epworth Press, 1934.

_____. *The Revival of Religion in England in the Eighteenth Century.* London: Robert Culley, n.d.

Sidney, Edwin. *The Life of Sir Richard Hill, Bart.* London: R. B. Seeley & W. Burnarde, 1839.

_____. *The Life of the Rev. Rowland Hill, A.M.* London: Baldwin & Cradock, 1835.

Smith, Timothy L. *Whitefield and Wesley on the New Birth.* Grand Rapids, Michigan: Francis Asbury Press of Zondervan Publishing House, 1986.

Smyth, Charles. *Simeon and Church Order.* Cambridge: University Press, 1740.

Southey, Robert. *The Life of Wesley and Rise and Progress of Methodism.* 2 Vols. London: : Longman, et al., 1846; 3rd ed. with "Remarks on the Life and Character of John Wesley by Alexander Knox."

Stephen, Leslie. *History of English Thought.* 2 Vols. London: Smith, Elder & Co., 1876.

Stevens, Abel. *History of Methodism.* 3 Vols. London: William Tegg, 1864.

Stevenson, George J. *Memorials of the Wesley Family.* London: S. W. Partridge and Co., 1876.

Stromberg, Roland N. *Religious Liberalism in Eighteenth Century England.* London: Oxford University Press, 1954.

Telford, John. *Life of Charles Wesley.* London: Wesleyan Methodist Book-room, 1900.

_____. *Life of John Wesley.* London: Epworth Press, 1886.

Thompson, D. D. *John Wesley and George Whitefield in Scotland. Or, the Influence of the Oxford Methodists on Scottish Religion.* London: Blackwood and Sons, 1898.

Toon, Peter. *The Emergence of Hyper Calvinism in English NonConformity 1689–1765.* London: The Olive Tree, 1967.

Townsend, W.J.; Workman, H.B.; and Eayrs, George. *A New History of Methodism.* 2 Vols. London: Hodder and Stoughton, 1909.

Treffry, Richard. *Memoirs of the Rev. Joseph Benson.* London: John Mason, 1840.

Tuck, Stephen. *Wesleyan Methodism in Frome.* Frome: S. Tuck, 1837.

Tulloch, John. *Rational Theology and Christian Philosophy in England in the Seventeenth Century.* Edinburgh: Blackwood and Sons, 1874.

Tyerman, L. *The Life of George Whitefield.* 2 Vols. London: Hodder, 1876.

_____. *The Life and Times of John Wesley.* 3 Vols. London: Hodder and Stoughton, 1890.

_____. *The Life and Times of the Rev. Samuel Wesley, M.A.* London: Simpkin, Marshall & Co., 1866.

_____. *The Oxford Methodists.* London: Hodder and Stoughton, 1873.

_____. *Wesley's Designated Successor.* London: Hodder and Stoughton, 1882.

Tyson, John R. *Charles Wesley on Sanctification: A Biographical and Theological Study.* Grand Rapids, Michigan: Francis Asbury Press of Zondervan Publishing House, 1986.

Tytler, Sarah. *The Countess of Huntingdon and Her Circle.* London: Isaac Pitman and Sons, 1907.

Vickers, John. *Thomas Coke: Apostle of Methodism.* London: Epworth Press, 1969.

Vulliamy, C.E. *John Wesley.* London: Geoffrey Bles, 1931.

Wainwright, Geoffrey. *Geoffrey Wainwright on Wesley and Calvin: Sources for Theology, Liturgy and Spirituality.* Melbourne: Uniting Church Press, 1987.

Walsh, John D. "Origins of the Evangelical Revival," *Essays in Modern English Church History: In Memory of Norman Sykes.* Ed. by G. V. Bennett and J. D. Walsh. London: Black, 1966.

Warfield, B.B. *Calvin and Augustine.* Philadelphia: Presbyterian and Reformed Publishing Company, 1956.

Watson, Richard. *An Exposition of the Gospels of St. Matthew and St. Mark.* London: John Mason, 1855.

_____. *Theological Institutes.* 3 Vols. London: John Mason, 1829.

Wedgewood, Julia. *John Wesley and The Evangelical Reaction of the Eighteenth Century.* London: MacMillan & Co., 1870.

Whitehead, John, *The Life of the Rev. John Wesley.* 2 Vols. London: Stephen Couchman, 1796.

Whiteley, J.H. *Wesley's England.* London: Epworth Press, 1938.

Wiggins, James. *The Embattled Saint: Aspects of the Life and Thought of John Fletcher.* Macon, Georgia: Wesleyan College, 1966.

Willey, Basil. *The Eighteenth Century Background.* N.c.: Chatto & Windus, 1940.

_____. *The Seventeenth Century Background.* N.c.: Chatto & Windus, 1934.

Williams, A.H. *John Wesley in Wales.* Cardiff: University of Wales Press, 1971.

Williams, Colin W. *John Wesley's Theology Today.* London: Epworth Press, 1960.

Winters, William. *Memoirs of the Life and Writings of the Rev. A. M. Toplady.* London: F. Davis, 1872.

Wiseman, Luke. *Charles Wesley.* London: Epworth Press, 1932.

Wood, A. Skevington. *The Burning Heart.* Exeter: Paternoster Press, 1967.

_____. *The Inextinguishable Blaze.* London: Paternoster Press, 1960.

_____. *Thomas Haweis 1734–1820.* London: SPCK, 1957.

Wynkoop, M.B. *Foundations of Wesleyan-Arminian Theology.* Kansas City: Beacon Hill Press, 1967.

Yates, Arthur S. *The Doctrine of Assurance with special Reference to John Wesley.* London: Epworth Press, 1952.

Secondary Sources: Periodical Literature

Austin, Roland. "Bibliography of the Works of Charles Wesley." *Proceedings W.H.S.* 10 (1915): 169–84, 211–23.

Baker, Frank. "John Fletcher, Methodist Clergyman." *London Quarterly & Holborn Review* 185 (1960): 291–98.

_____. "Wesley and Arminius." *Proceedings W.H.S.* 22 (1939-40): 118–19.

_____. "Wesley's Puritan Ancestry." *The London Quarterly & Holborn Review* 187 (1962): 180–86.

Bretherton, F.F. "Two Wesley Letters to the Countess of Huntingdon." *Proceedings W.H.S.* 27 (March, 1949): 2–4.

_____. "Wesley's Visits to Holland." *Proceedings W.H.S.* 19 (1934–35): 106–12.

Brigden, Thomas E. "The Ministry of George Whitefield." *Proceedings W.H.S.* 10 (1915): 33–59.

"John Cennick, 1718–55: A Bi-centenary Appreciation." *Proceedings W.H.S.* 30 (1956): 30–37.

Chadwick, W.O. "Arminianism in England." *Religion in Life* 29 (1960): 548–55.

Childs, Robert E. "Methodist Apostasy: From Free Grace to Free Will." *Religion in Life* 27 (1957): 438–49.

Clark, F. Stuart. "The Theology of Arminius." *The London Quarterly & Holborn Review* 185 (1960): 248–53.

Clipsham, E.F. "Andrew Fuller and Fullerism: A study in Evangelical Calvinism." *Baptist Quarterly* 20 (1963–64): 99–114, 146–54, 214–25, 268–76.

Cushman, Robert E. "Theological Landmarks in the Revival Under Wesley." *Religion in Life* 27 (1957): 105–18.

Dallimore, A. "George Whitefield." *Evangelical Library Bulletin.* Autumn 1964.

Edwards, Maldwyn L. "George Whitefield After Two Hundred Years." *Proceedings W.H.S.* 27 (October 1970).

Evans, R.W. "The Relations of George Whitefield and Howel Harris." *Church History* 30 (June 1961): 170–90.

Foster, H.D. "Liberal Calvinism; the Remonstrants at the Synod of Dort in 1618." *Harvard Theological Review* 16 (January 1923): 1–37.

Frairs, Geoffrey L. "The Death of William Seward of Hay." *Proceedings W.H.S.* 39 (1973–74): 2.

"Letter to Howel Harris," *Proceedings W.H.S.* 6 (1908): 111.

Harrison, A.W. "The Arminian Magazine." *Proceedings W.H.S.* 12 (1920): 150–52.

Heitzenrater, Richard P. "John Wesley's Early Sermons." *Proceedings W.H.S.* 37 (February 1970): 110–28.

Henry, Granville C. "John Wesley's Doctrine of Free-Will." *The London Quarterly & Holborn Review* 185 (1960): 200–07.

Hoenderdaal, G.J. "The Life and Thought of Jacobus Arminius." *Religion in Life* 29 (Autumn 1960): 540–47.

Hornsby, J.T. "Wesley. Hervey. Sandeman." *Proceedings W.H.S.* 20 (1935–36): 112–13.

Jones, M.H. "Attempts to Re-establish Union Between Howel Harris, English and Welsh Methodists and the Moravians." *Proceedings W.H.S.* 16 (1928): 113–17.

_____. "References to the Wesley's in the First Calvinistic Methodist Newspaper." *Proceedings W.H.S.* 12 (1920): 158–63.

"List of Local Methodist Histories." *Proceedings W.H.S.* 1 (1897) and "Supplemental List," 6 (1907): 70.

Marshall, I.H. "Sanctification in the Teaching of John Wesley and John Calvin." *Evangelical Quarterly* 34 (1962), 75–82.

Maycock, J. "The Fletcher-Toplady Controversy." *London Quarterly & Holborn Review* 191 (1966): 227–35.

"The Methodist Magazine 1778–1969." *Proceedings W.H.S.* 37 (1969): 72–76.

Newman, J.H. "Selina Countess of Huntingdon." *Essays, Critical and Historical.* London: Basil Montagu Pickering, 1871. Written in 1840.

Noll, Mark A. "John Wesley and the Doctrine of Assurance." *Bibliothecasacra* 132 (April–June, 1975): 161–77.

Paananen, Victor N. "Martin Madan and the Limits of Evangelical Philanthropy." *Proceedings W.H.S.* 49 (1975): 57–68.

Parker, T.M. "Arminianism and Laudianism in Seventeenth Century England." *Studies in Church History: Vol. 1.* Edited by C. W. Dugmore & C. Duggan. London: Nelson, 1964.

Parlby, William. "The First Methodist Martyr: William Seward. His Grave at Cusop. 1702–1740." *Proceedings W.H.S.* 17 (1929–30): 187–91.

Pask, Alfred H. "The Influence of Arminius on John Wesley." *The London Quar-*

terly & Holborn Review 185 (1960): 258–63.

Rattenbury, H. "The Historical Background and Life of Arminius." *The London Quarterly & Holborn Review* 185 (1960): 243–48.

Reist, Irwin W. "John Wesley and George Whitefield: A Study in the Integrity of Two Theologies of Grace." *Evangelical Quarterly* 47 (1975): 26.

Roberts, Griffith T. "John Wesley Visits Wales (October 15–21, 1741)." *Bathafarn* 13 (1958).

_____. "The Trevecka Manuscripts." *Proceedings W.H.S.* 27 (1950): 178–80.

_____. "Wesley's First Society in Wales: I. Origins." *Proceedings W.H.S.* 27 (1950): 111–16.

_____. "Wesley's First Society in Wales: Persecutions and Disputes." *Proceedings W.H.S.* 27 (1950): 125.

Simon, J.S. "Whitefield and Bristol." *Proceedings W.H.S.* 10 (1915): 1–10.

Smith, J. Weldon. "Some Notes on Wesley's Doctrine of Prevenient Grace." *Religion in Life* 34 (1964–65): 68–80.

Stafford, Darby. "A Dead Controversy and a Living Hymn. John Wesley and Augustus Toplady." *The Methodist Recorder* (July 12, 1906): 9.

"Extracts from the Trevecca MSS: An Account of an Association Held at Bristol, January 22, 1776–77. *Proceedings W.H.S.* 15 (1926): 120–21.

"Diary of Richard Viney, 1774." *Proceedings W.H.S.* 4 (1904): 194.

Wallington, A. "Whitefield's First Hymnbook." *Proceedings W.H.S.* 10 (1915): 60–62.

Wakefield, Gordon S. "Arminianism in the Seventeenth and Eighteenth Centuries." *The London Quarterly & Holborn Review* 185 (1960): 253–58.

"Wesley and William Cudworth." *Proceedings W.H.S.* 12 (1920): 34–36.

Whitebrook. J.C. "An Account of Tracts and Pamphlets on the Doctrines of Grace. Published by Hervey, Sandeman, Wesley, and others, from 1755 to 1773." *CCH* 10 (1925).

Williams, A.H. "The First Methodist Society in Wales." *Bathafarn* 15 (1960).

Williams, D.D. "George Whitefield." *CCH* 16 (1931).

Secondary Sources: Dissertations

Crow, Earl P. "John Wesley's Conflict with Antinomianism in Relation to the Moravians and Calvinists." Manchester University Ph.D., 1964.

Dale, James. "The Theological and Literary Qualities of the Poetry of Charles Wesley in Relation to the Standards of His Age." University of Cambridge Ph.D., 1961.

Heitzenrater, Richard P. "John Wesley and the Oxford Methodists, 1725–35." Duke University Ph.D., 1972.

Ireson, Roger W. "The Doctrine of Faith in John Wesley and the Protestant Tradition." Manchester University Ph.D., 1973.

Kinghorn, Kenneth C. "Faith and Works: A Study in the Theology of John Fletcher." Emory University Ph.D., 1966.

Lawson, Albert B. "John Wesley and some Anglican Evangelicals of the Eighteenth Century: a study in co-operation and separation, with special reference to the Calvinistic controversies." Sheffield University Ph.D., 1974.

Lawton, George A. "Augustus Montague Toplady—A critical account, with special reference to Hymnology." Nottingham University B.D., 1964.

Packer, James I. "The Redemption and Restoration of Man in the Thought of Richard Baxter." University of Oxford D.Phil., 1954.

Shipley, David C. "Methodist Arminianism in the Theology of John Fletcher." Yale University Ph.D., 1942.

Tyacke, N.R.N. "Arminianism in England, In Religion and Politics, 1604 to 1640." University of Oxford D.Phil., 1968.

Walsh, John D. "The Yorkshire Evangelicals in the Eighteenth Century, with special reference to Methodism." University of Cambridge, Ph.D., 1957.